HISTORY OF
THE 17TH (NORTHERN) DIVISION

HISTORY OF THE 17th (NORTHERN) DIVISION

BY

A. HILLIARD ATTERIDGE

GLASGOW

Printed for the Division by

ROBERT MACLEHOSE & CO. LTD.

THE UNIVERSITY PRESS

1929

PREFACE

HAVING been in command of the 17th Division from 13th July, 1916, until the close of hostilities, I am very glad, by writing this foreword, to be able from close personal knowledge to testify to the splendid work carried out by it in the Great War. From its arrival in France in July 1915 until the Armistice, the Division bore its full share of the fighting and hardships on the Western Front. Without prejudice one might say *more* than its share, for it seemed to have a peculiar faculty for having " nasty jobs " to negotiate. Throughout its career, in spite of the greatest difficulties and constant change of personnel through heavy casualties, it maintained a very high standard of military efficiency, being most gallant and determined in attack, dogged in defence, and always willing and cheerful to endure hardship under all conditions, no matter how difficult they might be.

The Division's first experience of war was in the trenches of the Ypres salient, a very trying sector for young troops ; but they at once proved their worth, and took part with success in several minor actions. After some months in the Salient it moved to the Armentières Area, and thence in June 1916 to the Somme, where it took part in the great attacks in July, suffering very severely in the heavy fighting which resulted in the capture of Fricourt, Fricourt Wood, and the trenches about Contalmaison. In August the Division was heavily engaged at Longueval and Delville Wood, again suffering most severely in the various attacks, and from heavy and continued shell and machine-gun fire whilst holding the line.

Throughout the winter of 1916-1917 it remained on the Somme, being engaged in constant hard fighting, and enduring great hardships through the severe and trying weather conditions.

In March 1917 the Division was attached to the Cavalry Corps for special service with it at the Battle of Arras, its rôle being to push forward independently in support of the Cavalry should a " break through " be made. It was subsequently engaged in the severe fighting about Monchy and on the Scarpe river. Remaining in the Arras sector until September it then moved north to play its part in the 3rd Battle of Ypres, and struggle for the Passchendaele Ridge. In the attack on 12th October it was signally successful, being the only Division to gain all its objectives on that date.

Transferred in December to the Cambrai Area the Division found itself holding the trenches astride the Canal du Nord on the north shoulder of the Cambrai salient when the Great German Offensive was launched on 21st March, 1918. All the enemy's attacks upon the Division on that date were successfully repulsed, but it had to retire at night in order to conform to the general withdrawal of the British Line. Throughout the 22nd March it completely defeated attacks made on it at Hermies and Havrincourt, earning special mention in F.M. Lord Haig's official despatches for its gallant defence.

The summer of 1918 was spent in the trench line directly north of Albert, until in August in the Great Final Advance, it swept forward across the Somme country, capturing Thiepval, Courcelette, Martinpuich, Transloy and other villages *en route*. It pressed on over the Canal du Nord, the Hindenburg Line, and River Selle, through the Mormal Forest, until the Armistice found it forming one of the advance Divisions of the Vth Corps at Beaufort.

In the record of such an epic as the above, in which all

played their parts so gallantly and well, it seems invidious to single out any event for special notice, but perhaps as being typical of the fine achievements of the 17th Division, I may mention the attacks carried out in the Somme battle in July 1916, the capture of Neuvilly on the river Selle on 21st October, 1918, the capture of Futoy and advance through the Mormal Forest on 4th November, 1918 ; the dogged endurance at Longueval and Delville Wood in August 1916 ; and the determined defence of Hermies and Havrincourt against the repeated German onslaughts on 22nd and 23rd March 1918.

I wish to take this opportunity of expressing my great appreciation for the loyal support and gallant service that I received from All Ranks of the 17th Division; whilst doing so, in addition to the Fighting Units, I remember with deep gratitude the excellent work carried out by the Administrative Units and the R.A.M.C. I cannot speak too highly of the perfect organisation and devoted services rendered by All Ranks of the latter from the A.D.M.S. downwards.

It is my greatest pride that I commanded such a splendid Division.

PHILIP R. ROBERTSON
Major-General

FOREWORD

To the preface which General Sir Philip Robertson has kindly written for this record of the 17th Northern Division I add this brief foreword, in order to express my very grateful thanks for the valuable help given to me by many officers who have placed at my disposal their personal diaries and letters, memoranda on special incidents and such helpful material as reconnaissance sketches and photographs, and maps marked with significant indications of the local situation on the fronts where they were engaged at various times—these last often supplying contemporary evidence of the highest value. I must also give my thanks to not a few who, in reply to my enquiries, supplied me with detailed information on special points, and for the friendly criticism on the work which I received while it was in progress.

While tracing the record of the Division, I have from time to time outlined the general situation on the western front so as to show how its operations fitted into the general scheme of the war.

I regret that it was not found possible to give more than incomplete statistics of the heavy losses incurred by the Division, though I have been able to supply these for considerable periods during its years of service at the front. Nor have I been able to add a list of the many decorations, British and Foreign, awarded to all ranks.

A. H. A.

CONTENTS

CONTENTS

LIST OF MAPS

17TH NORTHERN DIVISION

BATTLE HONOURS

Battles.		Dates.
Actions of Hooge, 1915 -	-	30th July-9th August.
Actions of the Bluff, 1916	-	14th-15th Feb.-2nd Mar.

BATTLES OF THE SOMME, 1916.

Battle of Albert, 1916 -	-	1st-13th July.
Battle of Delville Wood	-	15th July-3rd September.

THE BATTLES OF ARRAS, 1917.

First Battle of the Scarpe, 1917	9th-14th April.
Second Battle of the Scarpe, 1917	23rd-24th April.
Action—Capture of Roeux -	13th-14th May.

THE BATTLES OF YPRES, 1917.

Battle of Poelcapelle -	-	9th October.
First Battle of Passchendaele -	12th October.

THE FIRST BATTLES OF THE SOMME, 1918.

First Battle of Bapaume	-	24th-25th March.
Battle of the Ancre, 1918	-	5th April.

THE SECOND BATTLES OF THE SOMME, 1918.

Battle of Albert, 1918 -	-	21st-23rd August.
Second Battle of Bapaume	-	31st August-3rd Sept.

THE HINDENBURG LINE.

Battle of Epéhy -	-	-	18th September.
Battle of the Canal du Nord	-	27th Sept.-1st October.
Battle of Cambrai, 1918	-	8th-9th October.

BATTLE OF THE SELLE - - 17th-25th October.

BATTLE OF THE SAMBRE - - 4th November.

CHAPTER I

THE FORMATION OF THE DIVISION
1914-15

For nearly a hundred years after the Napoleonic Wars the only conflict with a European Power in which England was involved was the war with Russia in 1854-56. Comparatively small forces of professional soldiers were engaged in it, and there was no serious interruption of the ordinary round of life at home during the war years. Russia had no effective naval power and our merchant ships freely sailed the seas as if all the world were at peace. The battles in the Crimea and the prolonged siege of Sebastopol were far away at the other end of Europe. The recruiting for the small regular army and the embodiment of the militia for garrison duty withdrew only a limited number of men from their ordinary occupations. The total losses of the British army in two years of war were less than those of single battles on the Western Front in the Great War that came in 1914.

In the half-century after the Alma and Sebastopol, while we remained at peace with all Europe, there were many little wars in Asia and Africa, mostly with semi-civilised or savage races and their petty kings and chiefs —wars in which disciplined forces and superior armament made our victory a certainty—a victory won at trifling cost. In this long series of wars in the borderlands of the Empire the only conflict that at all seriously taxed our energies was that with the South African Republics. This too was a distant war and our opponents were irregular levies. The experience won thus threw little

light on the nature of warfare against the huge armies of
a first-class European power under modern conditions.
Our sailors and soldiers had never undergone the test
of battle with fairly-matched adversaries.   They studied
the conditions and problems of modern war and trained
themselves for the trial, and there was a patriotic confidence that if the occasion came they would prove equal
to it.   But even for them the coming of the Great War
meant a plunge into the unknown.

Still more was this the case with the civilian population.   No one in England had any adequate idea of what
war between Britain and a powerful European enemy
might mean for him.   In the countries of the Continent
war was well understood to mean, not a mere duel
between professional armies, but " the nation in arms,"
with the instant call for all men of military age to be ready
to take their places in the fighting line, unless they could
be more useful in some other department of the national
organisation.   Moreover everyone would realise that on
the result of the first contact of the armies it would depend
whether or not war would mean invasion.   But in
England there was neither this wide-sweeping call to arms,
nor this imminent possibility of the familiar fields and
streets being soon the scene of battle.   On the night of
August 4th, 1914, when the clocks struck eleven (the
midnight of Berlin) and cheering crowds in London and
other great centres greeted the coming of war, and next
morning when everyone read the news in the papers,
hundreds of thousands, who before long would be taking
part in gigantic battles, had not the remotest idea that they
would ever be called upon to fire a shot in the coming
conflict.

The popular opinion was that it would be decided—
and decided very soon—by the Navy and the highly-
trained Expeditionary Force that was to be sent to the
help of France.   The Territorial Army was being mobilised for home defence, but level headed men held that

invasion was the least likely of events. Expert writing in the newspapers gave comforting proof that even hostile air raids from beyond the sea were all but impossible contingencies. Leader writers and " military correspondents " settled that the war could not last many months, and predicted a speedy victory of the Western Allies, and an overwhelming advance of " the Russian steam roller " on the Eastern front. To suggest that the German army might prove a tough adversary and that the war might last for years was to risk being denounced as " pro-German." Some of the newspapers proposed the reassuring policy of " Business as usual." England might go on living its ordinary life and securing a profitable trade with the enemy's former customers beyond the seas, while French and Joffre were marching across the Rhine and Jellicoe was winning a new Trafalgar.

This highly patriotic but dangerously optimistic state of mind received a severe shock when there came the news of the collapse of the Belgian fortresses and the result of the frontier battles. The shock would have been still more serious if the English people had been allowed to know the whole truth, and if the average man, with his scanty knowledge of war, had not been too blissfully ignorant to realise the full significance of what was passing.

Our little army—little only in comparison with the vast armies of the Continent, but nevertheless the greatest army that Britain had every put into the field at the outset of any war in all its long history—had fought magnificently. But it had been involved in the disasters of that far flung opening fight, which the French call the " Battle of the Frontiers," a battle in which Mons was but an incident. The Allied Armies of the West were in full retreat; the invaders were pouring into France; Paris was preparing for a siege; the French Government had been transferred to Bordeaux; our bases on the Channel coast of France had to be hurriedly abandoned. Then from the Eastern front there was news of Hindenburg's victory and Russia's defeat in the Masurian marshes.

It all came as a terrible disappointment after the sanguine optimism of the first days.   But the people met it bravely.   There was a renewed rush of recruits to the Regular and Territorial Armies.   Offers of whole units of the latter for service abroad poured into the War Office. Men now realised that they were facing a far more serious crisis than they had anticipated, and that those who had predicted a long war were better judges of the situation than those who had been pleasantly prophesying swift success.   They heard without dismay that Lord Kitchener had talked of a three years' war.   The news of the Marne brought a temporary revival of the ill-informed optimism of the first days, but the prospect was overclouded again when the enemy stood fast, on the Aisne heights and met the attempt to turn his flank by extending his line northwards towards the sea.

The nation was now preparing for a long war, and had begun the expansion of its land forces to the dimensions of the great Continental armies.   Five Regular Divisions had gone to France in August.   A sixth reached the fighting front during the battle on the Aisne.   Other divisions were being formed that would bring the whole strength of the Regular Army into the field.   Territorial units had embarked for the Mediterranean garrisons, Egypt, India and the Far East, to set Regular units free to return to Europe.   Whole divisions of Territorials had assembled for field training and would go to the front as soon as this was completed.   The Dominions were about to embark the pick of their manhood for service side by side with the men of the Mother Country, and the Indian Army was preparing a contingent for the Western Front.

But besides all these reinforcements for the fighting line Lord Kitchener—greatly daring—had planned the creation of an army specially enlisted and organised for service during the duration of the war. This new army —the " Kitchener's Army " of popular parlance—was to number eventually many hundreds of thousands. It was to be an improvised army of Regular troops prepared for active service by intensive training. It was to be linked with the old Army by its infantry units being formed as new " service battalions " of the Regular regiments belonging to the districts in which they were recruited. The new battalions would thus inherit some of the traditional *esprit de corps* of the historic regiments by whose names they were known and whose badges they wore.

Lord Kitchener had hardly taken possession of his post at the War Office, when he drafted in brief outline a scheme for the New Army. An order issued on August 31st, 1914, called for the enlistment of its first hundred thousand men. These were to be organised as the first six of the new " K " Divisions, which were to be numbered from Nine to Fourteen. There was a rush of recruits, and by September 12th the "First Hundred Thousand " was completed. Then came the call for a second hundred thousand, which were to make up six more divisions of the New Army—the Fifteenth to the Twentieth. It was thus to the second hundred thousand that the Seventeenth Division belonged.

This raising of the new armies was a daring experiment and ran counter to the main current of received military tradition.[1] It had indeed been recognised that it was possible to improvise infantry battalions, but this recog-

[1] This was admitted and indeed emphasised by Lord Kitchener himself in the statement which he made to a meeting of Members of the House of Commons on June 2nd, 1916, when he said :
" Such an idea was contrary to the theories of all European soldiers. Armies, it had always been argued, could be expanded within limits, but could not be created in time of war. I felt myself that, though there might be some justice in this view, I had to take the risk and embark on what may be described as a gigantic experiment. I relied on the energy of this country to supply deficiencies of previous experience and preparation, and set to work to build a series of new armies, complete in all their branches." (*Life of Lord Kitchener*, by Sir George Arthur, vol. iii. p. 329.)

nition was qualified with the warning that they might be of somewhat doubtful value until they had undergone a hardening and sifting process in the stern and costly school of active service.   In discussions on the possibility of creating new armies, regular soldiers would recall the experiences of those improvised by Gambetta in the second stage of the Franco-German War of 1870-71, and point to these as a clear warning of disappointing results being more likely than any real advantage.

It was argued that the records of most of the battles fought by the new levies against the Germans in the months after Sedan told of success only at the outset, in the first contact with the enemy's advanced troops; after this would come a serious check as the hostile resistance gathered strength; then ill-combined and half-hearted attacks on the part of the French, the result of their lack of march discipline and battle training; and finally a general breakdown and a retreat with heavy loss in prisoners and stragglers.   When the Germans of 1914 heard of the new Kitchener Armies being organised, their newspapers wrote of them as likely to be nothing better than " Kanonenfutter " (cannon fodder, or as we would say "food for powder") and sought confirmation for their forecast in references to the Gambettist levies of 1870.

There was a very serious error in the comparison— for the new levies of 1870 had received only a brief and incomplete training—some elementary drill of the barrack yard type, a few shots fired at the fixed targets of a short rifle range, two or three route marches, and then they were hurried into the fighting line, and sent into action by improvised staffs that showed themselves unequal to the task of handling masses of men.   But in the Kitchener scheme there was no trace of this ill-judged haste.   It contemplated a prolonged period of intensive training, and it was only in a limited sense of the word that the New Armies could be said to be " improvised."

But even so there were—not unnaturally—many

doubts as to the possibility of thus preparing for active service in a few months, not only new infantry units, but also the various other arms that go to the making of a fighting division. There was especially not a little criticism of the project for forming new field and howitzer batteries for the Kitchener Armies. In the days before the Volunteers were converted into Territorials, the War Office had consistently opposed the idea that a force of mere " auxiliaries " could be provided with its own mobile artillery. The Volunteers were at most allowed to train with heavy guns in fixed coast defences and to form a few " position batteries " that would not be expected to manoeuvre with troops in action. It used to be said that it would take some two years to make efficient artillery drivers out of recruits, and since those days the whole work of the gunners in the field had become more complex and exacting. But despite all doubting criticism Lord Kitchener looked forward with confidence to taking some hundreds of thousands from the civilian population, and within a year turning them into efficient Infantry Divisions provided with every necessary arm of the service —artillery, engineers, signallers, transport and medical services. It was a tremendous task.

With the 17th Division and the other formations belonging to the Second Hundred Thousand the problem . to be solved was in some respects more difficult than it had been with the First. In the earlier days of the war, among those who crowded to depots and recruiting offices to enlist in the Regular and Territorial Armies, there came with the flood of new recruits large numbers of men who had had some military training and experience as officers and non-commissioned officers in one or other branch of the service and who were eager to resume their places among their old comrades. When the First Hundred Thousand were enrolled for the New Armies there were still some of these useful enlistments, and they helped to form the cadres for the units of the new divisions. But

by the time that the 17th Division and the other formations of the Second Hundred Thousand began their
organisation, comparatively few such men were available.
Battalions and other units had therefore in not a few
instances to begin their formation and training with only
one or two officers who had already a record of some kind
of service, and a few sergeants who had learned their work
in the Regular Army, or less completely in the auxiliary
forces.   The rest of their cadres was made up of newly-
commissioned officers, full of zeal and goodwill but with
everything to learn, while the required number of N.C.Os.
was provided by trial promotions of likely men from the
rank and file of the recruits.   It is easy to understand how,
especially in the first weeks, this state of affairs increased
the difficulties of making civilians into soldiers.

There was a further serious difficulty arising from the
fact that by the end of September the supply of uniforms,
arms and equipment had been all but exhausted, and
the organisation for meeting the deficiency was being only
slowly extended.   For some time no uniform of any kind
was available for the rank and file of the 17th Division
and the men paraded in a strange variety of civilian dress
and headgear.   There was a scarcity of blankets in the
improvised billets and crowded camps, and this became
a serious matter as the advance of autumn was marked by
a sharp drop in temperature.   As for arms, for months
the infantry battalions had only a few old rifles officially
known as of the " D.P." class, that is just good enough for
" Drill Purposes."   The men took it in turn to drill with
them.   When the first machine gun sections were formed
training started with " dummy guns " that left a good
deal to the imagination.

The men who were to form the 17th Division came
chiefly from the north of England, hence its official
designation—the " 17th Northern Division."   Of the
thirteen infantry battalions nine were raised in Yorkshire
and Lancashire.   Amongst these men from the cities

and towns, miners and factory hands, and recruits from the warehouse, the shop and the office predominated. This too was the prevailing element among the recruits of the battalion raised on Tyneside. In the battalion raised in Cumberland, and those from Lincoln, Derby and Nottinghamshire and South Staffordshire, there was a large element of men from field and farm. Besides these men of the north and centre, the Division had a battalion raised in its training area, townsmen and villagers of Dorsetshire. In accordance with Lord Kitchener's plan of linking up the units of the new armies with the old Regiments of the Line, they became " Service Battalions " of the regiments belonging to the districts from which they drew their recruits. On September 11th, 1914, the official existence of the Division began. It was to be made up of three Infantry Brigades, the 50th, 51st, and 52nd, and a divisional battalion, with the due proportion of the other arms. Anticipating a later stage in the progress of its organisation, the list of its infantry units and their brigade grouping may be given here:

50TH INFANTRY BRIGADE.

6th Dorsetshire Regiment.
7th East Yorkshire Regiment.
10th West Yorkshire Regiment (Prince of Wales's Own).
7th Yorkshire Regiment (Alexandra Princess of Wales's Own).

51ST INFANTRY BRIGADE.

7th Lincolnshire Regiment.
7th Border Regiment.
8th South Staffordshire Regiment.
10th Nottinghamshire and Derby Regiment (Sherwood Foresters).

52ND INFANTRY BRIGADE.

12th Manchester Regiment.
9th West Riding Regiment (Duke of Wellington's Own).
9th Northumberland Fusiliers.
10th Lancashire Fusiliers.

DIVISIONAL BATTALION.

7th York and Lancaster Regiment.

There were carping critics who asked what was gained by giving to completely new organisations the names of historic regiments, which were represented in their ranks by perhaps at most a regular officer attached to act as adjutant, a couple of sergeant-instructors and three or four old soldiers. Sometimes there was not even this small personal link between new and old. But Lord Kitchener's action was amply justified by two good reasons—the one a matter of fact, the other a matter of feeling. As for the former, most of the new recruits came from the districts of which these older units were the county regiments. As to the latter, there is Napoleon's often quoted saying that in war the moral element often counts for far more than the material. *Esprit de corps* is an all-important factor in every military unit, and the new battalions were given the first elements of this inspiring feeling supplied by the link of names, badges, and battle records of the famous regiments, to which they were thus attached. They inherited a tradition and a standard of conduct, which they were called upon to emulate. Thus it was a real help and inspiration to the officers and men of the Tyneside battalion to know that they had been adopted as comrades by the " Fighting Fifth '—the old Northumberland Fusiliers, with their record of good service in the Peninsula, India, Afghanistan and South Africa; for the Border recruits to be reminded of Albuhera, Inkerman and Lucknow; for the new unit of the Lanca- shire Fusiliers to feel they belonged to one of the Minden Regiments, and that they were to emulate the deeds of those who had fought under Moore at Corunna and Wellington in France and Spain; who had stood by Lawrence at Lucknow and marched with Kitchener to the conquest of Khartum. The record of the Lincolns went back to the wars of Marlborough. Two of the new Yorkshire battalions had as long a history, and the West Yorkshires had the still earlier battle honour of Namur. The Staffords had a tradition that included, besides

Peninsular and Crimean honours, a long roll of Indian victories, including the hard fought battles that won the Punjaub.   The Sherwood Foresters inherited the record of the winning of Canada, the victories of Wellington from Rolica to Toulouse, and good service in India, Burmah, Abyssinia and Egypt.   The record of the Dorsets began with Plassey, the victory that won India for the Empire.   It was surely a wise decision of Lord Kitchener that the officers and men of his new armies should begin their months of training for active service as the adopted comrades of these splendid regiments of the old Army, instead of being simply given a new battalion number that would suggest that they were only units in a makeshift force without any link with the inspirations of a glorious past.

Apart from the honoured titles under which they began their army life, there was at first little to remind the new recruits of the 17th Division that they were soldiers. Only the very first steps in the work of organisation could be attempted in the districts where they were enrolled. They were given a few elementary lessons in drill and discipline, but they had neither uniforms, equipment nor arms.   The first important move towards the real organisation and training of the Division was its concentration in its training area.   The new battalions were moved to it by rail, each under the charge of a couple of " Conducting Officers," and a few N.C.Os.   The march to the railway stations was more like an improvised procession than a military parade, the entraining was like the sending away of a large party of excursionists. Legally regular soldiers, they were practically still only the raw material out of which soldiers were to be made.

The district assigned to the Division as its training area was the south-west of Dorsetshire, with the town of Wareham for its headquarters centre.   The town is a small place of about 3,000 inhabitants.   Though now cut off from the sea it once ranked as a prosperous port

of the English Channel.   It stands on a strip of low land
between two small rivers, whose confluence once formed
an estuary opening on the land-locked waters of Poole
harbour.   But the estuary has long since been silted up,
and the approach to it is barred by extensive shallows.
On this side the open sea is miles away, and southward
all view of it is cut off by the range of grassy downs that
forms the backbone of the Purbeck Peninsula.   Thus,
near as it is to the sea, Wareham has the aspect of an
inland market town.   It has a long history with many
records of siege and battle, for it was once a place of
strength, protected by the marshy lines of its two rivers
and the ramparts now marked by green mounds that
stand outside its present limits, showing how far its
extent has dwindled since the old times when it was
a fortress and a port.

The little town gave but scanty scope for billeting, so
the units of the Division had to be scattered in camps and
improvised quarters in various parts of the district.   In
the last days of September they began to arrive from their
recruiting centres in the north—crowds of men weary
with a long railway journey, often interrupted by tiresome
stoppages on the way, for it was a time when much movement of troop trains was in progress all over England.
On arrival, lack of experience and their elementary organisation and deficiency of equipment made the settling down
into rough billets or open bivouacs a troublesome business.
Some of the battalions remembered this first movement
as an unexpected introduction to the hardships of
campaigning.

Thus, for instance, the 7th York and Lancaster, some
1,300 strong, entrained at Pontefract for Wareham in
two trains.   The first reached the town late in the evening.
The second however got no further than Wool station,
eight miles to the westward of the place, where they
detrained in a downpour of rain at a small village which
could find no proper shelter for six hundred tired men.

After a rough night they pushed on to Wareham next morning, and were given temporary billets mostly in churches and schools. It was a time when everyone was keenly ready to help, and the townsfolk lent them a change of clothes, dried their rain-soaked kit, and did everything to welcome and care for them. A poet of the battalion sent its thanks to " the people of Wareham " in verses, the sincere gratitude of which made up for any technical defects of composition. The opening and closing lines may be quoted here:

> " Here's just a line as a message of thanks
> For the way you have treated the York and the Lancs ;
> Because, till you're wet through, there's nobody knows
> The pleasure of wearing a suit of dry clothes.
>
> . . . .
>
> " Your kindness we'll speak of wherever we roam,
> And our wives and our mothers will bless you at home,
> So please take our thanks, and your townpeople share 'em,
> The York and the Lancs. bless the people of Wareham."

This was not the only act of kindness for which the new division had to thank the people of Wareham and the district. It was a time when all over England there was a fine spirit of helpfulness everywhere. In the billets officers and men were treated as welcome guests. When tents began to arrive and camps were pitched round the town there was a woeful deficiency of Quartermasters' stores, and with the first early touch of autumn chilly nights accentuated the lack of blankets. From Wareham, Bournemouth, Poole and many smaller places there came friendly help in the shape of hundreds of bulky parcels of blankets and warm rugs, and when the parcels were unpacked numbers of them were found to contain also packages of cigarettes, chocolate and other comforts.

By this time organisation and training had begun. The first days were a difficult time. With all their goodwill numbers of the men hardly yet realised what soldierly discipline meant; and they had to learn even the first elements of it under serious but inevitable disadvantages. The recruit of pre-war days found himself from the first day of his training in an atmosphere of discipline. Apart even from all instruction he learned it almost insensibly from living and doing his daily round of work and duty among men to whom it had more or less completely become a habit. Here this very atmosphere of discipline and order had to be created. It was no fault of the men that from mere ignorance of what the new conditions of their life were to be they committed glaring faults against its new code. As civilians it had been no serious matter to take a day or a few hours off from their work. Their week-end pay might be a little the shorter for it, but it was easy to find an excuse, and the excuse was sometimes hardly expected. So now there were cases of men being absent for awhile from duty or parade because fine weather tempted them to prolong a country ramble, and they had not the remotest idea that this might be treated as a " crime." They had never been taught the necessity of keeping their belongings in any particular order, and could not for awhile realise that for men crowded together in improvised quarters insistence on some standard arrangement of kit and belongings generally was a matter not of routine and " red tape," but a necessity for comfort and efficiency. At first, getting the men on to parade was anything but a simple business. There were laggards to be hunted out, not because they had even the remotest idea of shirking a drill, but simply because they had not yet learned the importance of everyone being in his place immediately, and were not all quite clear as to what their places were. Things however began to shape themselves fairly rapidly into something resembling soldierly order and discipline. It was to the credit of all concerned that the process was not a long one. It was decidedly helpful when in October the men began to change from their civilian dress to some kind of uniform. The quarter-master and fatigue parties were kept busy with the arrival, distribution and unpacking of endless bales and bundles of what was to be the general uniform till shortly before the move to France next summer.   The supply was made up of a collection of the peace uniforms of a number of regular and militia regiments, now discarded for khaki by all the mobilised units of the old Army.   Battalion after battalion thus became for some months "red coats," but even then for some time many of them had to combine civilian headgear with this military dress.   But then came an issue of old pattern peaked caps, and supplies of civilian overcoats.   One battalion was fitted out with a heavy pattern greatcoat which, combined with the peaked cap, won them for awhile the jocular title of " The Chauffeurs."

Before the end of September the original improvised billets were mostly abandoned, a supply of tents having arrived and the men went under canvas.   While the fine weather lasted this was a decided change for the better. Officers' messes were organised, and later messes for the sergeants ; canteen huts were put up; and the first steps taken to provide amusement in camp for the men and lessen the applications for short leaves to Bournemouth and Poole.

When the weather broke in November the camps, with numbers of the tents half worn-out and leaky, became anything but comfortable or healthy.   There was a good deal of sickness, and this led to the weeding out of a number of men whose physique left something to be desired.   In preparation for the winter, hut camps were being erected about Wareham, and a heavy storm that laid low numbers of the tents and converted much of the camping ground about them into a swamp led to a move into as many of these new hutments as were sufficiently advanced to be habitable.   Gradually all the infantry were transferred to these better quarters.

Another step in advance was the distribution in December of a large supply of the old pattern Lee-

Enfield magazine rifles, to replace the miscellaneous collection of old D.P. ("Drill Purposes") weapons that had so far been the only arms available. With these Lee-Enfields and a good supply of cartridges it was possible to teach at least the elements of musketry.

Christmas and the first days of the New Year of 1915 were a time when many were coming and going on leave. By the middle of January this holiday period was over and steady training began again. The Division was now taking shape. It is true that so far only elementary work had been done, recruit and company drill being the programme for the infantry, and equipment of all kinds being still utterly incomplete. In their training centre at Swanage the gunners of the Division were still in the same early stage of their military education, but by this time the men had ceased to be civilians and felt that they were soldiers and there was the prospect that the coming summer would see their departure for one of the war fronts.

Major-General Kenyon-Slaney, who had so far carried through the difficult work of organising the Division and conducting the earlier stages of its training now resigned his command to the General Officer who was to take it to the front a few months later. The new commander was Major-General T. D. Pilcher, C.B., an officer with a distinguished military record. Born in 1858 he had received his first commission in the Northumberland Fusiliers at the age of twenty-one, and saw his first active service in West Africa in 1897, when he held the rank of Major. It was a difficult time. The "entente cordiale" was still in the future ; the relations of France and England were already strained by the "race for the Nile," and this tension was soon to culminate in the Fashoda crisis. In West Africa there was a dispute as to the limits of the "spheres" of influence and territory of the two powers, and French and English columns moving in imperfectly-known country were engaged in "pegging out claims" to be made good at some future settlement.   Only the tactful conduct of the commanders on both sides averted a clash that might have led to a serious conflict.   Major Pilcher went to West Africa as a special service officer in a field of activity that required no little enterprise, the knack of handling native levies, and political insight, where an error of judgment might have had more than mere local ill consequences.   He served there for nearly three years.   He raised the 1st Battalion of the West African Field Force (the " Waffs "), and in 1899 commanded the expedition to Lapai and Argeyah. This brought him a brevet of Lieutenant-Colonel, and the command of the 2nd Bedford Regiment on leaving West Africa.

He was on active service through the whole of the War in South Africa from 1899 to 1902, mostly in command of mounted columns.   One of his successes, the raid on Sunnyside and Douglas on January 2nd, 1900, made his name popular at home, for although it was a minor operation it was skilfully planned and conducted and seemed to come as a first presage of better things after the " black week " of Stormberg, Magersfontein and Colenso.   His services in South Africa gained him several mentions in despatches, a C.B., nomination as A.D.C. to the King and promotion to the rank of full Colonel.

After his return to Europe he paid more than one visit to Germany to follow the autumn manoeuvres of the Kaiser's army and study its methods.   He was already well acquainted with current military literature of Germany.   He was promoted Major-General in 1907 and in the following six years held various commands in India.

Soon after the outbreak of the Great War he was recalled to England, with a view to his taking command of a division of the New Armies.   When he reached London he was sent by Lord Kitchener to spend some weeks on the Western Front and visited most parts of it. The report which he prepared on returning to England contained some useful suggestions.   In January, 1915, he was appointed to the command of the 17th Division and at once proceeded to its headquarters at Wareham.

When he took command of the Division the preliminary work had so far advanced that it was possible to begin higher training. A rifle range at Bovington had been completed on Hyde Heath, and here in January real musketry instruction and rifle practice began. Battalion training for the infantry succeeded company training, and brigade training followed. Route marches and tactical schemes on a small scale were followed by operations with larger numbers and occasional night operations. A system of trenches was marked out and gradually completed and extended on the hills of the Purbeck Peninsula above Wareham, and here detachments spent in turn spells of twenty-four hours, carrying out the regular routine of trench warfare. Besides all this, for the tactical instruction of the officers the G.O.C. carried out a series of staff rides and tactical exercises without troops actually on the ground.

Rumour is busy in war time, and there came the minor excitements of reports that the Germans were raiding or about to raid the south coast ; stories of espionage—all baseless—and reports of strange lights being seen at night at various points along the heights of the shore, with sudden musterings of emergency companies and patrols to investigate, always with negative and therefore reassuring results.

In March there was a limited issue of service rifles, and new leather infantry equipment was distributed. Later on further supplies of service rifles arrived, though the full armament and equipment of the infantry brigades was not completed till the eve of the embarkation for France.

At the end of May orders arrived for the transfer of the Division to South Hampshire. The move was to be made by route march. Measured in a direct line the distance was about 36 miles, but by the roads to be followed it was much nearer fifty. Early on May 27th the infantry columns set out from Wareham, and bivouacked that afternoon in Cranford Park near Wimborne. The second day's march was to Somerley Park near the river Avon; the third day's march lay through the New Forest to Lyndhurst, and on Sunday, June 1st, the troops reached camps and billets at various places to the south and west of Winchester. Here training was resumed. There was a good deal of work in digging, and detachments were sent by rail for field firing at the Fovant ranges on Salisbury Plain.

So far we have dealt mostly with the organisation and training of the infantry. During the time spent in the Winchester area they were joined by the other components of the Division. Something must be said of the raising and training of these.

The organisation of 1914 allotted to an infantry division twelve batteries of artillery, grouped in " brigades " of three batteries, one of these brigades being armed with field howitzers, the rest with the 18-pounder Q.F. gun. Besides this the artillery of the Division had to provide a divisional ammunition column, charged with the transport and supply of ammunition of all kinds. This considerable force of artillery had to be improvised for the new Division, and it had always been recognised that to improvise such a highly-trained force for special technical work was a more serious task than the rapid making of infantry battalions out of raw civilian material.

General Purvis, R.F.A., was given this task for the 17th Division, and he found himself handicapped by the raw material provided for him being hardly as promising as that of its infantry units, though for artillery work a higher standard of physique and intelligence might well be required. He had a few regular officers of the Royal Artillery to assist him. Captain J. Browne acted as his staff officer and Lieut.-Colonel Cardew and Lieut.-Colonel

Harrison took command of the first artillery brigades that were formed. Most of the other officers had everything, or almost everything to learn, and there were very few non-commissioned officers who were able to give them any efficient help. There were many good men in the ranks, but there was a considerable leaven of very unpromising material. These last were men from Glasgow and some of the large towns of the north of England, who apparently had not been taken on by the local regiments and were treated by the recruiting authorities as surplus recruits that might be disposed of by turning them over to some other arm of the service. The Divisional Artillery of the 17th received a large number of them. For not a few of these the medical inspection must have been somewhat perfunctory, and long before the training had made much progress it was realised that some 20 per cent of the recruits were not fit for military service, and they had to be replaced. Amongst those who had thus to be weeded out many were as weak in intelligence and education as in physique. All this unfortunately handicapped the officers who had to create the new divisional artillery. The fact that so many of the recruits came from large industrial centres also made it difficult to get the drivers into shape. Even when the most likely men had been selected, it was found that very few had ever ridden in their lives or had any experience whatever of horses.

Swanage, a pleasant seaside town, about ten miles from Wareham, nestling in the curving heights of a bay in the " Isle of Purbeck," had beeen assigned as the training centre of the divisional artillery, the choice of this locality being about the only satisfactory feature of its training conditions. The early autumn months had been fine, and the men were encamped in fields near the town, but later rain set in and camp life became more than difficult, and there was a good deal of inevitable sickness. At last the camps were evacuated and the men were crowded together in a number of empty houses in the town, under very unsatisfactory conditions.

The artillery material provided at the outset and used for some months was woefully inadequate—indeed almost ludicrous in its out-of-date inefficiency. There was not a single field gun or howitzer of the type with which the batteries were eventually to be armed. There were a few limbers and waggons and a number of old guns, some of them so obsolete that they might be regarded rather as dummy guns than artillery weapons. Among them were two old French guns dating from the Franco-German war of 1870. These guns, more fitted for an artillery museum than a training centre, had actually no sights when they arrived at Swanage. All the technical equipment of a modern battery was absent; there were no dial sights, directors, range tables, telephones, etc. However with the aid of local carpenters and blacksmiths all sorts of ingenious contrivances were made up to serve as rough and ready imitations of the missing material. The marvel is that any training whatever was possible in these first difficult months at Swanage.

By the New Year of 1915 things were looking more hopeful. The doubtful elements of the rank and file were being replaced. Two more regular officers of rank and experience joined the command, and it was now possible to organise the personnel of the four brigades. The commanders were — 78th Brigade, R.F.A., Lt.-Col. E. H. Willis ; 79th, Lt.-Col. Harrison ; 80th, Lt.-Col. Cardew ; and 81st (Howitzers), Lt.-Col. R. S. Hardman. Colonel Hardman had commanded a howitzer battery for some years, and had been on active service in France till December, 1914. In the first week of January he was sent to Swanage to assist in the training of the new divisional artillery there.

The officers attached to the batteries were a useful lot. A few were regulars, a few more had learned something in the auxiliary forces, and among the rest there were a number of young men from the Dominions and other Dependencies of the Empire, men who could ride well and were used to open-air life. It was decided that all officers should be able to ride and those who were quite new to artillery work were sent away in turn to the various artillery schools for short courses of instruction; and some were further sent over to France to spend about ten days at the front, and see the actual working of their arm on active service.

In the middle of February, 1915, the first batch of horses for the gun teams arrived and were distributed among the brigades. They came from America. Colonel Hardman writes of them:

" I must say a word of the merits of the North American horses we were fortunate to get. Without this splendid little beast I don't think we could have become a mobile unit in the time. He was the best of all draught horses it has ever been my fortune to have had to deal with in a long career—small, few of them over 15.2, symmetrical, round, standing on short legs, with good feet, he had all the virtues of the equine race, with few of its faults. He seemed to revel in hardship, mud, wet, neglect and short fare, a most honest worker. I seldom, if ever, saw a team gibbing. At the same time he was extraordinarily docile, tame and easy to handle. Bucking or trying to get rid of a bad rider seemed unknown to this paragon of horses. One had only to put any six of them together, and three untrained men on their backs and the outfit walked away with a gun or waggon as if they had had years of training at Aldershot or Salisbury Plain. As an old gunner with long experience of English and Australian horses it was a revelation to me."

It was not till April that the 18-pounder Q.F. guns, with which three of the brigades were to be armed, began to arrive. The first of the howitzers for the 81st Brigade did not reach Swanage till May 15th. The Brigade was to be made up of four batteries of four howitzers each, and for some days this one gun was the centre of strenuous training, successive detachments being busy with it as long as daylight lasted. Three more arrived within the next fortnight, and by the end of May each of the batteries of the Brigade was happy in the possession of just one howitzer. In the last days of the month the three other Brigades moved by rail to a practice camp on Salisbury Plain. The Howitzer Brigade remained for a few days longer at Swanage.

Since the fine weather began in the spring a good deal of work had been done erecting huts for the Divisional Artillery and stabling for its horses, but it was only in the second part of May that they were sufficiently advanced for much use to be made of them, and the last of the Artillery left Swanage just as its camp was nearing completion.

Orders were now received for the Howitzer Brigade to proceed to Larkhill, Salisbury Plain, for gun practice, and knowing the training value of such an experience Colonel Hardman obtained permission for the move to be made by road. The R.A.S.C. co-operated in the march arrangements, and sent two young officers to act as supply officers, and arranged for rations and forage to reach the halting places each evening by train. Two officers of the Brigade on motor cycles went forward each day to see to the arrangements for the camps. The weather was fine and the march was a great success. Leaving Swanage on June 3rd, the first night was spent at Wareham Camp; the second in a field lent by a brewer at Blandford; the third on a common at Shaftesbury, and the last in Lord Pembroke's beautiful park at Wilton.

On arrival at Larkhill on the 7th the Brigade had only one howitzer for each battery, and these had to be put together to make one completely armed battery for training. No dial sights had yet been supplied, and none of the gun-layers had ever handled or even seen one. Firing at the artillery ranges was to begin at 10 a.m. on June 10th, and no dial sights were available until 5 p.m. the evening before, when an N.C.O. arrived bringing four of them, sent on loan from another brigade. A very busy evening was spent trying to impart to forty-eight gun layers some elementary knowledge of the theory and use of No. 7 Dial Sight.   There was practice on the two following days, and considering the disadvantages under which the training had been carried out the results were satisfactory.

The Brigade left Salisbury Plain on June 12th and was moved to Winchester by train, where on June 13th all the Divisional Artillery was assembled, and the whole of the 17th Division was being concentrated in and around the city.   Guns, waggons, ammunition and stores of all kinds now began to arrive, and field days and other operations were being carried out in concert with the Infantry of the Division, beside whom the gunners now found themselves for the first time.   The Division was doing its last days of training before being reported ready for service.

Three field companies of Royal Engineers were formed for the Division by selecting men who had already in their civil capacity some technical knowledge of various trades that would be useful to the sapper.   Junior officers and the N.C.Os. were sent to short courses at Chatham, and the technical equipment, at first collected and improvised in a somewhat haphazard way, was gradually replaced by proper material for work on active service.   But by the end of 1914 it had been realised that spade work and field engineering generally would play a much more important part in the war than had been at first anticipated, and it was decided to supplement the Field Companies R.E. by converting a number of infantry units of the New Armies into "Pioneer Battalions," one of which was to be attached to each Division.

Such battalions, which besides their infantry training, received a considerable amount of training as engineers, and were provided with the necessary equipment for this special work, had long existed in the German Army and in our own Indian Army.   Instead therefore of an additional battalion as a reserve in the hands of the Divisional

Commander, and not allotted to any of his three Brigades, each Division was to have one of these Pioneer Battalions, and the 17th Division was directed to select one of its infantry battalions for conversion into a pioneer unit.

Large numbers of miners had enlisted in the northern battalions, and an investigation showed that the largest percentage of these skilled workers was to be found in the 7th York & Lancasters, the battalion raised at Pontefract. It was therefore selected for conversion into a Pioneer Battalion, and a number of officers of other battalions, who, thanks to their previous occupations in civil life, possessed technical or scientific qualifications and experience, were transferred to it. The reorganisation was effected in the first days of January, 1915, and the battalion was henceforth officially known as the " 7th Battalion, York & Lancaster Regiment (Pioneers)."

Training in its new duties was added to the earlier routine of infantry work, and though at the outset there was a marked deficiency of field engineering equipment, some practical work was accomplished in the course of the new training. A detachment under Major Armstrong, with the help of a locally borrowed motor roller, constructed a serviceable camp road at Bovington, and near Wareham systems of trenches and dug-outs were made, which though they afforded useful practice proved to be somewhat inferior imitations of the elaborate defences of the Western fighting front. It was the day of small beginnings for the Pioneers of the Division, but they became before long one of its most useful units, and and we shall see that during their years of war service they did excellent and in some cases exceptionally valuable work. It was one of the many instances in the New Armies in which the previous civilian experiences of officers and men proved to be a preparation for their duties in war.

The all-important R.A.M.C. contingent of the Division was supplied by attaching to it the newly-raised 51st,

52nd and 53rd Field Ambulances.   These were organised and trained at a special training centre for the R.A.M.C. formed at Tidworth Camp on Salisbury Plain early in September, 1914.   The R.A.M.C. training camp was placed under the command of a regular officer who had already had war experience, Lieut.-Colonel R. N. Woodley, D.S.O.   At a time when there was an overwhelming amount of work to be done by the R.A.M.C. at the front and in the great base hospitals, and military hospitals at home, he was fortunate in obtaining for his camp the assistance of a few Regular officers, R.A.M.C. and medical officers of the Territorials.   The newly-commissioned officers who came to Tidworth for special army training were of course all men who had already medical qualifications and experience of civilian practice.   The rank and file were mostly men who had everything to learn.

Colonel Woodley gives the following account of the work done under difficult conditions at Tidworth:

"In September, 1914, I was ordered to proceed to Tidworth Camp and take charge of the R.A.M.C. Training Camp to be formed there.   Shortly after two regular R.A.M.C. officers were sent there to assist me— Major Bramhall and Captain J. Sylvester-Bradley.   Two regular N.C.Os. also arrived.   Recruits began to arrive rapidly and eventually 3,000 men were in training. These formed the nucleus of fifteen Field Ambulances, and included the three Field Ambulances which eventually joined the 17th Division—namely, the 51st, 52nd, and 53rd.   They were commanded in these early days respectively by Captains W. Barclay, D. Dougal, and J. R. Robertson.   These three officers later served in the 17th Division with much distinction.

"While at Tidworth the officers and men were accommodated in tents.   As the weather was cold and wet and the men raw recruits, mostly from towns, considerable hardship was experienced, there being a shortage of blankets, and no tent boards were at first available.   The men still wore their civilian clothing, which was not sufficient protection from the inclement weather.   The discipline was good and desertions not frequent, everyone being then desirous of getting out to the war.   It was an amusing sight to see the men on parade in those days—civilian clothes of all types, and headgear that included caps, bowlers, velours and even straw hats.   One gentleman arrived in a tall hat!

"Training was somewhat retarded by a complete absence of Regular N.C.Os. and by a shortage of technical equipment, which latter was later supplied on a limited scale.   Warrant officers and N.C.Os. had to be promoted from the rank and file of the recruits.

"In December, owing to the severity of the weather, and as the result of representations to Headquarters, the Training Camp was moved into billets at Torquay, where the men were more comfortable and contented, and training progressed more favourably.   While here Lieut.-Colonel Gowlland, D.S.O. (then T/Captain) arrived and took over command of the 51st Field Ambulance.

"The Field Ambulances remained at Torquay until the early spring of 1915, when they left to join the 17th Division at Wareham, where they received their full equipment and completed their training.   They there came under the command of Colonel Henderson, R.A.M.C., A.D.M.S., with myself as D.A.D.M.S. Colonel Henderson was later relieved by Colonel A. D. Julian, C.M.G., before the Division embarked for France."

For its Divisional Cavalry the Division was fortunate in having allotted to it a very efficient unit of the mounted arm of the Territorials, namely A Squadron of the Yorkshire Dragoons.   It was supplemented by a cyclist company.

This necessarily incomplete record will give some idea of how the 17th Northern Division came into being as a military formation of the New Armies.   When it moved into the Hampshire country about Winchester it could be said to be nearly ready for service.   Here General Pilcher was able to carry out some of the final stages of training, exercises in which artillery and mounted troops could work with the infantry.   The Division was at last complete.   What had been eight months before a crowd of raw recruits was now an effective fighting force.

CHAPTER II

THE FIRST WEEKS IN FRANCE AND FLANDERS
(JULY AND AUGUST, 1915)

IN the early summer of 1915 the movement of the New
Armies to the fighting fronts began.   It had been originally intended that the move should come somewhat later
in the summer in order to give the " K." Divisions a
longer training in England, but the need for a reinforcement of the armies in the field was becoming acute.   The
Dardanelles expedition had encountered unexpected
resistance, and from a minor operation of the war was
growing into a campaign demanding supplies of man
power on a scale that no one had anticipated at the outset.
Sir Ian Hamilton had asked for a reinforcement of
100,000 men, and troops were being diverted from the
Western Front to this eastern field of operations.   In
France and Flanders the results of the spring had been
disappointing.   In the second Battle of Ypres, though
the line held fast, some ground had been lost and the
Salient had become dangerously acute ; the spring
offensive at Neuve Chapelle had shown that it was useless to attempt to break the enemy's entrenched barrier
on a narrow front.   Foch's operations in the Souchez
valley and other local French attacks had given very
limited results even where they succeeded.   The Allied
plans were therefore now centred on an offensive on a
wide front in the early autumn, and the British had agreed
to take over a larger part of the line.   It was accordingly
decided to send several of the new Divisions to France
early in the summer, to learn the ways of trench warfare
before the next " big push " was made.

In May, 1915, the first of K. Divisions (the 9th) had gone to France. In June five more of them left England, but of these three were sent eastwards to reinforce the army of Sir Ian Hamilton in the Gallipoli Peninsula. The whole of the First Hundred Thousand had thus left its training camps for the war fronts. In those midsummer days the rumour ran that they would soon be followed by the " K. 2." Divisions (15th-20th), though some of these might be kept for a while longer in England for " home defence " and some further training.

From the outset of the war the Government had been strangely anxious about a supposed peril of invasion. In the first weeks of the war, though six splendid divisions of Regulars had been detailed for the Expeditionary Force, only four were sent to France, the two others being for awhile held back by this groundless fear of a German landing in England. Groundless it was, because while the Navy held command of the narrow seas, no enemy could land even a division, and from the first day of the war that command of the sea was effective. Had it failed there would be no need for the enemy to attempt an invasion, for the supplies both of the armies in the field and the civil population at home would inevitably have been cut off, and the war would be lost. But strange to say, this elementary principle of the defence of Britain, verified by all the experience of history, seemed to be forgotten, and during the first three years of war huge armies were kept in England for " home defence," and much energy wasted on such useless matters as the digging of an entrenched line to bar the eastern approach to London, the elaboration of detailed schemes for the hurried evacuation of English towns by their inhabitants, and even plans for making it more difficult for an invading army to cross the Thames between London and Reading. So now in June, 1915, when reinforcements were needed on the Western Front, it was decided that of the six Divisions of the second " K." Army two should remain

in England, and General Pilcher was informed that the
17th Division was to be one of those thus detailed for
" home defence."

As the East Coast was considered to be the danger
front on this theory of a possible invasion, Home Defence
Divisions were placed in camps and quarters at various
centres in the Eastern and Midland counties, selected
with reference to rapid concentration by rail on any point
of the coast and usually near important junctions, where
troops trains were held in readiness on the sidings with a
certain number of locomotives always under steam.   An
outpost line was provided by detachments of troops who
watched and patrolled the coast, and there were occasional
practice alarms.   The 17th Division would therefore
have to be moved from Hampshire to one of these defence
centres; accordingly in the first week of July it was concentrated about Winchester so as to be ready to move
northward or eastward.   This concentration was completed on July 4th, when the 50th and 52nd Brigades and
the Pioneer Battalion were brought in from the musketry
camps at Fovant and Larkhill.   That evening the distribution of the Division was as follows :

Divisional Headquarters -   -   -   -   Winchester.
    50th Brigade   -   -   -   -   -   Ramsey.
    51st Brigade and Motor M.G. Battalion   Flower Down.
    52nd Brigade   -   -   -   -   -   Hursley.
Divisional Mounted Troops: A Squadron,
    Yorkshire Dragoons and 17th Cyclist
    Company   -   -   -   -   -   Pitt Corner.
Divisional Artillery: 78th, 79th, 80th, and
    81st R.F.A. -   -   -   -   -   Pitt Corner.
Divisional Engineers and Pioneer Battalion   Hursley.
    The 51st, 52nd, and 53rd Field Ambulances were
        detached for training at Sutton Vaney.

On the following morning the General Officer in
Command received definite orders that while the rest of
the Divisions of the K.2. group were to embark for active

service the 17th would be retained in England. The 15th Division was already moving to its embarkation ports, and the 16th originally detailed with the 17th for home defence was preparing to follow. But during the day there was a sudden change of plans at the War Office, and at midnight General Pilcher received a telegram cancelling the orders sent that morning, and directing that the 17th Division was to embark for France immediately after the 15th—the 16th remaining in England. All mounted units with the transport and horses of dismounted units, and a party of 3 officers and 108 other ranks from each infantry battalion were to march from Winchester to Southampton and embark for Havre on July 12th to 15th. The Infantry Battalions were to be conveyed by train to Folkestone for embarkation to Boulogne.

A tremendous amount of work had to be got through in the next few days as the result of this sudden change of plans. On the 6th Captain E. C. Packe of the Royal Fusiliers (D.A.A. & Q.M.G.) with nine infantry officers was sent over to Havre to make arrangements there for disembarkation and railway transport. At Winchester every unit had to carry through the closing up of accounts and returns, and the obtaining and issuing of an endless variety of stores and equipment for active service abroad. The makeshift old pattern rifles, that had mostly been so far used for drill and training, were dumped, and the new short rifles issued, many of the men now handling them for the first time. When on the 11th the Division was reported as mobilised for service the proviso had to be added that in several of the units various objects of minor equipment would be drawn and issued in France.

Large numbers of the men had not had any leave since they joined and were looking forward to a brief visit to home before being sent away for active service. Pressing requests for this leave poured into Battalion Headquarters, but with the brief time available and the heavy work to be done only a limited number could be granted. The leaves were of the shortest and mostly meant a long railway journey northwards, a day at home and a hurried return to Winchester. The Dorsets were the luckiest, for they were not far from their old homes, but most of the officers and men had to make the best of a disappointing experience, and in thousands of households in the northern counties, instead of the expected visit their came the goodbye letter from a soldier son, brother or husband, telling that leave was impossible and the next news would come from France or Flanders.

On the 12th the first movements began—guns, transport, mounted troops and other details by way of Southampton to Havre, the first units of the 50th Brigade by train to Folkestone, and thence to Boulogne. By the 16th the whole of the Division, except the small parties left at Winchester to hand over surplus stores, etc., was in France.

French people had long become used to the arrival of their Allies from England, and the period of enthusiastic popular welcomes was long past. The landing in France was therefore a very matter-of-fact business. French interpreters joined each unit as it arrived. Those landing at Havre were quickly entrained for the concentration area assigned to the Division in the St. Omer district. The infantry battalions landing at Boulogne were sent up to the rest camps on the heights, and within the next twenty-four hours marched to the military station at Pont-des-Briques to entrain.

As evidence of the perfect organisation on the part of G.H.Q., B.E.F., which attended the concentration of divisions arriving in France, even at this early stage, it may be mentioned that as each battalion arrived at its entraining point, the special train which steamed in within a minute of its time contained the regimental transport and details which had left England some days earlier via Havre. The effect of even such a small item as this on the confidence of all ranks was most marked.

A.N.D.   B

On July 17th Divisional headquarters were established at Lumbres about eight miles from St. Omer, the old town of French Flanders, which was then the G.H.Q. of the British Expeditionary Force. The Division concentrated in the area south-west of the town, in and about the villages of Lumbres, Vizernes, Arques and Tattinghem.

The headquarters of the 17th Division at the outset of active service was thus constituted:

Divisional Commander: Major-General T. D. Pilcher, C.B.
A.D.Cs.: Captain L. C. Rattray, 6th K.R.R.
   Temp. 2nd Lieutenant G. St. C. Pilcher.

STAFF.

G.S.O.: 1st Grade—Lieut.-Colonel T. R. C. Hudson, R.A.
  ,, 2nd Grade—Capt. E. L. Humphreys, Lancashire Fusiliers.
  ,, 3rd Grade—Capt. H. E. Franklyn, Yorkshire Regiment.
A.A. and Q.M.G.: Colonel F. C. Muspratt, Indian Army.
D.A.A. and Q.M.G.: Capt. E. C. Packe, Royal Fusiliers.
D.A. and Q.M.G.: Major W. O. Marks, A.S.C.

ADMINISTRATIVE SERVICES AND DEPARTMENTS.

A.D.M.S.: Colonel O. R. A. Julian, C.M.G., R.A.M.C.
D.A.D.M.S.: Major R. N. Woodley, R.A.M.C.
A.D.V.S.: Capt. W. W. R. Neale, A.V.C.
D.A.D.O.S.: Hon. Major H. Lovett, Comm. of Ordnance.
A.P.M. : Colonel R. F. H. Anderson, Retired Indian Army.
C.R.A.: Brigadier-General Jackson, R.A.
C.R.E.: Colonel H. R. Hale, R.E.

A few days were spent in the concentration area, completing equipment and carrying out the preparations for the first move into the line. The issuing of a ground sheet, reserve " iron ration," and 120 rounds of service ammunition to all the infantry told of serious work being near at hand. The fighting front was only some thirty or forty miles away, and though it was what was called a " quiet time " the dull thudding and rumbling of artillery fire could often be heard in the distance. There was a further reminder of the fact that this was not the peaceful

English land, but the countryside of war-stricken France, in the almost complete absence of men of military age. Only women, children and elderly men were to be seen in the villages or working in the fields.

For most of the men in the Division it was an interesting time, with the strange experience of the first sight of a foreign country, and contact with foreign ways. There was the eager curiosity excited by being about to see and take part in the great drama of war, and if there was a reminder of the risks to be run, there was the beginning of that curious mentality by which the soldier thinks not so much of his own coming danger as of the question who of his comrades would have good or bad luck when serious work began.

The first active service of the 17th Division was to be in the Ypres Salient.   It was to form part of the Fifth Corps under the command of Lieut.-General Sir E. H. H. Allenby, K.C.B., the other Divisions being the 3rd and 46th, the former one of the old Army Divisions of the original Expeditionary Force, the latter a Territorial Division from the Midland counties.   The Fifth Corps, with the Second and Sixth, formed the Second Army under Lieut.-General Sir H. C. O. Plumer, K.C.B., who, with his headquarters at Cassel, held the left of the British line, mostly on Belgian ground.

According to the methods then in use of gradually initiating new Divisions into the ways of trench warfare, the 17th was to move up in the first instance to a position in rear of the line, and send officers and detachments of their men into the trenches for brief spells of service amongst the experienced troops who held them.   The movement to the front began on July 21st, and on that day Divisional Headquarters were transferred from Lumbres to the village of Steenwoorde, four miles east of Cassel, and close up to the Belgian frontier.   The Division was to occupy camps and billets south of Ypres and in rear of the sector of the salient that formed its southern front, where the line was now held by the 14th Division.

On the morning of the 18th, as one of the columns of the Division marched along the St. Omer-Hazebrouck road, Sir John French with some officers of the G.H.Q. rode out from the city, took post at a cross road and for some time watched the troops moving by.

The weather was fine but intensely hot, and the men carrying full service kit and ammunition, and tramping in new boots on the rough pavé of the Flanders roads, felt their first marches as a trying experience. To lighten their task much of the movement was effected by night. The way lay over the low line of hills that runs westward from the ridges of Kemmel to the bold height of Cassel. It was while crossing the slopes of the Mont des Cats that many of the men had their first sight of war. The sound of the guns around Ypres came clearer as they neared the crest, and as they passed it to north and east over a wide circuit they could see the long flashes of the heavy artillery, the glare that came and went in the sky, and the red points of light in dusk or darkness that showed where shrapnel was exploding. They were far from the battle line, though it seemed strangely near, and with these young soldiers here and there the breakdown of a waggon and the sudden check in the march led to a report spreading that a shell had burst somewhere on the column in front.

By July 24th the movement was completed. General Pilcher had fixed his headquarters at the village of Reninghelst, and to the east of it the Division had settled down in its huts, tents and billets, the accommodation everywhere being of the worst description. During this march across the Franco-Belgian frontier the first losses had been incurred by the Division, one officer and thirteen of other ranks having to be sent back to hospital seriously ill.

Next day, July 25th, the real work began. The General in command and parties of officers of the Division made a tour of the trenches, small detachments of the 6th Dorsets and the 9th Duke of Wellington's spent some time in them for practical instruction in trench duties, and the Pioneer Battalion (7th Y. & L.) supplied working parties for the construction of a reserve trench in rear of the support line, later known as the " G.H.Q. Trench." This day the Division had its first casualties under fire. The Pioneers were spotted by enemy aircraft and the German gunners shelled them with shrapnel. Second-Lieutenant Frampton was wounded, and of the men one was killed and four wounded, one of these mortally. Under the intermittent fire in the trenches the Dorsets lost one man killed and one wounded, and the Duke of Wellington's had one man wounded—nine casualties in all for the first day. Next day General Pilcher while visiting the trenches was hit by a splinter from a bursting shell. The wound was not serious, and after receiving first aid he resumed his work. That night while a working party of the Pioneer Battalion was moving from the village of Vormezeele to a support trench in the defences of St. Eloi, Second-Lieutenant Dibbs was killed, and later in the night while directing the work Captain Palmer, who commanded the party, was also killed by a long ranging rifle bullet. Each day now brought its toll of losses. Officers and men were being trained in the stern school of active service and the cost had to be paid.

A detachment from the 51st Brigade thus sent into the trenches on the night July 27th-28th had a trying experience. It was made up of officers and men of the 7th Lincolns, 10th Sherwood Foresters, the 7th Borderers, and the 8th South Staffords—a company from each regiment of the 51st Brigade. They were to spend a few days and nights in the extreme point of the Salient about Hooge, then held by troops of the 14th and 46th Divisions, to the latter of whom the 51st Brigade contingent was attached. There were fifteen casualties in getting into

the trenches, and on the 29th.   That day the German
guns were fairly busy, and desultory artillery fire from the
enemy's batteries in front of Hooge continued long after
dark.   About three a.m. on the 30th the firing rose into
a violent cannonade and the apex of the Salient came under
an intense bombardment.   So heavy was the fire that it
seemed to presage a general attack, and the 17th Division
was held in readiness to move up into the line.   But
when the attack came the fighting was confined to the
trenches about Hooge.   There the night attack revealed
a new horror of war.   The brunt of it fell on the men of
the 60th (King's Royal Rifles), young troops of the 14th
Division, who were holding the advanced trench across the
road near Hooge, the very point of the Salient, a trench
with a lot of badly-cratered ground in front of it.   Through
this broken ground the enemy worked their way up to
close quarters.   Men peering through loopholes saw
that here and there in the attacking line heavy objects,
under which those who carried them staggered, were being
lifted and dragged into the nearer craters, and the first
idea was that these would prove to be trench mortars.
Then suddenly there was along the front the loud buzzing
hiss of escaping blasts of air, splashes here and there of
what seemed like heavy rain drops, a smell of petroleum,
and then long fierce jets of flame swept over the trench, and
men fell or staggered back with hands and faces scorched
and clothes on fire.   The " flame flingers "—the
Flammenwerfer—were for the first time coming into action.
They might be roughly described as adaptations on a
large scale of the device used by painters to burn old
paint away with hand lamps giving out a jet of flame.
Originally devised for setting fire to barricades and
wooden buildings in street fighting, they were now being
used against living men.   The defence of the trench
was utterly disorganised by this new horror, a nightmare
terror against which there seemed to be no resource, and
the enemy's rush that followed the burst of killing and

torturing flame carried the defences of the Hooge road. The enemy held the trench they had won against a hurriedly improvised counter attack and kept it long after.

The companies of the 17th Division had been attached to units of the 46th (Territorial) Division, which held trenches about Sanctuary Wood and in support towards Zillebeke, the sector being just to the right of the position held by the 14th Division in the Hooge apex of the Salient. The Lincoln company, attached to the 4th Lincolns, was on the extreme left of the sector and in touch with the 14th Division. As it was then the custom to keep the front trenches closely manned, there were some casualties during the bombardment, mostly in the Lincoln company. The men behaved well in this their first sharp experience of war's realities. The next day passed quietly. In the night there were a couple of hours of heavy fire which seemed to prelude a renewed attack, but none followed. Early on the 31st General Pilcher and Brigadier General Fell visited the advanced position held by the detachment. Enemy aircraft were becoming more active and enterprising, and on the 31st to secure better protection it was decided to billet the Divisional train as far as possible to the rear and it was moved back to Boeschepe, about four miles west of Reninghelst and on the other side of the frontier line.

The preliminary period of instruction in trench duties and of initiation into active service conditions was now over, and on August 1st orders were issued for the 17th Division to take over the sector of the front so far held by the 3rd Division. It was a line of a little more than two miles in length, on the southern front of the Salient, with its right marked by the Wytschaete-Vierstraat road, and its left about the ruined hamlet of Oosthoek, not far from the south bank of the canal. It had been held since the heavy fighting of the First Battle of Ypres, when the Wytschaete-Messines ridge was lost, and this had given the enemy the possession of the high ground north-east

of Wytschaete, from which they had a good view at short
range over the British trenches in this sector.   From
about Wytschaete on a fine day they could search the
ground far to the rear of the line.   This drawback however was not peculiar to the sector held by the 17th
Division.   In the First Battle of Ypres the Germans had
failed to break the line, but they had secured an important gain in forcing it back from so much of the higher
ground.   In any other country but a land like these
flats of Flanders the " heights " would be regarded as
little more then low gently sloping rises of ground, but
here they were relatively important from their command
of the dead levels over which their view ranged far and
wide, so once they were won, the enemy could look down
into all the defences of the Salient.

The line to be handed over by the 3rd Division to the
17th was divided into two sections, each to be held by a
brigade.   That on the right began at the Vierstraat-
Wytschaete road and extended to a point about 250
yards south-west of St. Eloi; the left section prolonged
the line through St. Eloi to Oosthoek, the ruins of which
were included in its entrenchments.   The trenches were
in good order.   They had been held by one of the old
Regular Divisions—a Division that had landed in France
in the first days of the War, fought at Mons, and begun
its experience of trench warfare on the Aisne.   Officers
and men had learned by long experience the new arts of
making themselves at home in the half-underground life
of the trenches, and the ways of keeping them in good
order and continually improving their defences by un-
remitting care and work that never wholly ceased.   The
weather had been fine for some weeks and the trenches
were dry, so they could be handed over to the newcomers
in first-rate condition.

The relief had to be carried out under the cover of darkness.   It began on the night of August 1st-2nd, when the
52nd Brigade under Brigadier-General Surtees, with the

93rd Field Company R.E., took over the right section of
the line from the 9th Brigade, 3rd Division.   The brief
entry in the War Diary that the relief was carried out con-
veys no idea of what a night of strange experience and
adventure it was to these young soldiers, men who only
a year ago had for their horizon that of the life in town
and village, shop and office, factory, shipyard and mine
in Lancashire, West Yorkshire and on Tyneside.   They
fell in for the night march in their cantonments about

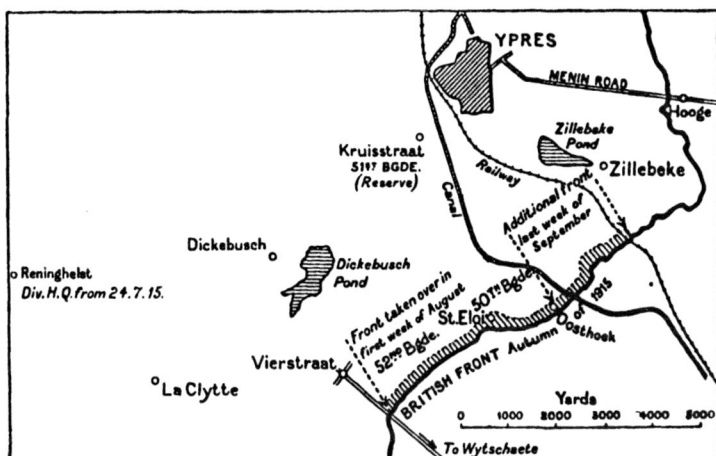

Sketch showing fronts held by the 17th Division in the
Ypres Salient. August and September, 1915

Dickebusch, with the new feeling that at last they were
moving into the fighting line.   Then came the march,
first on the rough pavements of the roads by Dickebusch
Lake, in the hot summer night, then westwards by the
main road that ran from Poperinghe towards the enemy's
positions on the heights round Wytschaete, a road that
in the darkness seemed endless, though the distance to be
covered was only some two miles.   Down the long slope
into the hollow below the lake, and up the ascent to the
low ridge where it traversed the shell-shattered village

at Vierstraat cross-roads, and then down again to the lower land where the trench line lay. Then came the sorting out of detachments to enter the labyrinth of the trenches, the movement out to the left of those who were to prolong the line northwards. There were guides to lead each party, but for most of the men all sense of direction was soon lost as they stumbled along narrow communication trenches, and felt the new sense of marching half-underground, while bursts of firing here and there in front seemed strangely near though often far away, and the occasional whistle of a shell overhead suggested danger. Other troops relieved by the Brigade were passing out. There was the endless work of settling down in advanced and support trenches, all the routine of " taking over," now an unfamiliar and some-what puzzling process to those novices in trench warfare. It was made somewhat easier for them because the troops they relieved were veterans of the old 3rd Division, who had ·had nearly a year's experience of the trenches, and were experts in " handing over."

On the same night General Banon's 50th Brigade—three Yorkshire Battalions and the Dorsets—left their quarters on the high ground near La Clytte, and marched by the Ypres road through Dickebusch, to bivouac north of the lake, not far from Kruisestraat village, ready to take over the left sector of the front assigned to the Division. Then General Fell's 51st Brigade—Lincolns, Borders, Staffords and Sherwood Foresters—began its movement to the grounds round an old château south-west of Kruisestraat, where it was to form the Divisional Reserve. Next morning it was rejoined by two of the companies which had been out near Hooge, the Lincolns and South Staffords. They had left their machine guns in the trenches there to help the 138th Brigade in case of a renewed attack.

On the night of the 2nd the 50th Brigade took over the trenches on the left of the 52nd, the line running through

St. Eloi to near Oosthoek, with its flank here not far from the Ypres-Commines canal. It was a dark night with heavy showers of rain, that overflowed into some of the dugouts, and made the trenches anything but desirable quarters. It was a lively night towards Hooge, and here and elsewhere along the line the guns were busy.

The German front line ran along the lower slopes of the rising ground immediately in front of the line held by the Division—a spur running north-east from the bold height topped by the ruins of Wytschaete at the north end of the famous Messines Ridge. Beyond the crest the enemy had masses of heavy long ranging artillery which indulged in bursts of fire from time to time by night and day. Their shells often reached or flew over the positions of the Reserve Brigade far to the rear about Kruisestraat Château. On the 3rd, to diminish their target here, General Fell moved two of his battalions—Lincolns and Sherwood Foresters—two miles further back. That day his brigade was rejoined by the last of the companies that had been detached to Hooge (Borders and Sherwoods), and it was now possible to ascertain the losses of the brigade in the days its four companies had spent there. These were: Lincolns, 27 casualties; Borders, 5; Sherwood Foresters, 15; and S. Staffords, 7—54 in all.

On the 4th the first reinforcement arrived from England, an officer of the South Staffords in charge of drafts for nearly every unit of the Division — a total of 687 men. That day the German artillery was particularly active. There were intermittent bursts of fire all day, and the trenches about St. Eloi were heavily shelled. Here there were nearly 100 casualties in the line held by the 50th Brigade, mostly in a company of the South Lancashires attached to them for instruction.

There were a few casualties in the Reserve Brigade near Kruisestraat, and next day it was heavily shelled for hours happily with small effect, for many shells failed to burst and many more fell harmlessly in the cornfields.

But it was evident that the enemy's gunners had marked the Brigade down as a good target, and General Pilcher decided to withdraw it to hutments near his headquarters at Reninghelst.   It moved off at midnight, and by 3 a.m. was settled down in its new and more comfortable quarters.

The ground held by the Division was regarded as a relatively " quiet sector " of the front.   People at home hardly heard of it, for since the heavy fighting of the First Battle of Ypres, when the enemy had won the Messines Ridge, the south front of the Ypres Salient was hardly mentioned in official communiqués.   It was one of the many sectors on which there was something like a permanent stalemate and deadlock.   But the enemy by unceasing activity with his artillery kept up the continual menace of an attack.   There was not a day without some casualties in the trenches, and the German guns intermittently shelled the positions far behind them, doing damage as far off as Vlamertinghe and Poperinghe, miles behind Ypres.   His aircraft were often busy overhead. His snipers, bombers and trench mortars were active in front.   For the young soldiers of the 17th Division the " quiet sector " seemed fairly lively.

The early hours of the 9th were lively enough about Hooge, and the batteries of the 17th Division joined in the preparatory shelling of the German front, which began with the first glimmer of dawn.   Then the 3rd Division successfully rushed and recaptured the trenches lost a few days before at the apex of the Salient.   The enemy's gunners replied heavily, and went on bombarding the front and the ground far behind it.   Shells burst repeatedly as far back as the streets of Poperinghe.   In the following days the enemy's guns and aircraft were very active.   In the artillery position of the 17th near Dickebusch Lake an 18-pounder was knocked out by a direct hit of an 8-inch shell, and some shells of the same calibre burst within a mile of the Divisional Headquarters at Reninghelst.

On the night of the 14th-15th August General Fell, 51st Brigade, relieved General Banon's 50th Brigade in the trenches on the left of the sector, taking over also part of the front so far held by the 52nd Brigade. The arrangement now made was that the 50th and 51st Brigades should alternately hold the front from the canal near Oosthoek southwards to the point where the little stream of the Diependaelbeck ran through the line. South of this the front on the right of the sector from the brook to the Vierstraat-Wytschaete road would be held by the 52nd Brigade under General Surtees, with two of its battalions in the trenches and two in reserve. This system was put into operation on the same night that the 51st Brigade took over the trenches on the right, and about St. Eloi two battalions of the 52nd being withdrawn into reserve, to form later the relief of those left in the line. Half the infantry of the Division would thus be in the trenches and half in reserve near Reninghelst.

The Pioneer Battalion (7th York & Lancasters) was employed in supplying working parties for the support trenches and the defences of St. Eloi. Its historian notes that for those who worked in one of these trenches (Q. 3) there was close at hand a reminder of home in the shape of " a derelict London motor omnibus, in which the scale of fares and discarded tickets of former passengers could still be seen."

The " No Man's Land " between the opposing lines of trenches was nowhere wide, and in some places was less than a hundred yards across. The enemy's artillery became very active in front of the trenches on the left, possibly to divert attention from the fact that a mine was being driven towards St. Eloi, where the front trenches were only about 80 yards apart. The South Staffords held this part of the line with the Borders on the right towards the Vierstraat road, the Lincolns on their immediate left, and the Sherwood Foresters on the extreme left near the Canal. The weather of the third week of

August was rather trying for the men in the trenches—
intensely hot with sultry nights and occasional rain storms.
To keep rifles and bayonets from rusting meant a lot of
work, and the trenches were now sodden with water, now
enveloped in a steaming haze when the sun shone out.
Festering half-buried bodies in No Man's Land added to
the discomfort of ·these conditions. Digging in the
trench line or repairs to parapets almost invariably
meant the exposure of bodies buried months ago.   In
the early hours of darkness and twilight on the 21st the
enemy's fire was heavy in the midst of a deluge of rain.
During the day the cannonade slackened off but was
resumed towards evening, and just after 7 p.m. there was
a heavy explosion in front of St. Eloi.   The Germans had
misjudged the distance of the mine they fired, which did
no damage to the trench line, but formed a crater twenty
yards in front of it.

This was the prelude to a good deal of "liveliness"
in front of St. Eloi during the last days of August The
enemy fired two more small mines, which did no damage
to our trenches.   One was so badly placed that it brought
down some of the enemy's own parapet in his front
trench.   There was day after day fighting with rifle,
bomb and trench mortar to keep the Germans from occupying the craters.   The enemy snipers were very enterprising, and sometimes elaborately disguised.   One
morning it was noticed that in one of the contested craters
some sandbags were moving slightly and suspiciously.
Probably a sniper was crouching behind them, and re-
adjusting his improvised protection.   Some rifle shots
were fired at the spot, and down into the hollow of the
crater rolled a dead sniper, disguised in sandbags, one of
which masked his face.   During these days the enemy's
artillery was busy not only shelling the front line but also
sending shells bursting far to the rear.   Our gunners
replied with good effect, and a novel use was made of the
machine guns of the Division.   General Pilcher was one

of the few commanders who at this stage of the war was a thorough believer in the power of the Vickers-Maxim, and held the theory, recognised and largely acted upon later, that its long range could be used for indirect fire. Twelve Lewis guns were placed at favourable points in and behind the trenches, and fired with high elevation so as to send their streams of bullets into the enemy's support and communication trenches, targets selected because it was now being realised that, unlike the British, the Germans held their first line lightly and kept most of their front line force in the support trenches. Air observation enabled the most likely points for this plunging M.G. fire to be selected. The result of this trench fighting was that the enemy had to abandon the attempt to push his line forward into the cratered ground, after losing a good many of his men in the effort. By the end of the month matters were again fairly quiet. Away to the east of Ypres the artillery was busy on both sides, and there were rumours of a coming " push " about Hooge, in which some battalions of the Division would be sent to co-operate. On the 26th and 27th the 51st Brigade was relieved by the 50th and became the Divisional reserve.

The total casualties of this first month in the trenches were:

	Killed.	Wounded.	Totals.
Officers - -	7	11	18
Other ranks - -	90	420	510
Totals - -	97	431	528

In the little wars of the past, this would have been considered a serious total of casualties. Campaigns of these earlier days had secured peerages for their commanders with lighter loss in action. But a year of European war had given the journalists and the people at home a better sense of proportion. Still these losses on what was considered to be a relatively " quiet sector " of the front showed what a costly business the new " warfare of attrition " could be, even though there were no battles.

The 17th Division had now been seven weeks in France and had passed its first month in the fighting line. It was less than a year since its formation began.   These last weeks had completed its training.   These thousands of men who in August, 1914, were still occupied only with the daily round of work in field and factory and mine, shop and office, had been transformed into soldiers. Many of the illusions of their earlier days of service had vanished, and in August, 1915, they had learned that the new war of the trenches was a dull kind of routine; but they had shaped themselves to it, and though it seemed so far to be a disappointing kind of way that led nowhere there was the cheering prospect that the second year of their service and of the war, now beginning, would bring a change.   For the early autumn was to see a combined Allied offensive on a vast scale.   There would be " real battles " that would bring the long deferred decision. The German line would break somewhere, and then would begin the victorious march to the Rhine.   It was something that after their long training in southern England and in the Flanders trenches they were ready to take their part in it.

CHAPTER III

EIGHT MONTHS OF TRENCH WARFARE
(SEPTEMBER 1915 TO MAY 1916)

FOR five weeks more the Division held the line which it had taken over in the first days of August. Broken weather and heavy showers of rain in the first part of September made the work in the trenches more difficult and conditions generally trying for the troops in the line. One night many of the trenches about St. Eloi were flooded. It was a foretaste of what campaigning on the Flanders flats would be in the winter. Then dry autumn weather set in and most of the month was fine, with at times windless days and at others a wind from the east blowing steadily, and suggesting doubts as to whether the elaborate preparations in progress for using gas in the coming autumn offensive might be useless. This new abomination of war kept the G.H.Q. hoping for a fair wind, as admirals watched for it in the old days of masts and sails.

This long-talked-of "great Allied offensive" had been fixed for the last week of September, and though the push was to be made far away to the south—by the British on the right of their line and the French in Champagne—the preparation for it and the course of the first operations had some influence on the experiences of all the Expeditionary Force in this autumn of 1915. As for the preliminary stage of the offensive the intensive artillery preparation would reveal to the enemy some days in advance, the sector against which it would be launched, unless he could be kept in doubt by increased activity

of our gunners on other parts of the front.   This was why
as early as the second week of September our guns began
a series of local bombardments on the Ypres front.   In
the third week this artillery action was further increased.
It seems to have misled the German command to some
extent, for when the attack was launched at Loos on the
25th that sector of their line was comparatively lightly
held.   They were more anxious about their front in
Champagne, where heavy artillery fire and an obvious
concentration for an attack suggested that the French
would play a chief part in the coming offensive and any
movement on the British front would be of minor
importance.

Further, the British plan included a number of subsidiary attacks to be made simultaneously with the main
push about Loos, in order to prevent the enemy opposed
to us from rapidly reinforcing his left from other parts
of the line in Northern France and in Flanders, and
especially to make him hesitate to draw such help from the
considerable force he kept permanently in front of Ypres.
Most of these minor attacks were to be mere feints,
pushed only so far as to give the impression that they
were serious.   But on our left at Ypres something more
was in view, and it was hoped that the position about the
Hooge apex of the Salient would be permanently improved
by winning some of the high ground so long held by the
enemy.

There had been early in the month some idea of making
this local push independently of the main operation, and
the Borders and the Sherwood Foresters had been temporarily detached from the 17th Division for some days,
which they spent in Sanctuary Wood waiting to assist
in the attack.   As they thus knew the ground, they were
again sent into the sector and attached to the 3rd Division,
which with the 14th was to make the advance on the
great day now definitely fixed for Saturday, September 25th.

On the 23rd the final instructions were issued.
During this and the following day there was a heavy
bombardment of the enemy's lines all round the Salient.
It began before sunrise, went on for some hours and then
ceased for awhile to be renewed from time to time during
the day.   Never yet had our gunners been able to maintain such a fire on the Ypres front—"4 a.m.—our artillery
going like mad," was the impressionist note with which
one of the brigadiers of the Division began his diary on
the 23rd.   He added that the enemy was replying
vigorously.   At first only lighter calibres were in action
on the German side, and it was conjectured that he had
perhaps sent away his heavier guns southwards, where our
bombardment, on these last days before the offensive, was
still more intense and sustained.   It never ceased, and
when there was a lull in the firing on the Ypres front, the
thunder of the massed artillery on the extreme right in
front of Loos and Hulluch, some forty miles away, could
be plainly heard.

But the enemy had not moved his heavy guns from the
Flanders front.   On the afternoon of the 23rd, and again
on the two following days, he threw some huge shells into
the trenches of the 17th Division, and some of these burst
far to the rear, and were identified as armour-piercing
projectiles from naval guns.   The Friday had been a dull
day with occasional rain and a good deal of mist hanging in
the still air.   In the early hours of Saturday the 25th it
was dull, with showers of rain and a slight wind from the
south-west.   It was still dark when at 3.30 a.m. all the
guns of the Salient opened fire, and the artillery of the 17th
joined in.   As the sun rose the attack of the two Divisions
was launched from the Hooge apex, the two battalions of
the 17th being here at first kept in reserve.   The rest
of the Division in its lines south of the Canal had only to
" demonstrate "—they were, as a diarist in the line put it,
" to play the giddy goat here and make the Bosche think
we were coming also."   One of these efforts at demonstra-

tion had unpleasant results for our own people, though it
may possibly have misled the enemy into the idea that he
was in danger of being gassed.   All the limited supply
of gas and gas projectors available was on the Loos front.
There a sudden change of wind had led to the British
troops in the front assembly trenches being the chief
sufferers.   The same thing happened with a sham gas
attack arranged near St. Eloi with the help of the York and
Lancaster Pioneers.   Working parties of these handy
men had fixed up trusses of straw in front of the fire
trenches, and when these were set alight it was hoped the
drifting smoke cloud would be taken by the Germans in
front to be the prelude of a serious attack.   But as at
Loos a trick of the wind sent clouds of stifling and blinding
smoke into our own lines.   It was nothing worse than
CO_2, but that is bad enough when there is plenty of it,
and a number of men suffered badly.   They were mostly
the York & Lancasters, who had contrived the show.

The artillery fire on both sides was so heavy that in our
lines south of the Canal the battle firing about Hooge
could hardly be heard, and even the explosion of a mine
that heralded the British attack passed unnoticed.   It was
not till 6.45 a.m. that the first news from the fight came
through to the 17th Division H.Q., and it was cheering.
The attack had broken into the German front line, and
the British bombers were working their way up his communication trenches.   At 7.30 another message said
simply that things were going well.   A few minutes
after 10 a.m. there was news that there had been good
gains of ground south of the Menin road, and the position
thus won was being consolidated.   There was no news
yet of the Borders and Sherwoods, only some days later did
the Division hear of the honourable part they played in
the Hooge fight.

In the afternoon the news was disappointing.   The
Germans had counter-attacked in force and won back all
they had lost north of the road about Bellewaarde, and the

result had been a retirement south of the road also. It was learned later that here the two battalions of the 17th had done good service. They had helped to cover the retirement, and their bombers had been effectively active. A month later one of their youngest officers, Second-Lieutenant John Christian White, received the Military Cross,—

" For conspicuous gallantry and determination, on September 25th near Hooge, when leading a bombing party to assist another infantry battalion. The bombers were driven back through heavy casualties, but Lieutenant White held on till only he and another bomber were left, when heavy shelling forced them to retire."

When the Borders and Sherwoods rejoined the Division on the 29th they reported their losses as—Borders, 16 killed, 66 wounded and three men and an officer missing; Sherwoods—10 killed, 90 wounded and 56 missing, mostly bombers, who were probably still with another battalion. This was a total loss of 222 for the two battalions.

The Hooge attack had thus failed, except in so far as it served to keep the enemy occupied, like the other subsidiary attacks. These latter were not intended to secure any further result than that of " demonstrating," but the Hooge attack was the most costly of all these " feints " because it was pushed more seriously. The affair was decidedly disappointing, all the more because the first messages from the fight had been so encouraging. Nevertheless, on the evening of the 25th, there was no feeling of discouragement at the local setback, for messages from Loos told of a victorious day, and there were further rumours of a tremendous success for the French in Champagne. There were high hopes that the decisive day, which would mark the turn of the tide, had come or was close at hand.

Next morning—Sunday, the 26th—there was a dead calm and a thick fog over all the Ypres front. Some of the German guns were firing through the fog, and here and there ours replied. About half-past ten the British batteries came suddenly into action, all along the front, and the Germans increased their fire, and for an hour there was a tremendous cannonade. It seems that all this expenditure of shells was the result of a S.O.S. message from the 14th Division at the apex of the Salient, reporting that a German attack was imminent. But it was a false alarm, and during the day there was nothing more serious than the usual desultory outbursts of trench fighting with bomb, mortar and rifle across the narrow " No Man's Land." A report from the Hooge sector placed the losses in the action of the day before at between three and four thousand casualties. News from the south was cheerfully optimistic. Fighting still continued at Loos. Some thousands of prisoners and 40 guns had been taken, and much ground won. There had also been large gains for the main French attack on the Champagne front. The brief information given by official communiqués was as usual supplemented by rumours of a tremendous success.

In war time dull matter-of-fact truth is at a discount. Official communiqués give the soldier abroad, and the civilian at home, only just as much as it is considered well for them to know, and no effort is spared to present what is told in a rosy light. So in our lines in Flanders, in those first days after the offensive of Loos began, little was known of what was really happening. Now after the lapse of fourteen years we know that such success as was gained on September 25th, 1915, was very limited, and, compared with what had been anticipated, a disappointing result. After days of intense bombardment six British Divisions had attacked on a line of about eight miles from the Double Crassier before Loos to La Bassée. The seven miles of enemy front south of the Bassée Canal was held by only thirteen enemy battalions, or about 11,000 men.[1] On the right about Loos a good deal of ground had

[1] Four line regiments, each of three battalions and a Jaeger (Rifle) battalion. They were all from the east of Germany, and many thousands were Poles from the Posen province.

been won and held, but elsewhere the gains were slight and much of the ground captured at the first rush had been lost before evening. All the Divisions engaged in the attack had suffered heavily. They fought well and were very near a real success. But there was poor staff work. Two new reserve divisions, hurried up to the fight by a long forced march, and flung into action in the afternoon, had gone to pieces. Other divisions were being called up to continue the fight against the now strongly-reinforced enemy.

On the Ypres front there were now happenings that told those who could think things out for themselves that the offensive was not going so well as official communiqués and unofficial rumour had told them. It was expected that at the end of September the 17th Division, having done two months in the line, would be withdrawn for " rest and training." But on the 29th there came orders from G.H.Q. that " in view of the situation in other parts of the theatre of war " it had been decided to withdraw the 46th Division from the Fifth Army, and the front occupied by it was to be forthwith taken over by the 3rd and 17th Divisions." The 46th was a Midland Territorial Division. It held the line on the left of the 17th between it and the 3rd. The 46th was to go south as a reinforce-ment for the Loos area, and the two other divisions were to extend left and right, each taking over half the front the 46th had so far held.

The new front thus assigned to the 17th Division began a little south of the Canal, and extended to just beyond the point where the Ypres-Lille railway passed through the line. This new front was about 2,500 yards in length, and would make the whole front held by the Division about 7,000 yards. On the night of the 29th-30th September advanced parties were sent into the trenches of the new line to arrange for taking over from the 46th. That day the Borders and Sherwoods rejoined the 51st Brigade from the Hooge sector. With the existing strain upon the Division it was not possible to give them the rest they had well earned, and almost at once they were sent into the trenches. The Sherwoods were not long in the line again, when an enemy mine blew in their front trench, burying an officer and 14 men.

In the night between September 30th and October 1st the extended line was occupied by the 51st Brigade. On October 1st, the Divisional H.Q. received from the Fifth Army H.Q. a general order that, till further notice, leave from France and Belgium was not to be granted unless " under exceptional circumstances "—one more indication that the situation was an anxious one. During the day units of the 9th Division began to arrive from the south for rest and reorganisation, during which they were to occupy rest billets of the 17th Division about Reninghelst and La Clytte. The 9th (Scottish) Division was the first of the New Army Divisions. It had been in action in the main attack on the Loos front on September 25th, where it fought on the left of the line. The Scots were held up on their own extreme left in front of Auchy, but on their right they broke through the front German line, capturing Fosse 8 and the northern trenches of the Hohenzollern redoubt. Then pushing on towards the second line they met a series of fierce counter-attacks, but though they had to abandon some ground, they held the enemy's works about Fosse 8. They lost heavily. One of their brigadiers told General Fell of the 17th that the casualties in his brigade were over 2,000, more than half its strength. Their report was that the fighting at Loos was still in progress, but the advance was held up and things looked like a new deadlock. From Champagne the news was that the French also were held up after the local gains won in the first rush.

On October 4th the 24th Division began to relieve the 17th, and by the 7th the Division had handed over all its positions to the new comers. The Division went into rest billets until the 20th, Divisional Headquarters being established on the 6th at Steenworde, eight miles west of Reninghelst, and just inside the French frontier on the main road from Poperinghe to Cassel. On the 7th General Allenby, the G.O.C. of the 5th Corps, came to Steenworde to meet General Pilcher and his Brigadiers. He told them it was a farewell visit, as he expected shortly to be transferred to another command. He spoke warmly of his appreciation of the good work done by the Division, and thanked the Generals for the help they had given him, adding that it was very likely that after its rest the 17th Division would not return to Ypres, but would be sent southward to the battle on the Loos front.

This was welcome news. It gave the prospect of a change from the endless, and apparently resultless, monotony of the Flanders trenches, where week after week went by without anything coming that seemed to have even the remotest influence on the ending and the winning of the war. This trench warfare was war reduced to deadly dull monotony—dull because " nothing happened that mattered much." Men lived a half-underground life; reliefs and fatigue parties moved stumbling along sunken paths in darkness; and always the front fire trench seemed to be the fixed limit that permanently barred all further advance. There was a ceaseless round of work to keep the trench system habitable and moderately safe. And that " safety " was only relative, for each month brought a toll of losses greater than the whole total of casualties in some of the little wars that had made the reputation of commanders in the recent past.

No one who had spent even a few weeks in the trenches of the Salient had any illusions left such as inspire poets, platform orators, leader writers in Fleet Street and composers of " drum and trumpet histories " with strange ideas of the romantic delights of war. In the trenches it was at best a dreary business, endurable only thanks to a steadfast patient sense of duty and discipline. " Battle " was a different thing. It meant at least a fair chance of some result that would count towards the final victory, of which no one doubted. There was a great battle in progress only a few miles away. At Steenwoorde, and still more plainly in the southern rest billets about Eecke, its gun fire could be heard day after day. Granted that the first results had been disappointing, and the enemy was showing an unexpected tenacity, yet there was a feeling that he must be badly shaken, and that under continued pressure the hostile line might give way at any moment, and the long-drawn battle give at last the hoped-for " decision."

The training done during this fortnight's " rest " suggested that it was a preparation for action on the offensive. Much time was given to attack drills, with the capture and consolidation of dummy trenches supposed to be held by the enemy. The sound of the cannonade and reports—official and non-official—from the south seemed to show that the battle was still in progress; but on October 17th there came disappointing orders that the Division was to return to Ypres and relieve the 3rd Division in the Salient.

Advance parties were sent forward on the 20th, and the same day the 51st Brigade moved up from Eecke to hutments between Busseboom and Brand Hoek, where a half-way halt was made before taking over the trenches in the Salient next day. The 50th Brigade from Steenwoorde followed on the 21st, and the 52nd Brigade on the 22nd. That day Divisional Headquarters were again established at Reninghelst. The Division was in the Salient for more than two months—until the first days of January, 1916.

On October 23rd Lieutenant-General Allenby bade farewell to the Fifth Corps with the following " Special Order ":

" On leaving the Fifth Corps, Lt.-General Allenby expresses his gratitude to all ranks for the constant support they have given him during the period of his command. He wishes them prosperity, and he is sure that, whatever the future may bring, the Fifth Corps will meet every trial with the determination and courage that have carried it to success and honour during the troublous times of the last six months."

He was succeeded in the command by Lieut.-General Fanshawe. The Fifth Corps was now made up of four Infantry Divisions—the 3rd, 9th, 17th and 24th, with their attached troops.

The 17th Division was now holding the apex of the Salient and guarding the Menin Road, on ground that had been the scene of much hard fighting ever since the autumn of 1914. The line it took over from the 3rd Division had its right a little to the north of the Ypres-Commines railway, in Armagh Wood, and ran north-wards by Observatory Ridge and Sanctuary Wood to Hooge, where its extreme left was just north of the Menin road. A little later—on November 8th—the extreme right of the line, including part of Sanctuary Wood, was handed over to the 9th Division and the left of the line of the 17th Division was prolonged further north by taking over from the 6th Division (Sixth Corps), the front to beyond the Ypres-Roulers railway, north of Hooge.

Before the front was thus altered the system of reliefs was that the 50th Brigade held the ground near Hooge, arranging its own reliefs and having two of its battalions always in the line; the southern sector was held alter-nately by the two other Brigades. After the change, the 50th and 52nd Brigades alternately held the Hooge sector, and the new ground was held by the 51st Brigade, arranging its own reliefs, and with its headquarters in the ramparts of Ypres near the Menin Gate.

In October, His Majesty the King paid a prolonged visit to the front. On the 27th he was at Reninghelst, where he inspected a force made up of composite bat-talions, each 500 strong, formed of detachments from all the units of the four Divisions of the Fifth Corps. The composite battalion representing the 17th Division was commanded by Brigadier-General Surtees, C.B., D.S.O., of the 52nd Brigade. On November 1st His Majesty addressed a Special Order of the Day to the Army in France and Flanders, which contained the following reference to the New Army Divisions:

" It is especially gratifying to me to have been able to see some of those that have been newly created. For I have watched with interest the growth of these Troops from the first days of Recruit Drill and through the different stages of training until their final inspection on the eve of departure for the front as organised Divisions. Already they have justified the general conviction then formed of their splendid fighting worth. Since I was last among you you have fought many strenuous battles. In all you have reaped renown and proved yourselves at least equal to the highest traditions of the British Army."

His Majesty ended by saying :

" I have seen enough to fill my heart with admiration of your patient cheerful endurance of life in the trenches, a life either of weary monotony or of terrible tumult. It is the dogged determination evinced by all ranks which will at last bring you to victory. Keep the goal in sight and remember it is the final lap that wins."

GEORGE, R.I."

"Nov. 1, 1915."

The line now held by the Division was a difficult one. About Hooge and in the northern part of Sanctuary Wood (all reduced to a wilderness of shattered tree stumps and shell holes), the German front trenches were close up to ours, with a very narrow belt of No Man's Land. The trenches were in bad condition, and as the ground sloped upwards towards the enemy's positions, and rose in a gentle slope in rear of our trench lines, it was difficult to drain them, and when the weather broke a deluge of surface water poured into the long hollow of Sanctuary Wood and the trenches were deeply flooded. In Flanders the winter of 1915 came early, with heavy rain storms and then hard frosts in the night, with a thaw in the early morning. Alternating rain, frost and thaw meant revetments giving way, sandbags rotting and breaking to pieces, and breastworks and traverses sliding down into heaps of mud. It was a never-ending task to keep the trench system in existence and to make it even barely habitable.

After visiting the front in the earlier period when conditions were better, the King had praised, in his message to the Army, the " patient cheerful endurance " and " the dogged determination of all ranks." The same soldierly qualities carried them through these winter months in the Hooge Salient. The " cheerful endurance " shown by these young soldiers of the 17th Division was a marvel. There were days and nights when the men in the trenches, soaked with rain from head to foot, stood to their posts with the water up to their knees. Commanding officers were worried, and the doctors at first puzzled, by numbers of men being incapacitated by a new kind of malady, which for want of a more scientific name came to be known as " trench feet." After a few nights in the sodden flooded trenches men found that they could hardly walk or even stand. Their feet were swollen and either numbed and dead or acutely painful. Rough and ready remedies proved useless, and attempts to stick it out and limp about ended in their being carried helpless to the hospital trains. Efforts were made to grapple with this new plague. The R.A.M.C. devised and issued a medicated oil to be rubbed into the feet as a preventive, and the Ordnance Corps provided a new article of equipment.

On November 11th the Staff diary of the 17th Division recorded the receipt of " 4,612 pairs of gum boots (thigh) for the use of men in the trenches." These measures reduced, but did not entirely obviate, the temporary losses through " trench feet."

During this tour of duty in the Hooge sector a number of new technical units were temporarily attached to the Division. These included No. 10 Anti-Aircraft Section,

gunners of the Royal Marines with quickfirers mounted
for dealing with the enemy's air raiders; the 6th Siege
Battery of the R.G.A.; the 5th Mountain Battery; the
2nd Siege Company, R.E.; the 2nd Entrenching Battalion; and the 175th Tunnelling Company, R.E.

The R.E. units were to help in the heavy work required
in the trenches and to assist in the countermining against
the German miners near the apex. The York & Lancasters, the Pioneer Battalion of the Division, with its
headquarters in Ypres, supplied skilled working parties
for many kinds of duty, including much work on the dugouts directed to making them not only shotproof but—
a more difficult business—to make them rainproof, and
safe from flooding. One of their companies was
employed in constructing a light railway from Kruistraat,
across the swampy ground south-east of Ypres, by which
supplies could be pushed up to the front on trolleys
without using either of the two roads available—that from
the Menin Gate and the road by Zillebeke. The work
was spotted by the German aircraft and the pioneers
were frequently shelled, and had a good many casualties.

During the sixteen days of October in which the
Division was in the line its losses were:

	Killed.	Wounded.	Missing.	Totals.
Officers -	4	9	—	13
Other ranks -	49	180	3	232
Totals	53	189	3	245

Besides, there were " evacuated sick," 20 officers and
441 men—461 cases in all—a large proportion of which
were due to " trench feet." Thus the losses by illness
were nearly double those due to the enemy's fire.

November began with two days of heavy and incessant
rain. The trenches were flooded, the Divisional camps
about Vlamertinghe a sea of mud, and the huts proved to
be hopelessly leaky. Then came brief intervals of
better weather, and again more rain, with later in the month

the first frosts and bitterly cold and dull weather. The reserve camps and supply depôts of the Division were about five miles in rear of the line, on very bad ground, but it was impossible to bring them nearer. Even in fine weather the movement of supplies each night, five miles up and five more back, would have been serious work, but under existing conditions it was an extremely trying task. The movement included marching by a ruined street kept open through Ypres, and day and night the enemy shelled the place intermittently, and sometimes put on a heavy bombardment, with something like a barrage by the Menin Gate, and at the road and railway crossing a little east of it, which came to be known as " Hell Fire Corner." Shells fell sometimes in the Vlamertinghe camps, others went screaming overhead to burst far off in Poperinghe.

In front of the left sector of the line held by the Division, north of the Menin road, the enemy's miners were busy. Here the defence was underground—pushing out countermines, listening for the sound of pick and spade, by which to judge where the German miners were at work and how near they had come, and then choosing the moment when an attempt might be made to blow his gallery in. It was a race in the dark with life and death as the stakes. Officers and men of the R.E. did the perilous work, helped by working parties from the Division—officers who a few months before had been mining engineers in England, and men who when the war began were miners in the coalfields of Lancashire and Northumberland. The aircraft helped at times by spotting the enemy's mineshaft heads behind his line, and our heavy guns tried to wreck them with H.E. shells. But day and night the countermining went on underground, and succeeded in preventing the enemy from driving his galleries under our defences. Our miners had the best of it.

Again in November the losses of effective strength by

sickness and exposure to the awful weather were far in excess of those by bullet, bomb and shell in the trench fighting.   The casualties were:

	Killed.	Wounded.	Missing.	Totals.
Officers	3	10	—	13
Other ranks	113	328	3	444
Totals -	116	338	3	457

The numbers " evacuated sick " were: Officers, 35; other ranks, 750; total, 785.

The bad weather continued in December.   There were many days of heavy rain; it became colder, and there were sharp frosts in the night followed by thaws in the daytime, keeping all the ground about Ypres in a sodden condition.   The enemy's artillery became more active, and by the middle of the month was so systematically busy that it seemed to be the prelude of an attack.

On the morning of December 14th the forenoon was fairly quiet.   It was a dull cold day with a thaw after the frost in the night.   At 12.45 the Germans started a bombardment of the trenches and of Ypres.   This lasted for two hours, during which there was very heavy firing, all the British guns available replying.   Then until evening there were intermittent bursts of hostile fire— periods of intense bombardment followed by a lull. Several 11-inch shells burst near the Menin Gate.   In the casemates close by, used as shelters and the headquarters of one of the brigades, men felt the old rampart shake as they exploded.   North of the Menin road the trenches were badly knocked about and there were many casualties. The Borders had 10 killed and 27 wounded, and the Sherwoods some 50 casualties.   Many of them were buried in the wreckage of the trenches.   About 6 p.m. the enemy's artillery ceased firing, but began again heavily about 8 p.m.   Then Ypres was shaken by a tremendous explosion that brought some of its tottering ruins to the ground.   The enemy had fired a large mine north of Hooge in front of the trenches held by the 7th Border Regiment. It made a crater 60 feet across and about 30 deep, but their miners had misjudged the distance, and it was forty yards in front of our line. The Germans rushed into it while the smoke still hung over it, but the Borders at once attacked with their bombers and drove them out after a sharp fight in the dark. In the night our possession of the crater was secured by wiring it and linking it up with the line by a short communication trench. The Borders had done a fine piece of work. Their losses for the day and evening were 26 killed and 78 wounded.

There was another bombardment of Ypres on the 16th. On the two following days there was nothing more than the usual intermittent firing. The weather was cold and damp, with a lot of fog and mist and hardly any wind. On the evening of the 18th, a light breeze began to blow from the north-east, a favourable point for a German gas attack, and this came early next day, Sunday, December 19th.

It had been a cold misty night, and with the first glimmer of twilight the German guns opened fire all round the Salient. Shells were bursting all over the trenches and the ground behind them. They rained on Ypres. At times there was something like a barrage by the Menin Gate. Then the enemy's long range heavies came into action, sending their shells far west of the town. Some of them burst about Poperinghe, and it was noticed that much of this long range fire was directed upon the roads and lines of communication from the reserve positions of our troops. It was a carefully-planned immediate preparation for an assault, with a bombardment of all the lines by which the defence of the trenches could be reinforced. Our guns answered the enemy's fire. The trenches were manned for battle. The 51st Brigade held those of the Divisional left sector, north of Hooge, and the 52nd was on the right. These Brigades called up their reserve battalions from the west of Ypres. The 50th Brigade forming the Divisional reserve was held in readiness to move if it was needed.

The bombardment had hardly begun, and these preparations to meet an assault were in progress, when helped by the steady north-east wind the enemy loosed off clouds of gas against the north front of the Salient. Weather conditions were perfect for its use—and it rolled forward in a dense cloud, and then began to spread over Ypres and make itself felt far to the west and south-west with remarkable rapidity. It was at 5.45 that a telephone message from the 51st Brigade informed the Divisional Headquarters at Reninghelst that a gas attack had been started by the enemy; within a few minutes after the smell of the gas could be noticed there, though the village was more than six miles from the point where it was loosed off. In the trenches the men had got their gas masks on and very few were affected by it, but further off many were taken unawares and suffered badly. It penetrated into the headquarters of the 51st Brigade in the ramparts of Ypres almost as soon as the warning of its approach arrived from the front. In his diary of the day Brigadier-General Fell writes: " I was slightly gassed and my eyes became extremely painful, not being able to see from the right eye. Nearly all of us were vomiting." The General suffered from the effects of the gas for many days after.

Besides the gas cloud, the Germans used gas shells freely in the bombardment. The gas hung about the place all day and the next. The bombardment of these early hours of the 19th was intense. The 9th West Riding Regiment, while moving through Ypres to the front, were caught in a storm of bursting shells. They lost their commanding officer and their adjutant, both wounded, and three other officers and 105 men killed and wounded. After they got through the ruined streets they reached the reserve line of the 52nd Brigade with only a few casualties. " Their advance under fire in skirmishing order over the open south of the Menin road was one of the prettiest movements I have seen," writes an officer of another regiment, who saw service to the end of the war.

North of Ypres soon after the first gas was loosed there had been a sudden burst of rifle and machine gun fire from the British trenches. Away to the left of the line held by the 17th Division the Germans were coming over their front trench. They did not come far. Not one of them got anywhere near our wire. They were caught by the sweeping fire from the British trenches, and then, with swift and timely artillery co-operation in the defence, a deluge of shrapnel fell upon them. Many dropped, the rest hurried back to the shelter of their trenches. The attack had failed at once, and seemed to those who watched it to be half-hearted. It was all over in five minutes.

The bombardment of the Salient and its hinterland continued. Gas shells rained upon Ypres—" tear gas " that half-blinded those it caught, and another variety that produced violent sickness and choking, stifling sensations in throat and lungs. For hours the trenches were kept manned in readiness to meet another attack, but the enemy made no further attempt to advance. By 7.15 p.m. with one exception all the telegraph and telephone lines of the Division had been cut and put out of action by the enemy's fire, and communication was for a while difficult. The one line from headquarters that held good throughout was a cable laid by the York & Lancasters. Luckily also a cross communication line between the 51st and 52nd Brigade positions was available. In his report of the day General Pilcher pays a tribute to the excellent work done under trying conditions by the R.E. and the Divisional Brigade and Battalion Signallers, and their repeated efforts to restore broken lines of communication. The R.E.'s early in the day, when shells were bursting freely about the Menin Gate bridge and other crossings of the moat, got their pontoons ready to improvise a way across in case any of the bridges were destroyed. They also sent forward working parties to the trenches, and helped to restore damage done to them under the bombardment. Two companies of the Pioneer Battalion the York and Lancasters also did useful work of the same kind. They moved out from Ypres in the first hour, crossed the open ground in artillery formation, and though under heavy fire thus reached the reserve trenches of the Division without loss.

At 9.45 the bombardment slackened, but it continued with less intensity all through the day and intermittently through the following night. Next day the artillery on both sides was at work, but it was rightly judged that there was now little prospect of the Germans attempting an assault. Undoubtedly on the day before everything had been prepared by the enemy for a serious attempt upon Ypres, and it had failed, thanks largely to the splendidly-organised and ideally prompt action of the artillery of the defence.

Gas was still hanging about on the Monday, and some more gas shells fell in Ypres. A number of men suffered from it though wearing their gas masks, for the chemicals in them had been exhausted during the long hours of the day before. The Divisional staff diary for this day (December 20th) contains an entry—" Brigadier-General Fell, 51st Brigade, wounded." The General's own personal diary says nothing of this. He had been gassed on the Sunday morning, and went back to Reninghelst in the evening for treatment, but on the Monday, though still suffering a good deal, he came back to Ypres with General Pilcher. All damage to the trenches and communications was made good during the nights of Sunday and Monday.

The Canadians, who were holding a sector of the line south of the Ypres Salient, had been making raids on a small scale on the enemy's trenches under cover of night.

Other divisions presently began to follow their example. There were for some time divided opinions as to whether these raids were worth their cost. They were supposed to be useful towards " keeping up the fighting spirit of the men," but one may well wonder if any such tonic was needed. Sometimes they provided for the Intelligence Officers of the Staff precise details as to the units in front, and secured prisoners to be questioned. But whatever was the balance of gain and loss they later on became fashionable, and a division that did not report a number of raids each month was regarded as showing slackness and lack of zeal. At first, except among the Canadians, they were rare adventures. The 52nd Brigade organised one in the early hours of December 22nd from the trenches near Hooge. The party was made up of an officer and sixteen men each from the Northumberland and the Lancashire Fusiliers (34 in all). They got up close to the enemy's trench, and threw about 100 bombs. The Germans manned their trenches and fifty rounds of shrapnel were rapidly fired into them by our artillery, while the raiding party retired, with only one casualty, a Lancashire Fusilier wounded. On the following evening shortly before 11 p.m. the enemy tried to retaliate. A few bombers, believed to be only four, crept up to the wire near Hooge, and threw bombs into the trench. They were driven off by rifle fire, leaving one of the party lying dead. The incidents are noted only as marking the beginning of raiding in its elementary stage of development.

Leave for home, suspended during the Loos fighting, had begun again in November. At Christmas some fortunate officers and men of the Division were in England on short leave. At the front parcels from home had arrived in abundance, and under difficulties some kind of effort was made at Christmas festivities. Orders had been issued that there was to be no attempt at renewing the fraternisation of the first Christmas at the front. On the German side the only sign of it was the appearance in the morning of a Christmas tree on the enemy's trench in front of the Borders north of the Menin road. It was fired at and immediately disappeared. There was some firing to the south of Ypres, and a number of shells fell near the Lille Gate, but most of the day was quiet. Commanding officers came round the trenches to wish their men a "Happy Christmas," but it seemed rather meaningless. Amongst the messages received during the day was a warning from Army H.Q. to be on the alert for a German attack from the south or south-east during the next few days as the wind was steady in that quarter, and favourable for the use of this latest development of "civilised warfare."

On the 29th, from midday for about an hour and a half, Ypres was heavily shelled. A barrage was put down on all its exits and gas shells were freely used. But there was no sign of an attack. In the following days there was desultory shelling, so in comparative quiet the end of the year came.

The casualties of the Division in the month of December were:

	Killed.	Wounded.	Missing.	Totals.
Officers -	4	25	—	29
Other ranks -	131	604	23	758
Totals -	135	629	23	787

Besides these losses there were "evacuated sick"— 29 officers and 758 other ranks, a total of 743. This made the losses of the Division from all causes 79 officers and 1,476 other ranks, making 1,555 in all for the last month of 1915.

The year 1915 had been disappointing for the Allies. Italy had joined them, but a new deadlock had been created where her armies were held by the Austrians along the Alpine frontier. Russia had lost all her earlier gains. The enemy held Warsaw, and the eastern front was pushed far into Russian territory. Serbia had been beaten. The Germans had joined hands with the Turks and Bulgars in the Balkan lands, and a new trench front had grown up round Salonika. The Gallipoli expedition had ended in withdrawal; the push for Bagdad in the siege of Kut. In the West the trench line stood much where it was twelve months before with the enemy's line unbroken. The newspapers at home wrote discreetly of the past, dwelt on the " inevitable exhaustion " of the enemy, which one sanguine critic declared to be close at hand, and with patriotic optimism the leader writers predicted that 1916 would be the " year of victory."

It opened in Flanders with dull skies, wild gusts of wind from the south-west and driving showers of cold rain. In the forenoon of New Year's Day our trenches were heavily bombarded, with much damage to the line north of Hooge. In the week that followed there was the usual intermittent artillery fire. On the 6th the 24th Division began to take over the front held by the 17th. By the morning of the 8th the relief was completed. The Division, thus set free, entrained at Poperinghe for a month of " rest and training " in France in the neighbourhood of St. Omer.

Divisional Headquarters were at Tilques, three miles north-west of the town, and the troops were quartered in and about the villages on or near the St. Omer-Calais road from Salperwick, near Tilques, to about Nordausques, some six miles away on the main road. The weather was better and there were many thoroughly fine days. The men could live in comfort, and even in the first days of their month's rest showed a marked improvement in health and fitness. Training of all kinds was carried out on a very full programme, beginning with steady drill and ending with field days, storming of dummy trenches and some instruction in wood fighting carried out in the Forest of Eperlecques. Rifle ranges had been prepared with the targets in chalk pits along the hills west of the

Calais road, and there was also a bombing school.   There
were abundant facilities for recreation, with plenty of
football, made more interesting by Brigade and Divisional
tournaments and inter-battalion matches.   It was the
best time the men had had since they left England.

The holiday ended on February 5th, when the Division
began to move back to the Ypres front, with orders to
take over the sector held by the 3rd Division.   On the
8th the movement was completed, and Divisional Headquarters were once more established at Reninghelst.
The sector assigned to the Division began near St. Eloi,
crossed the Canal and extended north-westwards to the
line of the Ypres-Comines railway.

It included some ground that had lately been won from
the enemy, on the north bank of the Canal.   This old
line of artificial waterway connects the flat lands of the
Yser with the valley of the Lys, and just in front of the
position on which the British lines were established after
the first battle of Ypres it cuts through the ridge that
divides these two regions.   The point chosen by the
canal makers for their cutting was the neck that connects
the Messines ridge with the heights that curve round the
south-east of Ypres to the high ground about Hooge.
From the Ypres flats these heights rise to a level of about
150 feet above the lower ground, and just north of the
canal there is a steep rise which gave the hill at this point
the name of " The Bluff " on the British war maps.
For some distance along the north bank of the canal the
débris dug out to make the cutting through the ridge had
been piled up into a long bank, 20 to 30 feet high,
extending to the lower slopes of the Bluff.   This had
consolidated long ago into solid ground, and when the
fighting about Ypres began was fringed with trees.   On
the Bluff and the high ground north of it there were
clumps of wood, fairly thick and moderately well grown.
The enemy had won the crest of the ridge in the fighting
of the winter in 1914, and the Bluff being the dominant

feature of the ground near the Canal the Germans looked
down on the British trenches on the slopes below.   Early
in 1915 a successful push had won back most of the high
ground, but it was by no means easy to hold, for the enemy

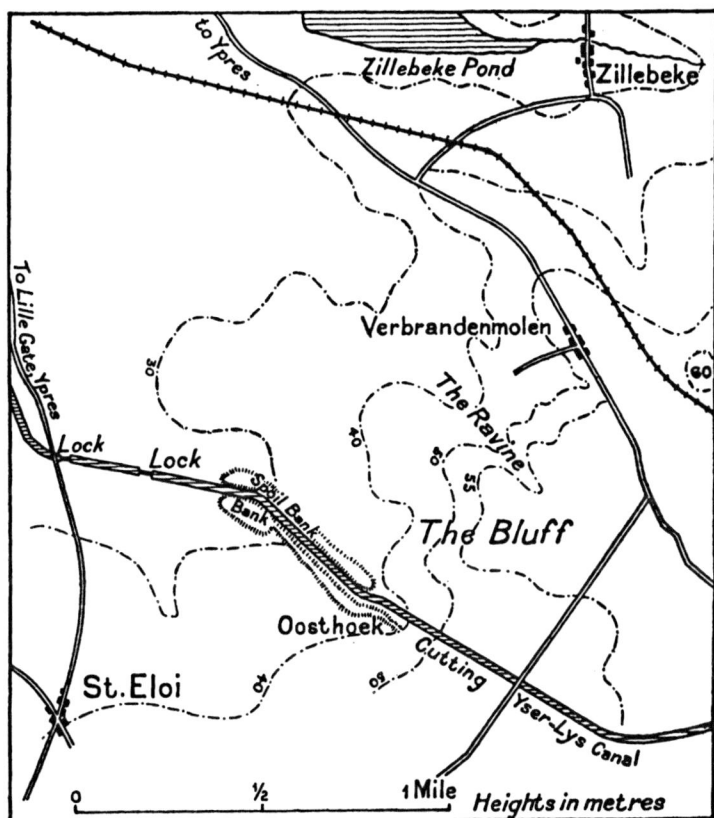

The Bluff. February, 1916.

had not been cleared off all the crest, and were still
entrenched close in front along the eastern margin of the
summit, with their supports on the reverse slope.   Their
batteries to the right on the Messines ridge, and in front
on the spurs that run out towards the Lys levels, could

bring a cross fire to bear upon the British position on and about the Bluff.

On February 8th, the very day when the 17th Division took over its new line, the Germans, after having for a while been comparatively quiet, became again active on the Ypres front. Their batteries began shelling the northern front of the Salient, and in the following days their fire became heavier, first against Hooge and the apex and then against the southern front. On the 11th the enemy's fire became more lively on the the 17th. Division front. They shelled the Bluff defences and threw a lot of gas shells into the trenches near the railway, and into the ruins of Verbrandenmolen, shells that caused some casualties and, to quote a diarist, " smelt abominably."

It had been discovered that the enemy's miners were driving their galleries into the Bluff. Countermining was in progress, and our airmen having spotted some of their mine heads and shafts east of the Bluff the heavies tried to demolish them with shell fire, but apparently without much success. This mining activity suggested that a serious attack was in contemplation, and a good deal of hard work was devoted to improving the Bluff defences.

On the night of February 10th-11th a party of Royal Engineers working at the head of one of our counter-mine galleries were surprised at seeing the face in front of them collapse and a German miner step through the opening. He was shot dead by the officer in charge of the party, and apparently was working alone, for no others were heard or seen. The German gallery was promptly blown in, and thoroughly wrecked. Next day there was a considerable amount of desultory shelling, and a down-pour of cold rain with a south-easterly wind made con-ditions in the trenches very uncomfortable. In the evening our counterminers succeeded in destroying another of the enemy's galleries in front of the Bluff.

On the 12th before dawn the enemy's batteries opened fire all round the Salient, and the heavy bombardment thus begun continued for several days. In the dusk the north front was attacked, and the Germans under cover of a smoke cloud got into the trenches near Pilkem, but were driven out about 7 a.m. Gas was loosed off in places on the south front, where the south-easterly wind was favourable. The 6th Division on the left of the 17th had several men gassed. But on this side of the Salient there was no attack, only continuous shelling until evening.

That day the Division received a useful reinforcement. In October, 1915, the War Office had given full recognition to the importance of the machine gun, by authorising the establishment of a " Machine Gun Corps," and for some time its M.G. companies had been reaching the front. One of these allotted to the 17th Division arrived on the 13th, and next day sent some of its M.G. sections into the trenches, with their Vickers-Maxim guns. On this day there was desultory bombardment of the south front, but heavy firing was heard towards Hooge, where the enemy having driven a number of saps towards our line had just joined them up by a new trench, from which they attempted an attack on the apex of the Salient, which ended in failure. A minor success of the day was the good work done by the howitzers of the 17th Division in demolishing a mine-head of the enemy's in front of the Bluff defences and near the Canal bank.

During the night the artillery was frequently busy on both sides on the Divisional sector. It was a sleepless night for most of those anywhere near this part of the front. At dawn on the 14th the enemy's shell fire became more intense. It slackened about midday but began again heavier than before at 3.30 in the afternoon. There had however been so much artillery work during the last few days that, though the trench guard was on the alert, it was not expected that a serious attack was impending.

That afternoon the distribution of the 17th Division was as follows: The right of the line was held by the 52nd Brigade under Brigadier-General Surtees. The 50th Brigade, under the temporary command of Lieut.-Colonel Edwards, was at Reninghelst as Divisional reserve, and was under orders to relieve the 52nd in the following night. Some of its troops were already moving out towards the front. The 51st Brigade, under Brigadier-General Fell, held the left front north of the Canal. It worked during this tour of duty in the line on the plan of having half its force in the trenches and the other half, which was to provide the relief, in the reserve, mostly about the Divisional H.Q. at Reninghelst. From right to left the battalions of the 52nd Brigade in the trenches were the 9th Northumberland Fusiliers, the 9th Duke of Wellington's, the 12th Manchesters and the 10th Lancashire Fusiliers. As the Brigade was entrusted with the defence of the point where the Canal passed through the line and held both banks of it, the Lancashire Fusiliers, under Lieut.-Colonel Wade, held the Bluff defences nearest the north side of the Canal. The rest of the front, including the left defences of the Bluff, was held by the 51st Brigade, with two battalions in the line— 10th Sherwood Foresters on the right and 8th Staffords on the left. The 7th Lincolns were in support on the spoil bank and the 7th Borders in reserve at Reninghelst. The Pioneer Battalion (7th York & Lancaster) had two companies in the front at work on the defences, one on the Bluff near the Canal, the other at St. Eloi, where for some days the German miners had been active. The other two companies were at Voormezeele, which was being converted into a strong point in support of the right. They were quartered in a ruined convent and some school buildings adjoining it. That afternoon General Pilcher was at St. Eloi, inspecting the right of the line. All along the front during the day there had been a desultory bombardment, with occasional bursts of heavier fire, and our gunners were retaliating. As the winter day drew to an end there was a general feeling that an attack was unlikely, though nevertheless all precautions were taken to meet it. There was to be a relief of the battalions in the line that night. The sun had set, and under the dull sky the twilight was deepening rapidly into night, when about 5.40 p.m. on the left of the Bluff near the Canal, there came a heavy mine explosion. It formed a large crater and wrecked the adjacent trenches. With their bombers in front, the enemy rushed the crater and the ruined trenches around it, and then with flank attacks from the ground thus seized, and frontal attacks from their advanced trenches, they began to work their way into the defences north of it, as far as and a little beyond the long sloping hollow known to the British as " The Ravine."

But after the first local gain on the Bluff the enemy, in face of the dogged resistance put up by our men, gained this further ground very slowly. For hours there was close and somewhat confused fighting, often hand to hand, along a front of some five hundred yards north-ward from the Canal bank, and less closely for some distance further to the left. At first the resistance was for the most part locally organised by company com-manders, who held on to their positions, and made counter attacks that held the enemy's progress. The heavy guns and howitzers of the Division brought their fire to bear on the German communication trenches, and on some of the artillery positions from which the enemy were putting a continuous barrage down on the western slope of the heights, between our support and reserve trenches.

The first reinforcement for the defence was supplied by the 7th Lincolns. On the right, near the Canal, Colonel Wade of the Lancashire Fusiliers sent a call for help to the company of the Pioneer Battalion under Lieut. Gillies, which had been working on the Bluff defences and was that evening on its way up to carry out a round of work during the night. On receiving the

message Gillies brought up his company of the York &
Lancasters to revert to their original status of a fighting
unit, and they did good service with bomb, rifle and
bayonet during the night battle.

As soon as General Pilcher at St. Eloi got the news that
a serious attack had begun north of the Canal, he hurried
back to his Divisional headquarters. The relief of the
52nd Brigade by the 50th, already ordered for the night,
was cancelled. One of the battalions of the 50th—the
7th Yorkshires—already on its way up to the front from
Reninghelst, was directed to halt near the Canal north of
Voormezeele, and remain in reserve there till further
orders. The Border Regiment and the remaining half-
battalion of the Lincolns were pushed forward north of the
Canal to support the defence. At 7.37 p.m. a reassuring
message reached Headquarters to the effect that the South
Staffordshires had retaken two of the lost trenches, and
apparently the German attack was being held.

The defence was already handicapped by the supply
of rifle grenades and bombs being rapidly used up.
Before General Pilcher reached Reninghelst a message
had been received from General Fell urgently asking for
a further supply of bombs. This request was complied
with, but by the unfortunate mistake of a subordinate
officer the bombs sent off were not detonated. It was
lucky however that some boxes of detonators were sent
with them. When these supplies at last arrived, and the
mistake was discovered, three companies of the Borders
were in the reserve trenches, the other company with a
company of the Lincolns having been hurried up to the
Ravine, where the Sherwoods were hard pressed. One
of General Fell's staff-officers took over the supply
of bombs in Kingsway trench, and organised working
parties of the Borders to fit them with the detonators, and
carrying parties to take them up to the fighting line. It
was dangerous work, and it had to be carried on for
hours in the darkness. There were some inevitable

accidents, and five of the Borders were badly wounded by explosions of the bombs they were fitting.   As supplies became available they were sent up into the line, and in this task the carrying parties of the Borders passed seven or eight times forwards and backwards through the German barrage.

Towards 9 p.m. steps were taken to organise a counter attack on the Bluff.   The Lancashire Fusiliers had been holding both sides of the Canal cutting at this point, and in preparation for the attempt to retake the crest Major Torrens brought across the Canal the two companies of the battalion that had been holding the south bank. Gillies with his Pioneers also joined in, as well as the remnant of the two companies of the Sherwoods that had been with the Fusiliers on the Bluff.   They had already suffered severe loss, a considerable number of one of the companies having being buried by the bombardment and the mine explosion that wrecked their trenches.   The counter-attack was started at 9.30, but, despite efforts renewed again and again till after midnight, failed with heavy loss, for the enemy had consolidated their gains on the Bluff, and the crest fairly bristled with their machine guns.

Well up the Ravine the enemy's further progress had been stopped by improvising a block armed with the guns of the M.G. Company.   Another counter-attack on the Bluff was repulsed about 2 a.m., and a third attempt failed a couple of hours later.

At 2 a.m. Divisional Headquarters had ordered the remaining three battalions of the 50th Brigade—now forming the Divisional Reserve—to move up to the ground about Dickebusch Lake.   The Dorsets went as far as Dickebusch and the West Yorkshires to Scottish Wood, a little east of the Lake.   The East Yorkshires pushed forward to the Headquarters of the 51st Brigade. Two companies of the West Yorkshires later on in the night were employed in providing carrying parties to take up supplies to the front. The Yorkshires already posted north of Voormezeele had been supplying carrying parties for the Lancashire Fusiliers for several hours. Though the 50th Brigade took no part in the actual fighting that night, these carrying parties of the two Yorkshire battalions came frequently under fire and suffered some casualties.

The last serious attempt at a counter-attack had been made by the defence north of the Canal about 4 a.m. on the Bluff, and the Pioneers again took a share in the fighting.[1] After this the battle gradually died down, though there was a good deal of firing along the front till daylight came—a dull cloudy dawn with a cold wind and driving showers of sleet.

The position now was that the crest of the Bluff and the front trenches north of it up to the Ravine were held by the enemy, but the support line lower down the slopes was intact in our hands. Losses had been heavy and the men were exhausted with the long struggle carried on all through the night. The Divisional artillery had been in action for sixteen hours, since early in the afternoon of the 14th. By 7.30 on the morning of the 15th the artillery fire had almost ceased, only an occasional shell flying overhead. Both sides were consolidating and reorganising. It had been decided that later in the day the artillery of the 17th would begin the preliminary bombardment in preparation for an attempt to retake the Bluff during the following night.

The day was miserably wet and cold and continual rain soaked the trenches and reduced the roads to tracks deep in mud. Early in the day, after a consultation between General Pilcher and Brigadier-General Fell, it was decided that the counter-attack on the Bluff should take place at 9 p.m., preceded by an hour of intense bom-

[1] General Pilcher wrote to Lieutenant Gillies congratulating him and his Pioneers on the good work they had done. Gillies was promoted to the rank of captain, but shortly after was severely wounded in the head and had to leave the York and Lancasters.

bardment. For this attack the East Yorkshires and the Dorsets were attached to the 51st Brigade. During the day, despite the difficulties of carrying out the relief by daylight close to the enemy and on lower ground, two companies of the East Yorkshires relieved the Sherwoods in the support trenches facing the Bluff, that now formed our front line. The other two companies moved in after dark. The Dorsets were to come up from Dickebusch so as to reach the assembly point assigned to them, near the Canal, and on the right of the attack shortly before the preliminary hour's bombardment began.

The main part in the attack was to be the advance of the Dorsets and East Yorkshires against the Bluff. To their right between the Bluff and the Ravine bombing parties of the South Staffords and Lincolns were to attack the trenches held by the enemy on that side. The Dorsets had not a long march to make from Dickebusch, not quite three miles even allowing for a devious line of march. But various circumstances delayed them. There seems to have been at the outset some hitch in the communication of the orders for the evening to them. For some time in the afternoon their commanding officer expected, from what he had been told, that he was simply to reinforce the right of the 52nd Brigade south of the Canal. This seemed a likely use of the battalion, for the Germans were lately very active in front of this sector, and there was some anxiety about a push on that side of the Canal following their successful dash at the Bluff. It was late in the afternoon, about 4.45, that the position was cleared up by definite instructions, and they were told to get ready to move and at once to send a couple of officers up to the front to get some idea of the Bluff position and act as guides in the advance against it.

When the battalion at last moved from Dickebusch their march in rain and darkness over sodden tracks deep in mud was very slow. They were only approaching the front when at 8 p.m. our gunners opened their heavy

preparatory bombardment. The enemy's artillery had
been in action at various times during the day. Whilst
replying, the Divisional artillery had taken the opportunity of carefully registering the targets for its guns in
readiness for the bombardment after dark. It had
hardly opened when the enemy put down a heavy barrage
on precisely the same line it had been placed upon the
night before. To reach their assembly positions below
the Bluff near the Canal bank, and in one place actually
on the old spoil heaps beside it, part of the Dorsets had
to pass through the barrage and here suffered their first
losses. By the time the battalion was in position it was
after nine o'clock, and the attack in which it was to take
part had been already launched. The unfortunate result
was that for nearly an hour the enemy had to deal only
with the attack on his right between the Bluff and the
Ravine, and successfully held our bombing parties, who
were trying to fight their way up by the old communication trenches. During this stage of the fight the attack
was reinforced however by a bombing party drawn from
the Border Battalion, the main body of which was closing
in for its attack on the Bluff.

When at last they attacked they made a very gallant
attempt to win the height. Two companies were
pushed forward, the right company from the Canal bank,
the left against the front of the Bluff. As it went up the
right company was caught in a heavy enfilading fire of
machine guns at point blank range, and suffered heavy
loss in a few minutes, during which all its officers were
killed or wounded, and it was brought to a standstill by
the cross fire from its immediate front. The left company
pushed up close to the enemy trenches, and one of its
platoons actually got into them, but was unable to maintain itself there. The remnant of the two companies then
held on to a position well up the Bluff, where they were
united under the command of Captain Mozley, the senior
surviving officer, bringing fire to bear on the trenches

above them.   Mozley held on till he received orders to withdraw, and during this time one of his sergeants (Orderly Room-Sergeant H. Bulkely) crept out from the position more than once to rescue wounded men lying close up to the German wire.

Meanwhile repeated efforts were made to press the attack of our left, but without success.   About 5 a.m. the attack was abandoned, and all the troops engaged withdrawn to the old support trenches.   During the action the enemy had kept up his barrage fire in rear of the attack.   One of the shells penetrated and burst in a dugout used as a dressing station, killing the medical officer, Lieut. Gough, R.A.M.C., and the wounded man to whom he was giving first aid.   The failure was due to the attack having been too rapidly improvised and the strength of the position consolidated by the enemy during the previous day being underrated, and finally to the right and left attacks not having been combined from the first.

It was now decided that the next attempt to retake the Bluff should be no hurriedly improvised affair, but an operation patiently and deliberately prepared so as to ensure a rapid and decided success.   The rest of the month was devoted to these preparations, and the success that was finally obtained was due to this patient thoroughness.   There was naturally a longing to get back the lost ground at the earliest possible moment, and there was some chafing at the delay.   But the delay itself was an element in the plans worked out by the G.O.C. of the 17th Division, who had in mind the object of lulling the enemy into the false idea that his position was secure, and giving the attack, when it came at last, the character of a surprise.

Before telling of the coming operation for the recapture of the Bluff, it must be noted that the enemy had been made to pay heavily for his success, but the persistent gallantry of the defence and first effort at recapture of the ground had cost the officers and men engaged on our side serious losses. There is no precise record of these, but they can be roughly estimated from the fact that the casualties in the fighting of February 14th and 15th north of the Canal formed the greater part of the total losses incurred by the Division during the whole month. And the losses in February were as follows:

		Killed.	Wounded.	Missing.	Totals.
Officers	-	12	66	11	89
Other ranks	-	212	1080	315	1607
Totals	-	224	1146	326	1696

The 326 reported as " missing " were practically all cases of officers and men buried by the mine explosion and the wrecking of the trenches by the bombardment, and of those who fell fighting on ground now held by the enemy.[1]

During the fortnight of preparation for the final attack on the Bluff there were many days of trying weather. First came a time of cold rain, and then hard frost and snow. This somewhat delayed the work that had to be done in our trench system north of the Canal, which included not only the repair of considerable damage done by the enemy's guns during February 14th and 15th, but also improvement of the communications, adaptation of the trenches for the assembly of the attacking force and some careful engineering work done to facilitate the advance immediately beyond our front trench, without revealing to the enemy the object in view. The snowfalls made it more difficult to conceal from his watchers the intended lines of advance. On the day of the 15th much heavy work had to be done clearing up and reorganising after the 48 hours of battle. The Dorsets relieved the South Staffords in the trenches. The Staffords had lost heavily, and their commander, Colonel Barker, had been dangerously wounded. On the 16th the rest of the line

---

[1] Besides casualties in action, 29 officers and 685 other ranks were returned as " evacuated sick " in the month, making the total wastage in the strength of the Division in February 2,410.

to the right was taken over from the Sherwoods and Lincolns by the 10th Royal Welsh Fusiliers and the 2nd Suffolks.

These were battalions of the 76th Brigade, belonging to the 3rd Division.[1]   The Brigade under the command of Brigadier-General Pratt had been placed at the disposal of General Pilcher by the G.O.C. of the Fifth Corps, General Fanshawe, as a reinforcement for the 17th Division.   It will be remembered that the 3rd Division had held this sector immediately before the 17th took it over, so that the reinforcing brigade was well acquainted with the ground.   They now took over the trenches held by the 51st Brigade, which was given a brief rest in Divisional reserve.

For three or four days after their success the enemy were nervously on the alert, apparently expecting an immediate counter-attack on the Bluff, and they repeatedly put down a barrage on their front.   Their aeroplanes were also busy, sometimes venturing on daylight flights behind our line, and making several bombing raids by night.   The result was a few casualties but very little material damage.   It was a time of cold and wet, and then came day after day of snow with hard frost at night.

Meanwhile the preparations for retaking the Bluff were being carried out with deliberate patience.   On February 17th a conference was held at Divisional H.Q. at Reninghelst to arrange the artillery preparation.   Long before and after this stage of the war there had been a kind of set pattern on both sides for the bombardment preceding a serious attack.   All available guns and howitzers opened an intense fire on the objectives for a day or two before the assault was launched.   It continued up to the last moment and then the sights were raised and the range lengthened just as the attacking troops went over the front trench.   This method gave fair warning of when an

---

[1] The 76th Infantry Brigade battalions were the 2nd Suffolks, 1st Gordons, 9th King's Own, and 10th Royal Welch Fusiliers.

attack was imminent. General Pilcher now adopted
another plan to avoid giving this warning and make the
attack, when it came, something of a surprise.

The Divisional artillery was reinforced, and each day
during the two weeks before the attack there was a desultory bombardment of the enemy's position and its
approaches, which was at times intensified into a prolonged heavy fire such as might suggest that an attack
was contemplated. The hour of this intense bombardment varied from day to day. It sometimes began at
dawn; then on another day it was towards noon or in the
afternoon or towards evening. Gradually the Germans
came to regard it as having no special significance, but
while it lasted it was directed to doing as much damage as
possible to the defence works of the Bluff and the ground
to the north of it.

To assist in this work of destruction all available trench
mortars were sent into the front line. They were kept
hard at work, and to supply them with abundant ammunition a lot of heavy work was done by carrying parties,
aggregating from 400 to 500 men, being detailed each
night for this task. It meant severe labour under the
difficult conditions imposed by the bad weather and the
resulting state of the ground.

As the day fixed for the attack drew near a new feature
was introduced into the artillery work at the suggestion of
Major W. Congreve.[1] There would be two bursts of
intense fire from every gun and howitzer, each lasting
only a few minutes, with an equally brief pause between
them. It was rightly anticipated that during the first
burst of fire the enemy would take cover in his trenches,
and would get into the way of lying low during the lull,
expecting the second blast of shells, and when it was over
manning his front line again and considering that the
annoyance was ended for the time being. It was intended

[1] A brilliant young officer then acting as Brigade-Major of the 76th Brigade.
He was killed in the fighting at Delville Wood in 1916.

that on the day of the attack on the Bluff the immediate prelude would be one only of these short bursts of heavy fire.   The assaulting troops would advance as it ended and while the enemy was still lying low in expectation of the second blast of fire.   Instead of this the brief pause would be ended by the artillery putting down its barrage beyond the enemy's first line and on his communication trenches.

The artillery of the adjacent sectors to right and left arranged for co-operation.   Further, the eastward curve of the front north of the 17th Division sector was examined to select a position from which the Bluff defences could be enfiladed with long range fire, and four heavy guns were posted on Observatory Ridge for this purpose.   Here they remained concealed and silent till the day of the attack.

The attack on the Bluff and the adjacent works was to be made by the 76th Brigade and two battalions of the 51st, with the other two of its battalions in support. On February 17th General Pilcher had a conference with the Brigadiers—Generals Fell and Pratt—at Reninghelst, when the 29th was provisionally fixed as the day for the attack.   On the 21st he submitted his plans for it to the G.H.Q. Fifth Corps, and these were approved.

On the nights of February 20th-21st and 21st-22nd the 50th Brigade relieved the 52nd in the trenches south of the Canal.   A good deal of work had to be done in this part of the sector, for it was thought that while the preparations for the Bluff attack were in progress the enemy might make a diversion on this side.   Night after night the pioneers and three R.E. companies and strong working parties supplied by the 51st Brigade were employed in strengthening the defences.   North of the Canal, besides constant work on the trenches facing the Bluff position, a considerable amount of work was done in improving the communications, and to ensure field telegraph systems from being broken by the enemy's fire on the critical day armoured cables were buried deeply, well back to Reninghelst, with the result that during the subsequent operations telegraphic communication was never interrupted.

Near Reninghelst a full scale model of the Bluff defences was dug, based on the latest aeroplane photographs. On the nights of the 22nd-23rd and 23rd-24th General Surtees with the 52nd Brigade relieved General Pratt's 76th Brigade in the trenches. The Brigade thus relieved was brought back to rest camps near Reninghelst, where in following days with the Lincolns and Sherwoods they practised the attack on the model enemy position. It is interesting thus to note some of the chief features of the elaborate preparations for what was counted in this great war as " a minor operation." It will give some idea of the colossal scale on which the greater offensives had to be prepared.

On the 26th it snowed heavily all night, and soon after dawn the enemy's aircraft raided and bombed the positions behind our line as far back as Reninghelst, and his artillery opened an intense bombardment. There was an order for all reserve battalions to be ready to move up to the front, but this was soon cancelled, and news came that the Germans had attempted to attack near the Ravine, but had been stopped by our gunners. After this the firing died down. This was the only show of a serious counter-attack made by the enemy during the period of preparation.

On the 28th it was decided to defer the attack until Thursday, March 2nd, when the assault on the Bluff would be made with the first glimmer of dawn. After a week of hard frost and snow the weather had changed. A sudden thaw broke up the ground and impeded all transport work, and for some days it was cold and wet, with occasional showers of sleet and snow that melted as it fell.

On the evening of March 1st the 76th Brigade, with two battalions of the 51st (7th Lincolns and 10th Sher-

woods), relieved the 52nd Brigade and took over the
trenches facing the Bluff positions.   General Pratt, who
was in immediate command of the attack, had thus six
battalions at his disposal.   General Fell, with the remaining battalions of his Brigade (8th South Staffords and
7th Borders), moved up to the north of Dickebusch as the
reserve of the attack.

It was a miserably cold and damp night, and few had
any sleep while waiting for the zero hour, 4.30 a.m. on the
2nd.   There was some desultory artillery fire after dark,
but this had been the case night after night for a week,
and care was taken that on our side it should not be
increased so as to put the enemy on the alert.

At 4 a.m. parties of our men began quietly crawling
forward from the front trenches, and silently gathered in
groups lying down near the German wire.   This was
found to be cut in many places and everywhere in bad
condition, with the posts loose in the ground, so that it
was easy to pull great lengths of it down.   At 4.30,
after our guns had been silent for awhile, there was a
sudden two minutes' burst of heavy fire.   It was the
usual general salvo fire, which the enemy had now become
accustomed to regard as being invariably followed by a
second short burst and then comparative quiet.   But
at 4.32 as the fire ceased the assaulting battalions went
" over the top " and up the slopes and into the enemy's
front trenches, and as they reached them the guns
reopened with raised sights, heavily barraging the enemy's
communications, and the four heavy guns on Observatory
Ridge, 1,800 yards away to the northwards, enfiladed his
support line.

The Germans were completely surprised.   Numbers
of them were found resting with their equipment off.   At
several points they hardly attempted a serious stand
against the rush of the attack.   The rapid capture of the
front line was followed by steady progress into the support
trenches.   The Lincolns rushed their machine guns up

and were able to take heavy toll of a mass of retiring enemies. The Welch Fusiliers (76th Brigade) actually got beyond their objective, and lost heavily through pushing too far to the front. This mistake was partly the result of the rapid collapse of the enemy, and partly of the fact that our repeated bombardments had so wrecked the German defences in this direction that it was no easy matter to recognise the trench they had reached. They were drawn back to the general alignment, and consolidation began, while the Germans, recovered from their first surprise, brought reinforcements up through our barrage, turned on all their available gunfire and began counter-attacking. A first batch of prisoners sent back included four officers and 177 rank and file.

The sending back of prisoners, removal of wounded, movement of carrying parties and runners with messages had to be carried out under a heavy barrage put down on the British trenches and communications and maintained for hours. Towards noon there was a determined counter-attack all along the front, but it was held and repulsed after some hard fighting. During this phase of the action in response to messages from the front, first two companies of the Staffords and then the rest of the battalion were sent into the fight. Towards 4 p.m. the battle gradually died down, and at sunset we were in secure possession of the Bluff and all the trenches that had been lost to the north of it, and further, of a small German salient locally known as " the Bean," which had been consolidated and linked up with the nearest of the recaptured works. The day had been a complete success. The prisoners taken numbered 252 (5 officers and 247 other ranks).[1]

---

[1] The History of the 27th German Infantry Division describes the first successful attack on the Bluff as having been carried out by the 124th Regiment. It is admitted that the German losses were heavy, and it is added that " the (British) counter-attacks, though unsuccessful, increased the casualties to a critical extent." The Regiment occupied the captured position till it was relieved by the 123rd

Losses were heavy (chiefly by the intense artillery fire of the enemy), the total from noon on March 1st to the evening of the 2nd being 65 officers and 1,599 other ranks. The losses of the 51st Brigade (included in this total) were :

7th Lincolns -	5 officers,	215 other ranks.	Total	220
10th Sherwoods -	3 „	97 „ „	„	100
8th S. Staffords -	2 „	21 „ „	„	23
Totals	10	333		343

This was the first important action in which the officers and men were all equipped with the steel helmet, and this saved many lives.

Divisional H.Q. had been informed in the last days of February that after the completion of the operations against the Bluff, the Division would leave the Salient and be transferred to the 2nd Corps then under the command of General Sir Charles Fergusson. On March 4th orders were received for the move into the 2nd Corps area.

The Division had a very short time in rest billets between the hills of the Belgian border and the flooded river Lys. It was less than a fortnight. The first week was a wintry time of frost and snow, but then came the first signs of spring. Headquarters were moved on March 7th to Steenvoorde, just inside the French frontier, and three days later to Merris, eleven miles west of Armentières. The troops were billetted in and around the neighbouring towns and villages—the Divisional

Grenadiers, the relief being completed on the night of February 21/22. The newcomers found the position " shot to pieces, with men cowering in shell-holes up to their shoulders in water." The narrative proceeds :—" There now occurred an absolutely tragic event. The position captured by the 124th Regiment was lost. . . . The defeat was due to the defences being destroyed and the men worn out after thirty-six hours' bombardment. But the 124th have never been able to forgive the Grenadiers, and there ensued a certain tension between the two Regiments to the end of the war. The Grenadiers, with the help of the 124th and 127th, tried to recapture the Bluff by a night attack, but enemy machine guns stopped every attempt to advance."

artillery about Hazebrouck; the 50th Brigade at Stra-
zeele; the 52nd at Outersteene; and the 51st near
Bailleul with its H.Q. in the town—" the first civilised
place we have been in since we landed last July," wrote
a staff officer in his diary. During this rest time Sir
Charles Fergusson, the 2nd Corps Commander, went
round the billets and inspected the troops, and there was
also a visit by General Plumer, the Army Commander.
When inspecting the Lincolns he praised the battalion
for its part in the capture of the Bluff.

The Division was now to relieve the 21st Division and
take over the trenches covering Armentières, east of the
bend of the River Lys. The town of Armentières was
then all that was left to France of the rich northern district of textile industry that has Lille for its centre.
Though it lay so close to the fighting front a large part
of its people still clung to their homes, and " carried on
bravely " just behind our trench line. During the latter
days of the short " rest " the G.O.C., brigadiers and staff
officers of the Division, visited the town and had a look
at the line they were to hold. From diaries of the time
one gathers some of their impressions. In Armentières
they saw many signs of damage done by hostile shell fire,
but nevertheless " shops were open everywhere." Crossing the flooded Lys they visited the sector established on
the flat land of its eastern bank. There was a lot of mud,
" nothing like that of Flanders in depth," but bad
enough, for the soil was clammy adhesive clay. The
support line was still incomplete in places, but what there
was of it looked fairly good, with " strong points " at
intervals of about 300 yards, where bits of dry ground
allowed more digging to be done, but, as one diarist
noted, " we did not think the men who laid it out had much
practical experience of heavy fire." The advanced
trenches did not give a good impression. " They are
mainly bad breastworks, old and not well constructed,
and would not stand an hour's ' crumping.' After

hearing a glowing account of them before we came we were disappointed. They don't know what shelling is, as carried on in the Ypres Salient." It must be added

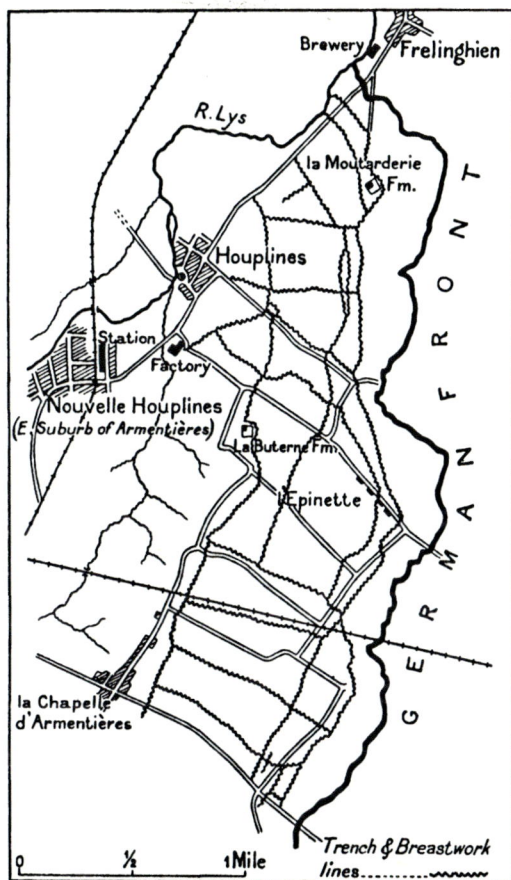

Front held by the Division in the Armentières Sector, 1916.

that on most parts of this ground, it was not possible to construct a trench system like that of the Salient. The water level was too near the surface, and no power on earth could have kept deep trenches from being permanently flooded. Hence the large dependence on breastworks, with shallow trenches behind them. There was a very narrow "No Man's Land," and enemy snipers were active in their front trench beyond it, but there was little shell fire.

On March 23rd the line was taken over from the 21st Division, and Divisional H.Q. were established in Armentières. The Division held the sector till the middle of May. There had been changes in two of the brigade commands just before the move to Armentières, Brigadier-General W. J. T. Glasgow taking over the 50th Brigade, and Brigadier-General J. L. J. Clark the 52nd.

The winter was nearly over. The river fell rapidly and the trenches were soon dry. A lot of steady work was done to improve the defences generally, one feature of it being the construction of machine gun nests, which may be described as something like large tubs sunk in the ground, and sheltered by splinter-proof overhead cover. But such fatigues as there were seemed a much easier matter than long marches and heavy work in the mud of the Ypres front. There were good billets in the factories and houses of Armentières; there were baths at Nieppe; there were shops, concerts, a cinematograph. It was like a return to civilised life. Then too after a few snowy days the coming of spring ripening into the early summer, with sunny days and flowers blossoming even among the trenches and breastworks.

The German snipers were often busy.[1]   On March 20th, while General Pilcher was going round the trenches of the 51st Brigade with Brigadier-General Fell and Major

---

[1] It was in this sector that the system of Intelligence Officers and observers was really developed. One of the first results was the discovery that the German snipers were using steel plate loopholes. An officer of the Lincolns had a 400 H.V. Jefferies sporting rifle sent out with a supply of solid steel bullets. This put an end to most of the enemy sniping on the Lincoln front in a week, for the bullets drilled through the loophole plates as if these were slices of cheese.

Graham of the Brigade Staff, Graham was shot through the head by a sniper and killed on the spot. The German machine gunners sometimes swept the crest of the front trenches with their fire, and one morning there was *Flammenwerfer* attack on a small scale. Aeroplanes made a few bombing raids with little effect. The German artillery fire was seldom heavy, though there was a good deal of desultory shelling. The comparative quietness of the sector was realised on the many days and nights when intense and prolonged artillery fire could be heard a few miles to the northward on the old front about St. Eloi.

Only once during the seven weeks spent in this sector did the enemy make anything like even an attempt at attacking, and this was no more than a raid. On April 26th there had been a good deal of artillery activity on both sides during the afternoon. Towards sunset this ceased, but at 7.30 p.m. in the twilight a German aeroplane flew over the trenches on our left near the river Lys and dropped first a white light and then two green ones. This was the signal for the enemy's guns opening a heavy bombardment against the left front, then held by the 52nd Brigade. The fire was most intense against trench 88, between the river and the moated farm of la Moutarderie. Its parapets and breastwork were quickly demolished, and at 8 p.m. a party of the enemy dashed forward to rush it. There were only about 50 of them. Most were stopped by the fire of the West Ridings, who held this part of the front, but a few got into the trench, only to be quickly driven out. The dead body of an officer of a Saxon regiment, probably the leader of the raid, was left in the trench. The West Ridings lost 5 officers and 23 other ranks, mostly as the result of the bombardment. A few days later on May 5th, the enemy opened a heavy fire all along the line after dark. It was especially intense against the Epinette Salient, and there were many casualties in the trenches. The Division on the right sent out a gas alarm and our artillery put down a barrage along the front, but the enemy made no attempt to attack.

On May 9th General Pilcher left for England on short leave and General Fell took temporary command of the Division. Four days later the New Zealand Division began to take over the sector, and the relief was completed on the 16th, when Divisional H.Q. were transferred to the village of Tilques, three miles north-west of St. Omer. The Division was assembled in the neighbouring district for a month of " rest and training." They knew the ground, for they had been here at the beginning of the year, when they were out of the line for about a month previous to their last tour of duty on the Ypres Salient. The troops reached it by route march by Estaires, the Forest of Nieppe and Arques. But the conditions were very different from those of their first training there in the winter. There was fine summer weather, and the country, with its wide stretches of cultivation and many orchards, had a holiday appearance. Billets were fairly comfortable, and the day's work was interesting, including not only training in the attack of trench systems, but also something of open warfare. By the end of the month everyone was in the best of health and condition, and it was generally known that the next active service of the Division would be in the expected great summer offensive.

General Pilcher returned and resumed command on May 18th. In the first week of June orders were received transferring the Division to the Fourth Army, as Reserve Division to the 15th Corps (General Horne), then on the right of the British line in the Somme region. Advanced parties started on their journey south on the 10th. Next day Divisional H.Q. were transferred to Allonville, a village three miles north of Amiens. The same day the 50th Brigade entrained at St. Omer, and by the 16th the movement of the Division was completed.

The train journey was a long one—first to Calais, then along the coast line by Boulogne and Étaples to Abbeville and by the main Paris line to Amiens, where the troops detrained at Longeau junction station on the eastern margin of the city.

CHAPTER IV

THE BATTLES OF THE SOMME, 1916
(FIRST PHASE, July 1916)

This southward move of the Division was drawing it into that tremendous concentration of fighting power which was soon to be flung into the greatest battle that the war had yet seen. At last a blow was to be struck with this concentrated strength that would, it was hoped, not merely win a few trenches in the German barrier line, but would smash through it on a broad front, and end the long-drawn warfare of the trenches.

These were the sanguine expectations of the early summer months of 1916. So far the two years of war had brought many disappointments. There had been in its first days hopes of speedy victory—hopes blighted for awhile by the Battle of the Frontiers, and revived after the Marne to be disappointed again as the opposing lines extended to the sea and became rigidly fixed in hundreds of miles of mud-sodden trenches in the late autumn. Then came the attempted breaks through of 1915— Champagne and Picardy, Neuve Chapelle, and in the autumn the indecisive gain on a narrow front at Loos. The German line held fast, and it became clear that success could be won only by a tremendous effort to breach it on a wide front in a gigantic battle. Any effort on a smaller scale would mean at best a limited gain bought at a terrible cost, and leaving the general situation none the better.

But such an effort could not be improvised. Men, guns and munitions had to be accumulated during weeks and months on a scale as yet unexampled in warfare. Nearly half the year would have to be devoted to preparing for the " great push." The blow must not be struck till a striking power that would make it irresistible had been gathered at the decisive point.

This is not a history of the Great War, or even of the war in France and Flanders, but only a record of the part the 17th Northern Division played in it. But to make this either intelligible or interesting the vast background of the war must be kept in mind, and there should be at least some general idea of the relation between the operations of this one Division and that of the armies of which it was a unit. We may therefore say a few words about the strategy of this " great push," which developed into months of battle in the region of the middle Somme.

The object of the push was to make a wide breach in the entrenched German line that extended like a fortress front from the North Sea shores to the Swiss frontier. The breaking of the line would end the stalemate that had lasted since the first autumn of the war. It would create to right and left two exposed flanks in what had hitherto been a line open only to frontal attack. A huge mobile army of operation pouring through the gap would break in upon the open country through which lay the enemy's communications. With this advance the hostile line for many a mile on either side would become unstable and untenable. The fortress front would collapse and open warfare replace the indecisive weariness of trench warfare.

As the strength of the British armies increased they had taken over a greater part of the Allied front, and their line extended in the early summer of 1916 from Flanders to the valley of the Somme near Albert. They thus faced the greater part of the entrenched enemy line that looked west from the North Sea to the bend in the line about Roye, Lassigny and Noyon, where the German front bending to the eastward made the bold Salient that had long been a menace to Paris.   From this bend the German front ran eastward till at Verdun it turned to the south, and their line, facing west, extended to the Swiss border.

It is easy to realise that the most rapid and extensive results would be obtained if a break through could be effected at or near a bend forming a great salient on the opposing line.   It would open the way to an advance not merely in flank but in rear of two long sectors of the broken line.   This was why in the late winter weeks, while the Allies were still unready for any operation of a large scale, the Germans in February, 1916, had attacked in force about Verdun, where they faced such a salient with the French fortress forming its apex.   The days when it seemed that Verdun was not unlikely to share the fate that had already befallen so many fortresses, were amongst the most anxious in the whole War.   There were moments when its fall seemed all but inevitable, and it would have been a disaster the results of which it would be difficult to estimate.

The front chosen for the Allied attack of 1916 was north and south of the point where the French and British fronts met on the Somme.   The French were so heavily involved in the struggle for Verdun that the chief share in the " great push " was allotted to the British.   The sector they were to attack was one of some twenty-five miles of front mostly a little north of the great bend in the enemy's line, where after running southward from the sea it began its trend eastward to its second great bend at Verdun.   It was thus to be a break through the apex and western face of the huge salient formed by the invasion.

It required, on the part of the Allies, some persistent adherence to the plans formed for the summer offensive, to hold on to the date approximately fixed for it, and complete the necessary preparations, instead of precipitating the advance in order to take off the hostile pressure from Verdun.   In the early days of June the French Head-

quarters Staff was becoming very anxious, but Verdun
held on, and the preparations for the advance were
deliberately completed.   These included the massing
of five British Army Corps and the Sixth French Army in
front of the sector to be attacked; the concentration and
use of a large flying force to dominate the German air
defence; the placing in position of masses of heavy
artillery exceeding in numbers and calibre of the guns
any concentration of artillery power hitherto seen in war.
These were to wreck the German defences and cover the
assault upon them.   To provide the necessary munitions
for the long artillery preparation vast stores of material
had to be collected in rear of the line.   It was a case of
piling up man power, gun power and every form of
aggressive power that science had so far made available
for war, in order to smash through the enemy line, and to
do this swiftly and decisively.   The long and costly
struggle that dragged on for months was not foreseen.
The proof of this was clear in the concentration behind
our lines of masses of cavalry, which were intended to
ride through the gap in the hostile barrier, and, pushing
on to the open country beyond, lead the way in completing
the victory.

     But on one point there were no illusions.   A heavy
price would have to be paid for the expected success.
So the base hospitals in France were cleared, and behind
the Allied front and along the lines of communication
there grew up new Red Cross camps, improvised hospital
towns, ready to receive the human wreckage of the coming
fight.   Like all the other preparations for it, that of the
Red Cross and the R.A.M.C. was on a colossal scale.

     The battle front at the outset was roughly some forty
miles in length, lying generally from north to south.   But
the prolonged struggle, the series of battles, which we
know as the " Battle of the Somme," was fought out
chiefly on about a hundred square miles of ground east of
Albert and north of the Somme—a space of about ten

miles by ten.   Before the prolonged war storm laid it
waste this tract of land was a green and pleasant piece
of country, a characteristic part of the well-tilled uplands
of Picardy.   It was a chalk land.   On our aircraft photographs every trench came out as a glaring white line, every
shell crater a bright white spot ; but the chalk was
covered by a good surface soil, deep enough for tillage—
no mere scanty surface of earth that could at most give
pasture for flocks of sheep.   Its rising grounds had
mostly a gentle slope, and it was a well-watered land.   So
it was closely dotted with strongly-built villages clustering
round their church towers, with walled gardens and
orchards.   There were a few detached farms, but the
villages were so numerous that these were an exceptional
feature.   There were many clumps of wood.

On the southern margin of this area ran the Somme,
winding in long curves between marshy banks, dividing
into back water channels and expanding into reedy pools.
Among the marshes at its sharp bend to the westward
stood historic Péronne, a famous fortress of mediaeval
times.   From near Péronne there ran north-westward
a main feature of the battle ground, the chalk down that
was known as " the Bapaume Ridge."   On the western
margin of the battlefield the little river Ancre cut its way
through the heights by a long gorge, on its way to join
the Somme near Corbie east of Amiens.   Where the
Ancre valley widened on the lower ground south of its
gorge stood Albert, huddled below its modern basilica,
with its tower crowned by the leaning figure of the great
bronze Madonna, bending over the house roofs as the
result of a hostile shell burst that had just failed to shatter
it or fling it to earth.   From Albert one of the two main
roads of the battlefield switchbacked over an outlying
ridge and then crossed the main height to Bapaume,
whence it ran on to Cambrai.   At Bapaume (which gives
its name to one of the battles of 1870-71), the road from
Péronne to Arras crossed it.   These two were the only

well-paved highways of the district. The rest were country roads and lanes, mostly following the hollows between the higher ridges or ascending by easy gradients of the complicated little valleys between their spurs.

The invaders had held this ground since the autumn of 1914, when they occupied it to counter the French attempt to turn their positions on the Aisne heights, as the long battle lines were extending northwards to the sea. Albert was saved by a hard fight, in which De Castelnau was opposed to Rupert of Bavaria. Its position at the important road junction at the crossing of the lower Ancre, and barring the way to Amiens, made it well worth holding. It faced a minor salient of the enemy's line, and it was the jumping-off point for what eventually became the main British push in the Battle of the Somme. For more than a year and a half the enemy had been converting the strong ground they held before it into an elaborately entrenched fortress. How strong it was, only the attempt to break into it revealed.

To resume the story of the Division :—It was assembled near Amiens in the second week of June. Divisional H.Q. had been established at Allonville on the 11th. The 51st Brigade and its attached details were billetted in this village and at Cardonette; the 52nd a little to the westward in Poulainville and Coisy; and the 50th some miles east of Amiens at Bussy, on the swampy banks of the Hallue brook. The 50th was placed here, as it was to be the first to be pushed forward into the line. The rest of the month was devoted to training and immediate preparations for going into the coming battle.

General Horne commanded the Fifteenth Army Corps, of which the 17th was now detailed as the Reserve Division. His two other divisions were in the line right and left of the sharp angle formed by the salient about Fricourt. On the left, facing eastward, was the 21st, a New Army division; on the right, facing northwards, the 7th Division, one of the Old Army formations, with a record beginning with the attempt to save Antwerp and the First Battle of Ypres in the autumn of 1914.

On June 13th General Glasgow was directed to move the H.Q. of the 50th Brigade forward to Morlancourt and send two of his battalions into the line with the 7th Division. They were in the trenches south of the Fricourt salient for ten days, till June 23rd, when they were relieved by units of the 7th Division and went back to rest at Heilly. On the 23rd two of General Fell's battalions—the 7th Borders and 8th South Staffords— were sent into the trenches of the 21st Division, west of Fricourt, and spent a week in the line, suffering a good many casualties from the fire of the enemy's long range guns, which knocked in some of the dugouts.

The detailed orders for the great attack directed that the greater part of the 17th Division was to remain in reserve at the outset, but the 50th Brigade was to be engaged on the first day. It was to be employed in attacking Fricourt, while the 21st Division on the left and the 7th on the right made an advance to cut off the point of the salient, their attacks converging north-east of the Park of Fricourt Château, marked on our maps as " Fricourt Wood." The date for the attack had been fixed for June 28th, and zero hour was to be 7.30 a.m. The 50th Brigade was not to advance against Fricourt until the converging movement of the two divisions had made some progress. A cheerfully optimist time-table for the day anticipated that by 11 a.m. the whole of the Fricourt salient would be taken and our advance pushed well on to the higher ground about Contalmaison.

The artillery of the 17th Division had been placed in position on ground already crowded with guns and howitzers engaged in the long preparatory bombardment of the enemy's defences. The ground here was not far from the extreme southern limit of the British lines, and numbers of French batteries were mixed up with our artillery. Huge dumps of munitions had been collected to feed the guns and many miles of light railways laid down for its distribution. Day and night the guns were in action; day by day the bombardment became more intense. It was directed with the help of observers in the cars of anchored sausage balloons behind our first line, and these were swaying on their anchor cables for miles to right and left as far as one could see. The enemy had tried to establish a similar line of aerial observation posts, but most of these had been shot down by our aeroplanes. The bombardment was mostly concentrated on the German first line, but some of our batteries were engaged with the enemy's long ranging artillery on the higher ground in its rear. But day after day, up to the very morning of the assault, the German gunners replied to our fire from well-chosen and carefully-entrenched positions.

Against these more distant gun positions our fire gave no very serious result, but the bombardment of the front line seemed to be appallingly effective. Hour after hour the German trenches were plastered with a steady shower of bursting shells. Parties of officers were taken to points of vantage commanding a good view of the German front, in order to obtain an idea of the general lie of the ground over which the advance was to be made. They saw the wide belt of trenches wrapped in smoke bursts, through which came the flashes of the explosions, and dark masses of earth and stones were hurled high in air. Mametz Wood was no longer green. Its leaves had been turned to brown and yellow by our high explosives. Fricourt village was crumbling into heaps of ruin. It looked as if the front line was being simply wiped out and that nothing could live under this deluge of fire. A little further back there was the contrast of a beautiful country-side, still all but untouched by the devastating bombardment. On the hill slopes the orchards and clumps of wood were green, and Contalmaison seemed to still cluster unharmed around its square church tower.

The weather in those last days of June was dull, with

frequent rain showers. As the appointed day for the attack approached the rain became a steady downpour. On the 27th the orders for the 28th were cancelled, and the attack deferred. The only reason was that the heavy rain, besides making movement on the sodden ground difficult and threatening to flood much of that over which the French would have to advance on the right, was shortening the limits of clear observation and would thus hamper the co-operation of the gunners. A change for the better was expected, and it was hoped the delay would be very brief. The alteration of the plan led to a variety of strange rumours being started to explain it, amongst others a story that Verdun had fallen and the whole situation was being reconsidered.

The two battalions of the 50th Brigade had been withdrawn from the trenches on the 20th and relieved by units of the 7th Division. They were sent back into the line before Fricourt on the 26th and placed temporarily under the orders of the 21st Division. On June 30th there was a change to bright summer weather, with clear air and blue sky, and that afternoon orders were issued by G.H.Q. for the attack to be made at 7.30 next morning.

Divisional Headquarters were moved forward from Allonville to the village of Treux, on the south bank of the Ancre, about five miles from Albert. The 8th Hussars were attached to H.Q. The 50th Brigade (Brigadier-General Glasgow), was moved up by Méaulte into the line. The 51st Brigade (Brigadier-General Fell) was assembled at Morlancourt, with the 73rd Field Co. R.E. The 52nd Brigade (Brigadier-General Clarke), with the 74th Field Co. and the 52nd Ambulance, was in huts and tents in the Bois des Tailles, a couple of miles east of the same village. The Pioneer battalion (York & Lancasters) were at Ville-sous-Corbie near Treux.[1] Of the Divisional Artillery two Field Artillery Brigades (less

[1] They had been some days in the trenches enlarging and strengthening dugouts and doing other engineer work.

one Howitzer battery) had been attached to the 7th Division, and two others to the 21st. The remaining 4.5 Howitzer Battery was attached to the Corps Artillery.

The last night of June was fine and warm. Few of those in the front line and the reserve positions got much sleep during the hours of darkness before the battle. The 50th Brigade were crowded in the trenches, the 51st and 52nd reached their concentration positions in and around Morlancourt and in the Wood of Tailles long after nightfall, for orders had not been issued till late in the day. All night long the guns were busy. As day broke their fire increased, and at 6.30 on the morning of Saturday, July 1, the last hour of intense bombardment began. During the week before, the fire of the Allied artillery on a front of nearly thirty miles had been heavier than anything yet seen in war. During these seven days the British gunners sent into the enemy's positions more shells than had been fired in the whole first twelve months of the War. But in the last hour the intensity of the fire exceeded everything yet attempted.[1] It was a bright morning. As the thin summer haze rose from the lower grounds, and the view to the front became clear, it seemed hard to believe that anyone could survive the shell shower that descended on the German line and half hid it in fire, smoke and flying débris. The men waiting in the trenches for the zero hour felt confident that in the first rush they would have to do little more than deal with handfuls of half-dazed men crouching in the shattered trenches.

At 7.30 there was a sudden lull in the roar of artillery fire, a few seconds of silence as the sights were raised and

[1] The sound of the guns was heard more or less clearly in many places in the south-east of England. At a seaside town in Sussex it was so loud that many went out to the sea front, and watched the morning haze rising from the water expecting that, as it cleared away, they would see a naval action in progress in the Channel. It was heard at many places on the high ground of the South Downs, and less distinctly even on the North Downs within a few miles of London—a strange murmur in the early morning air, now louder now less marked, but plain enough for many to feel sure there was hard fighting in France or Flanders.

the bombardment of the German front line changed to a barrage beyond it. The attack was launched at this moment on its twenty-five miles front, but the enemy was ready for it. The Germans were swarming out of the tunnels and deep dugouts where they had sheltered during the deluge of fire. In a few moments their half-ruined trenches were manned and bristled with machine guns rushed up from underground with the men who handled them.

The Fricourt angle of the enemy line was part of the sector held by General von Stein's 14th Reserve Corps. It was originally a Baden formation. It had been at the outset of the war in the 7th Army on the German left and had taken part in the attempted push for Nancy. Since October, 1914, it had been on the ground it now held north of the Somme, and for nearly two years had been strengthening its position. During this time it had become a partly mixed formation, mainly south German, receiving drafts not only from Baden, but also from Wurtemberg and Alsace, and some Prussians. Von Stein's officers and men were good fighters and put up a stubborn resistance.

For those who waited in reserve behind the battle line on that July morning at Treux and Morlancourt and in the woods of Tailles, the impression of the early hours was one of a great victory. Reports from the fighting line told of the front trenches having been carried without much resistance. On the extreme right of the British advance the 13th Corps had reached Montauban. The 7th Division was pushing into Mametz; the 21st was through the enemy's defences north of Fricourt. Early in the morning German prisoners were behind the wire fences in the compound near Morlancourt. Ambulances loaded up with casualties were arriving back in rapid succession. Streams of " walking wounded " were coming along by the roads from the front, but they told cheerily of ground being won, and among them were many slightly wounded prisoners.   Germans and British were helping each other to get back to the casualty clearing stations.   Our artillery had lengthened its range and was shelling Contalmaison and Bazentin-le-Grand.

At Divisional H.Q. definite news was coming in, and the impression was not so cheerful.   Ground was indeed being won, but won very slowly and at heavy cost, and behind his wrecked front line the enemy was making a dogged resistance.   North of Fricourt, after the first rush, the advance of the 21st Division was being held up.   As it crossed the front line Brigadier-General Glasgow, with the H.Q. of the 50th Brigade established in a dugout in our front line, had been asked to send in one of his battalions to cover the movement of the 21st by establishing a defensive flank towards Fricourt.   He sent in the 10th West Yorkshires on his left.   The two leading companies passed through the German front line with very few casualties.   But the two other companies, as they followed them, were caught in a storm of machine gun fire from the ruins of Fricourt.   It was a well-built village, with vaulted cellars under all its houses, and these had been converted into safe dugouts.   It was held by a strong garrison and its margin armed with machine guns.   The Commanding Officer of the West Yorkshires, Lieut.-Colonel Dickson, his second-in-command, Major Knott, D.S.O., and his adjutant were all killed.   The company officers tried to get forward, but the two companies were all but completely destroyed by the machine gun fire and cut off from all communication either with the first half of the battalion or the trench line.   The two advanced companies fared as badly.   They pushed on with heavy loss to the point they had been directed to reach, but unsupported, isolated, caught in a storm of artillery and machine gun fire and counterattacked by crowds of bombers, they were broken up into detached groups.   One of these succeeded in joining the right of the 21st Division.   But the battalion was all but completely destroyed.   Its losses in these morning hours totalled 733 casualties.[1]   Early in the afternoon the advance of the 21st Division had been brought to a standstill in front of the German trenches in Lozenge Wood on the Fricourt-Contalmaison road.

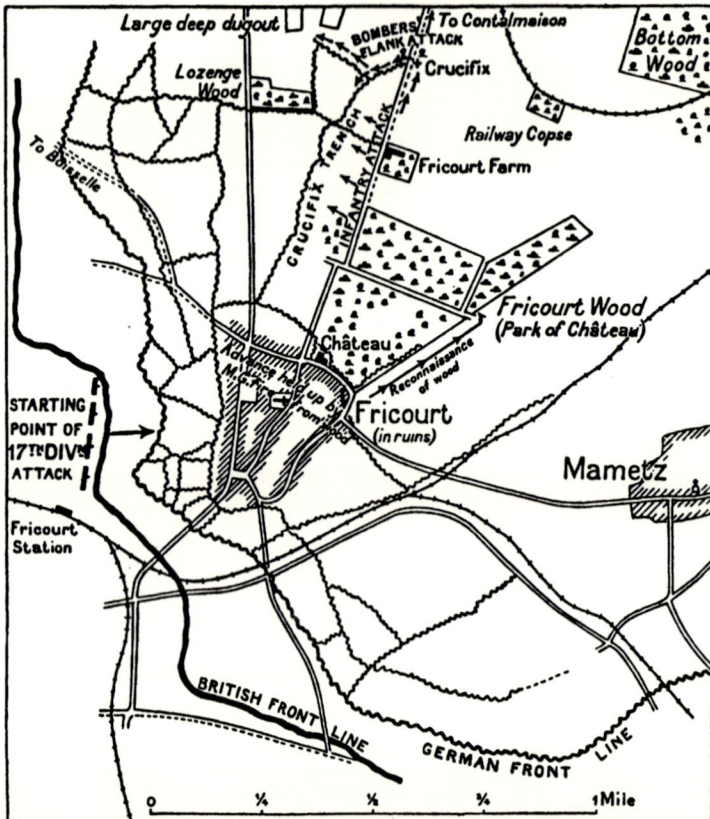

The Capture of Fricourt.

On the other side of the salient the 7th Division was held up in the southern outskirts of Mametz. The plan of cutting off the Fricourt angle by the two divisions joining

[1] The details of this heavy loss were :—Officers—killed 11, wounded 10, missing one ; other ranks—killed 264, wounded 304, missing 143.   Total :— Officers 22, other ranks 711—making 733 in all.

hands on the higher ground north of the village had so far failed.   There was a gap of nearly two miles between the furthest points they had reached.   So the 21st Division H.Q., in the hope of clearing up a difficult situation, directed Brigadier-General Glasgow to attack Fricourt village with the 50th Brigade, now reduced to three battalions.

The 7th Yorkshires were ordered to attack the west front of the village, with the 7th East Yorkshires in close support.   The 6th Dorsets were held in reserve in the front trenches.   At 2.30 p.m. the attack began, and in line after line the two Yorkshire battalions went forward, as steadily as if they were on parade.   They were at once caught in a barrage fire, and along the margin of the village machine guns opened on them.   In three minutes the 7th Yorkshires lost thirteen of their officers and over 300 men.   They struggled on through the hostile fire, and the East Yorkshires pressed forward to help them. The ground was strewn with lines of fallen men, but numbers reached the margin of the village where their dead and wounded were soon piled in heaps.   A few men actually got into the village, some were killed or wounded and captured.   A little handful, isolated in the enemy's position and helpless, took refuge in a cellar and lay there all through the following night.   The attack had failed but failed gloriously.   The Yorkshire men had done all that was possible, but the frontal attack was a desperate attempt, all but hopeless from the first.   The remnant of the two battalions straggled back to the trenches.   They had left more than 800 of their officers and men strewing the ground over which they had advanced.

At 5 p.m. the Brigadier received orders to try again. He had now in hand only the Dorsets and the remnant of the two Yorkshire battalions.   At 5.30, when the Dorsets were ready to advance, an order came countermanding the attack.   It was a wise counter-order that averted another useless sacrifice.

What happened at Fricourt on the first day of the
Somme battles was typical of much of what occurred in
this first phase of the great battle.   The optimist forecast
of the operations had not been realised.   Some ground
had been gained, but the enemy had hardly attempted to
hold long stretches of the cratered wreckage that marked
his first line.   The real resistance was behind it, and
against this well-organised opposition the advance of the
attack was held up.   Then came hurried orders to try
to make good the situation by improvised frontal attacks
against the strong points of the German support line, and
the result was all but inevitable failure.

That midsummer day had been one of at best partial
success.   On the Allied right south of the Somme the
French—up against less formidable defences had won
a good deal of ground.   On the left at the Gommecourt
Salient, and along the gorge of the Ancre by Serre and
Thiepval, the German line held fast, and all attacks ended
in failure with heavy loss.   In the Allied centre—the
British right in front of Albert—the most that could be
claimed was that the attack had pushed beyond the first
line of the enemy's trenches.   Everywhere it was held
for the time being by determined opposition.   Nevertheless people at home read next morning that a tremendous
victory had been won.   Berlin too was gladdened with
official stories of German success.   In war frank an-
nouncements of the truth are at a discount for the sake
of keeping up the fighting spirit of the soldier and the
civic courage of the civilian.   The plain truth was that
though there had not been the hoped-for success, a good
beginning had been made by the Allies, and there was an
expectation that it was the prelude to an early victory.
It was actually the beginning of a battle that was to last
far into the winter.   No one realised what a long and
costly task the conquest of the Somme uplands was to be.

On our side the impression of the High Command was
that the enemy was badly shaken, that his defence was

strained nearly to breaking point, and must give way if the pressure upon it was maintained. So the days that followed showed a series of hastily-improvised frontal attacks. The methodical attack began later.

At 8.50 p.m. on July 1st H.Q. of the 17th Division received orders from the Corps Commander, General Horne, to take over from the 21st Division the front held by the 50th Brigade and prepare to clear the enemy out of Fricourt next morning. General Pilcher was also notified that the artillery of the 21st Division (with the 17th Division batteries attached to it) was placed under his orders, and his trench mortar batteries that had been attached to the 21st and 7th Divisions would revert to the 17th Division.

On receiving this message he got his brigadiers together at the 50th Brigade H.Q. and gave them verbally the necessary orders. The 51st Brigade was to relieve the 50th before Fricourt, but the 7th Yorkshires were to remain for a while in the line in order to assist the newcomers with local information. The 52nd Brigade was to move from the Wood of Tailles to Morlancourt and remain there as Divisional Reserve ready to go forward at short notice. At 11 p.m. further orders came through from Corps H.Q. The Division, after clearing Fricourt, was to push forward by Fricourt Wood towards Bottom Wood (about a mile south of Contalmaison). The divisions on the right and left would co-operate in this final stage of the movement and the 17th would form a link between them. Late that evening Divisional H.Q. were transferred from Treux to Ribemont.

Brigadier-General Fell had already sent two of his battalions forward shortly after 6 p.m. on a request from the 21st Division. The rest of the brigade followed as soon as Divisional orders were received, but the roads were so encumbered with transport, ambulances, and men streaming back from the line (many of them " walking wounded ") that progress was slow, with not a few checks;

and when the line was reached the trenches were blocked with wounded, bearer parties and stragglers, and there was a good deal of confusion, so that it was not till broad daylight, about 5.30 a.m., on July 2nd, that the relief was completed.   All night the artillery had been in action, and shells were bursting over the roads well back behind the front.

In the early hours of the morning Colonel Fife of the Yorkshires went to the front trenches with General Fell and pointed out to him the enemy's machine gun positions in Fricourt, especially noting those of three guns that had inflicted the heaviest loss on his battalion.   Since dawn our artillery had been shelling the village.   The place was strangely quiet.   Early in the day a handful of the West Yorkshires suddenly appeared coming out of a ruined building on its nearest margin.   They dashed across No Man's Land, strewn with the dead of the day before, and reached our line in safety.   They had been hiding in a cellar since the attack of their battalion failed. They had not been disturbed there during the night, but in the morning shells bursting close overhead suggested the danger of their being buried in their place of refuge, and they had besides no food of any kind, so they made their successful bolt for freedom.   As to the situation in the village, they could tell nothing.

A strong patrol of the South Staffords was pushed forward to the eastern margin of the village at 8.50 a.m.   As they got near it a party of twenty-two men of the 111th German Infantry came out of the trenches, holding up their hands and bringing with them a couple of men in British khaki.   These proved to be wounded men of the Yorkshire Regiment.   The prisoners were brought back to our line, and from what they said it was gathered that the enemy was evacuating Fricourt.   This confirmed the impression already formed by the Brigade Command, and it was reported by telephone to Divisional H.Q.   On receiving this report General Pilcher hurried up to the front and met

the Brigadier in the advanced trench.   He agreed with
General Fell's judgment of the situation, and the order
was given for the brigade to push forward and occupy
Fricourt, with Fricourt Farm and Wood for its second
objectives.   Orders were sent to the gunners to cease
firing on the village and shell the wood.

The first line of the advance was formed by the
Lincolns on the right and the South Staffords on the left.
The Sherwood Foresters were in support and the Borders
were held in reserve.   The two leading battalions dashed
across the ground, that had been the scene of the terrible
slaughter of the day before, with only a few shells bursting
overhead.   The machine guns that had mown down the
advance of the Yorkshire battalions had already been
withdrawn.   The village was in a ruinous condition,
but its cellars and deep dugouts had to be cleared out,
and this took some time.   Ninety prisoners were secured,
most of them in a pitiable condition of exhaustion.   Only
at one point was there any resistance, a German officer and
a small party of his men putting up a fight and being
quickly disposed of.

Shortly after noon it was reported that the village had
been cleared, and patrols of the South Staffords had pushed
out northwards towards Fricourt Farm, while the Lincolns
were preparing for the attack on the Wood.   Orders were
now given that the advance should push forward to the
railway, the left to join up with the 21st Division (reported
to be getting forward to Shelter Wood), and the right to
push for Bottom Wood and gain touch with the 7th
Division in that direction.

The Lincolns had already come under heavy machine
gun fire from Fricourt Wood as they reached the north-
east margin of the captured village.   What was described
on our maps of the time as " Fricourt Wood " was the
park of an old country house, the Château of Fricourt, a
building just outside the village.   It had been badly
battered by our bombardment and the enemy had aban-

doned it.   But they were holding on in the park.   This was a fenced enclosure about 600 yards square, with a further broad belt of plantations extending for another 600 yards from its north-eastern angle.   From the park front of the château a wide clearing ran for about a quarter of a mile to a ride traversing the wood from east to west.   The clearing had once been a grassy lawn. It was now cratered in many places by our shells.   Right and left of it were densely-grown belts of wood with thick undergrowth, and the further obstruction of numbers of shattered and fallen trees.   Movement through it would be very slow and difficult.   The Germans had machine guns amongst the trees, and more of these were hidden away near the cross ride to sweep the central clearing of the park.   The Lincolns had suffered many casualties from their fire as they showed themselves on the margin of the village, and it was plain enough that to push straight on to make a frontal attack through the tangled labyrinth of the woods or by the broad central clearing would be to walk into a death trap and share the fate that had over-taken the Yorkshire battalions in the dash for the village on the first day of the battle.   The battalion was there-fore kept under cover in Fricourt, while a reconnaisance was made on the right of the wood with a view to substi-tuting a turning movement against it for a frontal attack.

Major Metcalfe of the Lincolns with an orderly went forward along a communication trench that followed the south side of the woods beside a country lane, and got as far as a point just beyond the transverse drive through the wood.   Having reached this place without meeting with any opposition, he entered the wood here and found no sign of the enemy holding it on that side and concluding that the Germans were withdrawing, he returned to Fri-court with this report.   The Lincolns then advanced into the wood and pushed right through to its further end. This was between 2 and 3 p.m.

On the left the Staffords and Sherwoods went forward

along the northern margin of Fricourt Wood. The advanced reached Fricourt Farm, but the enemy held not only a trench running from near it to the railway, but also a strongly wired trench parallel to the margin of the wood and only about 150 yards from it.   This was known to us as " Crucifix Trench," taking its name from a road-side cross on the slope near its northern end.   From Crucifix Trench a heavy fire of rifles and machine guns was directed upon Fricourt Wood.   Here the Staffords lost their second in command, Major Raper.   The Staffords and Sherwoods now faced to their left to engage the enemy in the trench, and began digging in along the margin of the wood.   Here were found hidden in the bush three field pieces abandoned by the enemy.

It was now getting dark.   There was a good deal of firing in front of Crucifix Trench, and our bombers were fighting at the end of the Railway Alley trench near the farm.   The ground won was being consolidated and further progress had to be deferred till next morning—all the more because the men were dead tired, many of them having had no sleep for more than forty hours.   Next day's work would be the capture of Crucifix Trench and the push up to the railway.   During the day patrols had gained touch with the 21st Division on the left and the 7th on the right.   Before the converging movement of these two divisions and the pressure of the 17th Division in the centre, the enemy had let go the point of the salient about Fricourt, and, as subsequent developments showed, were fighting a delaying action, while preparing for a determined stand in the Quadrangle position for the defence of Contalmaison against our advance from the southward.   On this side the approach to the large village offered admirable facilities for defence, the slopes below it forming a glacis, scarred by successive trench lines, while right and left the high ground about Mametz Wood and towards Boiselle flanked the line of advance of the assailant.

After dark on the Sunday evening the 6th Dorsets, the only battalion of the 50th Brigade which had not been closely engaged on the first day of the battle, was brought back into the line and temporarily attached to the 51st Brigade.   At 9 p.m. Divisional H.Q. issued orders that next morning the Brigade would continue its effort to take

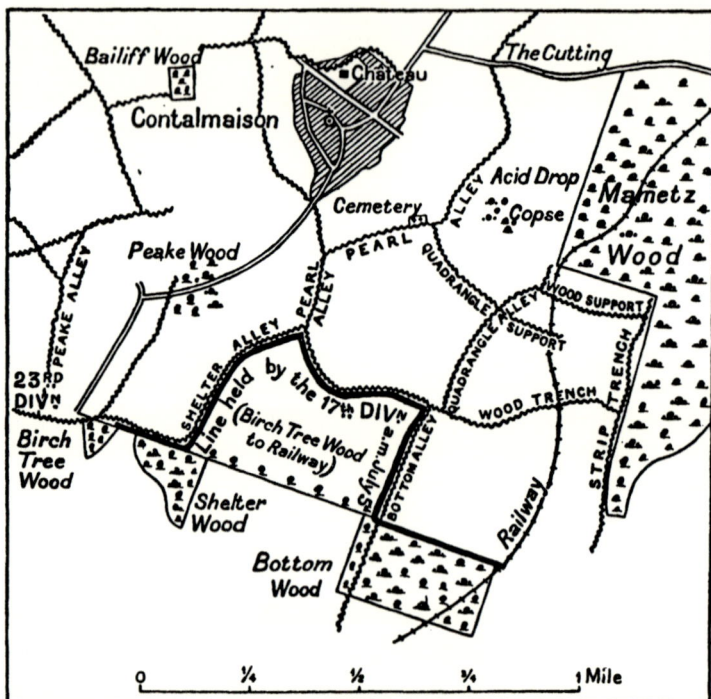

The Push for Contalmaison.

Railway Alley, the trench running east and north-east from near Fricourt Farm, by bombing attacks pushing eastward, and to attempt cutting its wire by parties advancing from Fricourt Wood.   Crucifix Trench was to be attacked at an hour to be named later, the attack being covered by an artillery barrage.   During the night the Divisional artillery would maintain its fire on the

positions named.   An hour later at 10 p.m.   General
Pilcher received orders from the 15th Corps H.Q. that
the attack along Railway Trench was to be pushed to
Railway Copse and Bottom Wood.   It would begin at
9 a.m. on the Monday morning, preceded by twenty
minutes of intense bombardment, beginning at 8.40.   It
would be simultaneous with an attack of the 21st Division
on Shelter Wood, and the left of the 17th Division's
advance was to join up with this Division along the line
of the hedge running to Birch Tree Wood.

During the night bombers of the South Staffords and
Sherwoods attacked in Railway Alley.   They forced their
way for a very short distance along the trench eastward
from the farm, and were then held up by a block or strong
point.   At 3.50 this was reported to Divisional H.Q.
with the request that the guns would try to break up the
strong wiring of the trench which was intact along most
of it.   Orders were issued accordingly to the artillery,
but by some oversight the promised barrage to cover the
advance on Crucifix Trench on the left of the attack was
not provided.   During the night much consolidation
work had been carried out, and working parties were also
busy removing the dead of the Yorkshire battalions on the
west side of Fricourt, one of the padres, the Rev. W.
Rushby, being active in directing this work.

The weather continued fine, and July 3rd was a bright
warm summer day.   At zero hour the attack was launched
against Railway Alley Trench on the right and Crucifix
Trench on the left.   Firing to the westward told of the
advance of the 21st Division, and from the eastward there
was the same token that the 7th was pushing on.   Just
as the advance began Divisional H.Q. received and passed
on to General Fell a report that an officer's patrol of the
7th Division had reached the south-east corner of Bottom
Wood, and found that side of it unoccupied.   General
Fell kept the Dorsets in reserve, and was thus able to
put all his own battalions of the 51st Brigade into the

attack, Borders and Sherwoods against Railway Alley, and Lincolns and South Staffords against Crucifix Trench. It was a successful day.

The Borders, suffering a good many losses from machine gun fire, forced their way steadily and fairly quickly along Railway Alley, the Sherwoods, at first in local reserve in Fricourt Wood, being brought up and sent into the attack in support of them as they went forward. The leading company of the Borders pressed on from Railway Alley into the western side of Bottom Wood. Though the 7th Division had reported from its east side that the wood was abandoned, the Borders here met with obstinate resistance, and there was some stiff fighting. The Germans held a trench running north and south a little inside the margin of the wood, where they had machine guns, and cross fire of other guns came on the left from Quadrangle Trench, a little higher up the slope towards Contalmaison.

Meanwhile Crucifix Trench had been attacked by the Lincolns from Fricourt Wood with the South Staffords on their left. The absence of the barrage was perhaps a gain, for the enemy did not expect the assault to be attempted when the Lincolns sent in their bombers against the north end of the trench from Fricourt Farm. As soon as it was seen that they were into it and bombing along it, the rest of the battalion dashed at it across the open from the Wood, and the South Staffords went forward on their flank. The rush was met by a hail of rifle and machine gun fire, but though they suffered many casualties the two battalions poured in wave after wave over the trench. As the enemy was being driven out of it an important capture of prisoners was secured. A mass of the enemy were seen to be trying to get away along a communication trench towards Shelter Wood. But the Lincoln bombers cut in on their line of retreat and drove them back into the victorious advance of the Staffords on their left. Thus caught, they held up their hands and surrendered. They were some hundreds of officers and men of the 186th Prussian Infantry, including their colonel.

Early in the afternoon Railway Copse was attacked and captured by the Sherwoods and parties of the Lincolns and South Staffords. By 2 p.m. the advance was being pushed on across the railway towards the line of hedge running from Bottom Wood by Shelter Wood towards Birch Tree Wood. The 21st Division had cleared Shelter Wood of the enemy; on the other flank he was abandoning Bottom Wood. The Germans were now concentrating on the Quadrangle trenches. Their artillery was bombarding the ground they had lost, throwing heavy shells, and many gas shells amongst them, into Fricourt and Fricourt Wood.

All the objectives of the 17th Division had been won, and it was in touch with the two divisions on its right and left. Nearly a thousand prisoners had been taken, and besides the large capture of the 186th Infantry, these included officers and men of the 15th, 111th and 118th Regiments. Eleven machine guns had been added to the trophies already secured, and an immense quantity of stores and material had been captured, particularly in a huge dugout a little south of Shelter Wood—an underground barrack. Considering the results obtained, the losses had not been very heavy. A rough estimate made in the evening told that the Lincolns had lost eight officers and some 200 men. The Borders had some 150 casualties, and the Sherwoods and South Staffords about 200 more.

At 7.45 on the evening of Monday, the 3rd, orders came through from the Corps H.Q. to General Pilcher that he was to bring up the 52nd Brigade to take over the ground held on his left by the 21st Division. The 21st had been in action since the early morning of July 1st. In the three days of fighting it had met with obstinate resistance, and won its way forward to Shelter Wood at the cost of very serious losses. In one of its battalions only three officers were left and more than half the rank and file had been killed and wounded.   It was so reduced indeed in numbers that a single brigade could take over the front it now held.

The general situation on this third evening of the battle may be summed up thus: On some ten miles of front on the left, from the Gommecourt salient southwards to near the Albert-Bapaume road, the attack made by three Army Corps, had been held by the enemy, and after the first day the British effort had been concentrated on the right sector of the line, from the great road southward and then westward round the Fricourt angle to where our line joined up with the French left at Maricourt. This was a front of about six miles.   Here the 15th Corps (Horne) was attacking the Fricourt angle, with the 13th Corps (Congreve) prolonging the attack on its right.   The German first line had been carried, and the advance was engaged with the strong points behind it. The 13th Corps had got as far as Montauban, the 15th had won the Fricourt angle and was up against the defences of the large entrenched village of Contal-maison and the woods near it.   Its possession was the immediate objective of the 15th Corps.[1]   Later in the long weeks of fighting which we know as " the Battle of the Somme "—really a series of battles—the more patient, deliberate and effective method was adopted of dealing with strongly-entrenched villages by pushing forward on their flanks, and only assaulting when they were menaced with envelopment.   But in these first days of July, after the initial disappointment, there seems to have been a disposition to rely on hurriedly-organised frontal attacks in the hope of hacking through by blow after blow delivered at an opponent who was supposed to be on the point of giving way if the pressure upon him could be maintained.

[1] La Boiselle, to the west of Contalmaison, was still held by the enemy after three days of hard fighting.

During the first three days the weather had been fine and intensely hot. On July 4th there was a change. The heat wave broke with thunderstorms and torrential rain at times that made the hollows into quagmires and filled the trenches with mud. In the night General Clark had brought up the 52nd Brigade through Méaulte, and taken over from the remnant of the 21st Division the ground it held with the front at Birch Tree Wood and Shelter Wood. The relief took most of the night, for the ground was in a chaotic condition, with most landmarks obliterated by the bombardments, and it was often no easy matter to identify the positions. In the early hours of the day there was something like a lull in the fighting. General Pilcher had moved his Divisional H.Q. forward near Méaulte and went up to the front. General Fell now holding with his brigade the right of the Divisional sector from near Shelter Wood to the margin of Bottom Wood (now held by the 7th Division), was able to report that patrols sent out in the hours of darkness had ascertained that the nearest German line—Quadrangle Trench—was not strongly held. It was agreed that its capture would be a comparatively easy matter. But after that there would be a much more serious problem to deal with. Beyond the trench the ground rose towards Contalmaison, and about 400 yards from the trench, Quadrangle Support looked down on a bare natural glacis without a scrap of cover except a few shell holes. To our right it was flanked by Mametz Wood, forming a strong bastion for the support line, and on the other side it was flanked by the high ground south-west of Contalmaison and the southern part of the village itself. The events of the following days showed that the enemy were concentrating their efforts on the defence of the Support, and counted the trench as a mere advanced position which they only lightly held.

At 3.30 p.m. orders came through from Divisional H.Q. that Quadrangle Trench and the enemy positions immediately to the east of it were to be attacked that night, the advance beginning at 12.45 a.m. on the 5th without a previous bombardment. The 17th Division was to rush Quadrangle Trench from Shelter Alley to its junction with Bottom Alley (the communication trench linking it with Bottom Wood). On their right the 7th Division would attack the extreme eastern end of Quadrangle Trench, the line east of it known as Wood Trench, and the southern salient of Mametz Wood. Later the orders were modified, and it was ordered that beginning at 8 p.m. the artillery should cut the wire in front of Quadrangle Trench. In the afternoon General Pilcher decided that the 52nd Brigade should relieve the 51st in the evening and carry out the attack. General Fell was to leave one of his battalions with the relieving brigade for another day. He chose the South Staffords. The relief, begun at nightfall, was not completed till just after midnight. The three battalions of the 51st Brigade thus relieved were all night on the move. They had trying experiences in the long communication trench running down through and beyond Bottom Wood. It was narrow and only waist deep, giving little cover. The movement was blocked at times by troops moving up, and heavy 5.9 shells from the German batteries on the heights above Contalmaison were continually bursting around it. There were times when all movement ceased for awhile, to be resumed at a snail's pace. Most of the officers and men were dead beat by the time they reached Méaulte towards 6 a.m. But they were in high spirits nevertheless. They felt they had done their bit well. Most of them were bringing back German helmets, weapons and other personal trophies, and the brigade had with it eleven German machine guns. General Ouseley, the Divisional artillery commander, had promised to send them during the day the three field pieces they had captured in Fricourt Wood. General Clark, with the 52nd Brigade, had taken over the front line, with the 10th

Lancashire Fusiliers on the left from Shelter Wood eastwards, and the 9th Northumberland Fusiliers on the right
at Bottom Wood.

At 8 p.m. our guns had opened on Quadrangle Trench,
drawing a heavy reply from the enemy's artillery.
Shortly after midnight our bombardment was intensified,
as the immediate preparation for the attack, and at 12.45
a.m. the sights were raised, and it became a barrage in
rear of the German line. Meanwhile the leading companies of the two battalions had crept forward to within
a hundred yards of the trench, and as the barrage crashed
down behind it the Fusiliers dashed forward and stormed
it after a short sharp fight, taking a number of prisoners
and suffering very moderate losses. The following
morning the 52nd Brigade received congratulatory
messages from General Pilcher and from General Horne,
the Corps commander.

On the right of the Brigade the 7th Division had
attacked Wood Trench and Mametz Wood unsuccess-
fully. As the result of this failure the ground won by the
52nd Brigade made the front of the 17th Division a
pronounced salient. On the morning of Wednesday,
July 5th, its front ran from Birch Tree Wood, held by the
right of the 23rd Division (which had relieved the 21st),
along the north side of Shelter Wood, then along Shelter
Alley and Quadrangle Trench, from which it ran back
by Bottom Alley and along the north margin of Bottom
Wood till it linked up with the left of the 7th Division
at the point where a light railway left the wood. The
day was spent consolidating the line, and there were a
good many casualties in the newly-captured trench, for
from morning till evening the enemy kept up a desultory
bombardment of it, mostly with big 5.9 howitzer shells.
With a view to reinforcing our reply the Pioneer Battalion,
the York & Lancasters, were busy making a plank road
through Fricourt and into the wood beyond the ruined
village to get some of our heavy howitzers into position there.

Out in front blocks were established at the junction of Quadrangle Trench with Shelter Alley and with Wood Trench, and an advanced post that had been pushed out into Peake Wood on the Fricourt-Contalmaison road was strengthened and held against hostile bombing attacks.   After dark posts were established some distance forward in Pearl and Quadrangle Alleys, with a view to the next advance.   That night the South Staffords went back to the 51st Brigade and were replaced by the 7th East Yorkshires from the 50th Brigade.   On the right the 7th Division was relieved by the 38th (Welsh) Division.   All through the night the enemy's artillery was very active, and he was evidently expecting another attack.

Shortly before midnight on the Wednesday evening Divisional H.Q. received a preliminary order from Corps H.Q. that next day (Thursday, July 6th), was to be devoted to preparations for taking part in an attack on the enemy's positions to be made in the night of the 6th to 7th.

This was the prelude to four days and nights of fighting, in which after eight attacks Contalmaison was at length won.   These preparations were carried on in very unfavourable weather.   It was dull and close with clouded skies and frequent downpours of rain that filled the trenches with clammy mud.

Corps orders for the attack came through the Divisional H.Q. early in the afternoon of the 6th, and operation orders for the division were given by General Pilcher at a conference held at his battle H.Q. near Méaulte.   In pursuance of Corps orders, the Division was to hand over to the 23rd Division on its left the ground it held west of Shelter Alley[1] and extend its right so as to take over from the 38th Division on that side the front as far as a point roughly opposite the south end of Strip Trench. Divisional boundaries for the attack were to be Pearl

---

[1] Shelter Alley itself was included in the Divisional front.

Alley on the left and on the right a ride running through
Mametz Wood northward just inside its margin and
Strip Trench. The objective of the attack for the 17th
Division was to be Quadrangle Support, Wood Trench,
and the west margin of Mametz Wood. On the left
the 23rd Division was to advance against Contalmaison,
and on the right the 38th was to attack Mametz Wood.
The attack of the three divisions was to be made at 2 a.m.
on July 7th, preceded by thirty-five minutes of intense
bombardment.

As for the 17th Division, General Pilcher ordered that
the 51st Brigade should be brought back by midnight
into the line on the right for the attack of Wood Trench,
leaving it to the 52nd Brigade to make the right attack
against Quadrangle Support and up Pearl Alley. As the
two Fusilier battalions had not suffered serious loss in
their capture of Quadrangle Trench, General Clark
detailed them for the attack with his two other battalions
—9th Duke of Wellington's and 12th Manchesters—
in support and reserve. General Glasgow brought up
two battalions of his brigade on the right to Bottom Wood
after dark. Another of his battalions, the 7th East
Yorkshires, was already in line. It was to attack with
the 6th Dorsets. The 7th Yorkshires were to be in
support. The remnant of the 10th West Yorkshires
was left at Méaulte and was to supply carrying parties.
Battle H.Q. of both brigades were established in the
cellars of Fricourt Château. Above ground the building
was in ruins, masses of fallen brick and rubble, with only
its south wall standing. But the strongly-vaulted cellars
had stood the bombardments that had wrought this
destruction. They had been the H.Q. of the German
defence of Fricourt.

These were the orders and arrangements for the great
attack which, it was hoped, would carry the Contalmaison
position. The 51st Brigade was to be Divisional reserve.
It was now under the command of Brigadier-General

G. G. Trotter, a Grenadier Guards officer, who had taken it over from General Fell on the day before.

While these arrangements were being carried out the enemy were preparing for a counter-attack on the 17th Division front to be made just before dawn on the 7th. One of the picked corps of the German Army, the 2nd Division of the Prussian Guard, had just taken over the defences on the south side of Contalmaison, and, towards midnight on the 6th, they were moving to their battle positions.

The night was dark and showery.   The artillery was active on both sides.   About half-past one our fire rose to the full intensity of the preliminary bombardment along the line of the three divisions, and at 2 a.m. the attack was launched.   The four front line battalions of the 17th Division went over the top and up the muddy shell-pitted slope towards their objective, while bombing parties pushed up Strip Trench and Quadrangle and Pearl Alleys.   Only here and there along the front did anyone reach the enemy trenches, for as our guns lengthened their range the Prussian Guardsmen had come downhill to meet the attack, and there was desperate close fighting in No Man's Land.   On the extreme left a handful of the Lancashire Fusiliers got well forward along Pearl Alley and, joining up with the right of the 23rd Division's attack, reached the southern outskirts of Contalmaison, but were soon driven out.   On this flank the 23rd Division was held by the enemy, and on the right the Welsh Division failed to penetrate into Mametz Wood. The wood was full of the dense undergrowth of two years, with here a confusion of shattered and fallen trees, there an abattis and a tangle of barbed wire barriers.   It was scored with trenches, with nests of machine guns.   No wonder the Welshmen failed to rush it.   The enemy felt so safe in the wood that they were able to reinforce the machine gun fire from its western side, and swept with a storm of fire from that flank the ground over which the 50th Brigade was advancing. This cross fire reached also the right of the 52nd. At the same time the German batteries on the higher ground in front maintained a heavy barrage. By 3 a.m. the attempt to get forward was abandoned for the time being, and the Prussian Guards were also falling back to their trenches. We might claim that we had held their counterattack, but it had brought our advance to a stop, and the attack of the three divisions had failed with considerable loss to all the units engaged.

During the fighting, and all through the hours that followed, it was difficult for the brigade commands to keep touch with the front. Telephone lines were so repeatedly cut by the enemy's fire that the only resource was to depend on runners. One and all of those thus employed showed unfailing gallantry, making their way backwards and forwards through the barrage and the gusts of machine gun fire.

At 5.25 a.m., in pursuance of an order from Corps H.Q., Divisional H.Q. directed that Quadrangle Support and Wood Trench should be attacked again at 8 a.m. There was very little time available for preparations. The 50th Brigade sent forward the East Yorkshires and the Dorsets again. The 52nd Brigade attacked with the 12th Manchesters on the right and the 9th West Riding (Duke of Wellington's) on the left. The 23rd Division was to attack at the same time on the left, and the 38th on the right was to endeavour to clear Mametz Wood. The 23rd gained some ground, but the 38th was held up before reaching even the edge of the wood. The 17th Division had thus an all but impossible task. It had to cross an open glacis, nearly a quarter of a mile wide, in broad daylight under a cross fire from the position in front and from the margin of the wood. To add to its difficulties our barrage was not as well directed as usual, and numbers of casualties in the advance resulted from it. The machine gun fire from Mametz Wood was deadly. The Man-

A.N.D.   E

chesters were its special target for some time, and their losses amounted to 16 officers and some 600 men.[1] Only at one point did any of our men get into the enemy's line. A party of the East Yorks reached the north end of Wood Trench, from Quadrangle Alley, but were soon driven out again, but they held on in the Alley and succeeded in establishing a block there. The attack was a costly failure. All day bomb fighting went on at the heads of the trenches leading to the enemy line.

Away to the left fighting continued during the morning, and shortly after 11 a.m. news came that the 23rd Division had penetrated into Contalmaison, but by noon the telephone reported that they had been driven out and were retiring, and with this the heavy fighting ended for that day.

About the same time General Clarke was informed that the 52nd Brigade would be withdrawn into Divisional reserve at Méaulte and replaced by the 51st. Out of a fighting strength of 3,900 it had lost—chiefly in the two attacks of the preceding night and that morning —60 officers and some 1,500 other ranks killed, wounded and missing. Such serious losses were the fate of brigade after brigade in these frontal attacks. But the men stood the trial splendidly, and with their ranks thus thinned they were all ready to face the same venture again and again.

Frederick the Great once said that if at the beginning of a battle one knew as much as one learns after it is all over, it would not be so difficult to be a great leader of men. Criticism after the event has to take into account this difference between forecast and after knowledge. But one cannot help thinking that after the experience

---

[1] Lieutenant-Colonel Harrison, commanding the Manchesters, was shot through the neck while directing the retirement of his men, the bullet just missing an artery. He had the double wound tied up by a stretcher-bearer and then walked back through Bottom Wood to the Brigade H.Q. through a rain of shells. Though exhausted with loss of blood he insisted on giving his report to General Clarke before going back to the nearest casualty clearing station.

of the first two attacks on the Quadrangle Support position it ought to have been fairly obvious that frontal attacks upon it were a more than doubtful policy so long as the forest fortress of Mametz Wood on its flank had not been effectively dealt with.   However, in these first days of the Somme battles the one idea seemed to be to smash through by blow after blow reckless of the cost.   There seems to have been always the idea that the enemy's defence was on the point of collapsing.   So again and again the Division was ordered to try once more over the same ground.

At 4.25 on this Friday afternoon, orders were received from Corps H.Q. that the Division was to attack again that evening, and it was added that there would be no attempt to advance by the divisions to right and left of it. The 52nd Brigade was now being withdrawn and the 51st was relieving it on the left of our front facing Quadrangle Support.   Corps orders had directed that the attack was to take place at an hour to be named later, but not earlier than 6.30, by which time all arrangements for it were to be complete.   It would have been impossible to be ready so early, and eventually it was settled that the attack should begin at 8 p.m.   This would be immediately after sunset, so it would be carried through in the early twilight of a dull rainy summer evening.   The 50th Brigade was to attack Wood Trench, Support, Strip Trench and the margin of Mametz Wood.   Quadrangle Trench was to be the objective of the 51st.

Again the attack was held by the enemy, after more than two hours of efforts to get forward.   The telephone wires were mostly cut by hostile fire, and communication by runners was slow and difficult, many messages not coming through.   At 9.30 from the right the 50th Brigade reported that their attack on Wood Trench had failed, owing to the amount of uncut wire before it.   The Dorsets were trying to bomb their way along Strip Trench on the edge of the wood.   A few minutes later the 51st

Brigade on the left got through a delayed message that, though the Sherwoods had reached a point about 40 yards from Quadrangle Support, the advance had been brought to a standstill by heavy rifle and machine gun fire and serious losses from the enemy's barrage.   Soon after this the attack was countermanded and the troops engaged withdrawn to our trenches.

At midnight on Friday, July 7th, the situation was: Shelter Alley on the left had been taken over by the 23rd Division (3rd Corps), the rest of the salient, formed when Quadrangle Trench was captured on the 5th, was held by the 17th Division along the Trench, Bottom Alley and the north side of Bottom Wood.   In front of this line we held about 200 yards of Pearl and Quadrangle Alleys, with stops at the north end of these sections of the communication trenches.   On the right the Welsh Division (38th) faced Mametz Wood.   The 23rd Division (3rd Corps) was on the left; the 21st Division (15th Corps) was in Corps Reserve.   The Battle of the Somme had now been a week in progress.

At 1 a.m. on Saturday, July 8th, Corps H.Q. having received the report of the attack on Friday evening, sent through an order that early next morning Quadrangle Support should be attacked from both ends by bombing parties working up from the posts held in Pearl and Quadrangle Alleys. Bombing parties were accordingly collected from the 50th Brigade for the right attack, and from the 51st for the left.   Covered by a barrage in their front the bombers advanced at 7 a.m.   On the right those of the 50th Brigade pushed on for about 100 yards.   The intermittent downpour of rain of the days and nights before had reduced the trenches to a wretched condition.   In Quadrangle Alley in places tenacious mud had accumulated nearly waist deep.   In Pearl Alley on the left the bombers of the 51st made more progress. They reached the junction of the Alley with Quadrangle Support, but could not force their way into it.   Our men were now fighting with counter-attacking parties of enemy to right and left. A flanking party pushed out in the latter direction drove back the German bombers and reached a point south-west of Contalmaison and close up to the outskirts of the village. Fighting went on all through the forenoon, but at last the attempt had to be abandoned, as the enemies' batteries on the higher ground beyond Contalmaison had concentrated a deadly fire on the junction of Quadrangle Alley and the Support, and were enfilading both the Alleys along which the attack was being pushed.

At 11 a.m., when the fight was drawing to an end, Corps H.Q. telegraphed that in the afternoon there would be a combined attack of the 17th and 38th Divisions, the latter assisting by assaulting Mametz Wood, but at 12.50 this was cancelled by a counter-order. The 38th would not attack, and the 17th was to carry on independently. Preparations were therefore made for resuming the bombing attack on Quadrangle Support, and it started again a little before 6 p.m. At 6.40 the 51st Brigade reported that the 7th Borders had fought their way into the west end of Quadrangle Support, but presently came news that they had not been able to maintain themselves there. After this there was no progress on either side and towards 9 p.m. the fight was broken off in both Pearl and Quadrangle Alleys.

While this bombing attack was in progress hurried preparations had to be organised to carry out a new order from Corps H.Q. The 38th Division was going to attack the south part of Mametz Wood, beginning at 2 a.m. on the 8th, and the 17th Division was to co-operate. The 50th Brigade (or, perhaps one should say, what was left of it) was directed to take part in this attack on the Wood. The operation orders issued from Divisional H.Q. included a preparatory move the same evening. Though our bombing attacks had failed to get into Quadrangle Support we had won the approaches to

it at both ends.   On the right the 50th Brigade now held
not only Bottom Alley to its junction with Quadrangle
Trench (and this line had been well consolidated since
it was occupied some days before), but had also won
Quadrangle Alley nearly up to the Support.   The
German position in Wood Trench was thus left completely
exposed and " in the air " at its west end.   Here it had
no direct connection with Quadrangle Trench and the
junction with the Alley.   It was separated from this
point by a short stretch of unbroken ground.   The
Germans communicated with Wood Trench at its other
end by Mametz Wood and Strip Trench; it was thus part
of the trench system of the forest position on its left,
rather than of the Quadrangle trench system on its right.

The exposed flank of the Wood Trench line gave an
opening for pushing the main attack of the 50th Brigade
on the tongue of Mametz Wood along this line, and as a
preparation for it, in pursuance of Divisional orders, the
6th Dorsets, just before 9 p.m., made a dash at its flank
from the south end of Quadrangle Alley across the narrow
neck of unbroken ground.   It was a complete surprise
for the enemy, and the Dorsets gained a secure hold on
the west end of Wood Trench, and made good their
position there, and a communication trench was rapidly
dug to link it up with the Alley.   Further orders were
that at 2 a.m. the Brigade was to attack the southern
tongue of Mametz Wood, bombing along Wood Trench
and across Strip Trench, and joining up with the advance
of the 38th Division in the Wood.

The attack, starting in darkness and drizzling rain at
2 a.m. on the Sunday morning, pushed steadily and
successfully along the Trench, reaching at last the margin
of Mametz Wood.   There was a good deal of artillery
fire all along the fronts of both armies, but no sign of anything like an attack on the Wood from the eastward and
no tidings of the Welsh Division, until at 3.35 a.m. news
came through to the H.Q. of the 17th that the attack of

the 38th Division had been deferred till 4 p.m. on the following afternoon. A stop was therefore established at the east end of Wood Trench, and the captured line was consolidated. All day there was intermittent firing and bombing, but the enemy did not counterattack.

While waiting for the co-operation of the 38th against Mametz Wood another attempt was made, just after noon, to capture Quadrangle Support by resuming the bombing attack on both ends of it. Heavy machine gun and rifle fire from both flanks held up our attack, and it was made all the more difficult because the men had to move by wading deep in mud in both Alleys. Early in the day Divisional H.Q. received a preliminary message that on Monday evening the Division would be relieved by the 21st, now in Corps Reserve.

At 2.30 p.m. there came another message from Corps H.Q. that the projected attack of the 38th Division against Mametz Wood was again deferred and would not be made till the following day. As there was therefore nothing to be done on the right that evening, General Pilcher gave verbal orders to the 50th and 51st Brigades that they were to make a surprise attack on Quadrangle Support under cover of darkness at 11.20 p.m.

That attack was the beginning of nearly twenty-four hours of continuous fighting—the last twenty-four of the 17th Division in front of Contalmaison, for it was to be relieved on the Monday evening after dark, but this last effort ended in success well won though dearly bought.

Half an hour after the attack began encouraging news came from the 51st Brigade on the left. The Lincolns had pushed up the prolongation of Pearl Alley to near Acid Drop Copse, thus covering the attack while the South Staffords pushed into the west end of Quadrangle Support. For a while there was no news from the right. Then came a message from the 50th Brigade Battle H.Q. asking how the attack on the other flank was progressing. They had no news of it, for all their telephone lines had

been cut by shell fire. Soon after 1 a.m. a further
message told that so far the attack of the 50th was unable
to make any progress. An hour later came another
message from the right telling that the attack of 7th
Yorkshires was held up by intense rifle and machine gun
fire with heavy losses. Communication with the left was
becoming uncertain, as the telephone lines on that side
also were put out of action, but the 51st were still fighting
in the west end of the Support. The 50th were directed
at 2.30 a.m. to make another attempt to help them at its
east end, and the 7th Yorkshires were sent in to join the
East Yorks in an attack on its junction with Quadrangle
Alley. Ten minutes after this came a disappointing
message from the left. Things were going badly with
the 51st Brigade and the South Staffords were hard
pressed and had lost most of their officers. Then came
a further message that they were being forced back out
of the Support to its junction with Pearl Alley. It was
now after three o'clock. Fighting had been in progress
for four hours and the dawn was coming. General
Pilcher, after consulting the two brigadiers, decided that
the attack must be broken off. Orders to this effect were
issued at 3.30, followed by an order to the 51st Brigade
to hold on at all costs at the junction of Pearl Alley and
the Support Trench.

A good reason for thus deciding to stand fast till daylight was that it was advisable to clear up the general
situation. Right and left of the Division for some time
there had been heavy firing, though information received
the day before had left Divisional H.Q. under the impression that neither the 23rd nor the 38th Division were to
attack that night. There had evidently been some
change of plans, and accidents to the telegraph and telephone lines had resulted in there being no warning of it
to the 17th Division. Presently it was ascertained that
the divisions to right and left were attacking. Between
5 and 6 a.m. came the good news that both were making

progress. The 23rd sent a message that they had captured Bailiff Wood west of Contalmaison and the 38th that they had got into the south side of Mametz Wood. By 6 a.m. parties of the Welshmen coming through the "tongue" of the Wood got into the southern end of Strip Trench and joined up with the men of the 50th Brigade holding Wood Trench.

There was now a pause in the advance on both flanks, though desultory firing continued in the Wood. At 7 a.m. (Monday morning, July 10th) Corps H.Q. sent orders to the Division to be ready to co-operate with the 38th on the right. Later in the morning came warning that the 23rd Division would attack Contalmaison from Bailiff Wood at 4.30 p.m. and the 51st Brigade was then directed to assist by demonstrating from Pearl Alley against the south side of the village. Contalmaison was meanwhile being deluged with shell fire from all our available batteries on a wide front.

The village had been held for some days by a Bavarian regiment. It was in a shattered state—its houses were mostly in ruins, its streets almost impassable with shell holes and heaps of débris. Many cellars used for dug-outs had been smashed in, and the deeper dugouts were overcrowded with wounded too numerous to be evacuated. Water was scarce, and supplies came in irregularly. The Bavarians were near the breaking point, now that the southern defences of the village were being won by the three divisions.

The rain had ceased, and this last day of the fighting was fine and clear. There was good visibility for our gunners, and the last stage of the bombardment did heavy execution.

At 2.40 p.m. the 50th Brigade sent a message to Divisional H.Q. that they had pushed along to the junction of Quadrangle Alley and Support, and on the extreme right a patrol had worked up Strip Trench towards Wood Support, and the enemy on the right front seemed to be withdrawing. Fighting in Mametz Wood still continued, the Welsh Division gradually forcing its way along its central north and south side.   About 3 p.m. the 50th Brigade saw through a gap in the Wood some of the 38th moving north-east of Wood Support, and expecting co-operation from that side which would catch the garrison of the Support between two fires, the 7th East Yorks attacked it.   But the men of the 38th were evidently intent only in flanking the attack of their own division and disappeared, moving away to the right.   The attack got into Wood Support, but could not hold on there and had to retire.

At 4.30 the 23rd Division on the left launched its attack against Contalmaison from Bailiff Wood.   The Bavarians put up a stubborn resistance, and it was not till two hours later that the attack had possession of the whole village, making most of the survivors of its garrison prisoners.   Meanwhile a battalion of the 51st Brigade was pushing on towards the sunken road that runs west from the village, and Quadrangle Support was being attacked by bombing parties from each end.   Even after the village was taken the enemy fought steadily in the trenches to the south of it.   The fight went on long after sunset, and it was not till towards 11 p.m. that it was at last reported the Quadrangle Support was clear of the enemy and the 50th Brigade had captured Wood Support and were in touch with the left of the 38th Division in the Wood.   On this side the Welsh attack was near the north margin of the Wood, from which the Germans were now everywhere retiring.

So at last all objectives were won, and this local phase of the great struggle ending.   The last of the fight was hardly over when the first relief detachments of the 21st Division began to arrive.   As they reached the front the captured trenches were handed over to them, and the weary victors of the 17th Division began their march back to Méaulte, taking many of their wounded with them. It was not till 4.40 a.m. on the Tuesday, the 11th, that

the relief was completed.   General Pilcher remained till
10 a.m. to hand over the command of the sector.   General
Ouseley, with the Divisional artillery, stayed on for ten
days more to co-operate with the 21st Division.

In our narrative of the last days of the battle we have
told of this or that " battalion " attacking.   It would
perhaps have been more correct to write not of battalions
but of remnants of battalions.   The Division had suffered
heavy loss in those days of persistent fighting, under
exceptionally difficult conditions.   A spectator who saw
the brigades setting out to entrain at a new railhead near
Méaulte told how the battalions were so reduced in
numbers that the marching columns " seemed to be
chiefly transport."   The casualties in action only show
part of the wastage in numbers, for exhaustion and
exposure, first under blazing summer weather, and then
for some days amidst drenching rain and in trenches deep
in mud, meant long sick lists.   But the men had stood it
all cheerily.

From July 1st to the 11th the casualties of the Division
were as follows:

	Killed.	Wounded.	Missing.	Totals.
Officers	70	97	20	187
Other ranks	779	2966	857	4602
Totals	849	3063	877	4789

The 877 returned as " Missing " did not, unless in a
few exceptional cases, represent prisoners unwounded
in the enemy's hands.   Practically all were officers and
men unaccounted for because they had been killed and
wounded in unsuccessful attacks, falling in the enemy's
positions or close up to them.

The losses of the Divisional artillery from July 1st till
they were withdrawn from the sector on the 22nd (partly
included in the above figures) were: Officers, 13 wounded;
other ranks, 38 killed and 150 wounded—a total loss
in action of 201.

APPENDIX TO CHAPTER IV

Detailed Statistics of Casualties of the 17/15th Division, July 1-11

Unit.	Officers.			Other Ranks.			Totals.
	K.	W.	M.	K.	W.	M.	
10th W. Yorks. -	11	11	1	270	304	143	740
7th E. Yorks. -	7	9	—	62	302	57	437
7th Yorks. -	5	11	1	73	322	44	456
6th Dorsets -	3	8	1	32	153	16	213
50th M.G. Co. -	—	—	—	—	16	—	16
50th T. M. Batty.	—	—	—	8	18	2	28
7th Lincolns -	7	6	—	56	237	30	336
7th Borders -	4	4	—	26	139	18	191
8th S. Staffords -	6	10	4	33	195	60	308
10th Sherwoods	5	9	1	32	223	84	354
51st M.G. Co. -	—	—	—	2	10	—	12
51st T.M. Batty.	—	—	—	3	18	4	25
9th Nthd. Fuslrs.	5	8	1	35	218	58	325
10th Lanc. Fuslrs.	3	6	5	35	204	82	335
9th W. Ridings -	7	5	2	42	176	47	279
12th Manchesters	7	5	3	50	275	210	550
52nd M. G. Co. -	—	1	1	4	21	2	29
52nd T.M. Batty.	—	1	—	2	26	—	29
7th Yk. & Lans.	—	—	—	2	33	—	35
Royal Engineers -	—	—	—	2	4	—	6
Royal Artillery -	—	3	—	7	54	—	64
R.A.M.C. - -	—	—	—	3	18	—	21
Totals - -	70	97	20	779	2966	857	4789

CHAPTER V

THE BATTLE OF THE SOMME (SECOND PHASE)
(July to December, 1916)

The rest billets assigned to the 17th Division were in what was officially known as the " Cavillon area," a few miles west of Amiens. It was a decided gain that for men coming straight from the last of a series of hard fights there was no long movement by rail. The entraining station was at Méricourt-l'Abbé near Treau on the lower Ancre, about five miles from Méaulte. The 52nd Brigade, which had been some days in reserve, got away first. The trains passed through Amiens and then by the Abbeville railway to the detraining station at Ailly-sur-Somme, the whole run being only about twenty miles.[1] The villages in the rest area that were furthest from Ailly (Oissy, Riencourt, Molliens, Vidame), were assigned to the first comers so as to give a shorter march to the rest of the Division. All the troops were in billets by next morning. Numbers of officers and men who had been in action at midnight and left the front in the early hours of July 11th, after living for days and nights amid the wreckage of the battle, found themselves resting before evening, still within distant sound of the guns, but in surroundings that seemed untouched by war. It was a bright sunny day, in a beautiful pastoral district with

---

[1] The long trains used for military transport in France moved slowly, and the " run " was more like a " crawl "—the 20 miles being covered in just two hours. There is an indication of the heavy losses of the Division in the fact that the first train was able to convey all the 52nd Brigade except half of the Duke of Wellington's, the Machine Gun Company, and the Trench Mortar Battery.

breezy uplands and sheltered valleys, well wooded and
watered, the fields a blaze of colour with poppies and
blue cornflowers.   Picturesque old country houses,
dignified with the name of châteaux, supplied quarters
for Divisional and Brigade staffs, and the troops were
billeted in villages and farmsteads that bore no trace of
war.

The H.Q. of the Division were at Cavillon.   General
Pilcher arrived late on July 11th and only spent one night
there.   Next day, July 12th, he visited the various
villages in which the troops were billeted in order to bid
farewell to the officers and men of the Division, which he
had trained and commanded in the months of trench warfare in the Ypres Salient, and in the days of battle that
carried our advance through Fricourt to Contalmaison.[1]
He spoke a few words to the officers of each unit, thanking
them for the good work they had done with him, and
wishing them all success under their new commander.
The diary of one of the brigadiers gives the impression of
the time in the Division: " To us, without knowledge of
all the circumstances, it seemed very hard that after the

[1] The operations that ended with the capture of the Contalmaison position
were undoubtedly a main factor in the first phase of the Battle of the Somme.
The 17th Division had been engaged from July 1st to the 11th as the centre
of this advance.   The Divisions with which it co-operated on its right and left
at the outset were relieved by others during these days and nights of almost
continuous fighting (the 21st by the 23rd, and the 7th by the 38th).   The 17th
was in action throughout.   In his *History of the War* (vol. iii. p. 174, 1922)
Lieut.-Colonel John Buchan thus notes the importance of the capture of
Contalmaison :

" On Thursday, 13th July, we were in a position to begin the next stage of
our advance.   The capture of Contalmaison had been the indispensable preliminary, and immediately following its fall Sir Douglas Haig issued his first
summary :

" ' After ten days and nights of continuous fighting, our troops have completed the methodical capture of the whole of the enemy's first system of defence
on a front of 14,000 yards.   This system of defence consisted of numerous and
continuous lines of fire trenches, extending to various depths of from 2,000 to
4,000 yards, and included five strongly-fortified villages, numerous heavily
wired and entrenched woods, and a large number of immensely strong redoubts.
The capture of each of these trenches represented an operation of some importance, and the whole of them are now in our hands.' "

Division had done really well in ordeal of battle its G.O.C. should be leaving it.   He visited all the units of the Division by motor car to bid them farewell, and I went with him to the billets of my brigade.   It was a painful tour round, and many of the officers were visibly affected, as the General had worked hard at the raising and training of the Division, and had been a year with it continuously at the front."

As the senior Brigadier-General, Clarke was directed to take command of the Division until a successor would be appointed.   In the afternoon of the next day, July 13th, General Philip R. Robertson, C.M.G., arrived at Cavillon to take over the 17th Division, which he commanded till the end of the war.

Born in 1866, he had received his first commission in the Cameronians at the age of twenty, and was with the regiment until he went to France in 1914 as Lieut.-Colonel commanding its 1st Battalion.   In June, 1915, he left it to take command of the 19th Infantry Brigade, which he held until in this second week of July, 1916, he became G.O.C. of the 17th Division.

The same evening orders arrived that the Division was to proceed next day to other rest billets a little further north, on the other side of the Somme near Abbeville. H.Q. were to be at Pont Rémy on the Somme.   The change was made by route march on the 15th, crossing the river at Hengest.   The Division remained in the Pont Rémy area till July 22nd for " rest, refitting, and training."   The Divisional artillery was still in the line, and the Pioneer Battalion, the York & Lancasters, were camped at Dernancourt near Albert, supplying working parties at the front.

Up to and including the date of its arrival in the Pont Rémy area, the Division received only small reinforcing drafts from England, amounting in all to 14 officers and 240 other ranks.   After July 15th, and before it again went into the line, drafts arrived amounting in all to 102 officers and 3,010 other ranks.[1]   The total (3,366) was 1,400 less than the aggregate of casualties incurred in the fighting of the first days of the month, without taking account of the further wastage by sickness.

The drafts included a number of officers and men who had already served at the front and recovered from wounds and illness.   But a considerable number were fresh from their first training in camps at home, and these, including some of the officers, had had no previous experience of active service.   There would be no opportunity of gradually introducing these new comers to the ways of trench warfare, as had been done when the Division arrived in Flanders, but happily in every unit there now were some hundreds of men who had hardened into experienced veterans.

On the 21st orders arrived that a move up to the Somme battle front would begin next day.   The Division was to proceed to camps and bivouacs on the north side of the Ancre below Albert.   Transport was to go by two days' march route starting on the 22nd.   The troops were to follow by rail on the 23rd.   On the 22nd, Divisional H.Q. were transferred to Ribemont on the Ancre, where they had been for a few days at the end of June and the beginning of July.   The H.Q. of the 15th Corps were close by at Heilly.   On the 23rd the troops marched to Hengest on the Somme, to entrain there, pass through Amiens and detrain near Ribemont.   The camp provided for the Division was mostly an open bivouac, with a very few tents.   Happily the weather was fine and warm.   The Divisional artillery was taken out of the line and rejoined.   Its commander, General Ouseley, R.A., had been wounded and was succeeded by General Buckle, R.A.

On July 27th, there was a Divisional parade for the

---

[1] Of these drafts, four officers and 1,458 other ranks came from units not belonging to the Division.   Till now all the battalions had received drafts from the regimental districts in which they were raised.

presentation of a number of Military Medals (or rather of their ribbons, for the medals were not available till long after), to N.C.Os. and men who had specially distinguished themselves in the recent operations. The Division was formed on three sides of a square, and as it was the first time he had seen it assembled, General Robertson took the opportunity of addressing it. The General said:

"OFFICERS, N.C.Os. AND MEN OF THE 17TH DIVISION,—The Corps Commander had hoped to be here himself to-day to present the Military Medals to the N.C.Os. and men of the Division, but he is very sorry that owing to press of work he is unable to come.

"As this is the first opportunity I have had of speaking to you on parade, I would like to tell you all how very proud I am at finding myself in command of such a fine Division, whose reputation stands very high in the British Army. I have heard from many how well the Division has always fought, and especially how splendidly they did during the first ten or twelve days of the present battle, and it is with the fullest confidence that I look forward to the time when you will again meet the enemy, and am certain that you will then add to the laurels already gained by the 17th Division.

"The N.C.Os. and men who are now to receive decorations have been brought to notice for special acts of gallantry and devotion to duty, and the names of others have been forwarded for rewards to higher authority ; besides all these I know that there are many officers and men who have done most gallantly, but whose deeds are unrecorded. In every big battle this must be so, but everyone of you whether rewarded or not has the satisfaction of knowing that it is your individual efforts which, combined, all go to build up the fine reputation of the Division, and also that each one of you has done his duty well, for the British Empire and a great and just cause."

The Division was now under orders to be held ready to go into the line at three hours' notice, and one brigade was warned each day to be prepared to be the first to move to the front. It will be useful here to note briefly what was the general situation at this time on the Somme. By July 11th the British attack had broken through the German first line, on a front of eight miles, and captured the woods and fortified villages behind it from La Boiselle and Contalmaison to beyond Montauban. On July 14th (the day of the French National Fête), the next great advance began against the second enemy line. This line ran along the upper slopes of the high ground which forms a round-topped chalk down extending roughly from the gap at Combles at its south-east end, north-westward to the heights beyond Thiepval above the gorge of the Ancre. The sector attacked was about four miles long, and its strong points were the villages of Longueval, Bazentin-le-Grand and Bazentin-le-Petit, each with its adjacent wood. It was a brilliantly successful day. The two Bazentins and their woods were stormed and a footing was won in Longueval and Delville Wood just beyond it. High Wood on the crest of the down north-west of Longueval, though outside the objective of the first advance, was reached but held only for a while. Large numbers of prisoners and many guns were captured. In the following days the ground won was consolidated, and further progress was made at Longueval and Delville Wood, under heavy artillery fire from the German third line with frequent counter-attacks about Longueval. Our position here was a sharp salient, and for some time it was the liveliest part of the Somme front. In the last week of July Delville Wood had been deeply penetrated, and away to the right attacks were being made on the village of Guillemont.

On July 30th, the 17th Division received warning orders to be ready next day to relieve the 5th Division, which had a brigade holding the trenches in the front at the north end of Longueval. The 52nd Brigade was next on the list for duty, and it received orders to march to Longueval in the afternoon of the 31st. Subsequently however this order was changed, and the start for the front was fixed for 9.15 a.m. on Tuesday, August 1st.

It was a fine summer day and soon became intensely hot and sultry. After crossing the Ancre near Albert the Brigade marched south-east to a bivouac near the ruins of Fricourt, where there was a rest for some hours. Close by an Australian battery was in action, shelling the German positions to the north-east on the ridge some five miles away. The gunners were stripped to the waist as they worked their guns and handled the heavy shells. In the afternoon the Brigade moved on to near Pommiers Redoubt, a captured German work half-way between Mametz and Montauban and about a mile from the latter village. General Clarke with one of his staff had gone on to the H.Q. of the 15th Brigade (5th Division), which he was to relieve after dark that evening. He found the Brigade H.Q. installed in a dugout in Montauban Alley, a long communication trench running from Pommiers Redoubt to the north of Montauban and the margin of Bernafay Wood, and branching off into several communication trenches leading to Longueval and other points already won in the German second line. Here the details of the relief were arranged.

Brigade orders directed that the front line taken over was to be held by the 9th Northumberland Fusiliers and the 9th Duke of Wellington's, with the 12th Manchesters in support, and the 10th Lancashire Fusiliers in reserve. Each battalion in the front line was to have with it a section of the M.G. Company and two Stokes mortars from the T.M. Battery. The move to the front began in the twilight of the evening, and there was a long march in the dark. As the men moved up shells were bursting freely right and left of the communication trenches. " The battle line that night was a marvellous spectacle," writes an officer of the brigade. " Flashes of guns, rockets, flares, and the variegated colours of the Very lights lit up the whole horizon, and for all the world looked like a gigantic firework display. Now and then an extra glare would indicate something explosive having been hit by a shell, and the village of Longueval was burning brightly from the incendiary shells that had been poured into it."

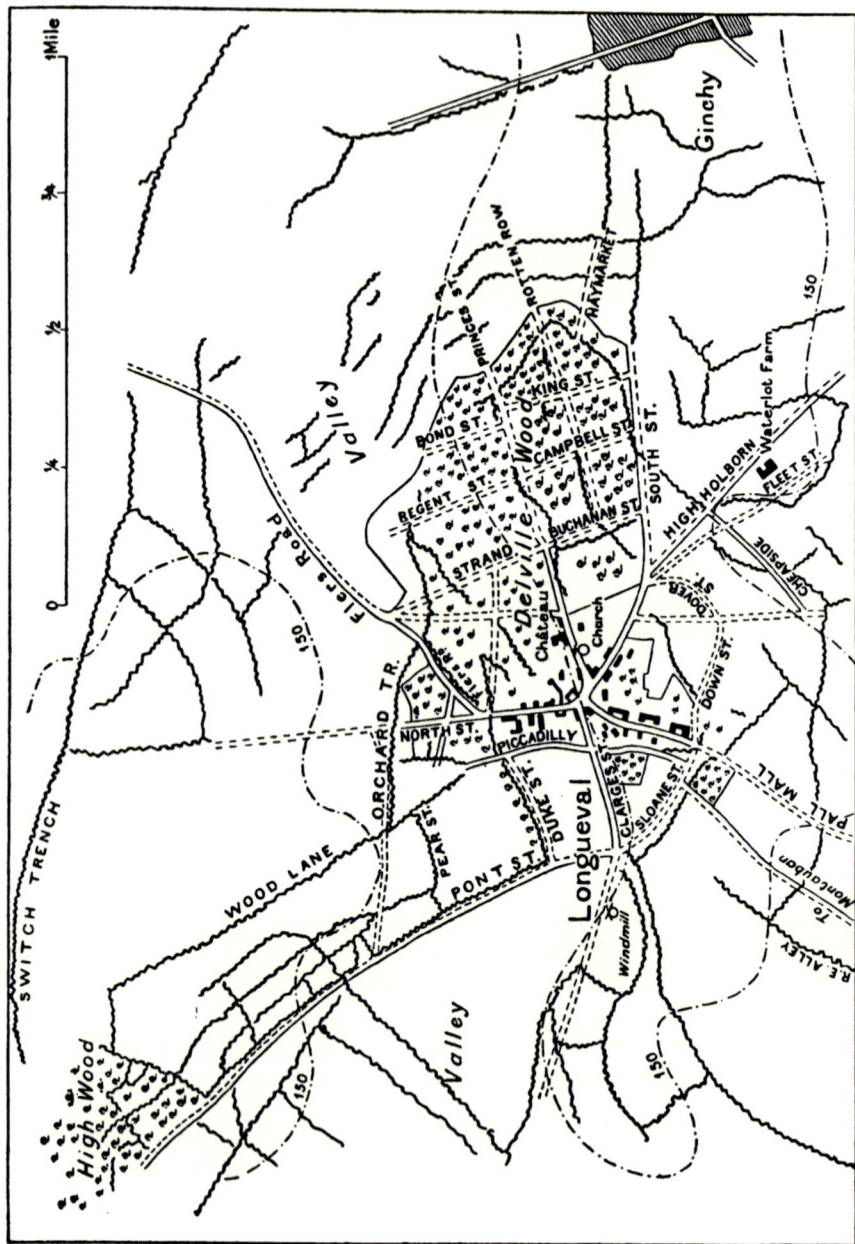

Longueval and Delville Wood, August 1916.

The relief was a difficult one, and was not completed till the dawn was coming. Longueval, the wood and the ground about both, had been heavily bombarded as a prelude to our attack of July 14th, when the greater part of the position was won. Then for a fortnight there had been confused fighting along the north margin of the wood and in the orchards at the north end of the long village. The day before the relief an attack on the enemy position at the latter part of the sector had failed. Day and night for more than a fortnight the village and wood had been persistently shelled by the enemy with guns of various calibres, from field pieces to the 5.9 howitzers, throwing big " crumps." The fire came from three directions—in front from the rising ground of the Bapaume ridge west of Flers; on the left from the ground north of High Wood still partly held by the enemy, and from the right about Ginchy. The village and Delville Wood were for the enemy on the sky line, for they stood on the crest of the Combles-Thiepval ridge, the outlying high ground running roughly parallel to the Bapaume ridge. From both ridges long spurs ran out and overlapped, giving on our left well-covered positions for batteries using indirect fire. The result of this prolonged bombardment was that all the ground was badly cratered, trenches had been reduced to strings of shell holes, and it was very difficult to identify the positions marked on our trench maps. In the information provided for the relief, posts were named as occupied which did not exist. To add to the difficulties of the sector our aircraft did not so completely dominate the situation as had been the case on July 1st, and the German planes were active and enterprising. The enemy was extending a new trench system in the immediate front and held positions close up to our ill-defined line, and from these kept up a deadly fire of snipers and machine guns, so that in the front any movement by daylight was difficult.

The orders for the relief, as recorded in the Divisional

Staff Diary, thus noted the information received from the 5th Division, which was handing over the sector to the 17th:

" Situation as given by 5th Division:—' Our line extends along Pont Street to Duke Street, thence across Piccadilly into Delville Wood, with posts believed to be at the following points:

(a) Junction of trenches in Pear Street at S. 11, c. 2. 5.
(b) Junction of Pear Street and Wood Lane.
(c) S. 11, d. 0.5.
(d) S. 11, d. 3.6. (in North Street).
(e) Corner of orchard at S. 11, d. 5.7.'

There appeared however to be considerable doubt as to the position of these posts, more especially as the existence of Orchard Trench, and the fact of its being held by the enemy had only just become known. The fact that Orchard Trench had been dug and occupied by the enemy was believed to have been the chief cause of the failure of the 5th Division's attack on the night of 30/31 July."

On the night of the 1st and 2nd August the 9th Duke of Wellington's took over the right of the position as indicated, a very ill-defined line, mostly in the west corner of Delville Wood, with two companies in front, and the two others at the south end of Longueval. The Northumberland Fusiliers occupied the line on the left, old German trenches in very bad condition. Posts a and b were identified and relieved, but posts c, d and e could not be found that night. No contact could be secured as yet with the brigade in the wood on the right of the position. There was obviously here a serious gap in the line. In Longueval there were some doubtful shelters in what was left of the village, but only one deep dugout near the ruined church. This was used as Battalion H.Q. for the right of the line. Of the two battalions in support and reserve, the Manchesters were in a valley close up on the reverse slope of the ridge, and the Lancashire Fusiliers were scattered in dugouts in Montauban Alley. One of the old German dugouts here was used as Brigade H.Q.

Divisional H.Q. had been established at Bellevue Farm near Albert, and close by the 50th Brigade was in Divisional Reserve. The 51st Brigade was sent forward to Pommiers Redoubt to act as support to the 52nd. The Divisional artillery came again into the line about Montauban.

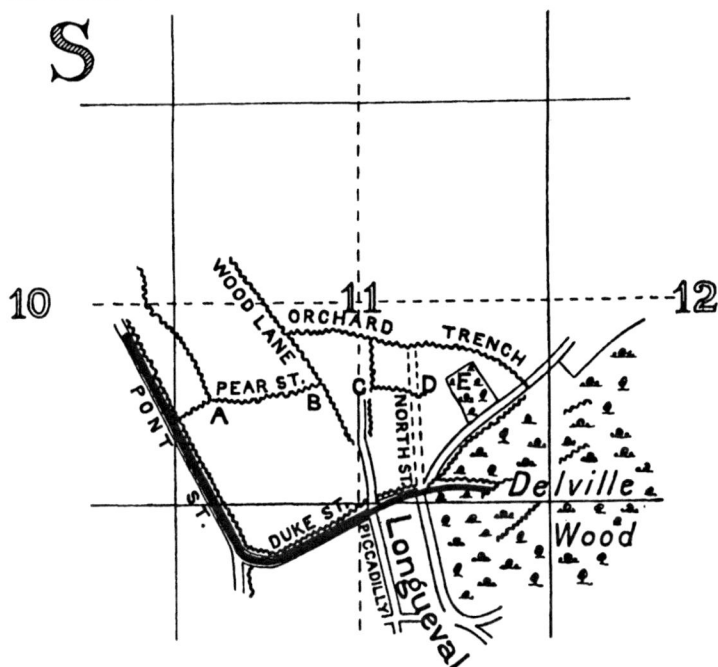

Line to be taken over...................
A, B, C, D, E ; Posts reported as held in front of line

Relief of 5th Division by 52nd Brigade at Longueval.

When day dawned on August 2nd an attempt was made to clear the situation. On the right in the Wood a defensive flank was formed to the right rear of the line to guard the gap, and patrols went out to gain touch with the 13th Division in the Wood. Other patrols sent to the front of the Wood discovered, in its north-west corner near Flers road, two machine gun detachments of the 5th Division, which had been isolated there for three days, under frequent shell fire, and the men were now without either food or water and in a very exhausted condition. They were relieved by an M.G. detachment of the 52nd Brigade. It seemed not unlikely that this represented post *c*, supposed to be in the orchard on the other side of Flers road. Further to the left, close to the line, an abandoned British machine gun and another that had been smashed up by a shell-burst were found. The enemy were not only in Orchard Trench, but also in the orchards at the north end of the village, and their extreme front seemed to run through the supposed positions of the three advanced posts reported at *d* and *e*, their real positions, while they existed, being close in to our front line. It is easy to say that such mistakes should not be made, but in warfare like that of the Somme battlefields there were times and conditions that made it no wonder they occurred, the only marvel being that they did not occur oftener. Positions where every marked feature by which a map can be set has been beaten flat and the outlook is amongst shattered woods and orchards and over ground churned by weeks of shell fire into a stretch of craters, with trench lines hardly distinguishable from the chaos around them,—this forms a prospect very different from the trim legibility of neatly squared maps full of clearly shown detail, some of which has ceased to exist in reality. These were the conditions in August, 1916, at the corner of Delville Wood and among the devastated orchards, at the end of the ruined village. It should be added that in the 17th, as in all the divisions that had been already heavily engaged at an earlier date in the great battle, there were now many young officers and non-commissioned officers who were having their first experiences of trench warfare under these difficult conditions. So far they had only seen the practice trenches of the training grounds, and it is more than doubtful if these dummy defences were ever designed to represent a trench position that had all but disappeared in a wild confusion of shell craters and heaps of débris.

On the afternoon of August 2nd Corps H.Q. sent a preliminary order that the 17th Division was to be prepared to extend the front it held, and to take over Delville Wood from the 13th Division on its right in the night of the 4th to 5th. Meanwhile, it was directed that the position actually held should be further consolidated.

The position was under continuous bombardment with all kinds of projectiles, including occasional bursts of gas shells, and consolidation meant unceasing work in restoring the damaged trenches, and in several places reconstructing them by connecting up lines of shell craters. There was a galling fire of rifles and machine guns from the enemy's line close in front at Orchard Trench, and the 52nd Brigade was directed to attack it shortly after midnight on August 4th after a preparatory bombardment during the 3rd.

Our gunners found it no easy matter to bring an effective fire to bear on Orchard Trench. Our advanced posts on the left were close up to it, and could not be withdrawn in daylight, and the position further to the right was ill-defined and awkwardly near our front in the Wood. The preparatory bombardment began in the afternoon of the 3rd, and the enemy at once replied with a heavy counter-bombardment on a wide front and of great depth. Shell rained on our batteries massed well to the rear about Caterpillar Wood; they fell in scattered bursts all over the ground behind our line and along the communication trenches, and the front itself was kept under intense fire, including discharges of phosphorus gas shells. As the evening came the hostile fire seemed to become more intense. The battalions in the front line—Northumberland Fusiliers on the left and the Duke of Wellington's on the right—had many casualties. The reports from the latter battalion told of numbers of men being gassed, many killed and wounded, and nearly all exhausted by the strain of holding on under intense fire in trenches that gave little cover. General Clarke decided to replace them by a fresh battalion for the attack, and the 12th Manchesters moved up under shell fire that at times enfiladed the communication trench they followed, suffering many casualties on the way.

At 12.40 a.m. on the 4th the attack started—Northumberlands on the left, Manchesters on the right. For a long time brigade H.Q. could get no news of what was happening. All communication lines had been cut by shell fire, and runners failed to get through the close barrage put down on Longueval and its approaches by the German batteries. It was not till 4.35 a.m. that messages came through that both on left and right the attack had failed. During the night the Lancashire Fusiliers had been brought up to the support position in Montauban Alley, and two companies were now sent forward to Longueval.

On the afternoon of the 4th General Robertson met his three brigadiers in a conference at Pommiers Redoubt, when arrangements were discussed for the reorganisation of the line, and its coming extension through Delville Wood. After this the extended front would be held by two brigades. In preparation for the move the 50th Brigade was brought up from Bellevue Farm to Pommiers Redoubt.

After the attack of the night before many of our wounded were lying in the cratered ground of No Man's Land. Some of these close up to the enemy's wire were taken into the German line. Others were rescued by our patrols during the night of August 4th. Captain Benton of the Manchesters was not thus rescued till he had lain for thirty hours in a shell hole without food, water or first-aid. He had been at the H.Q. of his battalion at the outset of the attack, and after the first check he had gone out to obtain information as to the position and help in reorganising the men for a second attempt. He was badly wounded, one of his legs shattered by machine gun fire. It was a marvel that he survived these hours of lonely agony in No Man's Land.[1]

On the night of Friday to Saturday (August 4th and 5th) the 50th Brigade relieved the 52nd on the left in Longueval, and the 51st took over the whole of Delville Wood from the 99th Brigade on the right. The dividing line between the two brigades ran along the upper part of North Street and then by " Piccadilly " to Sloane Street. The 50th Brigade thus held the trench line along Pont Street and Duke Street, with the advanced posts in front of it, and the 51st held the ruined village along the west margin of the Wood and in the Wood itself, a rather vaguely marked line, near its northern edge.

The 50th Brigade had one battalion in the front line, two in support and the remaining battalion in reserve. The 51st Brigade was to have two battalions in the front and the two others in support. The 52nd Brigade was the Divisional Reserve. It had gone into bivouac near Pommiers Redoubt, on being relieved, but the place was decidedly " unhealthy." It was close to one of our artillery positions, and in the following night when the enemy was persistently shelling Longueval, Delville Wood and the ground behind as far as Montauban, there were several casualties in the bivouacs of the Northumberland and Lancashire Fusiliers, so next day the brigade was moved to other ground west of Fricourt and near Bécordel-Becourt. Movement in rear of the sector held by the Division was, however, now facilitated by the work

---

[1] It was one of the horrors of this prolonged trench warfare that the firing was practically continuous, and it was rarely that there was even a local informal truce to clear the battle-ground after a hard fight. The dead lay unburied in No Man's Land or tangled in the wire ; the wounded were often left without help. Sometimes, but very rarely, a brief unofficial truce was arranged by the local commanders at the fighting front, and British and Germans worked together at succouring the wounded and getting them back into their own lines. But this was an irregular proceeding, and higher authority on both armies had a dread of anything like " fraternisation."

of the Pioneer Battalion the York & Lancasters, who,
by several days and nights of digging and revetting, had
transformed a ruinous old German communication
trench, running from Montauban to the left rear of the
Longueval position, into a comparatively safe road up to
the front.   It was given a zig-zag trace to protect those
moving in it from the deadly enfilade fire that had caused
a good deal of loss in the old communication trenches,
and the service rendered by the battalion was recognised
by the reconstructed trench being given the name of
" Y. L. Alley."

Conditions in the front line were now those of a severe
trial for the brigades that held it, and more especially for
the 51st in the Wood.   The enemy had been accumulating
a mass of artillery on a front of some four miles round the
salient formed by the Longueval-Delville Wood position
on a great curve from the spurs beyond High Wood, along
the Flers Ridge and then southward behind Ginchy and
Guillemont.   He was thus able to keep up a converging
fire upon the position from three sides.   But the salient
had to be held at all costs until a renewed advance would
straighten out the front by pushing it forward to the right
of the Wood.   In his detailed despatch on the Battle of
the Somme, written in the following December, Sir
Douglas Haig thus referred to the situation at Longueval
and Delville Wood in these trying days of August, 1916:

" This pronounced salient invited counter attacks by the enemy.
He possessed direct observation on it all round from Guillemont on
the south-east to High Wood on the north-west.   He could bring
a concentric artillery fire to bear not only on the wood and village,
but also on the confined space behind, through which ran the
French communications as well as ours, where great numbers of
guns as well as ammunition and impedimenta of all sorts had
necessarily to be crowded together.   Having been in occupation of
the ground for nearly two years he knew every foot of it, and could
not fail to appreciate the possibilities of causing us heavy loss there
by indirect artillery fire;   while it was evident that if he could drive
in the salient of our line, and so gain direct observation on to the

ground behind, our position in that area would become very uncomfortable.   If there had not been good grounds for believing that the enemy was not capable of driving from this position troops who had shown themselves able to wrest it from him, the situation would have been an anxious one."

It was plain enough that if our hold on the apex of the salient about Longueval were lost, the open slopes to the south of it and the valley by Montauban would be a " very uncomfortable " area.   But meanwhile the conditions on the protecting crest, where our men clung doggedly to the ruined village and the devastated wood, were such that it would be the feeblest of descriptions to call them " very uncomfortable."   They were simply horrible almost to the breaking point of endurance, and our men held on at the cost of heavy loss through days and nights of unceasing strain.

On the left we held the battered trenches at the north end of the village, trenches that it was no easy matter to keep in existence by constant labour, and which afforded only defective shelter from hostile fire.   The village had been rushed in the great attack of July 14th, but the enemy held the orchards at its north end.   But the ruins of Longueval could not have been defended for a day unless we also held the large wood on its eastern margin.   This wood had been assaulted on July 15th by the South African Brigade.   They had fought their way along its central ride and up the cross rides till they had nearly reached its eastern and northern boundaries.   Then they had been counter-attacked, and forced back to its south-western corner, where they made a desperate defence and won back some of the lost ground.   They were relieved by British troops when they were reduced to a mere handful.   It was then reported that the Wood had been captured, but at the end of the month the enemy still held parts of it on the north and east.   It was not finally and completely won till August 24th, after six weeks of fighting.

When the 51st Brigade took over Delville Wood on August 5th the struggle for its possession had been three weeks in progress. The official view seems to have been that the whole of it was within our front line. This however was optimism not entirely justified by fact. Only the western margin of the Wood and its central southern part were entirely clear of the enemy. There was not even any continuous trench front in existence traversing it from west to east. The line was at best a series of detached fragments of old German trenches, with between them strings of shell craters, improvised into posts. It was a mass of broken tree trunks and fallen branches, often blocking the rides that had once been open roadways through it, with shell holes everywhere, and a tangle of undergrowth, bristling here and there with rusty barbed wire. The enemy had freely used phosphor gas bombs in the three weeks' bombardment, and the poison gas hung in the hollows, and drifted among the undergrowth. But there was even a more noisome foulness in the air. Day after day from soon after sunrise the heat had been of tropical intensity, and the nights were close and sultry. From end to end Delville Wood was littered, and in many places heaped, with dead. They had fallen in the days of hand-to-hand fighting when the Wood was first penetrated, and under the persistent bombardment that followed. Many of them wore the German " field grey " uniform, many the British khaki, and of the latter numbers bore the badges of the South African Brigade and of Scottish battalions. " I never remember having seen so many dead in so small a stretch of ground; in one of the rides they lay five and six deep," writes one of the defenders of the Wood. In that August heat in Delville Wood the first signs of decay showed themselves within four or five hours of the fatal blow, and as so many of the unburied dead had been littering the place for days or even weeks, the air was poisoned with the odour of death. Under such conditions, added to the increasing bombardment, it was possible to hold the Wood only by short spells of service in its so-called trenches. The enemy in front, much less sorely tried, had to spare his men in the same way, and during the fighting for the Wood they were relieved after a very few days in the line. On July 14th, the 6th Regiment of the 2nd Bavarian Corps (Nurembergers) had held Longueval and Delville Wood. They were relieved by troops of the 8th Division of the 4th German Corps (Magdeburg) and then by the 5th Division of the 3rd Corps, the Brandenburgers, who claimed to rank next to the Guard as the best fighting men of the German Army.

When the 51st Brigade took over the line in the Wood on the morning of Saturday, August 5th, the Sherwood Foresters were in the line on the left and the Borders on the right. The other two battalions, Lincolns and South Staffords, were in support on the slope to the south and near Longueval Church, but even here they suffered from the bombardment. Patrols in the Wood discovered that the enemy still held its north-west corner and had re-occupied an old trench linking up with Orchard Trench. On the afternoon of Monday the 7th, after a preparatory bombardment by the Divisional artillery, the Staffords and Borders attacked at 4.30 p.m. to clear the Wood and establish themselves on its northern margin.

The attempt failed, the attacking troops being met by a storm of machine gun fire at point blank range and forced to take shelter in the craters of No Man's Land. The 50th Brigade tried to help by sending the Dorsets from Pear Street against the small orchard north of Flers road, but this advance also was held by the enemy's machine gunners. At midnight the Sherwoods again attacked, but the only useful result was that they established three posts in craters towards the south end of Flers road. Steps were being taken to renew the attack on the 8th, when Divisional orders were received that no further attempt was to be made by the two battalions, which would be relieved during the following night by those in support.

Accordingly during the night of Tuesday to Wednesday the Borders on the right and Lincolns on the left took over the line in Delville Wood. Something had been done already to improve this line, but it was not a continuous one, it was still made up of bits of trench with linked shell holes connecting them, and a gap in the centre by the Regent Street wood path, south of the north " horn " of the Wood. Patrols found that the enemy still held this north angle, and a trench running through the margin of the wood on this side, curving through its eastern portion, and linking up by a line running due east to the new German trenches outside it.

The Borders took over the line—such as it was—from about Regent Street eastward. The Lincolns had a company between Strand and Regent Street, another by Flers road facing Orchard Trench in the centre of their sector, and another on the left between Piccadilly and North Street. The centre and left companies were in close touch, but touch with the right company was only maintained by patrols. The fourth company was south of the central drive through the Wood near Longueval Château. A considerable part of the line was held by groups in shell holes. The trying conditions in the Wood have already been described. Every narrative of those who held it tells of its horrors, and the soldiers long after talked of it as " Devil's Wood."

Day and night the enemy's fire was unceasing—sniping in the bush at the front, shells of various calibres coming from three directions and including plenty of gas shells, and frequent pelting with machine gun fire, direct from the enemy's nearer trenches, and indirect fire from longer ranges sending in descending streams of bullets. The patient endurance with which the men held on is all the more to their credit, because for many of the newcomers it was their first experience of being under fire.

On Thursday, the 10th, the Borders attempted to reach the enemy's trench in the wood margin to the north of their line, by working along an abandoned trench, full of dead, that led towards it. The advance was held by heavy machine gun and rifle fire. On the left the Lincolns were busy improving the line and making good the frequent damage done by the bombardment. Casualties were numerous.

On the night of the 10th-11th, the 52nd Brigade relieved the 51st in the Wood, with the 10th Lancashire Fusiliers on the right and the 9th Northumberland Fusiliers on the left, and the other two battalions in support. As a final impression of what the position was now like we may quote the brigadier's note of how he found it when he took over: " Conditions in Delville Wood were appalling. It was full of gas and corpses; no regular line could be discerned, and the men fought in small groups, mostly in shell holes hastily improvised into fire trenches; communication both lateral and from front to rear was exceedingly difficult, dangerous and barely possible." The Brigade had a short tour of duty in the Wood, for before it went it was informed that the 17th Division would be relieved by the 14th on the night of August 12th-13th. Corps orders directed that an attempt should be made to establish advanced posts in the front, and three of these were secured on the 11th. The relief began on the following evening and was completed by next morning. The Divisional artillery remained in the line until the 17th. Fighting continued in the Wood for nearly a fortnight after the Division was relieved, and the enemy did not let go its eastern and northern margins till August 24th.

The losses of the Division while holding Longueval and Delville Wood were even heavier than those it had incurred during the first days of the battle, round Fricourt, and in front of Contalmaison. The returns of losses for the month of August are practically those of the opening

days of the month, as the Division was not again in close
action during the rest of August.[1]   We may therefore
take the return for the month as representing the losses
in the days at Longueval and Delville Wood.   The details
of these losses were:

		Killed.	Wounded.	Missing.	Totals.
Officers	-	78	172	21	271
Other ranks	-	1093	4194	991	6278
Totals	-	1171	4366	1021	6549

Besides these casualties, 36 officers and 360 other ranks
—396 in all—were " evacuated sick," making the total
wastage of the Division 6,945.   This was some 1,500
more than the losses in the July fighting, and amounted
to about half the combatant strength of the Division.

After coming out of the line the Division concentrated
at Buire Camp on the Ancre near Albert and was then
moved to rest billets in villages south-west of Doullens,
where Divisional H.Q. were established on August 16th.
The Division now came under the orders of the 7th
Corps (Lieut.-General Snow).   The artillery had
remained for a few days in position near Montauban after
the Infantry Brigades were withdrawn.   It was ordered
to rejoin the Division on the 23rd.

The rest was a brief one.   On August 18th Corps
H.Q. sent orders that the Division, now greatly reduced
in strength, was to relieve the 56th Division in the line
east of Doullens.   The sector to be taken over had a
front of nearly four miles, with its centre opposite the
Gommecourt salient, its right at Hébuterne and its left
opposite Monchy-aux-Bois.   On the first day of the
Somme battle the Gommecourt salient had been the scene
of the repulse with heavy loss of the attack made by the
46th and 56th Divisions, but since then there had been no
important events on that part of the front.   It was

---

[1] As we shall see, there was no serious fighting while the Division was in the
sector facing Gommecourt in the last days of the month.

reckoned to be " a quiet sector," and along much of its front there was a fairly wide " No Man's Land."

The relief was spread over three days, being carried out by a brigade each day taking over a section of the front, the 50th on the right, the 52nd in the centre opposite Gommecourt, and the 51st on the left. The trenches were in good order; there was little artillery fire and the villages behind the line showed hardly any trace of war damage, though those closest up to the trenches had been

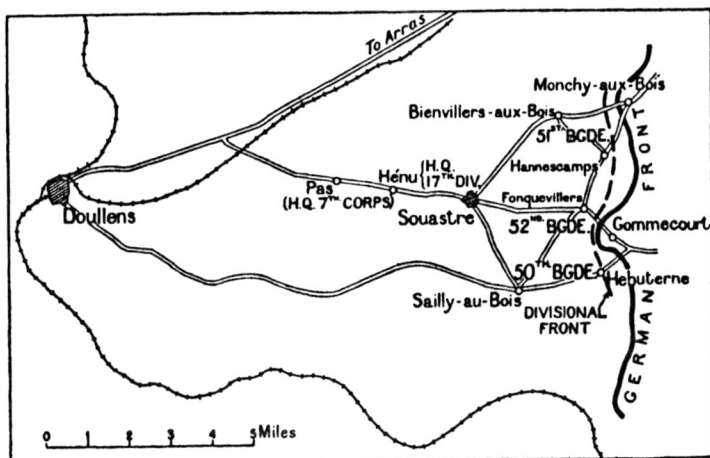

In front of the Gommecourt Salient, Autumn 1916.

evacuated by most of their inhabitants. Compared to Fricourt and the quadrilateral positions, and Longueval and Delville Wood, this sector of the line seemed almost a place of rest.

One of the surprises of the sector was the sight of the Château de la Haye, which for some time had been the H.Q. of the 56th Division, and was now to be the H.Q. of the 52nd Brigade. It stood on an emience about half-way between Fonquevillers and Souastre, a large semi-castellated country house, having a courtyard on its eastern front with extensive stabling on both sides of it. Though it stood on the sky line at a range of not more than

4,000 yards from the enemy's batteries near Gomme-court Wood, it did not seem that they had ever made it their target. It was true that many of the windows on the east front were broken and boarded up, but this damage might have been the result of concussion, for right and left of the château the artillery of the 56th Division was in position close by, a fact that made it all the more remarkable that the château had not attracted the enemy's fire. On its roof there was a carefully-camou-flaged look-out station that gave a wide view over the German lines far to the south. A fine room on the ground floor had been converted into a messroom. An officer slept near it, beside a telephone, to receive any messages during the night. For the rest of the staff there were well-built and comfortably-fitted rooms in a deep trench on the west side of the building. These had been constructed by the French when they held this sector and were using the château as a headquarters.

But General Clarke and his officers had not been more than a couple of days in possession, with their horses in the courtyard stables, when one night the Germans suddenly pitched shells into the château. One burst in the ground floor and brought down the messroom ceiling. Another dug a small crater in the courtyard. After this it was considered advisable to withdraw the Brigade H.Q. to a large house in the eastern outskirts of Souastre.

Sheltered in a hollow of the higher ground, the large village or small town of Souastre had enjoyed comparative immunity from hostile shell fire though it was only about three miles from the German salient at Gommecourt. Many of the inhabitants had remained and several shops were open and doing good business. Numbers of the new and temporary establishments, characteristic of an advanced divisional base, clustered in and around it—transport lines, workshops, stores, canteens and the like. To these was now added a new place of entertainment for the men of the Division. Two officers, who in the days before the war had had some practical experience as entertainers, had been for some time organising a Divisional concert and theatrical party, which took the unassuming title of " The Duds." A large barn at Souastre was converted into an improvised theatre, and here on September 6th " The Duds " gave the first of many successful performances, which was honoured by G.O.C., General Robertson occupying a front seat in the " stalls " supported by many of his officers.

By this time Army Orders had arrived that the Division was to begin preparations for an intended attack on the Gommecourt salient and the adjacent sector of the enemy front. General Robertson was invited to submit a plan of operations, and worked it out in considerable detail, in consultation with his Divisional artillery commander, and there were conferences on the subject with the Brigade commanders. Gas cylinders were brought up and installed in the front trenches, and on the evening of September the 7th the gas was loosed off against the salient and Gommecourt Park. It was a useful preliminary practice, and was also intended to test the readiness of the enemy and make him show what arrangements he had made for defence. The wind was fair and the gas cloud swept over the German front and into the woods beyond it where he had his artillery positions. There was a good deal of excitement on the German lines, and a brilliant display of Very lights and signal rockets was followed by an outburst of his artillery fire. The expert verdict on the performance of enemy gunners was that it was somewhat feeble. The firing was desultory and irregular. Shells fell here and there, but obviously there was no careful ranging on selected targets and no attempts at concentration, and the fire on our front never amounted to a barrage. The Divisional artillery (which had now replaced that of the 56th Division) replied. But when the enemy realised that no attack was developing the cannonade rapidly died down, and the front relapsed into its relative quietude.

The Divisional artillery was now reinforced by bringing up several batteries of the Corps heavy artillery, which were concentrated on the high ground behind Hébuterne, and wire cutting by gunfire began. Corps orders received on September 17th directed that this should be suspended, and next day there was a further order that the 17th Division would be relieved by the 33rd and would proceed by march route to the St. Riquier area for a fortnight of intensive training in preparation for the projected attack.

On the 22nd, Divisional H.Q. were transferred to St. Riquier, a small town about sixteen miles west of Doullens. The same day the march of the Division began, and by the evening of the 25th it was billeted in the villages of the new training area, where it remained until October 6th.

The weather was fine and it was a time of hard work, including day and night operations against lines of dummy trenches. There was a tank training centre in the neighbourhood, with a wide stretch of broken ground, furrowed by open trenches and banks and dykes eight or nine feet high. Parties of officers and men were taken to see the new monsters at work and to receive some instruction in co-operating with them. The tanks had made their first appearance in actual fighting on September 15th on the Somme front. It was a day when the largest gain of ground in a single push since the battle began had been secured, our line being carried forward on a front of five miles from near Pozières on the left to Delville Wood on the right for a distance of over a mile everywhere and in some places for the best part of another mile. The attack had pushed down the slopes of the Combles-Thiepval Ridge and won a footing on the spurs of the Bapaume Ridge, taking the villages of Courcelette, Martinpuich and Flers. The tanks had certainly been a considerable factor in this fine day's work, though at the time their contribution to it was somewhat exaggerated and nothing was told to the public at home of the inevitable failures that occurred in the handling of this new weapon.[1]   At St. Riquier other minor stunts were demonstrated by experts, including a device for starting work on the digging of a communication trench by laying numbers of tubes of high explosives (ammonal) along the marked line, and firing them in rapid succession.

On September 29th the Divisional artillery began its march eastward to resume its place in the line, and on October 6th Divisional H.Q. were transferred from St. Riquier to the village of Pas near the former H.Q. at Hénu.   The three brigades were now moving up to the front.   The Division was in the sector before the Gommecourt salient till October 17th.   Preparations were still being made for the projected attack.   The Pioneer Battalion had even been engaged in digging assembly trenches near Hébuterne.   These however were never used and were knocked to pieces by the enemy's artillery, for the G.H.Q. changed its plans and the Division was ordered to return to the south to take further part in the main advance on the Somme battlefields.   Accordingly, on October 17th, it was relieved by the 48th Division, and began a five days' march southward in cold and wet weather, the first sign of winter being near at hand. Some help was given by transporting detachments on lorries and motor buses, but several units did most of the

[1] The tanks concentrated on the Somme front for the attack of September 15th were of the first, almost experimental, type.   Their utmost speed was only 2 miles an hour, and they turned slowly and sometimes uncertainly. Though the plates were bullet proof, bullets and lead splashes came through the joints of their armour and caused casualties, and their engines and steering gear were very liable to break down.   Only about half of them succeeded in getting into action, the rest being ditched or brought to a standstill by trouble with their gear.   Of those that actually reached the German line few escaped mishaps of greater or less gravity.   Later they were made more effective, and their tactics and those of infantry co-operation were worked out.   But even at the outset the temporary scare they produced among the enemy was very useful.

journey by heavy marching over sodden roads. On October 27th Divisional H.Q. were transferred from Pas to the Citadel Camp near Bray, and the Division was concentrated in various rest camps of huts and somewhat ragged tents in the neighbourhood. Orders were received that it was to relieve the 8th Division in the front line south of Gueudecourt.

Since the great success of September 15th, there had been another important gain of ground ten days later (advance of the 25th and 26th), and the British line northeast of Flers now formed a bold salient curving round the ruined village of Gueudecourt. Henceforth, till the cold and rain of the winter brought the operations to a standstill by making the ground all but impassable, it was a time of minor operations with small local gains when they were successful. The advance was slowing down to a temporary stoppage. It was truly said that our front had now two No Man's Lands—a narrow one in its front towards the German line, and behind it a much wider one, of cratered ground, wrecked woods, ruined villages, and roads and tracks that were deep in mud. Wheeled traffic could only move slowly and uncertainly with wheels sinking in the water-logged ground. Efforts were being made to organise a new form of transport immediately behind the front. Mule trains were being collected and on the south slopes of the Combles-Thiepval Ridge light railways were being constructed on which trollies could bring up supplies. But much reliance had to be placed on the man-power of carrying parties, whose toilsome duties were " fatigues " in a very literal sense of the word, and the movement of troops over the No Man's Land behind the line meant a slow plodding through a sea of mud, often under a storm of cold wind and pelting rain.

On the night of October 29th-30th the relief of the 8th Division began, and on the 31st the H.Q. of the 17th was established in hutments in Bernafay Wood, to the east of Montauban and about a mile south of Longueval. All the three brigades of the 17th Division sent some of their battalions into the line, the dispositions being—on the right the 50th with two battalions in the front and two in the support trenches; centre, the 51st with one battalion in front and another in support; and on the left the 52nd with two battalions in the front and two in the support line. The Guards Division artillery and that of the 20th and 4th Divisions, already in position, covered the Divisional front. The Brigade H.Q. were in the old Flers line, in small dugouts cut into the chalk.

The narrative of one of the brigadiers gives a very striking word picture of the condition of affairs in the sector when the Division took it over, and these were at the time the general conditions of the front. He saw the men of the 8th Division leaving the trenches soaked with rain and plastered from head to foot with mud—" it was impossible to transport blankets for them, so the troops had only greatcoats and ground sheets wherewith to withstand the wintry conditions that had already set in." The way up lay through Delville Wood and the fringe of Longueval and we are told how " Longueval had been flattened into heaps of bricks and rubble." Then followed a walk through Delville Wood, " but what a different scene to my last acquaintance with that accursed spot! Now there was scarcely a vestige of a wood left— a few trunks of not more than four or five feet high, the rest tree stumps and shells holes jostling one another, with a duckboard walk zig-zagging its way to the northern edge, when it traversed a downward sloping crater field until a hollow valley was reached, into the opposite slope of which dugouts had been tunnelled ; away from the duckboards nothing but mud, shell holes and débris." Here were the Brigade H.Q. On a slight eminence above the dugouts an extraordinary panorama presented itself. In the foreground to the left and left front were the ruins of Flers and Gueudecourt, while to the front was a crater field gradually sloping down to the valley below the Transloy Ridge, the diagonal line of Needle Trench (originally a German switch trench) sharply defined in the middle distance across a welter of shell holes. Away on the horizon the chimneys and spires of Bapaume showed above the ridge, which was still in possession of the Germans. To the right were the ruins of Lesbœufs and Morval. " It was a scene of abomination and desolation indeed, with barely a vestige of life or movement visible to the eye on the surface, though not so in the air where the bursts of shrapnel and ' archies ' were continually in evidence, with occasionally the dull thud of an H.E. shell, throwing up its geyser of mud, stones and débris."

The trenches taken over by the Division had not been long in our occupation, and consequently gave very imperfect cover, and dugouts were scarce and flimsily constructed. The front line was some way up the slope of the Bapaume Ridge, while the support line was nearly a mile further back in Needle Trench, which gave better cover and contained some deep dugouts of German construction.

During the fortnight spent in the sector the most important incident was the capture of a section of the enemy's front trench forming a small salient close to the centre of our line, which was here held by the 51st Brigade. The work captured was known on our maps as " Zenith Trench." The south-east end of it had been captured while the 8th Division was in the line, and was now held by a company of the Lincolns, with British and German blocks separating them from the enemy in the uncaptured section, which curved round at a sharp angle at its north end, to join another enemy trench known as " Eclipse." Both Eclipse and Zenith trenches were in very bad condition, part of the latter being only a string of craters, joined by a trench knee-deep in water, which in some of the craters was even waist deep. The ground in front was full of shell holes.

The attack was made just after dark on November 2nd
by a company of the 7th Borders, and was planned as a
surprise with no preliminary bombardment.   Only the
usual night firing was going on on both sides.   The

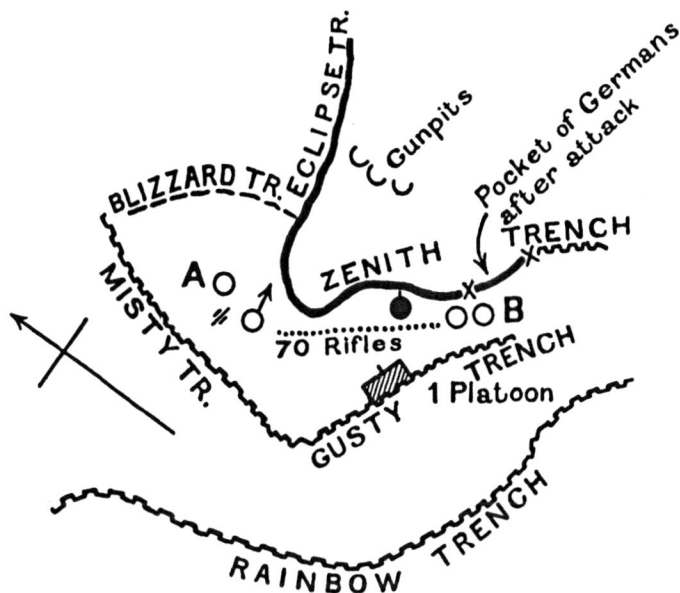

Officer   OO *Bombing Squads*   ‖ *Lewis Gun*
A B *Position where Co. lined up*
〰〰 *Trenches held before attack*
‒‒‒‒ *Trench dug after attack*
━━ *Portions of enemy trench line*

Capture of Zenith Trench, November 2nd, 1916.

company slipped quietly out of Misty Trench, and formed
in the broken ground on a line parallel to the front of
Zenith Trench, with its bombers on both flanks.[1]   It
then crawled forward and was not discovered till it was

[1] Some of these bombers were temporarily attached from the Yorkshires
(50th Brigade).

within 25 yards of the enemy, who then suddenly opened fire on our right. The company dashed forward and after a sharp bomb and bayonet fight cleared the trench, except where on our right a handful of Germans held on to its left. Twenty-five German dead were found in the captured trench, and the losses of the Borders in this stage of the attack were only one officer and five men.

The artillery now became more lively on both sides. Our gunners put down a barrage about 200 yards behind Zenith Trench and the enemy's artillery, apparently expecting a more serious attack would develop, barraged our front line. About thirty of the enemy who had taken shelter in some old gun-pits on our left front attempted a small counter-attack, which was easily beaten off, leaving four prisoners in our hands. At 1 p.m. the Lincolns took over the captured line of trench from the Borders.

During the night there were occasional small bombing attacks. A company of the Borders was engaged in digging a communication trench linking up Misty Trench with the junction of Eclipse and Zenith trenches, where a block was made. This was later pushed 150 yards further up Eclipse Trench.

At 6.30 a.m. on the 3rd, just as dawn was coming, the enemy tried to counter-attack Zenith Trench. They were allowed to come close up and then swept away and beaten off by Lewis gun fire. Half an hour later a party of some eighty of them stood up from the craters where they had been sheltering and made signs that they wished to surrender; the signal was made to them to come forward, but just then a rifle, by some unlucky blunder, was fired and one of them killed and the rest bolted back to cover. In the afternoon at 4 o'clock the enemy made another counter-attack covered by a heavy barrage, but it was held and broken by our barrage and rifle fire 200 yards from the trench. Some fighting went on till 6 p.m. with parties that had sheltered in shell holes. During this final attack the Lincolns surprised and captured the small section of the trench at its south end, making prisoners the thirty-five Germans who had held on there since the evening before. Zenith Trench was now securely in our possession.

On November 9th the G.O.C. of the Fourth Army paid the 17th Division the high honour of circulating among all the units under his command a detailed printed narrative of this successful minor operation, with an explanatory trench map.

The narrative was thus prefaced:

" The Army Commander wishes the following account of an attack carried out by two battalions on Zenith Trench on the 2nd November, 1916, to be circulated, as a good example of the result of initiative shown by Battalion and Company Commanders, the good leading by officers, the fine fighting spirit shown by all ranks under very difficult circumstances owing to the weather and the state of the ground. The fact that the majority of the officers and men who took part had but lately joined, and that this was their first experience of fighting, makes the incident all the more creditable to all concerned."

After this till the Division was relieved by the Guards on November 14th, there were no important events, but only the daily and nightly round of service in the muddy trenches, with occasional skirmishes between patrols. The losses incurred in this fortnight near Gueudecourt were serious, considering that there had been no fighting on any large scale. The casualties were:

	Killed.	Wounded.	Missing.	Totals.
Officers -	16	37	2	55
Other ranks -	247	799	192	1238
Totals -	263	836	194	1293

A number of those returned " missing " disappeared through being drowned in flooded shell craters or buried in mud during night patrols and encounters. Besides the losses on the casualty list there was a further heavy wastage of men through officers and men being evacuated sick as the result of the trying weather and ground conditions.[1]

The Pioneer Battalion, the York & Lancasters, had been at work on improving the communications and erecting huts in Bernafay Wood. They had then been moved to the ruined sugar refinery at Waterlot Farm between Longueval and Ginchy for further work on the communications. Here no tents or other shelter was available, and officers and men slept in shell holes or under waggons in miserable weather. The result was long sick lists. When in the middle of November the Division was taken out of the line and went for rest and training to the Cavillon area, a few miles west of Amiens, the Pioneers did not accompany it. Until the early weeks of 1917 they were in a hut camp near Montauban, or in temporary camps further to the front, assisting in the construction of light railway lines from near Montauban to beyond Ginchy towards Lesbœufs. Numbers of men were invalided during this spell of hard work in wintry weather, and on December 18th Lieut.-Colonel Byass, C.M.G., went back to England, handing over the Pioneers to his second-in-command, Lieut.-Colonel C. S. Sharpe, D.S.O.

While the Division was at Cavillon there were two changes in the brigade commands. Brigadier-General Glasgow handed over the 50th Brigade to Brigadier-General C. Yatman, and Brigadier-General Clarke, who had now completed two years' service in France, was

---

[1] An extract from General Robertson's personal diary may be quoted here as striking evidence of what the Division endured during this tour of service near Gueudecourt. On November 11th, 1916, he writes :

"We went to see the W. Yorks, just in from the trenches ; they are in an awful state, only 200 able to walk ; a very large number of cases of frost-bite on both hands and feet. This last fortnight has undoubtedly been the most trying of the war. The weather conditions have been simply appalling and trenches awful—men *buried* in mud for two or three days at a time before they could be dug out—several deaths from exposure alone—cases even of men *drowned* in mud. The men have borne it splendidly in spite of all—with no hot food or fires and very little drinking water. I wonder if those behind the lines have the slightest conception of what it is like."

seconded for temporary service in England, and for the time being replaced by Brigadier-General G. D. Goodman in command of the 52nd Brigade.

About the time that the 17th Division went to its rest billets in the Cavillon area, there began a marked break of continuity in the operations on the Somme front. Any important advance was all but impossible now that the cold wet winter had set in, reducing all the ground to a morass-like condition that made it difficult even to supply and maintain the troops holding the front line. It is a matter of somewhat arbitrary choice to fix the date at which this long-drawn battle of months and of millions of men came to an end. One might round off its complete record by saying that its final episode was the following up of the enemy's retreat to the Hindenburg line early in 1917. But the great battle had by December, 1916, subsided for a time into monotonous trench warfare in the midst of a wilderness of mud, and the Allied Commanders were already discussing not any immediate operation of importance, but the plans for the continuation of the offensive in the coming New Year, and trying to forecast the earliest date at which it could be resumed.

CHAPTER VI

LAST DAYS ON THE SOMME—THE BATTLE
OF ARRAS
1916-17

BEFORE resuming the story of the 17th Division it may be well to say something of the general situation in the mid-winter of 1916-17 and of the Allied plans for the coming year. It can only be a brief survey of some salient points, but without this one cannot realise the significance of the great events in which the 17th Division played a part in 1917.

In December, 1916, the war was in the fifth month of its third year. The record of 1916 included both failures and successes for the Western Allies, and with another New Year's Day at hand, and the progress on the Somme battlefields slowing down, people in both Britain and France were taking stock of the situation. In both countries there was a persistent patriotic feeling that decisive success must come sooner or later. But it seemed to be a long time coming, and over-optimist predictions from both press and platform that it was near at hand had so often been disappointed, and—to use an Elizabethan phrase—there had been so many " half-doings," that despite all their patriotic anxiety to make the best of things many thoughtful men did not fully realise the value of such success as had been obtained.[1]

[1] This was, by the way, what happened when after Howard broke off his pursuit of the Armada, Walsingham wrote to the Lord Chancellor on August 8th, 1588, and used and perhaps coined the phrase : " I am sorry," he wrote, " that the Lord Admiral was forced to leave the prosecution of the enemy by the wants he sustained. Our half-doings doth breed dishonour and leave the disease uncured " (*Armada Papers*, ii. 69).

For the Battle of the Somme—so far the greatest battle in the world's history—was a success.   It is true that it had not realised the exaggerated expectations of its first days.   It had not brought the oft-talked-of " decision."   The enemy's line had been pressed back, but not broken.   The entrenched lines he held on July 1st had been forced so slowly that other lines had grown up one after another behind them.   The progress secured had been terribly costly.   In five months, on a front of a few miles, there, had been over 400,000 British casualties, without counting the wastage by invaliding and the losses of our allies.   The strain on man-power and on all the services for supplying the army was becoming serious, all the more because besides the huge battle in France, there were a number of side shows that absorbed great armies which had to be supplied at the cost of withdrawing whole fleets of shipping from the supply service of the home country and the army in France and Flanders. Salonika, the desert border of Palestine, and the river region of Mesopotamia were three new theatres of war, in all of which there were larger British armies operating than had ever been engaged in any of our wars of the past. So far, in these subsidiary theatres of war, no important results had been secured, and our Allies, except France, had not been fortunate.   The Italian armies had made little progress anywhere;   a large Russian territory was in the hands of the enemy;   Serbia had been crushed out;   and the Rumanian intervention in 1916 had not only been followed by defeat, but had revealed the unpleasant fact that Russia was unable to give the promised help to our new ally.

All this seemed on the surface a disappointing result for nearly two and a half years of war culminating in the immense effort of the Somme.   The disappointment found expression in a change of government in Britain and a change in the High Command of the French armies. But few at the time realised that, costly though it was, and though it had yielded no clearly decisive result, the Battle of the Somme had been a success of the highest value. It had averted a disaster and saved Verdun by forcing the enemy to divert to his endangered Somme front the reserves available for continuing his great push further east.   Seven divisions originally held the German front of the Somme.   Before the end of November forty more, including some of his best, had to be flung into the Somme battle.   We know now from Ludendorff's Memoirs how terrible was the strain on the German, defence; how difficult it was to maintain the spirit of the troops as line after line gave way before the persistent Allied attacks; how anxious was the German High Command, and what fears there were that this seemingly inevitable progress of the Allied offensive would result in a break through when operations were resumed on a large scale in the coming spring or the late winter months.   There was much debate as to how the menace of disaster could be met. The position seemed so serious that in December, 1916, the German Government threw out guarded suggestions for peace negotiations.

On the Allied side the question was that of the exploitation of the solid success so far secured.   The Government and the H.Q. Staffs of Britain and France were discussing the plan of campaign for the New Year.   Here a divergence of views soon developed, of which there were some indications at the time, but the full story of which was only known after the war.   On one point there was agreement. As the winter hardened and steady frost succeeded the trying broken weather of the early winter months, movement and supply would be somewhat easier, and it would be both possible and highly advisable to resume minor operations on the Somme front.   On this small scale there would be no important gains of ground; but the front could be improved and at the same time the enemy would be compelled to keep a large force on this side in view of these minor operations being perhaps only the prelude to a continuance of the advance of 1916.

But was an advance from the new Allied front on the Somme battlefields the best course to adopt ?   Might not larger and more fruitful results be obtained under better conditions by a push from another front.   Both the British and the French High Commands had plans for such a new stroke.

Here again, though the two plans of campaign were mutually exclusive, on one point there was again complete agreement, and that point was the approximate date for the starting of the new offensive.   It must come as early as possible in the New Year, but not before there could be reasonable prospect of a Russian advance on the eastern front.   Chiefly at the cost of the British Government an immense amount of arms, munitions and equipment had been supplied to Russia in the summer and late autumn of 1916, through the White Sea in the far north, and it was anticipated that the Russian Armies, thus rearmed and refitted, would be able effectively to assist the Western offensive by an advance that would keep large enemy armies occupied in the Eastern front.   It was agreed that weather conditions would not make a Russian move on a great scale possible before April, and this fixed the earliest date for the Western move.   The chief points of the two plans—British and French—may be thus summed up.

The British plan was for an offensive against the enemy's right in Flanders.   In this operation Haig's armies would play the chief part, but they would have the immediate help of the Belgian army and the French corps on the left of our Ypres lines, and the indirect assistance of French pressure on the German front from the Somme to Verdun.   The Flanders offensive would also receive valuable co-operation from the British Navy.   The first step would be the driving of the enemy from the high ground dominating the Ypres position.   This would be followed by a push north-eastward along the Passchen-

daele Ridge, an advance of the Belgians and French on the
extreme left, and a naval attack on the coast defences held
by the enemy from Ostend to the Dutch border, with the
surprise landing of a specially trained and equipped
British Division.   The submarine bases at Ostend and
Zeebrugge would be captured; the enemy deprived of
aerodromes which were the starting point of his raids
on England; Bruges set free; and the way opened for an
advance eastward, turning the flank of the main German
line, and menacing the bottle neck between the Ardennes
and Holland, through which lay the main railway communications on which the very existence of the German
occupation of Northern France depended.

The French plan, on the other hand, was directed to
the immediate liberation of the occupied departments in
France.   It was an ambitious scheme devised by General
Nivelle, who had replaced Joffre as the Commander-in-
Chief of the French armies.   When the war began Nivelle
was a colonel of artillery.   He had rapidly risen to high
command, and in the late months of 1916 he had become
the popular hero of France by winning back in a series of
brilliant operations much of the ground lost at Verdun in
the earlier months of the year.   Not only with the general
public in France, but also in the mind of not a few prominent politicians both in France and Britain, Nivelle was
supposed to have discovered an infallible formula of
victory.   It was even suggested that he might with
advantage be given the supreme command of both the
French and the British armies on the Western front.   The
French army was to play the chief part in his plan.   The
British were to co-operate by an advance from Arras into
the lower lands towards Douai and Cambrai watered by
the tributaries of the Scheldt, but though a large army
would be concentrated for this attack it would be a subsidiary operation and diversion to facilitate the main
French offensive.   This was to advance northward on a
wide front, against the heights of Aisne and the German

front in Champagne west and east of Rheims.   The plan included a time-table forecasting a series of rapid successes, the first of which would outflank the German line on the Somme and cut off the salient, from which the invader had long menaced Paris.   The early summer was to see the whole German front in France collapsing, and Haig was then to make his push in Flanders.

After much debate, in which both eminent politicians and generals took part, Nivelle's plan was accepted, and though he did not become Commander-in-Chief of the Western Front, it was understood that Sir Douglas Haig was to conform generally to his directions while the great plan was being executed.   After an initial limited success the Nivelle plan failed disastrously.   The advance in Flanders was then attempted, but it began too late in the year, and was brought to a standstill by the early coming of wintry weather making it impossible to carry through more than its first stages on the Ypres heights.   In 1917 the 17th Division took part in all three phases of the Allied plans—the minor operations on the old Somme front, the battle of Arras and the offensive in Flanders.

The Division was training and refitting in the Cavillon area from November 15th to December 12th 1916.   At a conference of senior officers held by General Robertson at Divisional H.Q. during this period, many practical details of administration and training were dealt with, and it is interesting to note that it was mentioned that the Division had been ordered to provide fifty candidates per month for commissions.   Losses in the commissioned ranks had been very heavy in the long-drawn battle.   Reference was made at the conference to the difficulties that would arise if a battalion commander found all his best N.C.Os. thus selected for promotion.   The official request for candidates at the rate of 600 per annum had its drawbacks, but it was a tribute to the efficiency of the Division.

On December 11th orders were received for the Division to move from the Cavillon area into Corps

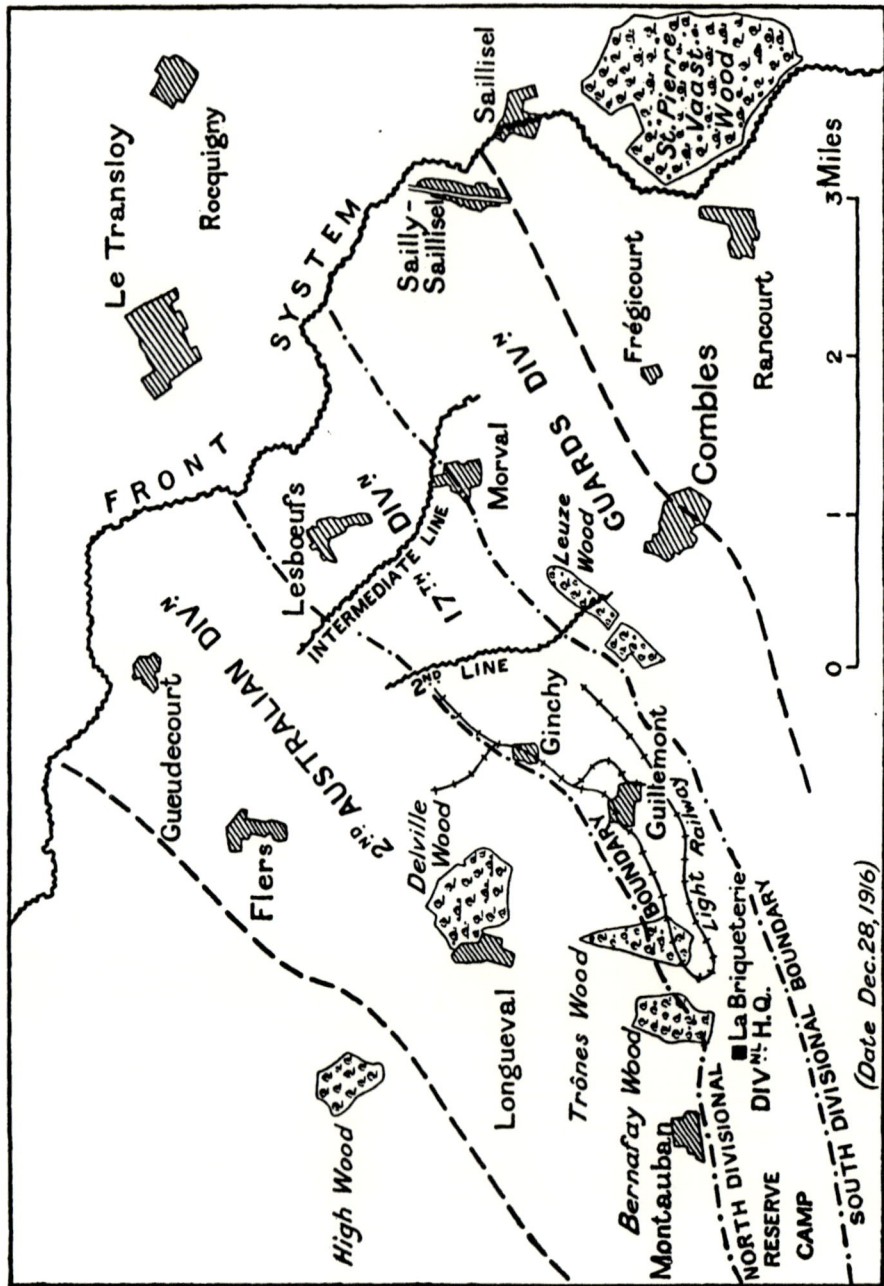

The Lesbœufs Sector, December 1916.

Reserve, and the move began next day by the 51st
Brigade being sent forward to Corbie, a little town on the
Somme near its junction with the Ancre—a place famous
in the history of Europe.   On the 13th the 50th Brigade
entrained for Méaulte and Divisional H.Q. were transferred to Corbie.   The move was completed on the 14th,
when the 52nd Brigade was sent forward to Méricourt-
l'Abbé on the lower Ancre.   On the 19th orders were
received for the 17th Division to relieve the 20th in the
trenches in the Lesbœufs sector in front of Le Transloy.
On the 24th the relief was completed, the 52nd Brigade
taking over the right of the line, and the 50th the left.
Next morning—Christmas Day—Divisional H.Q. were
established at the abandoned farm and ruined brickworks
of La Briqueterie, about 400 yards south of Bernafay
Wood.   The sector to the right (Sailly-Saillisel) was held
by the Guards, and that on the left (Gueudecourt) by the
2nd Australian Division.

The weather was cold and wet, with frost at night,
when the prevailing rain showers would turn to sleet or
snow.   As it always thawed quickly the ground was in a
bad condition, but the state of the sector was better than
that which the Division had last occupied near Gueudecourt, for there were now plenty of duck boards, and the
moving of supplies to the front was facilitated by the light
railway, which started from near Bernafay Wood, nearly
the whole of the line being in the sector.   The Division
felt grateful to its Pioneer Battalion, which had done so
much of its construction.   Near Guillemont and further
back along the road that runs south-west from Montauban
there were standing camps of the new Nissen huts, which
gave good shelter to the battalions in reserve, and other
troops out of the trenches.

To lighten the strain on the men actually holding the
front a new system of reliefs was temporarily adopted.   The
Division was worked as two groups of six battalions each,
one group for the right and the other for the left half-

sector.   Each battalion was alternately three days in the trenches and three in reserve, and no battalion took more than 400 men up to the front.   While there the battalion spent two days in the front trenches and one in support. Two of the brigadiers were in command at the front, and the third with the reserves.   The relative quietness of the sector made this arrangement possible   It meant a lot of marching, but this was well compensated by the shortened terms of trench duty and the larger amount of rest.

Little of importance happened during the three weeks passed by the Division in this sector.   An incident on the night of December 29th-30th is worth noting as showing the extent to which the wintry weather had made even No Man's Land fairly safe and quiet after dark.   It was a cold night, with driving snow showers that made visibility nearly as poor as in a dense fog.   A young officer of the Lincolns, Lieut. D. A. Jones, D.S.O., M.C., going up to the front with his soldier servant, passed through a narrow gap in the forward trench line and only discovered he had lost his way and gone too far when he found himself among abandoned communication trenches half-full of mud and water, and with unfamiliar pieces of equipment and rusty farm implements lying here and there.   Just as he realised this, a German patrol passed close by without seeing him, and a stronger party in full equipment became visible for a few moments as they burned a Very light.   They were only a few yards away but they took no notice of the two Lincolns.   They seemed to be engaged in relieving another party in a trench which had no wire before it.   As the light vanished the two wanderers made their way back as quickly and quietly as possible to their own front line.   A patrol of the Staffords, which went out on another snowy night a little later, had much the same experience of getting close up to the enemy's front line, and passing German patrols without being seen, even though some Very lights were burned close by.

A good deal of useful work was done improving the wiring of the trench system, double duckboarding the line of communication, strengthening and extending the dugouts, and putting up more huts in the reserve camp near Guillemont and at the starting point of the light railway.   This work however was interrupted and retarded by a rearrangement of the front being carried out during this tour of duty.   On the last day of the year G.H.Q. orders were received that by January 4th, 1917, the front was to be " adjusted " by the Division taking over 900 yards of the front trench system from the Guards on the right and handing over 600 yards of front to the Australians on the left.   On January 6th there was an order for a further readjustment by taking over an additional 700 yards from the Guards.   This " readjustment " was the result of the British extending their front southwards, and taking from the French all the ground north of the bend of the Somme at Cléry, a couple of miles north-east of Peronne.   It carried the front held by the 17th Division to near the north of the end of the ruined village of Sailly-Saillisel, which the French had captured in November.

The casualties of the Division during December, 1916, were:

	Killed.	Wounded.	Missing.	Totals.
Officers	1	4	—	5
Other ranks	23	100	16	149
Totals	24	104	16	154

Losses by sickness were much heavier, the number " evacuated sick " being 903 (24 officers and 879 other ranks).

On the night of January 16th-17th, 1917, the 17th Division handed over the reorganised Lesbœufs sector to the 29th Division.   Divisional H.Q. went back to Corbie and the troops spent the next ten days in rest camps along the lower Ancre.

On January 20th orders were received for the relief of the 14th Division in the Sailly-Saillisel sector before the end of the coming week.   On the 28th the relief had been completed and Divisional H.Q. were established at Arrow Head Copse.   The Copse had disappeared but gave its name to a hut camp about half-way between Trônes Wood and Guillemont and on the line of the light railway.   The sector taken over thus included some of the back area occupied by the Division in its tour of duty a fortnight earlier.   The front to be held began at the right of the readjusted front of the Lesbœufs sector.   Our front line ran southward, just east of Sailly-Saillisel, and then curved closely round the western margin of the ruins of Saillisel village, the British line here forming a re-entrant opposite a strong enemy salient, and divided from it by a narrow No Man's Land, mostly only a hundred yards across.   Moreover at this point the German defences were on higher ground, giving the enemy a good view over the British front system.

The most important incident of the Division's three weeks' stay in this sector was the improvement of this part of the line by a brilliant minor operation resulting in the capture of the enemy's main position at Saillisel.   This success was announced in the British official bulletin, given to the public at the time, in guarded words and with discreet reticence as to what our gain of ground actually was.   This was because more than two months before, on November 12th, 1916, the French official bulletins had claimed the capture of Saillisel village.   But when the British took over this part of the front it was found that the German front line marked on the French maps as the " Tranchée de Saillisel," and renamed on our maps as " Sullivan Trench," ran through the western part of the ruined village, more than half of which was still held by the enemy.   The line taken over was on the margin of the village and was dominated by the German front line. The successful operation soon to be described was

reported in the news given to the British press simply as
" resulting in the capture of an important enemy position
on the highest part of Sailly-Saillisel Hill." This
avoided any suggestion either that our Allies had never
captured Saillisel, or that if they had scored this success
and taken the village, they had lost it since the advance
claimed in November.

The weather in the last days of January and the first
week of February, 1917, was cold and frosty with frequent
snow showers.   There were nights when the patrols went
out wrapped in white sheets across snow-covered ground.
There were bright days of partial thaw, and others when
the ground was so hard that enemy shell bursts were more
dangerous than usual.   The front line had been handed
over in a somewhat unsatisfactory state.   There was a
good belt of wire, but behind it, instead of a continuous
trench, there was a string of separate posts.   Behind this
there was a continuous support trench, but it was neither
completed throughout nor everywhere wired.   No Man's
Land was very rough ground with many shell holes half
full of water, foundations of ruined houses, and fallen
tree trunks and broken branches lying about.   Every
night some work was done in digging to convert the front
line into a continuous trench by linking up the existing
posts, but it was slow work on account of the frozen condition of the ground.

On February 1st preparations began for improving the
general situation by an attempt to capture Sullivan
Trench.   To mislead the enemy there were day after day
frequent bombardments of differents parts of his line and
wire-cutting where no attack was contemplated.   The
divisions on the right and left co-operated by similar
bombardments.

General Robertson prepared the plan of the attack.
The actual capture of the trench was to be entrusted to one
battalion and surprise was to be an important element in
the expected success.   " I propose," he wrote, " to make

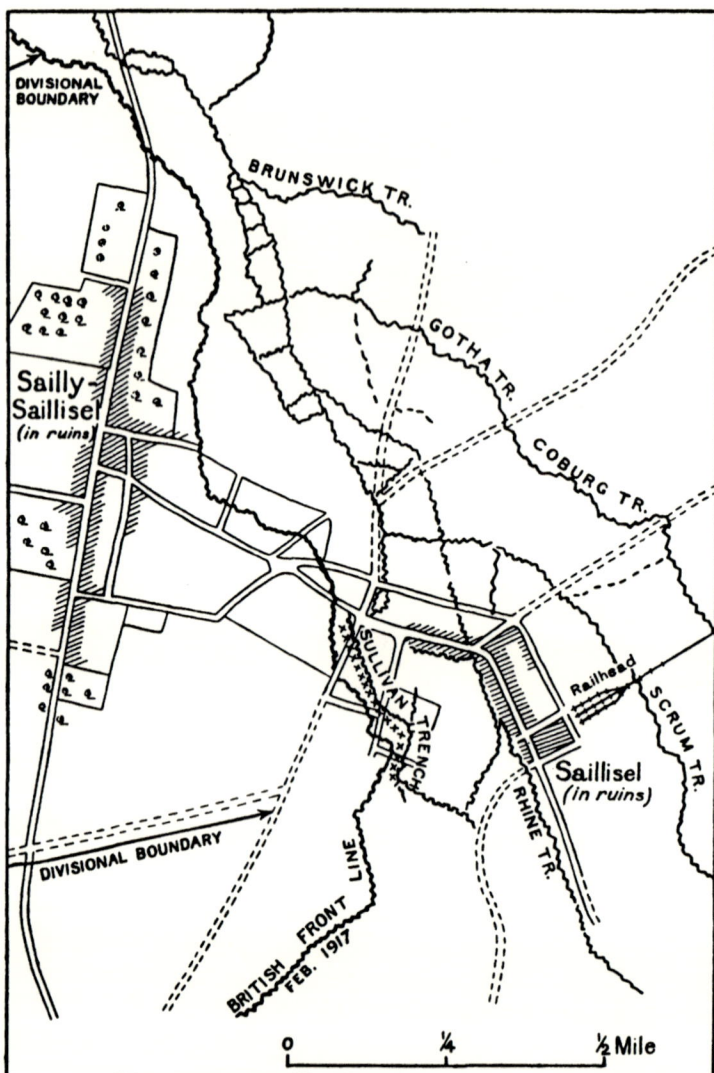

The Sailly-Saillisel Sector, 1917.

the attack in the early morning in daylight after the enemy has assumed his day dispositions. I think that at this time the enemy is to be caught unawares, night duty men being probably asleep, others engaged cooking, cleaning arms, etc., and, according to prisoners' statements, the machine guns placed in the dugouts. I also consider that the less time the troops have to wait after daylight to advance, the better."

There was to be no preliminary bombardment, to give notice of the attack to the Germans, but at zero hour a barrage was to be put down on the enemy trench, and this would be the signal for our advance to begin. Three minutes after zero the barrage would lift, and it was anticipated that by this time the attack would have got across No Man's Land and be breaking through the wire and rushing into Sullivan Trench. Heavy fire would be opened on the enemy's support and communication lines with artillery and indirect machine gun salvoes, and the flanks of the attack would be protected by Stokes mortar, rifle grenade and Vickers and Lewis gunfire. The last wave of the attack would carry forward additional bomb supplies and wire and other material for consolidation. It was noted that a standing barrage on the enemy's front, lifting to longer range as the attack closed upon it, would be better than a creeping barrage, which might be more deleterious than helpful with a narrow broken No Man's Land, and difficulties of accurate ranging increased by actual ground and weather conditions.

The idea of a creeping barrage therefore found no place in the proposed plan, when it was sent to Corps H.Q. for approval. But creeping barrages were now the accepted fashion, and the General Commanding the Corps Artillery insisted on a creeping barrage starting at 50 yards from the enemy's front. This feature was added to the plan in the final orders with unfortunate results.

The attack was fixed for Thursday, February 8th, with zero hour at 7.30 a.m. The 52nd Brigade under General

Goodman held the trenches in front of the objective. The 7th Yorks under Colonel Fife were to be the assaulting battalion, the 12th Manchesters were in support. Some batteries of the Guards Division on the right were ready to co-operate with the Divisional artillery in the bombardment, and the Guards machine gunners got their Maxims into position to enfilade the German support trenches, from the south flank of the salient formed by the enemy position at Saillisel.

There had been hard frost all night. The shell holes in No Man's Land were covered with thin ice, and there was snow on the ground. This with the bright moonlight made the assembling of the assaulting companies in the front line difficult to conceal, but neither the German lookouts nor the patrols discovered anything of these preparations.

At 7.30 a.m. the artillery opened fire, putting down a barrage on Sullivan Trench and starting the creeping barrage in front of it. At the same time some forty machine guns began to sweep the German communications with indirect fire. The Yorkshires began moving forward in three waves across the broken ground of No Man's Land as the first salvo rang out. Amongst the rubbish heaps well out in front of the enemy's wire three of his snipers were lying. The advance passed on without paying any attention to them, taking them for dead men lying in the snow. Two telephone wires were carried forward, one communicating with the artillery command the other with the battle H.Q. of the Brigade. One of these wires was actually laid across the body of a sniper, who kept quiet "shamming dead." He and his comrades later surrendered as prisoners and were sent back with the other captures.

Unfortunately there was a good deal of short shooting in the creeping barrage. It caused some casualties in both the forward waves of the Yorkshires and still more in the third among the men struggling under their loads of

consolidation material. They were thus badly caught in
our own shell fire, and as many of the carriers were hit a
considerable amount of useful material was left in No
Man's Land. But the assaulting waves got quickly
through the wire and into the trench where the surprise
was complete. Little resistance was offered. Two officers
and seventy-seven of their men were quickly made
prisoners and forty or fifty German dead lay in and around
the captured trench, mostly killed by the barrage.

The enemy's artillery had now opened fire on a wide
front. The Germans put down a barrage along the
trench, and, misled by a smoke barrage sent out on the left,
threw a shower of shells on Sailly-Saillisel and the ground
about it, evidently expecting a second assault from that
side. The firing was very wild, shells bursting here and
there far back in the area behind our front. One of these
chance shots wrecked a dressing station and killed some
of the wounded there.

The enemy soon counter-attacked with bombing parties
along the communication trenches, which had been
rapidly blocked with barbed wire. This and two succeeding attacks were repulsed, but there was a critical
moment when the supply of bombs in the hands of the
victors ran perilously short. Luckily many officers and
men had been taught how to handle German bombs,
and a large supply of these was discovered in the trench
in the nick of time, and this saved the situation.

Two machine guns and a Stokes mortar had been
brought up with the attack. These were placed in
position and did useful service. A Lewis gun post was
established in a shell hole beyond the trench, wiring was
pushed on rapidly, and by the afternoon the position was
secure.

The telephone lines carried forward by the attack did
not last long. They were cut by shell fire almost immediately. Information during the fighting depended on
runners, a carrier pigeon and the useful help of a low-flying

aeroplane, which twice dropped successfully within reach of Brigade H.Q. reports of the situation with marked sketch maps.

Our losses were almost entirely by shell fire, and on the 8th and the two following days several units besides the actual assaulting battalion suffered loss in this way. The casualties from February 8th to 10th—chiefly on the first day—were:

		Killed.		Wounded.		Missing.		Totals.	
		O.[1]	O.R.[1]	O.	O.R.	O.	O.R.	O.	O.R.
7th Yorkshires	-	1	50	5	1·10	—	14	6	174
7th E. Yorks	-	1	13	—	36	—	—	1	49
12th Manchesters	-	—	16	3	43	—	5	3	64
4th Northumberland Fusiliers -	-	—	6	—	14	—	5	—	25
8th S. Staffords	-	1	2	3	17	—	1	4	20
17th D.A.C. -	-	—	—	—	—	—	—	—	1
		3	87	11	221	—	25	14	333

Totals: { Killed, 90, Wounded, 232, Missing, 25 } In all 347 casualties.

[1] O.—officers ; O.R.—other ranks.

The operation gave the solid gain of cutting off a dangerous enemy salient, and substituting a strong front line for the very defective position here taken over by the Division in the last week of January. No attempt was made to push the advantage further, and the Germans held the east side of Saillisel until they abandoned it on March 15th during their retirement to the Hindenburg line.

The rest of the Division's stay in the sector was uneventful. Except for occasional outbursts of activity on the part of the enemy's gunners the front was fairly quiet. On February 12th General Robertson was able to go away for a fortnight's leave in England, and in his absence the Division was commanded by General Yatman, the senior brigadier. On the 21st the 29th Division

took over the sector from the 17th, and next day Divisional
H.Q. were moved back from Arrow Head Copse to
Heilly, on the lower Ancre, and the troops were once more
quartered in the neighbouring rest camps of that now
familiar ground. It was announced that the Division
was transferred from the 14th Corps to the G.H.Q.
Reserve. This was the first step towards its employment a few weeks later in the coming great push at Arras.

There was a welcome rest of a week in the Ancre camps,
a pleasant time, for the weather had become warmer and
there were bright sunny days. The Pioneer Battalion had
come back with the Division, but the very day after their
arrival on the Ancre they were recalled for work in the
communication trenches, and were then sent to Méaulte
to attend a bombing school. They did not rejoin the
Division till the following month.

It was during this week's rest that, after rumours on the
subject had been circulating for a few days, an official
communication, dated February 25th, was issued conveying the news that the enemy had begun a retirement
all along his front north and south of the bend of the
Somme. Optimists took it to mean that the German line
was collapsing and the end of the war was at last coming
into sight.

Before Christmas our airmen, flying behind the enemy
lines, had seen great bodies of workmen throwing up new
lines of entrenchments covering Cambrai and St. Quentin.
Since the war we have learned that still earlier, in the last
week of November, the higher command of the German
Army had been warned that soon there would be a retirement from the Somme front to shorten the line, cut out
the now perilously exposed salient towards Roye, econo-
mise man-power and set free a number of divisions to
strengthen the reserve. A spell of milder weather
towards the end of February facilitated the withdrawal.
A thaw reduced the back areas of the new allied fronts to
a quagmire, but behind the German lines unbroken roads

were available.   The withdrawal was skilfully organised. It was only in the last week of February that it was discovered that line after line in the German front system was first lightly held and then abandoned   As the Germans fell back they left nothing undone to make the pursuit difficult, burning villages, destroying supplies, and cratering every crossing of the roads with high explosives. Small detachments with plenty of machine guns acted as rearguards when our pursuit began, and a wide zone of country was reoccupied without any serious fighting. The enemy at last halted in a new line of works of a formidable character, know to the Allies as the " Hindenburg " line.[1]   It started from the western end of the Aisne heights passed a little west of St. Quentin and Cambrai, and joined up with the enemy lines before Arras.   Between Cambrai and the Arras trenches a branch line started at the village of Quéant and ran nearly due north through Drocourt to Courrières north-east of Lens.   This line, marked on our war maps as the Drocourt-Quéant Switch, was a reserve line in case the positions held by the enemy round Lens and east of Arras were lost.   When the enemy retirement began the Hindenburg line was already a formidably-entrenched position, the switch line was little more than marked out.[2]

[1] The Germans gave their new entrenched positions names taken from the heroic figures of the Nibelungen legends, popularised in recent times by Wagner.   What we called the " Hindenburg line " was officially known in Germany as the " Siegfried position," and the switch line starting north from Quéant was the " Wotan position."

[2] During the German withdrawal the Pioneer Battalion of the Division, 7th York and Lancasters, was at Méaulte and at Harponville, west of Albert. Many Pioneer and R.E. units were pushed up to accompany our advance to repair the cratered roads, and deal with ground mines and other explosive traps left by the enemy as he retreated.   The York and Lancasters, however, were not called up for this duty, but Captain Gilvary, in his interesting history of the Battalion, tells how they were inundated with official circulars on the subject of clearing away " land mines and booby traps."   He adds that besides suggesting quite obvious possibilities " every despatch further enlarged upon the enemy's diabolical ingenuity in such matters ; while all those things which the enemy had not yet done, but might be expected to do, were duly tabulated at Corps, Army and General Headquarters for the encouragement of the troops."

The German withdrawal was already beginning, though concealed by the front line being still lightly held, when the 17th Division went into the rest camps on the lower Ancre in the last week of February, 1917, and it was notified that the Division no longer belonged to the 14th Corps, but till further orders was in G.H.Q. Reserve. By the end of the week orders were received for the first stage of what proved to be the move towards Arras, and the month of March was devoted to training in various areas in the country north of Amiens, with intermediate moves, which by the end of the month brought the Division into the great concentration for the coming battle.

On March 1st the move began by a short march route to villages north-west of Amiens, and on the 3rd Divisional H.Q. were transferred to Contay on the Hallue brook, about five miles from Heilly. During the twelve days of training here there was a sudden return of cold wintry weather. There were heavy snowfalls, but the cold was interrupted by some warmer days which produced a temporary thaw and reduced the country roads to quagmires. Then there were ice and snow again. Spring came slowly in Northern France this year and the wintry weather lingered on far into April.

From the Contay area there was a second northward move into billets in the villages about Doullens, with H.Q. established on March 15th at Willeman. A week was spent here, and then there was a third move north-eastward towards Arras, and from March 23rd to April 8th Divisional H.Q. were at the château of Le Cauroy about eighteen miles west of Arras.

Both in time and space the great battle that was to open the serious fighting of 1917 was now near at hand. The York & Lancasters were called up to Arras to take part in the final preparations. They were set to work on bringing into good condition the roads by which the main attack would pour out of the city against the enemy's centre. Arras was in a strange position, a cathedral city of some 30,000 inhabitants in a salient of the British line, with the German trenches within a mile of the eastern suburbs. It was closer even than Ypres to the fighting front. But while Ypres was now a mass of ruins, Arras survived with only local damage from occasional shell fire. Lofty buildings, that might be good observation posts, had been targets of the enemy's gunners. The cathedral, a modern building, was wrecked; the Hotel de Ville, dating from times when Arras was a city of Spanish Flanders, had been knocked to pieces, and many of the quaint gabled houses of the great square had suffered. The eastern suburb near the railway station had been badly knocked about. But much of the city had escaped damage. Most of its people had left it, but many remained. There were hotels, cafés, shops still doing business, though the city had been for over two years in the front line.

And there was another Arras, an underground city below its streets that was now full of life. There were great crypts and subterranean storehouses and a labyrinth of the galleries of abandoned quarries, with long tunnels that had once been drains. All these had been explored, cleaned up and cleared of rubbish, provided with ventilation and lighted with electricity. Roadways had been opened and marked off from west to east, linking up by ascending tunnels with the roads on the one side and the British trenches on the other, and here whole brigades were living in improvised quarters—" confined to barracks " during daylight lest the enemy's airmen should mark this concentration, but free to crowd the streets after dark. The fact that a battle was imminent could not be concealed, but it was thus possible to hide away some of the concentration against the enemy's centre, and to provide covered ways for the movement of troops along the underground streets, while others were marching through the city above ground.

At its various halting places since it left the Somme front the 17th Division had had training in open as well as in trench warfare, and this indicated that the plans for the coming battle included some hope of a break through the triple line of the enemy's defences. During the training around Le Cauroy the special mission of the Division was revealed first to the higher ranks and then in operation orders.

A Cavalry Corps was to exploit and carry forward our success in case the coming attack on the German lines, now fixed for Easter Monday, April 9th, should result in a sufficiently wide breach being made in the enemy's third line. The Cavalry Corps was made up of three Cavalry Divisions with the 17th Infantry Division in support. It was to be assembled west of Arras, and if the expected opportunity for its intervention occurred, the advance of the mounted troops through the city and the enemy's broken lines north and south of the Arras-Cambrai road was to be closely followed by the infantry. As the cavalry seized its first objective, the infantry were to take it over and consolidate it, setting the mounted troops free to push on to a second objective, where they would be supported in the same way, the aim of the operation being to secure a position as near as possible to the western defences of Cambrai. Officers and men of the 17th Division felt it was a high honour that they should have been selected for this adventurous dash with the cavalry into the open country beyond the enemy's third line.

In these last days before the battle there was special instruction in co-operation with cavalry, and the details of taking over a line from the mounted troops were carefully studied and elaborately explained in memoranda issued from Divisional H.Q. On April 5th the Division in successive detachments began its march from the billets about Le Cauroy to the concentration area of the Cavalry Corps west of Arras. The movement was com-

Battle of Arras, 1917. Projected break-through of the Cavalry, supported by the 17th Division.

pleted on the 8th (Easter Sunday), when Divisional H.Q. were transferred from Le Cauroy to Haute Avesnes, six miles west of Arras on the road to St. Omer.

The three brigades and the troops attached to them were in the villages immediately to the south of the road, the 50th Brigade in and around Agnetz-les-Duisans, the 51st at Habarcq, and the 52nd at Simencourt. The 1st Cavalry Division was north of the St. Omer Road. To the south towards the Arras-Doullens road was the concentration area of the 3rd Cavalry Division and still further south, beyond the road, lay the 2nd Cavalry Division. Corps H.Q. were at Duisans.

Operation orders directed that the cavalry should go forward to Arras in two columns—left column, the 1st and 3rd Cavalry Divisions by the St. Omer-Arras road ; right column, the 2nd Cavalry Division, by the Doullens-Arras road. The 17th Division was to be organised in two columns to follow the cavalry advance as closely as possible. The 50th Brigade was to support the 3rd Cavalry Division on the left, and the 52nd Brigade was to follow the 2nd Cavalry Division on the right. The 51st Brigade was to be the Divisional Reserve.

To each brigade there were attached a Field Ambulance and a Field Company R.E. Further, an Artillery Brigade (three batteries R.F.A.) was to be attached to the 50th and 52nd Brigades. A company of the Pioneers (York & Lancasters) was to be with the 52nd Brigade and the remainder of the Pioneer Battalion with the 51st. The Divisional Artillery, already in action north of Arras, was to draw out of the line and rejoin the Division as it advanced.

It was anticipated that about eight hours after zero the attack would have made sufficient progress for the Cavalry Divisions to have the heads of their columns on the eastern outskirts of Arras ready to push forward. The first objective to be seized would be a line along the left bank of the river Sensée, the second objective would be on the line of the Quéant-Drocourt switch.

The preparatory intensified bombardment of the German position was in progress while the 17th Division was moving up to its concentration area west of Arras. The bombardment had begun on April 4th. These early April days were cold, with a north-east wind that brought clear skies and good visibility. It was a heavier and more effective artillery preparation than that which preceded the Somme battle, more than 2,800 British guns were in action, and they threw 80,000 tons of projectiles into the enemy's lines. The rapid progress made on the first day of the battle was largely due to this thorough preparation. Another element of success was derived from the long experience of aggressive trench warfare in the months of battle on the Somme front. Zero hour was 5.30 a.m. on Easter Monday morning. In the evening before there had been a sudden change in the weather. The wind backed to the north, and there came first rain squalls, then a drizzling mist, which towards morning changed to a steady fall of snow.

Through mist and snow the attack surged forward, covered by a heavy barrage, on a front of some fourteen miles, from the margins of the old Loos battle ground fronting Lens, over the Vimy ridge, and by the Arras front to the northern sector of the Hindenburg line. The rapid progress of the first hour seemed to promise a tremendous success. On the left the Canadians, supported by a Scottish Division, were winning their way steadily across the Vimy plateau; before Arras the first enemy line, a mass of mere wreckage, had been carried at a rush, and our men were into the second line. A group of tanks trampled their way through the fortress-like position of the "Harp," and the north end of the Hindenburg defences was turned.

The Cavalry Divisions began to close up towards Arras. The left and right columns of their infantry support, the 17th Division, assembled at Agnetz-les-Duisans and Simencourt, and soon after the outburst of our artillery

fire told the battle had begun warning orders came that
they were to be in readiness to advance at eighty minutes'
notice.   But hour after hour went by without further
orders.   Cheering messages circulated telling that steady
progress was being made, but it was evident that after the
first rush the advance was being met by more stubborn
resistance.   At 1.30 p.m. Divisional H.Q. was informed
that it was not likely that there would be any move until
about 4 p.m.   It was after three when at last orders came
through that the infantry columns were to move off so as
to clear their starting points by 4.45 p.m.

Shortly after four the troops were on the move.   The
left column marched by the main St. Omer-Arras road;
the 50th Brigade (General Yatman) leading, followed by
the 51st (General Trotter).   On the right the 52nd
Brigade column moved by country roads through Walrus
and Daimville to the main Doullens-Arras road, reaching
it north of the citadel.   It was now again under the command of General Clarke, who after some months of duty
in England had returned to France a month before.   He
had been given the command of the 3rd Brigade in the
1st Infantry Division, and had the interesting experience
of following up for a few days the German retirement to
the Hindenburg line.   But he had at once asked General
Robertson to get him brought back if possible to the 17th
Division, and during the stay in the Le Cauroy area he
had been transferred to it, resuming command of the
52nd Brigade.

It was a dull cold afternoon with a bitter wind, and the
sky was dark with heavy clouds ominous of another snow-
storm.   The roar of the gunfire beyond Arras told that
heavy fighting was still in progress not far east of the city.
As the left column approached its suburbs it received an
order to halt and bivouac or find billets in the villages for
the night.   The right column got further forward.   It
had moved into Arras, and the head of the column was
near the railway station in the eastern suburbs, when

about 6.30 p.m. a cavalry officer brought the news that the 2nd Cavalry Division had been held up and was halted at Tilloy-les-Moufflaines in the captured German first line. Immediately after came a message from Colonel Blockley, commanding the advanced guard of the brigade, that he had been brought to a standstill in the original British front line, where he was in touch with the rear of the cavalry column. The sun was now setting, but under the clouded sky it was already getting dark and snow was beginning to fall in thick flakes. The column was strung out through a long street of Arras from the railway station nearly as far back as its western suburb. Further movement was obviously impossible. General Clarke therefore sent orders to his advanced guard to find what local shelter they could for the night, and got the rest of the brigade into the houses along the street. The first line transport and most of the artillery were at the west end of the city near the public gardens. The road was cleared by sending them to bivouac in the gardens, where the men found some shelter under their waggons. By 9 p.m. all these arrangements were completed. The brigade staff found quarters in the cellar of a partly ruined house near the railway station, putting the horses into a room still intact on the ground floor. There was a stove in the cellar, so a fire was started and after supper of biscuit and tinned beef, the officers slept on the stone floor. It snowed heavily all night, but there was no shelling of the city. Late in the evening orders came through from Divisional H.Q., now established in a house in the Place de St. Croix in Arras, to carry out the plan already adopted for getting the men into improvised shelter.

It had been a day of success. The first and second German lines had been stormed and the third line pene-trated on a small front about Fampoux on the north bank of the Scarpe. Thousands of prisoners and many guns had been taken. But for the 17th Division it had been a disappointing day. There was a feeling that the particu-

lar part of the plan that concerned them had somehow
gone wrong. The anticipated break-through and onward
dash of the Cavalry Corps had not been effected, and the
visions of " open warfare " were disappearing. The two
brigades of the left column had mostly bivouacked in the
snow along the high road west of Arras, and the advanced
guard of the right column had passed a miserable night in
the open. Early in the Tuesday morning the battery
attached to it was sent back to the public gardens, and the
men were told to find shelter in the houses on the fringe
of the eastern suburb.

The day was intensely cold with frequent snow
blizzards. Divisional orders were that the two columns
were to stand fast and await further developments.
Officers reporting at H.Q. in the Place de St. Croix were
told of the successes gained on the Monday, but were also
informed that the 2nd Cavalry Division had attempted
to push through by the Cambrai road, but had been held
up by wire and machine gun fire west of Monchy-le-
Preux and Guémappe and had to abandon the attempt,
suffering heavy loss.

The battle had been resumed at dawn, and further
ground was gained though much more slowly than on the
first day. The Easter Monday battle had been the greatest
success yet won by the British arms since the war began,[1]
but progress was now slowing down, and the awful weather
was helping the desperate efforts made by the enemy to
hold our advance and stiffen his badly shaken front. On
Tuesday amid driving snowstorms the Canadians won

[1] Of the opening day of the battle Ludendorff writes in his *Memoirs*:
" The battle near Arras, on April 9th, formed a bad beginning for the serious
fighting of the year. April 10th and the days that followed were a critical
time. A breach of 12,000 to 15,000 yards wide and 6,000 yards and more in
depth takes some mending. It meant even more to replace the resulting
wastage of men, guns and munitions. The High Command had to find
reserves on a large scale, but it was simply impossible to have a division ready
to replace each division forced out. Thus a day like April 9th upset all our
calculations. And it was a matter of many days before a new front could be
established and consolidated."

from the enemy his last footing on the Vimy Ridge, and in the centre the 6th Corps won its way to the western slopes of the hill of Monchy-le-Preux, the dominant point between the Scarpe and Sensée rivers.   But the enemy held on there and checked with heavy machine gun fire an attempt of the cavalry to work round it on the north and south.

The left column of the 17th Division had been brought into shelter in Arras early in the day, and all three brigades spent the rest of it in the city, waiting for orders. At 8.50 a.m. Divisional H.Q. had a wire from the Cavalry Corps, directing that at 11 a.m. the 17th should have its advanced guards ready to move at half an hour's notice and the rest of its two columns ready to move off half an hour later.   At 10.35 another message came through saying that it was unlikely that any move would be possible before 2 p.m.   No further orders arrived from the Corps H.Q., for the attempt to push forward round Monchy-le-Preux was held up at the very outset.

Next morning, Wednesday, April 11th, the cavalry tried again.   They scored a success, a terribly costly one. It had snowed all night and the men as they waited for the surprise dash that was to win the village and the hill of Monchy, were white with the flakes that clung to helmets and cloaks.   The snow ceased at dawn, and Monchy village, still little damaged by shell fire, showed up with its roofs sharply defined by their white covering.   Our guns still spared it, for this strange attack of mounted troops was to come as a surprise, and its success was no doubt largely due to its seeming impossibility.   To right and left of the village and straight for it the cavalry rode, dismounting to clear the houses as the first rush carried them into the place.   The village was lightly held and the attack was a swift success, and then the price was paid. A storm of German shells descended upon Monchy.   An enemy plane buzzing overhead marked the mass of the cavalry supports standing by their horses below the hill, and another deluge of shells found them. There was a fearful slaughter of men and horses, and the leader of the gallant charge, General Bulkeley-Johnson, was brought back dead. The cavalry were replaced in the captured village by detachments from the 6th Corps and withdrawn to near Arras. Any idea of a push by the mounted troops and their support, the 17th Division, towards Cambrai was abandoned, and at 1.45 p.m. Divisional H.Q. received orders that the Division was transferred from the Cavalry Corps to the 6th Corps (Lieut.-General J. A. Haldane), and was to relieve the 15th (Scottish) Division in the following night in the line between Monchy-le-Preux and the river Scarpe.

Ludendorff was now closing the breach in the German line by building up a new trench system between the rivers on this side, and a British advanced trench line was coming into existence facing it. The Arras battle was slowing down into the routine of trench warfare, but for some days there had to be continuous pressure on the enemy front, to assist the now imminent advance planned by Nivelle to sweep the invaders out of France.

Divisional orders, issued in the afternoon of April 11th, directed that the 50th Brigade would relieve the 44th Brigade (15th Division) in the front line. The 52nd would be in support and the 51st was to be the Divisional Reserve.

The relief proved to be a long and a rather difficult business. The 50th Brigade moved out from Arras by the Cambrai road at 4.15 p.m. and the 52nd followed an hour later. Both found themselves at once involved in a dense double stream of traffic. The cavalry were moving back from the front, convoys of supplies and detachments of various units were moving out to the front, and where the road passed through the old German lines a disabled tank encumbered the roadway and produced a local block that affected the movement for a mile on either side. By the time the head of the 50th Brigade reached a point near the old German third line, where it was to turn off north towards Feuchy, darkness had come on and it was snowing heavily.   At this turn matters became worse, for the infantry had to cross the track of the cavalry, and there were repeated halts of the intersecting columns of route as they alternately gave a passage to detachments, mounted or on foot, and long trains of waggons.   Occasional bursts of shell fire added to the confusion.   It may have been pure chance, but it seemed as if the enemy, despite dark- ness and snow, had some uncanny knowledge that there was a huge congestion of traffic at the road crossing.   As the brigade column cleared the block and headed for Feuchy it was found that battalions and even companies had been broken up in the crush, and at the halt near the ruins of Feuchy there had to be a sorting out and reorgani- sation.   From this point the move was eastward parallel with the line of the river, and on reaching the front north-west of Monchy it was found that the brigade had to take it over not from the 44th Brigade but from various units of all three brigades of the 15th Division, which the trench fighting of the preceding days had placed here and there in the new front line.   It faced a German trench front running down the slopes from near Monchy to the swampy hollow of the Scarpe at the bend west of Roeux, where marshes and wide pools, lightly frozen over, protected the enemy's flank.

The 52nd Brigade, involved in the same block of traffic on the Cambrai road, took four hours to reach its support position, though this was only three miles from the starting point.   In orders the place was indicated only by a co-ordinate (H. 21. d. 2½. 3.), and there were no guides from the troops to be relieved.   When the supposed place was reached it was found to be an open snow- covered field, and as the brigade halted it was discovered that two battalions were missing, perhaps still wedged in the traffic on the Cambrai road.   It was now 9.30 p.m. There was no longer any shelling, and half an hour later the snow ceased falling. It was a pitch-dark night with a clouded sky and bitterly cold. The men tramped about to keep themselves warm, and a staff officer went off towards Feuchy to try to find the support position held by the 15th Division, of which the orders gave no helpful indication, and meanwhile a look-out was kept for the missing battalions. They arrived about 1.30 a.m., and the situation was cleared up by news being brought back from Feuchy that the troops to be relieved were holding the old German third line south of the village, with H.Q. in its ruins. It was after 5 a.m. when the relief was completed. The 51st Brigade occupied the reserve position at the Railway Triangle, a German strong point before the battle, where there was abundance of shelter in well-constructed dugouts.

The 9th Division was on the left of the 17th on the other side of the Scarpe, and the 29th on the right on the hill and in the now ruined village of Monchy-le-Preux and the new trench line immediately to the south of it.

During the twelve days the Division spent in the line there was only one general attack along the whole front, but each day saw attempts with varying results, to gain ground at several points. These were met by an increasing vigour in the enemy's resistance, and a greater disposition to counter-attack. The net result was how-ever a moderate gain of ground on the whole front, but no success even remotely approaching in importance that of the first day of battle.

Thursday, April 12th, was a day of snowstorms, with fighting along a considerable part of the front and satis-factory gains on the extreme right and left. In the centre the 9th Division attacked, from its position east of Fam-poux, the German trench line north of the railway. This was its first objective, and in case of success it was to make a push south of the railway to capture the village of Roeux. The 50th Brigade was directed to co-operate on the south side of the Scarpe by pushing forward as far as the bridge across the river at Roeux. As a preliminary step the brigadier sent the Dorsets forward to seize the crest of a spur, east of Lone Copse, running down from the high ground towards the wide pools and marsh flats opposite the west end of Roeux. The Dorsets won the crest with little opposition and began to consolidate there, but as the first move of the 9th Division on the other bank ended in failure, no further advance was attempted on the south side. On the situation being reported to Divisional H.Q., General Robertson telegraphed an order for the Dorsets to be withdrawn from the spur, where, with Roeux still safely held by the enemy, the battalion was in a dangerously exposed position with the line on which it was consolidating open to enfilade from the north bank of the Scarpe.

On the morning of the 13th the enemy's artillery was very active, the bombardment extending to the support line, where a heavy howitzer shell made a direct hit on the Battalion H.Q. of the 12th Manchesters, completely wrecking it and causing many casualties. Amongst those killed were the battalion commander, Lieut.-Colonel Magnay, and his adjutant, Captain Tower. There had come a change in the weather, a thaw followed by some dull days with frequent rain showers. A good deal of work was being done improving the trench system, and the Pioneers were employed in " making Feuchy a tidy ruin "—clearing the roads through the village of fallen débris and filling up shell holes. Some useful discoveries were made. A well yielding a good supply of excellent water was found, and the clearing away of fallen bricks and rubble opened several strongly-built cellars which could be used as ready-made dugouts. After this the Pioneer Battalion was called away to work on a light railway north of Arras.

The orders for April 14th, so far as they concerned the front immediately south of the Scarpe, were that the 29th Division was to make a push from Monchy and seize and consolidate a line running from the high ground east of the village to near the Bois des Aubépines. It would be an advance of a thousand yards in the wide No Man's Land at this point, and the 10th West Yorks (50th Brigade) were to co-operate with the left of the advance by establishing posts on its flank. Shortly before 1 a.m. the German artillery began throwing quantities of gas shells into the ground behind our front, and these fell continuously in the support position of the 52nd Brigade, with the result that the men had to put on their gas masks and got very little sleep. The apparent object of this gas bombardment was to embarrass reliefs and supply of our front during the night. Early in the morning reports came in that the enemy were moving out in extended order from the Bois du Sart, towards the hill east of Monchy, and that the sunken road south-west of Pelves village was full of Germans. The 29th Division had started their advance from Monchy. It was a case of both sides having planned an attack for the same day in the same sector of the front.

The enemy put down a heavy barrage from Monchy northwards to the Scarpe and their advance developed into a well-sustained counter-attack. The 50th Brigade checked them on their flank with machine gun fire and the West Yorks suceeded in consolidating two advanced posts on the right of the brigade front. Early in the afternoon the fighting died down with no important result for either party. Each claimed that it had held the attempted advance of the other side.

In the following night the 52nd Brigade relieved the 50th in the front line. On Sunday, April 15th, there was a conference of Divisional Commanders at Arras. As one of its results the 52nd Brigade was ordered to extend its right, and in the following night take over from the 29th Division the line as far as the road from Monchy to Pelves. The 51st Brigade was to be in support, and the 50th was withdrawn into Divisional Reserve at Arras, where most of its units were quartered in caves under the city.

The British operations on the Arras front had now been a week in progress. On Monday, the 16th, Nivelle launched the French offensive, to which they were a preliminary. At midnight the news reached Arras that the first day of the great push had been a splendid success, some miles of the enemy's first line won and 11,000 prisoners taken. The front attacked was from the heights of the Aisne on the left to the Moronvillers Hills east of Rheims on the right. The French advanced amid driving snowstorms. (Later in the day the same wintry weather extended to the Arras front.) The attack met with a rather feeble resistance, and the first impression was that Nivelle's " victory plan " was working out so well as to presage further and greater results.

The morning after this encouraging news arrived the 17th Division received warning orders to begin immediate preparations for taking part in a general advance of the whole line on the Arras front, at dawn on Friday 20th. But on the 19th there was a change of plans and the advance was deferred to St. George's Day, Monday, April 23rd.

On the front held by the 17th Division the first objective was to be the clearing of the enemy positions that formed a salient of his line on the south bank of the Scarpe opposite Roeux and north of Monchy-le-Preux. The orders contemplated a further advance to Pelves village if this ground was won. In preparation for the attack the 51st Brigade had been brought up to the front line, and the two battalions that were to lead the assault, the 7th Borders on the right and the 8th South Staffords on the left, were in the assembly trenches dug on a line running north and south through Lone Copse. The 9th Northumberland Fusiliers (52nd Brigade) were attached to the 51st and posted so as to cover the right of the attack and connect up with the 29th Division north-east of

Monchy. Two tanks were to be at the disposal of the
G.O.C. 51st Brigade, but unfortunately both broke down
on their way to the assembly position. Trench mortars
were placed near the south end of Bayonet Trench to
enfilade it and fire also on Rifle Trench. Bayonet
Trench followed the crest line of a spur running from
the direction of Monchy towards the Scarpe, and Rifle
Trench joined it at right angles about half-way along its
length. On the left, near the Scarpe, other mortars were
placed to put down a smoke barrage on the line of the
river covering the left flank, and doing something to
shelter the advance from fire from the north bank. The
50th Brigade was in support, and the 52nd (less the
Northumberland Fusiliers), was in reserve at the Railway
Triangle.

Covered by a barrage, the assaulting battalions left the
assembly trenches at zero hour, 4.45 a.m. on St. George's
Day. Hardly had they gone over the top when the
enemy's barrage came down, and at the same time a well-
sustained bombardment opened upon Monchy and the
ground on its neighbourhood, and a tremendous enfilade
fire of machine guns came from the north side of the
Scarpe. By an unlucky mistake the wire in front of the
German line was hardly anywhere cut. Twice the
Staffords, on the left, attacked the north end of Bayonet
Trench, but both attacks were repulsed with serious loss.
On the right the Borders fought their way into and along
the south end of the trench nearly up to its junction with
Rifle Trench. They also made a push for the latter
trench across the cratered ground in the angle between it
and the front line. This attack did not reach it, but
parties of the Borders held on in shell holes till they were
withdrawn after dark that evening.

The two other battalions of the 51st Brigade—7th
Lincolns and 10th Sherwoods—had meanwhile been
brought up into the Lone Copse assembly trenches from
the old front line. The G.O.C. 51st Brigade ordered

the Lincolns to attack the north end of Bayonet Trench, after the remnant of the Staffords had been withdrawn to Lone Copse, and sent a request through for a barrage to cover their advance.　By some mischance a message from Divisional H.Q. countermanding the attack as the artillery was not just then able to help, came through too late, just after the Lincolns had begun to move forward at 8 a.m.　They reached the enemy's wire with a rush,

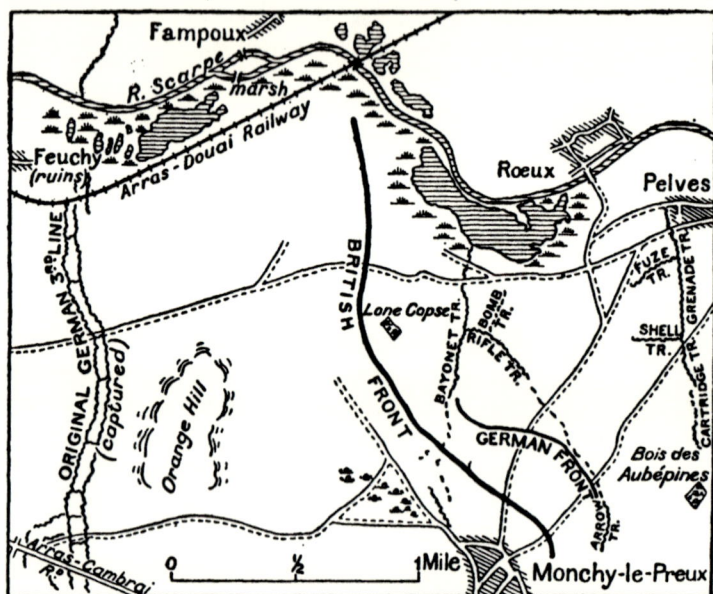

Operations East of Arras, April 1917.

but there the attack was held.　Under a cross fire from the trench in front and the storm of M.G. bullets from the other side of the Scarpe, officers and men lay down trying to work under or cut through the barrier of intact wire.　The attack failed with losses amounting to nearly 200 of all ranks.　On the same ground the Staffords had already lost 214 officers and men.

After this there was for some hours a lull in the battle until early in the afternoon the 50th Brigade was moved

up from the support position with orders to pass through
the 51st Brigade and renew the attack on Bayonet and
Rifle trenches, and if this succeeded endeavour to make
further progress eastwards.   The Brigade came under
heavy artillery fire during this movement.[1]   When at
3.30 p.m. the leading battalions attacked Bayonet
Trench it was believed that Roeux was in the hands of the
Division next to the northward on the further bank of the
Scarpe, and that the left flank was therefore secure.   But
Roeux had been retaken by the enemy, and the advance
of the 50th Brigade was held and repulsed by cross fire
from the Trench and from machine guns in Roeux.
After the failure of this attack no further advance was
attempted that day and all efforts were devoted to consolidating the position.

Although on both banks of the Scarpe the day had been
disappointing, at many other points on the line of eight
miles covered by the attack on St. George's Day a fair
amount of ground had been won, despite the obstinate
resistance everywhere made by the enemy, who had
seven divisions in action.   At this stage of the Arras
Battle the chief object of the operations was to occupy as
many German Divisions as possible, and so lighten the
task of the French.   This was all the more important
because Nivelle's offensive was now faring badly.   His
advance was everywhere held with enormous loss, and
after the sanguine forecasts spread broadcast on its first

[1] An interesting note made by an officer of the 51st Brigade who watched
the advance of the 50th, gives an instance of the small effect sometimes resulting
from the fire of H.E. shells against infantry on the move, under circumstances
where shrapnel fire would probably have caused heavy loss.   " The sun was
shining," he writes, " and the visibility was extraordinarily good.   In company
with the late Lieut.-Colonel Barker, O.C. 8th South Staffords, I was sitting in
a hole under the bank at Lone Copse, when the Dorsets came over the ridge
and down the forward slope from the old German 3rd line in three waves.
They were literally blotted out by a storm of H.E. shells, and we both remarked
that ' that was that.'   But presently out of the smoke there emerged the three
waves, stolidly arriving at Lone Copse.   They had, I believe, *about five
casualties.*—But many men 800 yards away were hit by the shells which burst
among the Dorsets ! "

day a wave of disillusion and depression was spreading through France.

On the 17th Division front the 52nd Brigade was brought up in close support into the line north-east of Monchy during the night following the St. George's Day battle.

The 24th was a fairly quiet day, the only incidents being two attempts of bombing parties from the 52nd Brigade to work their way further up Bayonet Trench—both of them failing in face of a concentrated machine gun fire from Rifle Trench. The Division was to be relieved on the evening of the 25th, but in the afternoon of the 24th orders were received that in co-operation with the 3rd Division, now holding Monchy, a surprise attack was to be made at 3.30 a.m. on the 25th, the objective being the enemy front line from Arrow Trench, east of Monchy, to the junction of Rifle and Bayonet Trenches. A couple of tanks were to be available for the left of the attack—that of the 52nd Brigade—which had Rifle Trench for its objective.

One of its battalions, the Northumberland Fusiliers, had been for some days in the line facing this position, with the 7th East Yorks of the 50th Brigade on its immediate left. Brigadier General Clarke replaced the Northumberlands with the 12th Manchesters at dusk. They were to attack the right end of Rifle Trench across a wide and much cratered No Man's Land. The 9th Duke of Wellington's were brought up to the front line after dark. They were to pass through the East Yorkshires and attack the left of the trench. Each of the assaulting battalions were to have the help of one of the tanks.

At 3.35 a.m. the advance began. It was hoped that the omission of any immediate artillery preparation would make it a surprise for the enemy, but the Germans were on the alert and discovered the movement almost immediately. Their artillery put down a wide barrage on No Man's Land. The two battalions had at once numerous casualties and both the tanks were knocked out by direct hits as they went through our own front line. On the left the Duke of Wellington's were mostly held by the sweeping machine gun fire from the trench that met them as they struggled through the shell shower over the broken ground, but some 50 or 60 got into Rifle Trench, only to be driven out by a counter-attack before any support could reach them. The right attack of the Manchesters fared better. Two companies effected a lodgment in the further end of the trench, and held on there all next day, succeeding at last in consolidating their hold upon it. In the afternoon of the 25th General Robertson saw General Clarke and discussed the possibility of completing the capture of Rifle Trench, but it was decided that with the relief impending in the following night it was better to be content with consolidating what had been won.

In this fight for Rifle Trench the Duke of Wellington's had nine officers and 250 other ranks killed and wounded. The loss of the Manchesters was four officers and 110 men. During the night of the 25th to 26th, the 17th Division was relieved by the 6th, and during the following day the troops (with the exception of the Pioneer Battalion left at Arras), were moved back by rail and bus convoys to the villages about Le Cauroy, where Divisional H.Q. were established. It was understood that after a short rest the Division would return to the Arras front in the first days of May.

On April 27th General Robertson issued the following Special Order of the Day :

" The G.O.C. wishes to express to all ranks of the 17th Division his sincere thanks for, and high appreciation of, the most excellent manner in which they have carried out the late active operations against the enemy from 9th to 25th April, and in particular in the pitched battle of April 23rd. Where all have done their utmost and so gallantly, he feels that it would be invidious to make any distinction between units by name. The unfailing spirit of cheerfulness in enduring hardships under most adverse weather conditions, and the way in which attack and defence have been carried out reflect the greatest credit on all, and fully uphold the splendid traditions of the British Army.

" The work of the Field Artillery, Field Companies and Field Ambulances was on the same high level as that of the Infantry.

" It is the G.O.C.'s greatest pride to have the honour of commanding so fine a Division."

CHAPTER VII

ON THE ARRAS FRONT—PASSCHENDAELE—THE LAST WINTER OF THE WAR (1917-18)

In this last week of April, 1917, when the 17th Division came out of the line for a few days to rest and refit, General Nivelle's plan, on which the whole arrangements of the Western front had been based, had already broken down. At Arras the British had fulfilled their subsidiary part of the scheme, which was essentially a diversion to facilitate the ambitious plans of Nivelle and the French Government, for which over a million men had been concentrated on the Aisne-Champagne front. On April 16th the French offensive had been launched, and by the evening of the 17th it was so plain that it had miscarried that Nivelle was modifying his plans and tacitly abandoning any idea of realising the immense results which he had promised to secure. On May 16th—exactly a month after the first shots of the great battle were fired on the Aisne front—he was deprived of his command and replaced by Pétain. Henceforth he was a mere spectator of the warfare on the Western Front, in which he had so confidently hoped to play a decisive part by one tremendous and far-sweeping victory in these early months of 1917. His failure and downfall was one of the tragedies of the war.

We have seen that when the date of the Allied offensive in the West was fixed for April, one of the chief reasons for choosing that month was that it was the earliest date at which the weather on the Eastern Front would permit the Russian armies to operate on a large scale, and thus force the enemy to carry on the war in two fronts. But in April 1917 the Russian armies were inactive. The paralysis of all activity resulting from the Revolution, that had overthrown the Czardom in March, 1917, had begun. Indirectly the events in Russia affected to a singularly perilous degree the situation in France, for after the failure of the Nivelle offensive there came a crisis of which the secret was kept until the war was over. That the secret was so well guarded was a marvel. The Germans heard some vague reports of what was happening, but discredited them as impossible of belief. On the French front regiment after regiment, and division after division, were refusing to obey orders. There were no violent outbreaks of disorderly mutiny. The peril lay in the widespread attitude of quietly determined and orderly resistance to authority among the rank and file, with the support of many of the junior officers. The malcontents declared that they were being uselessly sacrificed by incompetent chiefs, and that it was time to patch up a peace of some kind. They formed soldiers' committees on the Russian model to discuss the situation. At one dangerous moment the talk was of a march on Paris, to impose their will on the politicians. What lulled the Germans into ignorance of what was happening was the fact that there was no vestige of fraternising with the enemy, and even where discipline broke down after the battle on the Aisne front had gradually died away, the routine of the outposts was everywhere maintained. Pétain dealt with the mutiny in the summer months by a policy mostly of conciliation. There were few court martials, but many concessions to meet real grievances of the French rank and file. During these anxious times it was hopeless to think of any serious operations on the French front, and the whole brunt of the war fell upon the British. They had at all costs to keep the Germans busy. The United States had joined the Allies in April, but it would be many months before the American armies would be able to take the field in Europe. They had first to be created. So in the early summer of 1917 it was for a while only the British army that counted on the front. The policy adopted was to maintain pressure on the enemy's front in France, and put into action the plan of an offensive in Flanders, which before the Nivelle plan was accepted was intended to have been the chief operation of the year.

At the end of April and in the first days of May, Nivelle was still trying to effect something on a more limited scale than that of his original " victory plan," and Haig was giving him loyal co-operation by continuing the operations east of Arras. What may be called the second phase of the Battle of Arras had begun, and it was gradually becoming a new development of the apparently interminable trench warfare. In this form it continued through the summer and autumn months, and some ground was gradually won towards Cambrai, but Flanders soon became the chief theatre of operations for the British Army in the West. Until September the 17th Division was employed in the operations east of Arras.

Its stay in the Le Cauroy area only lasted a few days. It was a pleasant time, for the long spell of broken, wintry weather was ending and spring began with bright warm days that promised an early summer. Drafts arrived from England to fill up the depleted ranks of the Division. Training was taken in hand, but on lines that left a large margin for rest and recreation. The " Duds " were rehearsing a new series of entertainments, and plans were in progress for sports meetings and a horse show, the expectation being that there would at least be a fortnight, perhaps even three weeks, out of the line. But on April 29th there came warning orders of an immediate move to the front.

Next day it was notified that the Division was to be attached, from May 1st, to the 17th Corps (Lieut-General Sir Charles Fergusson), which was operating on the north side of the Scarpe.   The other three Divisions of the Corps were the 4th, 9th, and 51st.   The 4th was an Old Army formation, which had gone to France in the first month of the war and fought at Le Cateau.   The 9th was the earliest of the New Army Divisions to be formed.   The 51st (Highland) Division was a Territorial formation with a fine war record.   The front held by the 17th Corps was about five miles east of Arras, with its right flank resting on the north bank of the Scarpe between the villages of Fampoux and Roeux, of which the latter was still held by the enemy.   The 4th Division held the left of its front line, and the 9th Division the right.

On April 30th Divisional H.Q. issued to the higher ranks under the title of " 17th Division Preliminary Instructions, No I," a forecast of the part the Division would play in the coming operations.   In the next advance, provisionally fixed for May 3rd, the first objective of the 17th Corps would be a line about a mile and a half east of the existing front.   It was described as running from Plouvain to " Square Wood " (near the Arras-Douai road).   This meant that the attack would have to capture the strongest feature of this sector of the enemy front, the bold height of Greenland Hill, dominating the ground immediately north of the Scarpe.   It was anticipated that the 17th Division would be in Corps Reserve.   Should this first objective be captured it was " to push through and secure a line between Biache and Fernes, and harass the enemy's retreat."

From midnight of May 2nd and 3rd the 52nd Brigade was to be attached to the 9th Division " as a reserve only to be used in emergency," and was to revert to the 17th Division when the latter went forward.   There was the forecast that in the event of the enemy " being thoroughly disorganised and his strength spent in repeated counter-attacks," the battle might be followed up by a night attack, made with the bayonet and without M.G. or rifle fire, the artillery co-operating only with counter-

battery work.   It was an optimistic forecast and suggested
that the advance in the first week of May was meant to
be something more than a mere diversion to keep some
German Divisions busy east of Arras.

On the morning of Tuesday, May 1st, Divisional H.Q.
were transferred from Le Cauroy to the château of
Hermaville, about eight miles west of Arras.   On this
and the next day the infantry of the Division moved up
to billets and hut camps between Hermaville and Arras
by bus convoys, the transport by route march.   On May
2nd the 52nd Brigade moved up into camp at St Nicholas,
the northern suburb of Arras, and was attached to the
9th Division.   This was because the Division was now
short of one of its own Infantry Brigades, the South
African, which had been reduced to a small remnant by
heavy casualities in action, and was receiving no drafts to
replace its losses.

May 2nd was a bright warm day of early summer.   In
preparation for the advance next morning our artillery
was active along a twelve mile front and the enemy was
making a rather feeble reply.   Going forward to confer
with Sir Henry Lukin, the G.O.C. of the 9th Division,
as to the co-operation of the 52nd Brigade, its commander,
General Clarke, found the Divisional H.Q. installed in
a former German dugout in a cutting of the Arras-Lens
railway about a mile north of the Scarpe.   This cutting
was a kind of advanced base for the sector now held by
the 9th Division, which was to be the scene of the trench
warfare of the 17th during various tours of duty in the
coming summer.   It was in places some fifty feet deep,
cut in the chalk, with steep sides dazzling white in this
summer weather.   The enemy had held it until our
advance in the second week of April, and its western side
was tunnelled and honeycombed with German dugouts.
To support their roofs the rails and sleepers had been
removed from the railway line in the cutting.   The dugouts provided useful cover, but with the defect that, as

they were constructed to give shelter from fire coming from the westward, and the enemy's batteries were now some four miles away to the east, their entrances looked in a dangerous direction. Sandbag traverses had been piled up to protect them, a necessary precaution as shells not infrequently reached the cutting from the batteries on and beyond Greenland Hill.

From the high ground above the cutting there was a good view of the country eastward and north of the Scarpe as far as Greenland Hill. For about a mile and a half from the railway the chalk down extended eastward, a scene of desolation, for the war storm had but lately swept over it. It was traversed and intersected by lines of old German trenches. In some of its nearer folds British batteries were installed. Of the old trenches many were in ruins, others had been improvised into British trench and support lines, and several of the communication lines were now in good order. North of the ruined village of Fampoux on the Scarpe the ground sloped eastward into a long valley beyond which it rose again to the summit of Greenland Hill. The enemy's front ran along its lower slopes, and then to the Scarpe by the ruins of Roeux village and the chemical works between it and the hill. Our advanced trenches ran along the hollow and over a spur of the hill, separated from the German front by a No Man's Land varying in width from 150 to 400 yards. The situation was not a satisfactory one. Our front was defended only by a somewhat haphazard system improvised out of captured trenches, hastily dug by the enemy after the first days of the Arras battle, sited to be held against an attack from the west, and without the traverses and dugouts that would have been found ready made if we had taken them after a long occupation. They were all overlooked from the hill, and in many places what we held was a German trench, commanded at close quarters by its original support trench, a little higher up the slope.

In the afternoon of May 2nd the 52nd Brigade was moved forward to the neighbourhood of the railway cutting and settled down in dugouts, tents and huts. The 51st Brigade replaced it in the camp and at St. Nicholas, and the 50th was brought into Arras.

Next day, Thursday, May 3rd, just before dawn, the German positions were attacked on a front of over twelve miles from near Vimy on the north to Bullecourt in the Hindenburg line south-east of Arras. On the extreme right and left there were important gains, but in the centre, on both banks of the Scarpe, the ground won in the early morning was mostly lost under the pressure of persistent counter-attacks later in the day, which continued long after dark. The 52nd Brigade had been held in readiness to move at brief notice, but was not called upon to intervene, and the results fell so short of the optimistic forecast issued a few days before that the rest of the 17th Division never moved from its billets.

On the evening of the 4th, the 50th Brigade had a disagreeable experience in Arras. Several of their units were billetted in sheds at the north side of the city, and in one of the larger of these the East Yorkshires were assembled to enjoy a boxing tournament, when there was a sudden alarm of fire. They cleared out in good order in three minutes, only to find that the fire was rapidly spreading along the line of huts which were their quarters. It had been started by a party of gunners who, while getting an improvised supper ready, upset a small petrol stove. The huts and sheds were so dried up with the hot summer weather prevailing that they blazed up like a train of crackers. It was impossible to save more than a trifle of the arms, packs and equipment of the East Yorkshires, and the fire spread to an ammunition dump. Thousands of cartridges were destroyed, and amid the crackling clatter as they took fire there came the explosions of bombs, several of which fell among the working parties who were fighting the fire, causing ten casualties.

The battalion machine guns were saved and all the trench mortars except two. Late in the evening the Brigade was ordered to move out of Arras to the camp near St. Nicholas.

On the night of May 10th to 11th the 17th Division took over the sector facing Greenland Hill from the 9th, after having received warning orders that it would take part in an attack on the enemy's position before the Hill on Saturday, May 12th.

The orders for the attack had been issued on the 8th and discussed at a Conference at Divisional H.Q. on the following day. Zero hour was to be 6.30 a.m. on the 12th, and the attack "was to be made by surprise, the putting down of the barrage being the signal for the infantry to leave their trenches." Up to zero artillery activity was to be normal. The 50th Brigade was to be in reserve in the railway cutting and the old German trench system to the west of it.

On the right of the 17th Division the ground north of the Scarpe was held by the 4th Division, which here faced the outlying defences of Roeux village, from the railway station near the ruined Chemical Works by the cemetery to the river bank. Corps H.Q. directed that, as a preliminary operation, these points were to be attacked by the 4th Division on the evening of May 11th. The 6th Dorsets (50th Brigade) were ordered to attach two companies to the 4th Division to cover the flank of this advance and clear the enemy trenches immediately north of the railway and the Chemical Works. The attack was made at 7.30 p.m. on the Friday evening, and proved a complete success. The 4th Division captured the Works, and the Dorsets, with trifling loss, pushed forward on its left over a number of trench lines which were lightly held and were abandoned by the enemy as soon as the Chemical Works were lost.

For the attack of the morning of the 12th, Roeux village was the objective of the 4th Division. The whole place was in ruins, but had been converted into a strong point, guarding the river flank of the enemy's main line in front of Greenland Hill. It had been taken in the attack of May 3rd but recaptured by a vigorous German counter-attack later in the day, which had also won back all the ground west of the village, including the Chemical Works.

For the 17th Division the objective was the main enemy trench line on the western slope of Greenland Hill. The advance had to be made from old German trenches on lower ground. The 52nd Brigade on the left had for its objective the long line of trench known on our maps as " Charlie." It was to be assaulted by two battalions, 10th Lancashire Fusiliers on the right, 9th Northumberland Fusiliers on the left, with the 12th Manchesters in support. The 9th Duke of Wellington's were left in reserve at the railway cutting.

The 50th Brigade (right attack) had for its objective the trench lines known as " Curly " and " Cupid," north of the Arras-Douai railway. They were also to clear the cutting by which this line ran through the south slope of Greenland Hill, and to keep touch with the advance of the 4th Division to the south of it. The assaulting battalions were the 7th Yorkshires on the right, the 7th East Yorks on the left, with the 10th West Yorks in support and two companies of the 6th Dorsets in reserve.

All the arrangements for the attack had been completed before sunrise on Saturday the 12th. There were still three hours to go by before zero, and long before it came it was only optimists who expected that it would be possible to bring off a surprise attack. It was a bright clear summer morning, and at dawn German aeroplanes were making daring low flights over our front, and must have had no difficulty in finding out that the forward trenches were full of infantry ready to advance. The German gunners showed no unusual activity, but there was ample time to make preparations for meeting our attack, and the enemy were quite ready for it.

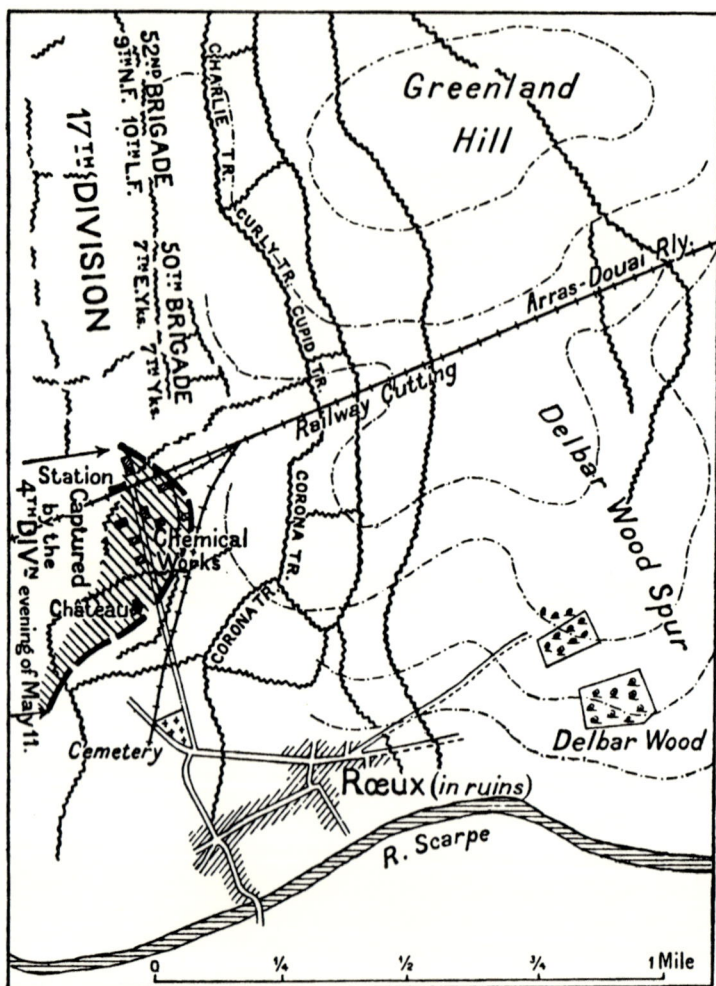

Operations East of Arras—Attack of May 12th, 1917.

At 6.30 our barrage was put down on the enemy's front, with a creeping barrage to cover the move across No Man's Land, which was from 100 yards to a quarter

of a mile wide.   As our guns opened fire the enemy put
down a heavy counter-barrage, and the advance was at
once wrapped in such a dense fog of smoke and dust
clouds that from the observation posts behind our front
it was for a while impossible, even with field glasses, to
make out what was happening.

The left attacks on Charlie and Curly Trenches were
a failure.   The advance came under heavy fire of all
arms, inflicting serious loss, and only one company of the
Lancashire Fusiliers got into the south end of Charlie.
With their flanks in the air they were counter-attacked
and driven out in about twenty minutes.   The losses
of the three companies of the Lancashires that made the
assault were 11 officers and 182 other ranks killed and
wounded.   Their gallant leader, Major David Comyn,
was among the dead.   On the right, near the railway
line, however, the 7th Yorkshires got into Cupid Trench,
made the position there good, and tried to bomb their way
to the left into Curly Trench, in front of which the East
Yorks had been held up by intense machine gun fire.
Trench fighting went on intermittently during the day,
the chief point of contention being the junction of Cupid
and Curly Trenches.   There were several minor counter-
attacks, but what looked for a while like an attempt to
mass for an advance in force by the enemy was broken
up by our gunners shelling their troops as they showed
coming over Greenland Hill, and bringing indirect fire
upon their supports on its reverse slopes.

A Victoria Cross was won by Private Thomas Dresser
of the 7th Yorkshires.   The official record stated that it
was awarded :

" For most conspicuous bravery and devotion to duty on May 12,
1917.   Private Dresser, in spite of being twice wounded on the
way, and suffering great pain, succeeded in conveying an important
message from battalion headquarters to the front-line trenches,
which he eventually reached in an exhausted condition.   His fear-
lessness and determination to convey the message at any cost proved
of the greatest value to his battalion at a critical period."

By sunset the fighting died down, and in the twilight of the evening there was for a while a kind of informal truce, parties of both British and Germans carrying off their wounded without molestation.   At 10 p.m. fighting began again, the 7th Yorkshires rushing the junction of Cupid and Curly and establishing a post in the latter trench about 30 yards north of this point.   But a simultaneous attempt of the East Yorks to rush the north end of Curly was driven back by heavy machine gun and rifle fire.   The attempt was renewed at 2.30 a.m. on the Sunday morning, but was again unsuccessful.

The results of the day were disappointing.   There had been only a limited local success on both sides of the Douai railway where, south of it, the left of the 4th Division had won some ground, and north of it the right of the 17th Division had captured the front trench to the north of the line.   During the following days there was fighting at the block in Curly Trench, and some half-hearted counter-attacks on the captured position.   A very unusual incident was a message on the morning of the 13th from one of our aeroplanes reporting that it had flown low over Charlie Trench without being fired on, and that this trench and its southward extension, Curly Trench, seemed to be unoccupied by the enemy.   Patrols sent forward to verify this report were promptly and heavily fired upon by the Germans, who had been only " lying low " while the aeroplane went over.   That evening the 50th Brigade, which had relieved the 51st, made an unsuccessful attempt to rush Curly Trench. Orders from Corps H.Q. now intimated that for the present the policy to be adopted was that of " exploiting gains by energetic patrolling and gaining ground wherever possible as a prelude to operations for taking Greenland Hill and Delbar Wood Spur."

The 4th Division, on the front between the Douai Railway and the Scarpe, was relieved by the 51st Highland Division.   They had not been long in the line when the enemy made a vigorous counter-attack on all our front from Cupid Trench southwards to the river.

At 3 a.m. on Wednesday 16th—in the dark hour before the dawn on a moonless night—the German guns, till then fairly quiet, opened a tremendous bombardment north of the Scarpe, and an infantry attack was at once launched against our front west of Roeux, and for some distance to the other side of the Douai railway.   S.O.S. signals from the right soon told that the situation on that side was becoming serious.   The Divisional and Corps artillery opened fire, and supports were hurried up to the front, but the Germans with their first rush won all the ground south of the railway up to the Chemical Works and then rapidly stormed these.   This success of the enemy left the flank of the 51st Brigade in Cupid Trench exposed, and the right of the attack, coming along the railway cutting and over the ground north of it, recaptured the Trench, and there was some confused fighting among the old German communication trenches in No Man's Land.

Early in the morning a counter-attack by the 51st Division recovered the Chemical Works, but an attack on Cupid Trench failed.   During the day the fighting along the front gradually came to an end, the net result being that the opposing fronts were left very much as they were before the advance of May 12th.   During the rest of the month the sector quieted down into the normal routine of trench warfare, and there was no incident of any real importance.   The Corps Command directed preparations for a new attack on the line of Charlie, Curly and Cupid Trenches, but it was deferred to a date not named, after warning orders had more than once been issued and then countermanded.   This was perhaps the result of information obtained from prisoners that the enemy was preparing to abandon the Greenland Hill positions and fall back on the Drocourt-Quéant switch line, which our aircraft reported was now heavily entrenched. On at least one occasion the 17th Division received orders to send out patrols to verify a report that the evacuation of the Greenland Hill front was actually in progress, and the Charlie trench line already abandoned. The patrols found it was strongly held by an alert garrison.

On May 29th, the 34th Division began to relieve the 17th, and the relief was completed early on the 31st, when Divisional H.Q. were transferred from St. Nicholas Camp to Couturelle, 14 miles west of Arras. The troops were conveyed by rail and motor-buses and the transport went by route march to the rest billets in the villages between this place and Doullens, and in the Forest of Lucheux. The area was immediately to the south of that in which the Division had carried through its training before the Battle of Arras.

The York and Lancasters, the Pioneer Battalion, had more than once been left in the line during these intervals of rest and training. On this occasion it was brought back with the other infantry units and had a well-earned three weeks at Warluzel village, spent in rest and refitting. While in the line during May it had done heavy and continuous work, remodelling and improving such of the captured enemy trenches east of Arras as were chosen to form the new British defence system. The Battalion had been frequently under shell fire and during its three weeks of trench work in May it had had ten killed and more than a hundred wounded.

There were two changes in Brigade commands during the rest in the Couturelle area. Brigadier-General G. F. Trotter was succeeded by Brigadier-General G. S. Bond in command of the 51st Brigade, and Brigadier-General L. J. Clarke, who had been ill for some days before leaving the line, handed over the 52nd Brigade to Brigadier-General A. J. F. Eden.

On June 19th the Division began to move back to the Arras front with the help of a fleet of motor-buses, a

Brigade group being transferred to the camp at St. Nicholas each day. The movement was completed on the 21st and next morning Divisional H.Q. closed down at Couturelle and re-opened at St. Nicholas. The sector facing Greenland Hill was being taken over from the 34th Division. On the 20th the 50th Brigade took over the left and next day the 52nd went into the trenches on the right. The 51st Brigade was the Divisional Reserve at St. Nicholas Camp. A Territorial Battalion, the 3rd Service Battalion, Royal West Kent, was attached to the Division for training.

There had been some ground gained on this part of the front since the Division had held the sector before Greenland Hill in May. The British front line support had been carried forward for about 500 yards to what in May had been the support trench line beyond the enemy trenches attacked in the fight of May 12th. The enemy front was now a line of trenches a little higher up the slope of the hill, beyond a rather narrow No Man's Land. The Germans had dug themselves in very thoroughly and still overlooked all our front trench system. The right of the line taken over by the Division was at first just north of the Douai Railway, but it had hardly been occupied when orders came from Corps H.Q. to " side-slip " to the right and take over some of the ground immediately south of the railway, which included the ruined Chemical Works of Roeux.

This additional front was taken over on the night of June 26th to 27th. There was an unfortunate incident just when the relief was being completed about 3 a.m. A covering outpost near the railway made up of a sergeant and eight men of the Manchesters had been placed in a short trench near the brink of the railway cutting—a trench which was only a string of shell holes as yet unconnected with the front at this point, and with no wire in front of it. The sergeant challenged a small patrol approaching from the front, and not receiving an answer ordered his men to fire.   The patrol disappeared into the darkness, and at the same moment the Sergeant's group was rushed from the left rear by another patrol, about twenty strong, which had crept round the flank of the so-called trench.   The enemy raiders dashed through the line of shell holes throwing bombs as they came, and then pushed for their own line.   Two of our men were wounded, and the sergeant was knocked down and carried off a prisoner by the raiders.   The whole affair was over in a minute.

On July 2nd the York and Lancasters were detached from the Division, and temporarily transferred to the Army in Flanders.   They had had some experience of railway construction on the light lines near Montauban during the latter stage of the Somme battles.   They were now to be employed on light railway making and maintenance for some months, often under exceptionally trying conditions.   The Battalion was conveyed by rail from Arras to Poperinghe, and after a brief period of intensive training with an R.E. Company they began the construction of a light railway on the west side of the Yser Canal, north of Ypres.   This was the starting point of a light railway system that eventually was carried across the Canal and to a point a little beyond Langemarck, following up the advance of the British.   For the great push in Belgium, originally intended to be the main operation of 1917, was beginning.   Already on June 7th an all-important operation had been successfully carried out when General Plumer retook the Wytschaete-Messines Ridge on the southern side of the salient—a dominant position, which the Germans had held since November, 1914.   It had been decided that the main advance in the autumn would be a difficult and perhaps impossible enterprise, if the supplies of the Allied Army as it moved forward had to depend entirely on motor lorries working on the country roads of the district, or making their way across improvised tracks on the swampy levels that a few days rain would make impassable for wheeled traffic, and that it would therefore be necessary to construct a number of light railway systems, linking up the advanced supply bases on the Ypres and Yser front and carried forward eastward as the new ground was won. The rails were largely secured by dismantling other lines on the permanent railway systems outside the war zone. R.E. Companies and Pioneer Battalions were collected from all sectors of the front in France and Flanders to carry out the work, and for " No. 1 System " on the extreme left of the British front the York and Lancasters supplied the chief body of workers.[1]

It was an arduous task. Though officially known as " Light railways " the new lines had to be very solidly constructed. They would have to carry not only food supplies and munitions, including loads of big shells, but it was also intended that they should be used for handling such trying loads as heavy howitzers when, as the advance won its way forward, the guns and gunners were pushing on to a new position. Much of the ground was not only swampy but also cratered by shell fire. The shell holes were full of water and the gases of the explosions had reduced the ground to a spongy consistency, so that much of the low-lying land had become permanently water-logged. Under such conditions the preparation of the road bed was a difficult problem. It often meant draining, pumping or bailing whole systems of shell holes and craters, digging out tons of mud, and dumping and ramming in loads of clay, earth and broken rubble. When the canal was passed the new line was laid for about two miles along the old road bed of the Ypres-Bruges railway. But roughly parallel with the line another had to be constructed nearly half a mile south of it on the flat swampy land. Without this second track there would be risk of the communications being cut at a critical moment by the only available line being badly wrecked by shell fire.

[1] For the Light Railways, " No. 1 System," cf. plan No. 16, p. 246.

Both construction and maintenance had to be secured by frequent spells of work under fire, and the York and Lancasters had a long casualty list.   In August and again in October the work was rendered more difficult by persistent deluges of rain.   It was some comfort however that officers and men had the advantage of transport on the sections of the lines already completed, instead of long tramps through mud and water to their daily and nightly work, and their standing camps gave them good shelter from the weather.

Instead of the stations, or halts and unloading points, on the new lines being merely numbered they were given the names of English stations.   To mention some of these—on the northern line of No. 1 System, one started from " Euston " and passed through Harrow, Bushey, Birmingham, Warwick, Coventry, and Stafford—all in a six-mile run.   From Rugby Junction one could reach Chester by way of Broad Street and Oldham.   When the system reached its greatest extension there were 18 miles of new main and branch lines.   Amongst other gains was that during the autumn battles wounded men were brought back almost from the actual fighting front in well-equipped hospital trains.

Having thus anticipated future events in order to say something of the good work done by the Pioneer Battalion after its departure from the Arras front, we must return to the story of the Division's long tour of duty in the Greenland Hill and Chemical Works sector, which lasted for three months, from the third week of June to near the end of September.   With the main operations developing in Flanders, the Arras front was now relapsing into secohdary importance, but though no serious operations were in progress there, the trench system north of the Scarpe could hardly be described as a " quiet sector."

After the brilliant recapture of the Messines Ridge in the first days of June, there was until August no operation on a grand scale on the Ypres front, and the German

High Command were very slow in discovering that important preparations for a late summer and early autumn campaign in Flanders were in progress behind the Allied front in the Salient and along the Yser Canal. So for a while the enemy was anxious about the Arras front, and an immense amount of labour was expended by the Germans on strengthening and extending their new trench systems covering the approaches to Douai and Cambrai. On the Greenland Hill front and the whole line north of the Scarpe the German artillery indulged in frequent bombardments of our lines with H.E. and gas shells, the latter now including shells carrying a new and particularly offensive chemical charge of what was known as " Mustard Gas." It blistered the skin and caused painful irritation of eyes and nose, throat and lungs. It temporarily disabled far more than it either killed or permanently invalided, but its most detestable quality was that wherever it was successfully discharged it remained a source of danger and trouble for many days. It hung about in dugouts, cellars and even shelters above ground. It often soaked into men's clothing, and loosed off again its exhalations in sunlight or by a fire. It saturated patches of ground so that men were gassed as they dug them. There had to be a warning against allowing horses to browse on grass or leaves where the mustard gas shells had fallen. From the summer of 1917 onwards to the end of the war it was one of the worst of the scientific nuisances invented by the enemy's chemical experts. It was in the earlier weeks of this last long tour of duty on the Arras front that the Division had its first unpleasant experiences of this new " progress of military science." Its victims hardly appreciated the suggestion that as the percentage of fatal results was not high it was, after all, a " humane invention."

The record of the Division during these last months east of Arras was one of somewhat monotonous trench warfare routine. It was the longest tour of duty yet

Operations East of Arras, Greenland Hill Sector, July to September, 1917.

assigned to the Division, and few formations had been anywhere kept so long in the line without even a week or two of relief for " rest, refitting and training." The Greenland Hill Sub-Sector on the left and the Chemical Works Sub-Sector on the right (which included trenches on both sides of the Douai Railway), were each held by a Brigade, with two battalions in the front line, a third in support and a fourth in reserve. The remaining Brigade in Divisional Reserve at St. Nicholas Camp, while waiting for its turn to relieve one of those in front, had not much rest, for it supplied carrying and working parties to the two Brigades in the trenches.

When the Battle of Arras began in the first half of April the Germans held, close in to the east side of the city, a trench system of three strong lines, the result of two years and a half of steady work since November 1914. Behind their third line (which lay just east of the Arras-Lens railway), there was open country as far as the suburbs of Cambrai. The Drocourt-Quéant Switch was at that time marked out, but little work had been done upon it, hence our project for a break through of the Cavalry supported by the 17th Division, which formed a feature of the plans for the Arras battle. We have seen what a surprise to the enemy's High Command was our rapid progress on the first day of the battle, when a wide breach was effected in the first and second German lines and the third was in danger. As Ludendorff notes in his *Memoirs :* " A breach 12,000 to 15,000 yards wide and 6,000 yards or more in depth takes some mending." While the third line still held, the enemy began digging new trenches further east, and the Germans were first-rate diggers.

Not one but several new lines were hastily marked out, and as our advance slowed down a new trench system came into existence to mend the broken front. North of the Scarpe it extended not only to Greenland Hill but to its reverse slope. But these new trenches were not like those of the original line.   One cannot, even with the most efficient work, produce in a few days and weeks an improvised fortress line like that which grows up under the patient toil of months and years.   So as our front was pushed forward, east of Arras, beyond the old German third line, we came into possession of an improvised and half-completed enemy defence system, with trenches sited to meet an advance from the west, and most of them and their communication trenches badly battered by our own gunners, so that many a so-called trench was only a line of shell holes.   Thus, when in June the new British front north of the Scarpe was stabilised on the line running along the lower slopes of Greenland Hill, and the centre of interest was shifting to Flanders so that there was little prospect of further progress east of Arras, we held a badly-sited and defective front, with behind it, for a depth of from a mile to a mile and a half, what might be not inaptly described as the wreckage of the new trench system improvised during the previous seven or eight weeks.   All the ground was heavily cratered first by our gunfire then by that of the enemy.   It was a tangle of trenches, mostly shallow, never thoroughly revetted or traversed, all more or less damaged, some practically ruined.   As we pushed forward some rapid work had been done, here and there, but nowhere could this somewhat haphazard trench system be compared with the front we had held before the great battle began in April. Among the most serious of its defects, were the almost complete absence of good dugouts and the insufficiency of traverses, and this was all the worse because the enemy's position on high ground gave him a good view over our forward trenches and over the lines of communication as far back as the ridge near the Lens railway.

The whole captured trench system had therefore to be reorganised, improved and in many places constructed afresh.   It was to be remodelled and made into a habitable and defensible sector of the front before the end of the summer. This was the task carried out by the Division, entailing a much more serious amount of continuous labour than the mere maintenance of an existing well-constructed system. It was a loss that the Pioneer Battalion had been sent away to Flanders. An effort was made to replace this highly-skilled and experienced body of workers, and on July 9th it was ordered that the 3/4th Royal West Kents should be attached to the Division as its Pioneer Battalion during the absence of the York and Lancasters. The Battalion therefore changed its training in trench warfare for intensive courses in Pioneer Work under the direction of one of the R.E. Field Companies, but on the last day of July orders were received for the 9th Northumberland Fusiliers to be transferred from the 17th to the 34th Division, and it was directed that the West Kents should replace it in the 52nd Brigade. So until the Division itself went north in October it was without a Pioneer unit.

The enemy's activity on this front in these summer months was almost entirely limited to his not infrequent bombardments of our lines, which drew very effective retaliation from our gunners. During the three months the Germans never attempted anything like a counter-attack. Their patrols were often out at night in No Man's Land, and the incident (already described) in the early morning of June 27th, when the Division was taking over the ground south of the railway, seems to have been only the improvised enterprise of a patrol that discovered the isolated post of the Manchesters, and went for it. During the whole period there were only two instances of regularly organised enemy raids on our front, one in August, the other in September, almost on the eve of the Division being relieved.

The first of these took place just after 4 a.m. on August 8th. The chief attempt was directed along the cutting on the Douai Railway and on both sides of it against the front here held by the 7th Lincolns astride of the railway line.   The day was dawning, but there was a damp fog that made the range of vision very limited and so favoured the raiders.   But the raid was a failure and General Robertson, in reporting to Corps H.Q., noted that it failed on account of the strength of our wire, which was penetrated only at one point, and also because " the enemy employed faulty artillery methods which gave us adequate warning, and enabled our artillery and barrage machine guns to intervene effectively and interfere seriously with the raiding party during its advance."

The patrols of the Lincolns had as usual been out in No Man's Land during the night, but reported no sign of activity in the enemy's trenches, when they came in and " stood to " with the rest of the trench guard just before dawn.   The Germans threw away any chance of surprise that the fog might have given them, by opening a heavy bombardment on the Lincoln position as their raiding parties started on their advance.   This gave the opportunity for our gunners to put down a barrage, supplemented by the fire of trench mortars, and Vickers and Lewis guns from our front.   A wounded raider who was left in our hands said that the barrage caught the enemy well before he reached our wire and inflicted many casualties.   On three-fourths of the front attacked, in the cutting and on the ground immediately south and north of it, the raid was an immediate and complete failure.   The Germans nowhere got through the wire, and while it held them they came under an intense fire of rifles, machine guns and bombs, including rodded rifle grenades.   After a few moments of confusion they broke and disappeared into the fog, now made more opaque by the smoke and dust of the bombardment and barrage.   But on the extreme left of the Lincoln front a strong party of raiders with a machine gun found a weak point in the wire, cut it, hitched on a rope to pull it away, and made a gap through which they broke into the front trench. A Lewis gun that should have flanked the front here had been buried by the bombardment and was being dug out and cleared for action at the critical moment. Another gun had been knocked out by a direct hit from a heavy T.M. shell and the explosion had killed or wounded all near it. The enemy made a brief bomb fight in the trench before they were hustled out. They left some dead in it and one badly wounded man. Here and at other points near our wire seven boxes of high explosives were abandoned by the raiders. This was taken to be an indication that they hoped to penetrate to the support trenches and blow in their dugouts. A good deal of damage to the trenches was done by the German bombardment, and the casualties of the Lincolns by shell fire and in the fight on their left were 10 killed, 25 wounded and two missing, probably prisoners.[1]

The only other enemy raid was that attempted at dawn on September 24th, after a heavy bombardment of the front from the railway to the Scarpe. The raiders were stopped and driven back by our artillery and M.G. fire, leaving one prisoner in our hands, a wounded man who was found entangled in the wire. He was a private of the 368th Company of Pioneers.

On all the front of the Division our patrols were out every night in No Man's Land. On July 16th a patrol of the East Yorkshires found a cache of enemy war material in one of the abandoned communication trenches that traversed it. They retrieved and brought in from this find a Maxim gun, two light trench mortars, three Lewis guns and two boxes of spare parts. Prisoners were sometimes taken by the patrols. On August 23rd a

[1] With reference to the German raid of August 8th, General Sir Philip Robertson writes : " I find the following gallant act noted in my diary—after the raid—' During the morning nine Germans crept up to No. 2 Sap and threw a volley of bombs, wounding all the post of four men. 2nd Lt. Wicks and his orderly, who were there, at once killed three of them, then the rest bolted. Lt. Wicks shot two with his revolver.' " Sir Philip adds, " Wicks was, I think, a Sherwood. He was given the M.C. for the above act, but was killed on 16th September in the raid made that night by the Sherwoods."

private of the 464th Infantry Regiment was captured in the railway cutting.   Under examination by the Intelligence Officer he spoke very freely.   He belonged to the 3rd Battalion of his regiment, which was holding the trenches on each side of the railway.   No work was done in these trenches at night as they were strongly held from sunset to dawn with the trench guard " standing to," for there was constant expectation of a renewed British attack.   He said that everyone was confident as to the war ending at an early date, as the result of the Submarine Boat campaign.   The German troops had lately been assured that in the month of July the total British merchant shipping sunk by the U-Boats was 820,000 tons.[1]

There were several successful raids on the enemy trenches.   On July 15th at 10 p.m. the 7th Borders (51st Brigade) on the extreme left raided Wit Trench. Covered by a barrage the raiders got across No Man's Land in the darkness of a rainy night and lay down inside the wire waiting for the barrage to lift.   On the way a German sniper, lying out in a shell hole, was bayoneted before he could give the alarm.   The trench was lightly held and its guard bolted as the Borders rushed it.   They fired on the retreating enemy, explored the trench, found two dugouts under construction, and secured and carried off a machine gun.   In twenty minutes they fell back to the line, suffering some casualties from the barrage put down by the enemy.   After they were back in Conrad Trench in our front, they heard the Germans bombing up the communication trenches to Wit, under the impression that it was still occupied.   The conclusion from this raid was that the enemy's front trenches here were lightly held as a mere outpost line, and his real line of resistance

---

[1] This was a propagandist exaggeration, but the losses by submarine attacks were very serious in the spring and early summer of 1917, so serious that Admiral Sims of the U.S. Navy, who came to London as liaison officer with the British Admiralty soon after America's entrance into the War, was told that the losses were causing very grave anxiety, and were so heavy that the Admiralty did not publish the full totals in their monthly communiqués to the press.   In the summer the defence against the U-Boats began to improve rapidly.

was the support line. Suggestions were made that this first line should be rushed and held, and Divisional H.Q. even prepared plans for the operation, but the Corps Command did not give the necessary permission.

The accepted policy at this time was to stand fast and consolidate the ground we had won east of Arras. But G.H.Q. seems to have received more than once information suggesting that the Germans were preparing a retirement to the Drocourt-Quéant Switch line, and on two occasions elaborate instructions were sent to the Division for "action in the event of a German retirement." These instructions directed that a close watch should be kept for such an eventuality, and if a retreat began it should be followed up step by step, securing each evacuated trench line and pushing out patrols to keep touch with the retirement. The enemy however had no intention of going unless he was pushed back, and the new dugouts in Wit Trench showed he was busy strengthening his position on Greenland Hill.

On July 21st a raiding party from the 50th Brigade got into Wart Trench (the enemy front due west of the Hill); but the Germans bolted out of it so promptly and rapidly that neither prisoners nor identifications could be secured. A week later, shortly after midnight on July 29th, the enemy trenches on both sides of the Douai Railway cutting were raided by the 7th East Yorkshires, the wire in front of them having been cut by trench mortar fire a few hours earlier. The raid led to some sharp fighting, as south of the railway the enemy was repairing the wire and had a covering party out. The Germans here dashed forward to meet our raiders, but were outflanked and driven in, and not only the front line but the support trenches immediately in rear of it were cleared of the enemy. Three dugouts in the support trench were blown up, and the raiders brought back a machine gun and fourteen prisoners, privates of the 190th and 464th Infantry Regiments. The East Yorks lost in this successful raid 2 killed, 23 wounded and 8 missing: 33 casualties in all.   The enemy's loss was much heavier.

This was the most successful raid during the three months.   It gained a congratulatory message from the Army Commander, General Byng.   Raids on the same front in September, on the 8th and the night of the 16th-17th, found the enemy on the alert, but got into the front trenches, blew in a number of dugouts and brought back prisoners.[1]

On September 25th the relief of the 17th Division by the 61st began and was completed next day.   Divisional H.Q. were transferred to Le Cauroy and the troops were encamped and billetted in the Fosseux area between that place and Arras.   It was announced that the Division was now to leave the 17th Corps and be transferred to the Flanders front.

On September 24th, the day before the relief began, Lieut.-General Sir Charles Fergusson issued the following farewell message to the Division:

"On the occasion of the 17th Division leaving the 17th Corps, I wish to express to all ranks my appreciation of the fine soldierly spirit which has been conspicuous in the Division during the last few months, while serving on this front.

" Its activity in patrolling, its keenness in raids have both been admirable.   But most conspicuous of all has been the splendid spirit shown in the work done in consolidating the line.   In spite of weakness in numbers and the absence of the Pioneer Battalion, the work done has been remarkable, showing not only excellent organization on the part of the Staff, but also energy and zeal on the part of the regimental officers and men.   All ranks may be proud of their record in this respect, R.A. and R.E., as well as Infantry.

---

[1] The raids on the night of September 16th/17th were carried out by the Sherwoods and Manchesters.   At 9 p.m., covered by a barrage, the Sherwoods raided Crust Trench, in four parties, total strength 4 officers and 60 men, with an R.E. officer and 12 sappers.   Several dugouts were destroyed and one prisoner taken.   The raiders lost one officer (Lieut. Wicks) and two men killed and a few wounded.   At midnight the Manchesters raided Wit and Wool Trenches with a stronger party of 9 officers and 220 men, with an R.E. officer and 15 sappers.   There was some stiff fighting.   Five of six dugouts were blown in, and four prisoners and two machine guns taken.   Our losses were four or five men killed and three officers and about 25 men wounded.

" I wish goodbye and good luck to all in the Division, with every confidence that they will fully maintain the reputation they have gained wherever their duty may call them."

After its exceptionally prolonged tour of duty in the trenches the Division had only a few days' rest. On September 30th orders were received that in the first days of October it was to move to the Flanders front, where it would be attached to the 14th Corps, forming part of the Fifth Army.

On the afternoon of October 3rd the entrainment of the Division for the Flanders front began. Next day at noon Divisional H.Q. closed down at Le Cauroy to reopen at 6 o'clock that evening at Proven behind the Ypres front and four miles north-west of Poperinghe. The Division was assembling in the neighbouring camps as the trains arrived from Arras. Orders were received here from Corps H.Q. that, on the evening of the 5th, the 51st Brigade was to march about six miles westward to Herzeele village, on the other side of the Franco-Belgian frontier, to do a few days of intensive training in the neighbourhood. The Brigade was to be the first to go into the new front north of Ypres.

The great battle in Flanders had already lasted for two months. It had begun on July 31st, after a tremendous bombardment of the German lines for nine days and nights. Almost on the eve of the attack the enemy had abandoned the line of the Yser Canal and his ruined front trenches before Ypres, and the first day's fighting had secured an advance of from 1,000 to 3,000 yards in depth on a front of nearly fifteen miles. Instead of the sharp and dangerous salient, we now had a new front on a long flatly curving line, with a footing on the high ground the enemy had held for years. It was a success that seemed to presage the reconquest of Western Belgium.

But on this first day of the advance the fine weather abruptly ended, and a persistent deluge of rain began that

The Advance North of Ypres, August to November, 1917.

lasted all through August. There was slightly better weather in September, but the downpour began again in October. Under these conditions, with even the higher ground deep in mud and the wide flats between the hills and the water-line of the Yser converted into a morass, progress became a slow and costly business. There were days of battle when another step forward was made, and a narrow zone was won on ground where all ordinary features had disappeared in a tangle of water-logged shell holes, with the streams and drainage channels blocked here and there with débris and spreading into wide pools and deep swamps. The tanks had been helpful on the first day. After that they were helpless, and many of them came to such swift disaster that there was some peril of the new arm being permanently discredited. Our men were fighting their way forward step by step against the lines of wired defences full of strong points of a new type—concrete machine gun nests, the little forts that our men knew as " pill-boxes," and ruined buildings concreted into improvised fortresses. Both sides in this long battle in the new swamps of Flanders suffered endless misery and losses that finally exceeded even the terrible total of the Somme.

By the end of September the original plan of the capture of the Ypres ridges being only the prelude to a joint naval and military attack on the German coast fortresses from Ostend to Zeebrugge, and a push for Bruges and Ghent, had been abandoned, and the objective was the winning of the Passchendaele Ridge and a line along the lower undulations of the ground south of Houthulst Forest. For the left of our advance this meant pushing onward over the water-logged and cratered flats on both sides of the railways that run north-east from Ypres to Staden and Roulers.

When the 17th Division reached Flanders, in the first days of October, the 14th Corps, under Lord Cavan, formed the extreme left of the British line, next to the sector where the French contingent was operating. Lord Cavan had the 29th Division astride of the Ypres-Bruges-Staden railway near the road that runs north from Poelcappelle[1] to Houthulst Forest, with the Guards Division facing the margin of the Forest north of the line on the left, and the 4th Division on the right. The 17th Division was presently to relieve the 29th in the centre.

When the Division was withdrawn from the Arras front in September it was greatly reduced in strength. Several of its battalions had only 50 per cent of their full numbers and every one was more or less short of its full war establishment. At G.H.Q. during the summer and early autumn this front east of Arras had been classed as " a quiet sector," and little or nothing had been done to make up for wastage of trench warfare. The anxious time was beginning when the problem of man-power was by no means an easy one. It was not only that besides re-cruiting for the army, a huge navy had to be kept manned, and workers provided for mine and factory and munition works, but besides this, if we take into account our commitments in the various " side shows " that had developed since 1914, it might be said that land forces were being maintained not for one but for several wars. Then there was the great army maintained at home, and the numbers of officers and men necessarily employed in various subsidiary but essential services behind the Western Front. It is no wonder that " quiet sectors " were in danger of being starved of a due allowance of reinforcing drafts.

[1] The Flemish word " poel " means " pool, swamp, morass," so the village name of " Poelcappelle " means " the Church in the Swamps." It throws some light on the condition of the adjacent flat country before its network of drains was dug and its streams were embanked. The name was fully justified in these autumn days of 1917, when the whole drainage system was knocked to pieces, the banks of the streams broken down, and the ground closely pitted with shell craters, while weeks of heavy rain had brought down flood upon flood from the higher ground to the eastward about Westoutre and Passchen-daele, and the lower heights of the Forest and the spurs of rising ground running west from the Passchendaele Ridge.

As the Division moved up to Flanders, and during the few days before it went into the line, there was a hurried and belated effort to make up at least some part of its wastage. The experience of one battalion—the 7th Lincolns—may be taken as typical. They came out of the trenches before Greenland Hill with a strength reduced to about 450 of all ranks. On the way north, and during the few days at Herzeele before going into the line and into action, the battalion received drafts amounting in all to 275 men, bringing its strength up to a little over 700. The new arrivals were all men of middle age, " combed out " by the Q.M.G. from detachments doing duty on the Lines of Communication, and from Kite Sections, etc. Before being sent off in the draft, numbers of them had been given such hasty musketry instruction as they could gain from firing some twenty rounds on a miniature range at the Base. They were keen enough, and their goodwill was worthy of all praise, but by no stretch of the imagination could they be classed as " trained soldiers." They learned something by working and drilling with the older hands at Herzeele, and every opportunity was taken for special training and lectures by the Company officers. Particular emphasis was laid upon the necessity of keeping close up to our creeping barrage, and their conduct in action showed they had grasped the lesson that this gave the best chance of getting through safely and successfully.

The training of the 51st Brigade at Herzeele was shortened to three days. On October 8th it began its march back to take over the new front, and next day the machine gunners of the 17th Division began relieving those of the 29th. The relief was completed in the night between the 10th and 11th, and on the morning of the 11th the 17th Division held the sector, with one Brigade in the front line, the other two in support and reserve and its Divisional Artillery covering the ground in front. Divisional Headquarters were moved that

morning from Proven Central Camp to the château of
Elverdinghe, near the starting point of the light railway
system on the west side of the Yser Canal.   Orders had
been issued for a new advance of the British left next day
—Friday, October 12th—with zero hour at 5.25 a.m. in
the autumn twilight about half an hour before sunrise.
There had been heavy rain on the 10th.   Next day there
were some signs of better weather, but on that Thursday
evening the sky was packed with heavy low-lying clouds,
and as the troops moved into their assembly stations there
began a downpour of cold rain that lasted for hours.
The night was pitch dark, and the rain helped to conceal
from the enemy the preparations for our attack.   On the
front held by the 51st Brigade these took a new form that
entailed some risk, but as the event proved it was a risk
that under the circumstances was worth taking, and the
bad weather probably helped to its success.

There was no regular trench system on the front held
by the Division, this front line being nothing but strings
of shell-holes protected by a very incomplete stretch of
wire.   Its total length was about 1,600 yards, astride of
the Ypres-Staden railway, and extending about 500
yards to the north of it.   On its extreme left it linked up
with the Guards Division, the front of which formed an
obtuse angle with its line, the Guards facing north
towards the outskirts of Houthulst Forest and forming
a defensive flank to the position held by the 14th Corps.
On the right of the 17th Division, the 4th prolonged the
front to near the ruins of Poelcappelle.

In this stage of the Flanders Battle fixed and limited
objectives were assigned for each advance.   There was
no attempt to push on to any considerable depth ; what was
aimed at was a moderate gain on the front, and when the
further boundary line of the captured zone was reached
there was a halt for the time being to consolidate (so far
as consolidation was possible on this semi-fluid ground),
and begin preparations for another forward step, a few

days later.[1] The objectives assigned to the 51st Brigade
would mean the pushing back of the enemy's front for
about 600 yards in two successive bounds, each of about

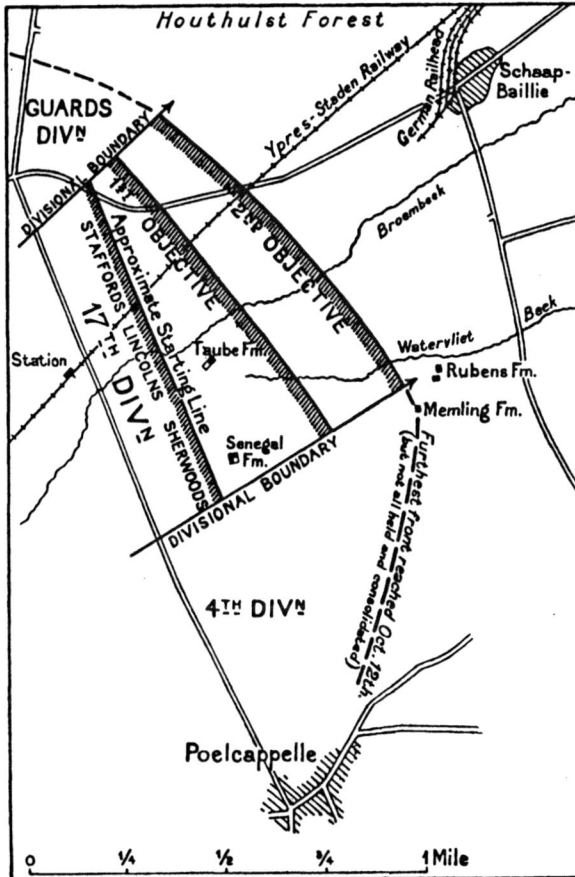

Action of October 12, 1917.

[1] Under existing conditions this was sound policy, but it had sometimes its
inevitable drawbacks. Thus, for instance, on October 30th the objective was
a line in the outskirts of Passchendaele. There is no doubt that when this line
was won the enemy was so badly beaten that there was a kind of panic, in which
the village was for a short time evacuated and at our mercy. It was reoccupied
by hurrying up the German troops that had been held in reserve for a counter-
attack, and it was not captured till November 9th after hard fighting.

half this depth. The two lines to be reached by the assault
were defined only by co-ordinates on the squared map, for
in this flat war-wasted tract of ground on the Brigade front
there were no dominant or prominent features to be
assigned to the first and second objectives.

The ground over which the advance was to be made was
a waste of mud, cratered with shell holes, with wide pools
along the line of the flooded Broembeek, south of the
railway; ruined farm-buildings here and there converted
into strong points; concrete pill-boxes, and lines of
shell-holes organised as a substitute for trenches. The
difficulty of movement across such ground may be judged
from the fact that the creeping barrage covering the
advance was to move forward at the rate of only a hundred
yards in ten minutes. The Corps artillery was to put
down lines of barrage on the communications of the
enemy's front.

The 8th South Staffords were to attack on the left,
north of the railway, the 7th Lincolns in the centre
immediately south of it, and the 10th Sherwood Foresters
on the right, where the 7th Borders were to follow in
close support. Of course there could be no question of
preparing assembly trenches. A line of shell holes was
the front from which the attack would start, but a novel
plan was adopted, and after dark, covered by patrols in
No Man's Land, tape lines were laid out, on which the
battalions were to assemble in advance of the front. In
dense darkness, under a steady downpour the battalions
massed in close order on these lines. They were to open
out into successive waves for the attack in the first stage of
the advance, and it was hoped—and the hope was realised
—that quickly as the German barrage might come down,
most of the assaulting battalions would be out in front of
it by the time its descent began. If this massed assembly
were discovered by the enemy before zero hour it would
have drawn a destructive fire under conditions that would
have made swift and serious losses inevitable. But the

absolute silence of the men, the mud that muffled every footfall, the torrent of rain that intensified the darkness, and the careful patrolling out in front, all combined to conceal the situation to the last moment. An enemy patrol of seven men was encountered, in front of the Brigade centre and close up to it, but they were all bayonetted without one escaping to give the alarm.

In the twilight at 5.25 a.m. our barrage opened and the advance began. The enemy's barrage was slow in opening and somewhat irregular. On the Divisional front it mostly came down along the Poelcappelle-Houthulst road, and the advancing battalions almost entirely escaped it. What few losses there were, were mostly in keeping close to our own barrage. But the Germans opened a heavy machine gun fire, and on the left the Staffords were caught badly in it and had many casualties at the very outset, including several of their officers. They slightly lost direction, getting out of touch with the nearest Guards Battalion on their left, and crowding to their right. This left a post of the enemy for awhile immune from attack, and the machine guns installed there were firing into the right rear of the Guards after the first objective was won.

This was for the 51st Brigade a line running at right angles across the railway, east of the road, and crossing south of the railway line the swampy course of two streams, the Broembeek and the Watervlietbeek. To reach it several strong points established in ruined buildings had to be dealt with. By eight o'clock the whole objective on the Brigade front had been won. The enemy put up a good fight at most points, and reinforcements were rushed up to support the defence. According to the accounts of prisoners these suffered considerable loss in coming through our heavy barrages. On the right, the 4th Division made slower progress, coming under a cross fire from Poelcappelle, and a defensive flank had to be formed on this side.

In the centre, one of the strong points was passed without being explored and " mopped up "—the result apparently of the garrison, dazed by our shell fire, having themselves ceased firing, and our men, in their eagerness to get forward, missing it. Its capture was a curious incident. Major Peddie, D.S.O., of the Lincolns, the Signalling Officer, Captain King, and an orderly carrying a basket of messenger pigeons, were following up the advance when, as they approached the concreted ruin, a crowd of Germans came streaming out of it. There was however no fight in them, and many of them were in a pitiable condition on the verge of complete shell shock. They were apparently the garrison of the strong point plus a number of fugitives who had taken cover there. The three Lincolns were unarmed, for the orderly had lost his rifle when he slipped into a flooded shell hole on the way up and thought only of saving his pigeons; the Major had left his pistol at Battalion H.Q. and the Signalling Officer, though he wore a revolver, had no cartridges. But the Germans were anxious only to surrender and they were sent back in charge of the orderly, some 90 in all being thus captured. The orderly summed up the situation by saying:

" The Bosches came out of their pill-box, and we had nothing to shoot them with but a basket of blinking pigeons."

By 11 a.m. the second and final objective was won—up to time-table. The right of the Brigade was now at the apex of a sharp salient at Memling Farm, the result of the advance of the 4th Division on this side being delayed and partly held up. Two companies of the Borders had been pushed in here to prevent a dangerous gap. From Memling Farm the new front ran back at an angle to Requette Farm near Poelcappelle. Such consolidation as was possible was now begun. The Germans did not even attempt a counter-attack, and in front of the Brigade all that could be seen of them was a confused group along the hollow of Watervlietbeek, out of which they were shelled by our gunners. Here and there groups held on in shell holes out in front, and there was some desultory firing during the afternoon. But by noon the battle was over. Poelcappelle had been cleared by the Division attacking south of the Corps front, and that flank was now secure.

The Brigade took 218 prisoners (nine of them officers). They belonged to thirteen different battalions. The captures included also an abandoned field gun and four machine guns. Such a good supply of ammunition was taken with these that they were mounted and in action on our new front next day. It was a very satisfactory morning's work, all the more because an attack over the same ground had failed with heavy loss not many days before. General Lord Cavan, the Corps Commander, telegraphed in the evening to General Robertson:

"Well done everybody. Wonderful performance in awful conditions. Hearty congratulations to you and all your great troops."

The line won that day by the 17th Division represented the furthest advance made on this flank during the operations of this autumn in Belgium. A little further east on the higher ground of the Passchendaele Ridge the push was continued until the first fortnight of November, but under the " awful conditions " prevailing on the lower lands it was decided, after the fight of October 12th, that further progress was for the time being out of the question—this although a few days before staff maps had been marked with the lines for further objectives that were to include finally the capture of the enemy's railheads about Schaap-Baillie. The whole campaign in Flanders was being smothered in mud and brought to a dead stop like Napoleon's operations in East Prussia in the winter after Jena, when he said that he had discovered that besides earth, air, fire and water there was sometimes a fifth element to be reckoned with in war, and that was mud.

Arrangements were therefore made for holding the ground that had been won, through the coming winter. It was decided to modify the line so as to get rid of the

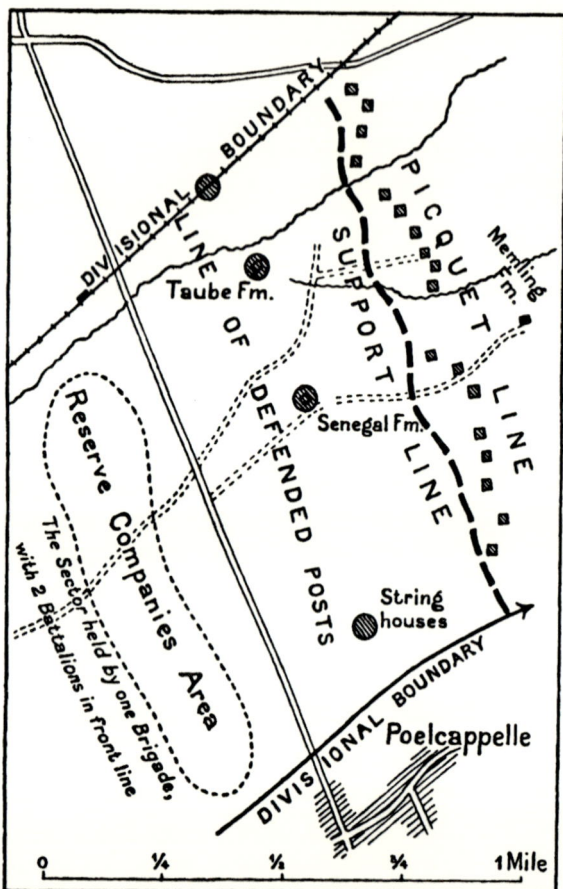

Front consolidated and held by the 17th Division after the action.

sharp salient at Memling Farm, and a new alignment was marked out and occupied by a slight withdrawal of part of the front. The Division took over the front on its right flank up to the outskirts of Poelcappelle and handed

over to the Guards Division its left front north of and
including the Ypres-Staden railway, which became a well
defined Divisional boundary on that side. Two battalions
held the new front, with a picket and support line established in shell holes, and four strong posts in the rear of
these east of the Poelcappelle-Houthulst road. West of
the road the reserve companies were given some improvised shelter and the Battalion H.Q.s were installed
here.

Weather conditions made it impossible to keep the
men in the front line for more than a few days at a time,
and in the posts of the picket and support line the stay
was limited to two days. So great was the difficulty of
bringing up supplies that the men occupying these
points brought their two days' rations with them. The
lines of communication were not trenches, but mere
duck board tracks on the ground level through a wide
expanse of mud, and running between the margins of
shell craters. The enemy's aircraft and artillery were
very active. The German airmen marked the tracks and
the gunners kept them under intermittent fire. New
tracks were made as alternatives to minimise danger and
loss, but it was impossible to conceal them. The movement along these narrow lines was always risky, and a
stumble in the dark might mean death. Men were
drowned, or rather suffocated in the deep mud of the
shell craters. Others were half-buried in them, and sometimes not discovered till daylight, when it was sometimes
a difficult business to extricate them. There were cases
of men sunk above the waist line, who could be rescued
only by taking the risk of putting a rope round them, and
dragging them out by main force. The rainy nights
were intensely cold. Leather jackets were provided for
some of the guards of the picket and support line, but
there were not enough for all. Even with shortened
tours of duty and every effort to provide abundant rations
and warm clothing, the sick list rose steadily and each

twenty-four hours had its casualty list from the shell fire
of the enemy artillery and the day and night bombing of
his aircraft.

In the earlier days of this trying time on the Flanders
front the Division was visited by a distinguished officer
of the American Army, General O'Ryan, U.S.A.,
commanding the 27th (New York) Division. (Before the
end of the war he rose to be first a Corps and then an
Army Commander.) With some of his staff officers he
was the guest of General Robertson at Elverdinghe
Château, saw the troops both on parade and in the line,
and made a careful study of our army methods. At the
end of the month he wrote to the G.O.C.:

> Hôtel de Crillon, Paris.
> 29th October, 1917.
>
> My dear General Robertson,
>   After leaving you at Elverdinghe we were for a time
> with the 31st Division in the vicinity of Arras, and for the past
> ten days were with the French during the attack north-east of
> Soissons.
>   General, I want you to know that we appreciate very much
> indeed the manner in which you received us and made us feel part
> of you. Our experiences with your army were most instructive,
> and I am sure we shall find them profitable in the future.
>   I hope to have you visit my division, which is the New York
> Division (27th), after it arrives here and gets settled. Be assured
> of a warm welcome.
>   The other officers join in sending you best wishes.
> Sincerely yours,
> John F. O'Ryan,
> Major-General U.S. Army.
>
> To Major-General P. R. Robertson, C.B., C.M.G.,
>   Commanding 17th Division, B.E.F.

On the night of October 13th/14th the 50th Brigade,
which had been in support about Langemarck and Pilkem,
relieved the 51st, which went into reserve near Elverdinghe, the 52nd moving up into the support position.
On the night of the 16th/17th the 57th Division took

over the sector. The H.Q. of the 17th Division were transferred to Proven Central Camp, where there was rest for a few days, and then a move on the 20th to the Recques training area west of St. Omer. Two days after reaching the training area, the 51st Brigade was suddenly ordered back to Proven as Corps Reserve, and entrained at very short notice. On reaching Proven it was ordered to take over the front held by the 35th Brigade, north of the Ypres-Staden railway in the Wijdendrift sector, facing the enemy's position on the south-west margin of the Houthulst Forest. The troops thus relieved were in a very exhausted condition after a long tour of duty on a front that was mostly made up of posts in badly-cratered and waterlogged ground with little shelter of any kind. The 51st Brigade held the line here for a few days. They were then relieved and returned to Corps Reserve in the Proven area. Here on November 7th they rejoined the remainder of the 17th Division, which on that day entrained at Recques for Proven and Elverdinghe to take over again the front it had held in October.

The Division held the sector for a month, under an accentuated form of the " awful conditions " of October. Hard frost and dry weather would have meant more cold, but it would have been tolerable and would have made life comparatively easy. But instead of changing weather, with snaps of early winter frost, there were days and nights of almost ceaseless cold rain. The troops were living and moving in a morass under frequent bursts of gunfire, with intermittent and poisonous experiences of the horrible new mustard gas shells, and bombing raids of enemy aircraft. It was no longer trench warfare, but mud-hole warfare. After the capture of Passchendaele on November 9th any idea of a further advance even on the Ridge had been abandoned. But the menace of an advance was maintained, and the enemy was still anxious about his Flanders front. A change of weather might make renewed operations possible, so the Germans still kept a huge army massed on our front. In November, prisoners taken by patrols and deserters confirmed the information obtained by our Intelligence Department that the enemy, with his hands freed in Eastern Europe by the Russian collapse, was moving several Divisions westward. Some of these reinforcements reached Flanders. In the last week of October German troops had reinforced the Austrians on the Alpine front and our Italian Allies had suffered the disaster of Caporetto. Their armies were being hustled back across the Venetian plain and soon British and French divisions were being hurried to Italy to avert a catastrophe. Thus, as the Flanders offensive came to a dead stop in the mud, there were omens of the tremendous crisis of the new year.

At the end of November there came rumours that the enemy was preparing a withdrawal in Flanders, like the retirement of the Hindenburg line after the long-drawn battle of the Somme. On November 29th the Staff Diary of the Division recorded that: " In view of an intercepted German wireless—' Dismantling wireless '— all concerned were informed of a probable enemy withdrawal." Orders were issued for keeping close watch for the first stage of the expected move and for following it up. But nothing happened, and the message intercepted probably referred only to the shifting of some local wireless post in the hostile line.

Apart from this disappointed hope the month in the sector was a time of dreary routine and patient endurance. The three Brigades took their turn in reserve, support and front line.[1] The probable outlook was that of tours

[1] The Brigade movements in this last month in Flanders may be thus tabulated :

		In Divisional Reserve.	In Support.	In the Front.
Nov. 7-13	-	51st Brigade.	50th Brigade.	52nd Brigade.
,, 14-19	-	52nd ,,	51st ,,	50th ,,
,, 20-25	-	50th ,,	52nd ,,	51st ,,
,, 26-30	-	51st ,,	50th ,,	52nd ,,
Dec. 1-5	-	52nd ,,	51st ,,	50th ,,

of duty in the line with alternate short periods of rest
behind it all through the winter. But in the first week of
December there came a welcome and unexpected move
from Flanders.

In the late hours of the evening on December 5th, the
35th Division completed the relief of the 17th in the sector.
The Division concentrated west of the Yser line and began
to move by train to Recques area near St. Omer, where,
on December 8th, Divisional H.Q. were established at
the château of Cocove. Three days later came orders
from G.H.Q. that the Division was to be held ready to move
at short notice to the Third Army Area—*i.e.* to the front
extending from the old ground east of Arras to the
trenches before Cambrai and St. Quentin.

During these first days of December G.H.Q. had been
anxiously taking Divisions from other parts of the line to
reinforce the Third Army. On its front great events
had been happening. In November, by masterly organisation a surprise attack on the enemy front covering
Cambrai had been prepared, and a leading feature in
these preparations had been the secret concentration of
a large array of the new tanks. The scheme was based
on our knowledge that the German front here had been
weakened, the enemy's attention being riveted on Flanders
and his offensive in Italy. The attack was launched on
November 20th, and at the outset was brilliantly successful. Some unfortunate accidents prevented its full
results being secured, and during the days of hard fighting
that followed the enemy hurried up reinforcements.
There was a lull in the battle, and then on November 30th
the Germans carried out a successful counter-attack with
a surprise at the outset. The result of hard fighting in
the first week of December was that some of the ground
we had won was lost, and on our right the enemy gained
part of the trench system we had held in our own front
for many weeks before the battle opened on November
20th. When the new orders reached the Division the

battle was over.   The front before Cambrai was being
reorganised and Divisions that had suffered heavily
during a fortnight of close fighting were being withdrawn
from the line and replaced by others.   The 17th Division

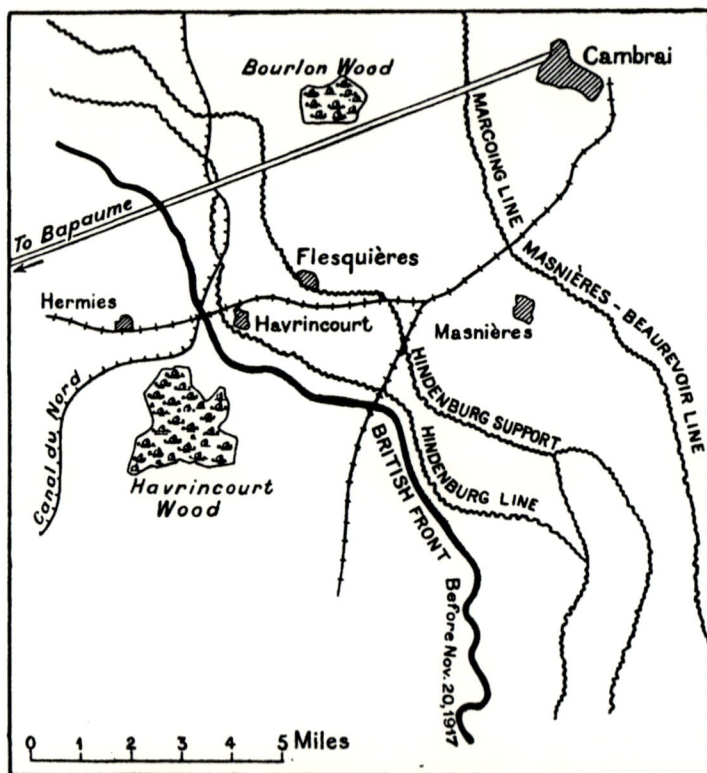

British Front and Main German defence lines before the
Battle of Cambrai.

was now held in reserve as available for these reliefs, and
the order to be ready to move at short notice meant that
G.H.Q. was not quite certain that the enemy would not
renew his counter-attacks.

On December 13th orders were received for a move

eastwards to begin that evening. Next day Divisional
H.Q. were transferred to Achiet-le-Petit, a village on the
margin of the old Somme battlefields, about four miles
west of Bapaume. The troops, as they detrained after
a long and cold journey from St. Omer, were encamped
and billeted in and around the neighbouring villages,
some of them as far east as Le Transloy.

Here it was hard frosty weather with some snow on the
ground, but it was a relief from the conditions on the
Flanders front. Some of the villagers and farmers had
already returned to the former battle-ground, and were
at work rebuilding their ruined or badly damaged homes
and making the first efforts to clear and cultivate a bit of
land, in happy, hopeful ignorance of the near future, when
the war storm would pass and again repass over the same
ground that it had already wasted.

The Division was now the reserve of the 5th Corps
which was holding the front before Cambrai. The
scheme for the defence of this part of the line was received
and all units of the Division were ordered to reconnoitre
the routes for an early move up to it. On the 16th the
Pioneer Battalion and the R.E. Field Companies were
sent forward to work on the reorganisation of the line,
and the Divisional Artillery began its march to the front.
On December 21st the Division took over from the 47th
Division the left sector of the 5th Corps front. The
Division was to hold the northern face of a sharp salient
opposite Bourlon Wood west of Cambrai. Its right was
near the village of Flesquières; behind the front line were
the villages of Hermies and Havrincourt—all names to
be famous in the coming year. The 17th Division was
now in the position which it so gloriously defended when
the great German offensive of March, 1918, bore back
the British line along a front of miles right and left of the
Flesquières salient. But here the Division held its own,
only retiring when at last to hold on any longer would
have meant complete isolation and destruction. It was

the most splendid episode in the record of the Division, and the heroic prelude of a long series of great days, first in the dogged fighting of the long retreat in the face of overwhelming odds, and then in the victorious advance that ended the war.

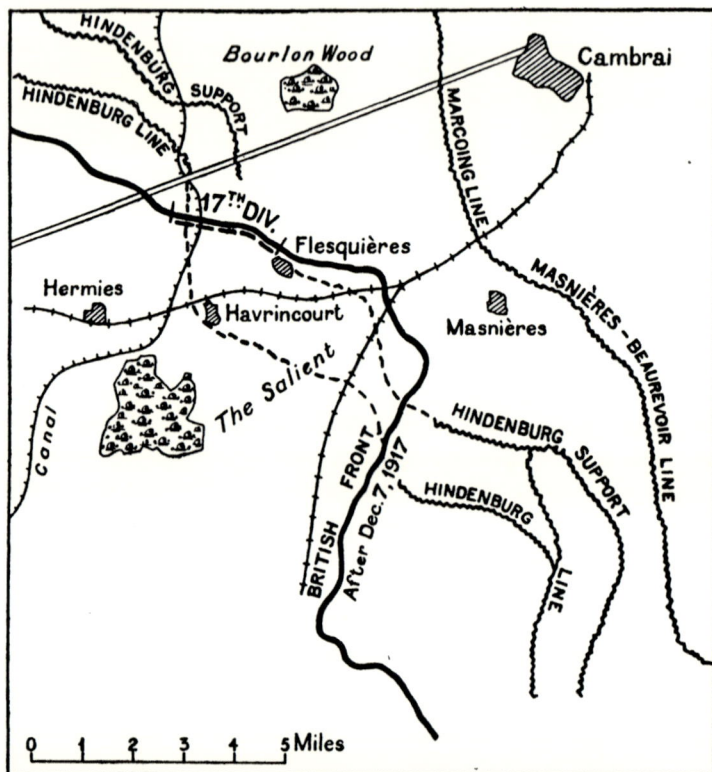

Salient towards Cambrai, formed as result of the Battle and the German counter-attack.

CHAPTER VIII

THE OPENING OF THE GREAT GERMAN
OFFENSIVE (1918)

WHEN the Division took its place in the Third Army front near Cambrai in the last days of December, 1917, there was among all who gave any serious thought to the immediate future a fair certainty that the New Year would bring a time of trial. Prophecy is always a thankless business in war time, for, even for those who are in possession of all the essential facts, there is an element of incalculable chance that often defeats the most careful attempts to predict results. During the first three years of this tremendous war optimistic prophets of a coming decision had fared so badly, and patriotic forecasts of early and wide-reaching success had so often ended in disappointment, that most people had settled down to a patient expectation of the long-drawn struggle ending at last in victory, but a victory that would most likely be won after living through many anxious days like those that had followed the first failures of 1914.

The gigantic scale of the operations made it difficult even for those who were actively engaged in them to know much more than what was happening in the particular front where they were employed. As for the great mass of the people at home, under modern war conditions a rigid censorship and a well-organised patriotic propaganda necessarily keeps them ill-informed as to what is really happening, and often gives them a very misleading idea of the situation of the moment and the possibilities of the immediate future.

But at the opening of the New Year in 1918, the broad dominant facts of the situation were so plain that it was hardly possible to conceal them, and once they were realised it was easy to read their significance. It required neither political insight nor military judgment to grasp the obvious fact that the collapse of the Allied Eastern front in Europe had radically altered the whole situation in the West; and that, while we were still waiting for the promised reinforcements from America, Germany would be able to concentrate superior forces for the attack of our main war front. A great German offensive with many factors favouring at least its temporary success for the enemy was inevitable.

That broad fact was clear enough. But there were two points open to debate. First, what was the earliest date at which the enemy could complete his preparations for the offensive, and launch it under conditions of ground and weather that would favour a gigantic and continuous advance? Before Verdun in 1916 the attack had come in February, so any preparations for defence must be pushed through in the first six weeks of the New Year. Then there was the question of what part of our Western front would be attacked. The French High Command persisted in the belief that it would be the front in Champagne. The British G.H.Q. made the correct forecast that the most likely point of attack would be the right of our line between Arras and the Oise, with a specially heavy blow directed against the extreme right to effect a break through between the two Allied armies, French and British.

The Sector assigned to the 17th Division was thus on the fighting front of the expected attack, which began precisely three months after its coming into the line on December 21st, 1917. These three months were a time of assiduous preparation for the coming crisis. Before noting some minor incidents of the time, it may be well to say something of special features of this period of waiting and working, and of the general scheme of defence adopted.

On December 7th Sir Douglas Haig had held a conference with the five Army Commanders to consider a scheme of defence for the threatened front. It was approximately a front of some sixty miles from the trenches east of Arras southward to the Oise valley. The plan adopted was the organisation of three lines of defence, on a depth of from four to six miles. The three lines were known as the Forward Zone, the Battle Zone, and the Rear Zone. The Forward Zone was to consist of two sections, subsequently known as the Advanced and the Intermediate Systems. Of these the former was to be treated as an outpost line. It lay along the existing front lines, and on these at intervals of about 2,000 yards there were to be constructed redoubts and machine gun-nests, placed so as to bring a cross fire on the enemy's advance between them and break up his attack. The Intermediate System was to be the support of this advanced line. Behind this lay a deep belt of defences, the real line of resistance, divided for purposes of organisation into a Second and Third System, and known as the " Battle Zone." It was to be elaborately wired and studded with strong points, and there was a not unreasonable expectation that the attack, after suffering heavy loss in coming through the Forward Zone at any point, would be held by this formidable defence system.

But the possibility of its being forced in places was kept in view and was to be provided for by creating a " Rear Zone," which, however, was very incomplete when the attack came. Still further back plans were worked out for meeting what was then regarded as the remote possibility of a retirement. The bridges of the Somme were to be prepared for demolition, and bridgeheads were to be constructed for the defence of the reach of the river from Peronne southwards. This elaborate defence scheme would entail an immense amount of hard work, and, as the event proved, the weeks before the crisis came were an insufficient time for its completion.   Behind the Battle Zone little was accomplished and in the Battle Zone itself on the right in the Fifth Army Area (where some miles of front were taken over from our Allies) the plan was in places only partly realised.   This was the result of insufficient man power, that made it an all but insoluble problem to provide the working parties and at the same time carry out the ordinary routine of the front and find time for giving the troops a thorough training for the defence of the system.

It will be remembered that when the 17th Division moved to Flanders in the autumn of 1917 its battalions were all under strength and it was by no means easy to provide drafts for them.   As the winter went on the situation as to man-power became more serious.   In a despatch, published long after, Sir Douglas Haig told of the difficulties of the time, but a vital passage was suppressed.   " The lack of adequate reinforcements," he said, " and my constant inability to keep the ranks of the fighting units within a reasonable measure of their establishment gave me cause of anxiety.   The strenuous efforts made by the British forces during 1917 had left the Army at a low ebb in regard both to training and numbers."[1]

The anxieties of the time were increased by persistent requests of the French Government and its General Staff for the British Army to take over a longer front.   It was even suggested that, to make matters easier for our Allies, we should extend our line along the Aisne front as far as Berry-au-Bac, north-west of Rheims.   Finally an extension as far as Barisis, a little south of the Oise, was agreed to, and this meant that two Divisions had to be provided to take over the new front.

In February the difficulty of keeping our battalions

---

[1] The first of these two sentences was cut out when the despatch was published, and did not appear till the complete edition of Sir Douglas Haig's despatches was published after the war was over.

something near fighting strength was met by an expedient
that had serious drawbacks.   The organisation of our
Infantry Divisions on the Western Front, with the exception of those of the Colonials, was radically changed by
reducing the number of Battalions in each Brigade from
four to three.   The Division would thus have, including
its Pioneer Battalion, ten infantry units instead of thirteen.
The Battalions thus taken out of the Brigades were to be
disbanded and their officers and men allotted in drafts to
other units of the Regiment to which they belonged.
The change not only introduced a new tactical working
of the Brigades in action, but altered disadvantageously
the conditions for holding the trenches.   With three
battalions instead of four each unit had to spend a longer
time in the front line, while the Brigade was doing its
tour of trench duty; there was a smaller reserve on which
to draw for working parties, and this too at a time when
extra work had to be done; and it was by no means easy to
give the men any time for rest or training.   That recourse
was had to change like this, in order to have three fairly
strong battalions instead of four weak ones, shows how
serious the problem of man-power had become.

The front taken over by the Division in the last days of
December was slightly modified after it was occupied,
but the change thus made amounted only to a slight
extension on the left.   The front line, as thus finally
organised, began on the right at a sunken road, just west
of Flesquières village, and was nearly two miles long,
running in a generally westerly direction across the hollow
of the Canal du Nord to a low spur of the higher ground
north-east of Hermies village, and between the line of
the Canal and the Bapaume-Cambrai road.   The depth
of the area to be held behind this front, with the help of
successive defence zones—largely to be reorganised or
constructed in the coming three months—was over
10,000 yards, or nearly six miles.

The ground then occupied by the British front before

Defence of the Hermies-Havrincourt Sector, and distribution of the 17th Division on the eve of the German Attack.

Cambrai—of which the Flesquières salient formed a most important part—belongs to the eastward fringe of the uplands that extend from Cape Gris Nez between the valley of the Somme and the plain of French Flanders and Southern Belgium. It is a chalk country, and in remote ages of geological time it was linked up with our own South Downs. Shakespeare's Cliff and Gris Nez still mark the wide rift that cut through the chalk ridge and made the British Channel. These uplands of northern France are known to French geographers as the " Collines d'Artois," but the " hills " are nowhere of any great height. The features of the country are not as bold as those of our South Downs. It is mostly a plateau, rising here and there into low ridges and furrowed by the streams that run on one side to the Somme and on the other to the Scheldt.

The head stream of the Scheldt, here near its source, runs down a hollow to the east of Flesquières, presently to flow past Cambrai about eight miles away to the northeast. The cathedral and the tall factory chimneys of the city were in sight, on any fine day, from the low spurs right and left of the Divisional front. Nearer at hand and due north was the forest-crowned knoll of Bourlon Hill, an outlier of the high ground which we held.

The most important feature of this ground in the sector assigned to the 17th Division was the ridge on which stand the villages of Hermies, Havrincourt and Flesquières, then all more or less in ruins. One of its higher points, a knoll close to Hermies, reaches the 120 metre level, but its general elevation is about 100. Towards the front the ground falls in easy slopes, with long spurs pushed out over them, but the difference of elevation between the general level of the ridge crest and the lowest ground in front is nowhere more than 70 or 80 feet.

Through the ridge, midway between Hermies and Havrincourt, ran the deep cutting of the Canal du Nord, after following on its south side the hollow between the ridge and the high ground of Havrincourt Forest.   The Canal, which formed an important tactical feature in many of the later battles of the war, was still " under construction " and for a considerable part of its long course—as here before Cambrai—there was as yet no water in it, and great masses of chalk and surface clay, brought up by the excavators, encumbered its banks at several points. It was nearing completion, for work had begun upon it as long ago as 1903, and it was intended that it should be finished by 1917, but nothing had been done since August 1914.   It was to link up Paris and Central France with the industrial and mining regions of the north, its southern terminal being at Noyon on the Oise and its north at Douai on the Scarpe, by which its traffic would reach the Scheldt and the Belgian waterways.   In this country west of Cambrai the Germans, in fixing the plans for the Hindenburg line, had made it run for some miles close to the Canal cuttings, which, where they were still dry, formed a sheltered roadway, and barriers often more difficult to cross than a narrow waterline would have been.

The Flesquières salient was a result of the wide breach made in the Hindenburg Line and its Support at the Battle of Cambrai in November, 1917.   The greater part of the front line held by the 17th Division west of Flesquières was actually on the captured section of the Hindenburg Support.   Its extreme left cut across the Hindenburg Line itself.   From this point the captured Hindenburg defences lay nearly north and south (and thus vertical to the general lie of the front) through the Divisional sector, following very nearly the west bank of the Canal.   Just below the final rise of the ridge it turned east, crossing the canal cutting and passing over the crest of the high ground at Havrincourt.

In reorganising the position some portions of the Hindenburg Line entrenchments could be worked into the new scheme, but in several ways it rather complicated than facilitated the problem of reconstruction. Its captured trenches on the two-mile section along the Canal presented a flank to the enemy, were open to enfilade, and were now in the position that suggested lines of communication rather than of defence   Throughout, the wide ditch and the broad tangle of wire obstructions were on the wrong side of the line.   Helpful in places, the captured line entailed a tremendous amount of difficult work in the remodelling of the position.

When the Division took over the Sector just before Christmas, 1917, the Germans were busy constructing new lines of defence from the point where the Hindenburg Line and Support were cut north of Hermies, eastwards along our new front, and well in advance of the Marcoing and Masnières-Beaurevoir line that covered Cambrai, and was the reserve position of the Hindenburg system. It was just a fortnight since the end of the Cambrai battle and on the front of the Divisional sector a good deal of useful consolidation work had been done.   The trenches of the Hindenburg support had been " turned " to the new front, and linked up west of the Canal with our old front line on this side.   The new lines of defence had been marked out and some work begun upon them, but all this was only the preliminary to many weeks of continuous work by day and night on the projected " Forward," " Battle " and " Rear Zones " of the new defence system.

For the officers and men of the Division the move from the waterlogged flats of the Flanders front to these uplands of Artois was a welcome change.   It was fine wintry weather.   There was some snow on the ground and there was hard frost at night, but the dry keen air was invigorating; working and tramping on hard ground was a pleasant experience after perpetual struggling through wide fields of mud, and picking one's way among dangerous craters on narrow duckboard tracks under frequent shell fire and torrents of cold rain.

The 51st Brigade went into the sector on December 20th, and was temporarily posted in shelters in the old British line, south of Havrincourt and on the margin of the Forest. For the time being it was the reserve of the 59th Division which still held the front. Next day it moved forward to take over the front trenches from the 140th Brigade; the 52nd Brigade moved up to the reserve position; and the 50th Brigade was posted in the old British support line close by. During these two days the sector had been "quiet"—indeed almost peaceful, but on the night of the 22nd to 23rd enemy aircraft flew over the front and dropped bombs as far back as Ytres. The only damage done was in the transport line of the 50th Brigade, where two bombs burst with deadly effect. Eight men were killed and 24 wounded, and 49 horses were killed and nine badly injured. On the 23rd the relief of the 59th Division was completed, the 52nd Brigade taking over the right of the sector. At noon Divisional H.Q. closed down at Achiet-le-Petit and were established at the château of Ytres.

Before dawn on Christmas Day one of the patrols in No Man's Land took the first prisoner secured on this front, a private of the 107th Reserve Infantry Regiment. Havrincourt was shelled intermittently during the day and snow fell heavily in the afternoon and evening. With the help of an extra ration issued and parcels from home the social side of the day was observed as fully as possible under existing conditions. There were cheerful fore-casts that it would probably be the last war Christmas, but at the same time it required no extraordinary fore-sight to realise that a trying time was coming early in the New Year.

During the last week of the old year there was hard frost with occasional heavy snow. The enemy's artillery indulged in frequent bursts of activity, Havrincourt village being a favourable target. The reserve Battalion of the right sub-sector had been posted there, for the place

had escaped the almost complete ruin that had overtaken
most of the front line villages.   Many houses were in
fairly sound condition and there were good cellars.   But
the enemy bombardment became so serious that the men
were removed from it, and found cover in the neighbouring trenches of the Hindenburg Line.   Then came a lull
in the bombardment, and the last day of the old year, the
New Year's Day of 1918, and the day after were all a
quiet time.

The front line was held by two Brigades, the boundary
between their ground running along the Canal cutting from
the ridge through the Battle Zone, and being about a quarter
of a mile east of it in Forward Zone.   A succession of
strong barriers armed with machine guns blocked the
cutting in the Forward Zone.   Each sub-sector of the
front line was held by two battalions, with a third in
support, and the fourth battalions near Hermies and
Havrincourt.   The Brigade in reserve was kept well
back between Bertoncourt and Haplincourt in the old
British support line of the days before the Battle of
Cambrai.   The artillery positions were in the hollow
behind the ridge on its reverse slope and on the high
ground beyond it.   The Pioneer Battalion, several R.E.
Field Companies and working parties from the infantry
units were kept busy on the reorganisation of the
defences.

The York and Lancaster (Pioneers) had been moved up
to the sector some days before the Division took it over.
They were for a while at Hermies and then encamped on
the margin of Havrincourt Wood.   Hermies proved a
very inconvenient base of operations for the Battalion,
which at the outset was chiefly engaged in constructing
and linking up the new posts of the front line east of the
Canal.   The movement to and fro of the working parties
often took nearly two hours.   During daylight with
snow on the ground it was impracticable, as the slopes
in front of the ridge were in full view from the enemy's

look-out stations on Bourlon Hill, and any movement drew heavy artillery fire.   So the move to the line between Flesquières and the Canal cutting had to begin in the evening twilight and be completed in the dark, and much of the ground was encumbered with the partly demolished broad belts of wire of the Hindenburg Line, and the working parties had to pick their way through the labyrinth of its trenches or over the unbroken ground between them.

In those first days of 1918 the front line of the sector was still in a somewhat indeterminate condition.   It had come into existence in rather haphazard fashion as the fighting died down at the close of the Cambrai battle. Blocks had been constructed and armed in the gap of the broken Hindenburg Line west of the Canal; parts of the captured support trenches turned and given a new front facing north; and a straggling line of posts was established along the actual front, some of them in positions determined merely by the chance that a party of our men had taken cover in a shell crater or had dug themselves in on the furthest ground gained. Some of the more advanced posts were abandoned as the line was rectified and reorganised.   This was why no attempt was made to recover three small advanced posts, well out in front of the line east of the Canal, which the enemy rushed in the early twilight on the evening of January 3rd.   At sunset the Germans opened a heavy barrage fire on our front, chiefly with trench mortars in his lines facing the sector immediately to the left, then held by the 2nd Division. A few minutes later the three posts in and near a sunken road between the Canal and Flesquières were attacked and taken.   Patrols sent forward reported the enemy was holding them strongly.   Some other posts were abandoned next day in the pursuance of the reconstruction scheme.   It was thought that this activity of the enemy might be a prelude to a more serious attack, and when the 50th Brigade went into reserve, on the night of the 7th

to 8th, it left a battalion at the bend of the Canal in the
hollow behind Hermies, to be at the immediate disposal
of the Commander of the left front.

In the second week of January, there was a change of
the weather—a thaw, some rain, and then mild days with
slight frost in the nights.   The 10th was a fine clear
day, and our observers on the higher ground reported
that they saw signs of considerable activity in the enemy's
front.   Numerous small bodies of infantry were to be
seen moving forward in the area on our right front beyond
Graincourt and south-west of Bourlon Wood.   Similar
reports came from the 2nd Division on our left.   As a
precaution, the Reserve Brigade was brought up to the
bend of the Canal behind Hermies.   But the day passed
quietly with intermittent artillery fire.   After dark, at
8.25, the guns of the 2nd Division opened a heavy fire
and an S.O.S. message came from their H.Q. asking
for the support of the 17th Divisional artillery.   Its
guns at once came into action and drew a vigorous reply
from the German gunners, but nowhere was there any
infantry advance.   Patrols on the Divisional front
reported everything normally quiet in the enemy's lines.
One of them brought in a prisoner, a soldier of the 104th
Reserve Infantry Regiment, who protested that there were
no preparations in progress for an attack.   As all was
quiet next morning the Reserve Brigade went back to its
original position.

The record of the rest of January is that of the routine
of trench warfare, an immense amount of fatigue work on
reconstruction, occasional artillery fire, some bomb-
dropping by hostile planes without any more serious
result than damage to huts, a couple of attempts at raids by
the Germans and a successful minor raid by the Borders.
Patrols brought in prisoners from time to time, who all,
when questioned, told of no exceptional activity on their
side that could indicate any serious attack at this early date.

Some drafts from England joined the Division during

the month.   Opinions were divided about their quality, and perhaps the unfavourable opinion at first formed of some of them was the result of a hasty judgment that, now that conscription was in force at home, recruits would not be of the willing class with their hearts in the work.   Some of these recruits were decidedly young, and it was obvious that the medical examination was far from being as strict as at an earlier date.   The Pioneer Battalion was greatly under strength and was given a good many of the newcomers.   It was disappointing to find that few of them had any previous experience of technical or manual work, and that they would have everything to learn, just at a time when so much pressing work had to be done, with a time limit on its completion.   There was also a suspicion—perhaps unfounded—that the best of the new recruits had been given to the Brigade Battalions. A number of young officers also joined, fresh from the O.T.C. Battalions at home, with no previous experience of soldiering either in peace or war.   But it must be said, anticipating what happened later, that all shaped well, and with a few weeks of experience of realities at the front stood the terrible test of March 1918 splendidly.

With the first days of February came orders for the reorganisation of the Infantry of the Division on the lines outlined in our general survey of conditions preceding the German offensive—that is the cutting down of all the Infantry Brigades to a three battalion strength.   At the same time all Pioneer Battalions were reduced from four to three companies.   On February 1st the order was issued that—" Owing to the reorganisation of the British Army in France the following Regiments from the 17th Division have been nominated by G.H.Q. for disbandment and drafted into units of the same regiment in other Divisions, at dates to be notified later:

" 7th Yorkshire Regiment   -   -   50th Brigade.
8th South Staffords   -   -   -   51st Brigade.
3/4th Royal West Kents   -   -   52nd Brigade."

Entries in the Staff Diary at various days in February record the departure of drafts of officers and " other ranks " of these units, which were completely disbanded by the end of the month.   There is however no mention of any compensating reinforcement of the remaining Battalions by drafts received from their disbanded regiments in other Divisions.   The Royal West Kents had only been a short time in the Division, but the South Staffords and the 7th Yorks had been with it for all the three and a half years since it was first formed at Wareham. Both had done good service on many a difficult occasion, and their disappearance was very keenly regretted.

The composition of the three Brigades was now:

50th Brigade.	*51st Brigade.*	*52nd Brigade.*
6th Dorsets.	7th Lincolns.	12th Manchesters.
7th E. Yorks.	7th Borders.	9th Duke of Wellington's.
10th W. Yorks.	10th Sherwoods.	10th Lancashire Fusiliers.

With Brigades thus reduced the system of holding the sector had to be modified.   Ever since the Division arrived in France and took its first tour of trench duty before Ypres in 1915, whenever a two-Brigade front had to be held, of the eight Battalions available four held the front line of the sector, with two more in support, and two others in Brigade Reserve.   This, besides giving an adequate front line garrison, made it possible to carry out a system of reliefs within each Brigade, and the Reserve Brigade had some chance of rest and training while out of the line, and the supply of extra working parties was seldom a severe strain upon it.   For the Brigades in the front line it was now no longer possible to do more than keep the four battalions in front with two more in support. They had no fourth battalions to act as reserve units. But of the Reserve Brigade one battalion was kept as an immediate reserve to the front line garrison, and thus for the available Divisional Reserve there were left only two instead of its former four battalions.   This seriously handicapped the defence of the Flesquières salient, now one of the critical points in the British line.

It was on February 21st, 1916, that the Germans had launched their tremendous attack upon Verdun, and as this February of 1918 began most people, who ventured upon a forecast, felt fairly certain that the new attack would come before the month was over. There was the sound argument for such a view in the now well-known fact that the movement of guns and men from the eastern front to the west had been in progress since the autumn, and it was obviously the enemy's interest to strike as early as possible in the year, and have a longer time for his operations to develop before the Allies could be notably reinforced by the armies that America was organising.

But the month went by without any serious incident on the menaced front in France. On the whole the weather was fine and not unfavourable for artillery work and movement of troops on a large scale. There were some rainy days, but it was a fairly dry month. Even when the rain came it was not the persistent deluge that had drowned in mud the offensive in Flanders a few months before. There was some snow, but many days of clear weather, often with hard frost in the nights. Many of the mornings began with a white haze hanging low over the hollows and the lower heights, just the condition that would mask the first stage of a new offensive.

The German aircraft were active and enterprising. They sometimes made daring flights low down over our lines and further back even than the Rear Zone of the defence. Some were shot down by our ground defence, one falling to a blast of machine gun bullets that found a target in its engine. They dropped some bombs but did little damage in this way, and probably they were chiefly engaged in reconnoitring and securing photographs of our new defence system. The enemy's artillery was intermittently active, probably a good deal of this activity being the result of numbers of guns registering from new positions.

There were a few attempts at raids in the Divisional front.   On February 4th, a fine clear morning after a quiet night, the enemy put down a box barrage on a section of the front just west of the Canal, where a little valley ran into the rising ground.   The barrage came down at 7 a.m. in bright daylight a few minutes before sunrise, and almost at once a strong party of raiders made a dash up the hollow, in which their front line was only about 200 yards away from ours.   A Lewis gun was promptly turned on them and the leader and some twenty of his followers were seen to fall.   The rest of the raiders mostly turned and ran back, carrying off some wounded men with them.   Four of them however got close up to a post in our line, and were killed as they tried to enter it.   Patrols sent out later in the day failed to get any identifications from the dead bodies lying near our front, badges having been removed before the raid started.

Further east towards Flesquières there was a wide stretch of No Man's Land on the Divisional front.   Here the first continuous trench of the new German defences, that had been growing up since the battle of Cambrai, was nearly half a mile away.   But nearer our line were some of the posts held by the British for a short time after the battle, and evacuated as our new front line was reorganised.   On our trench maps they were coloured as part of the enemy trench system, but a patrol which entered the nearest of them—"Reindeer Post"—on February 12th found it unoccupied.   It appeared that these advanced posts of the enemy front were not all of them permanently garrisoned.   A dugout at Reindeer Post was examined and some British signalling equipment was found in it, and brought back to our line.   A few days later our patrols reported it as strongly held, but soon after a party, sent out one night to seize it and destroy the dugout, found it again vacant. The patrol blew in the dugout by wrecking its two entrances with explosives, and withdrew without encountering any opponents.

Our patrols were out beyond the front night after night, but the enemy's patrolling did not seem to be so regularly kept up, and especially in the wide section of No Man's Land on the right it was not often that German patrols were encountered. On the night of the 12th a patrol of the E. Yorks captured near the sharp bend of the enemy line on the western part of this broad ground before our right, two privates of the 123rd Grenadiers (27th German Division). Examined separately, they talked freely enough, and gave the same information. From their statements it was gathered that the line before our Divisional front was held by four regiments (12 battalions). One of these was west of the Canal and the three others east of it. In each regiment two battalions were in the trenches (five companies in the front system, three in support) and the remaining battalion was in reserve at Cambrai. Reliefs within each regiment took place every six days by the Cambrai battalion coming into the line, and a front battalion going into reserve. The prisoners reported that there were many casualties in the front system, mostly from the fire of our trench mortars. This information showed that in the opposing front systems and in close support the enemy had eight battalions against six of ours and a reserve of four more while we had only three.

On February 8th the Commander-in-Chief, Sir Douglas Haig, with the Chief of the General Staff, and the Army and Corps Commanders paid a visit to the 17th Division H.Q. at Ytres. It was a brief and informal incident in a rapid tour of the front which Sir Douglas was making. The Third Army Commander, Sir Julian Byng, and General Fanshawe, who commanded the 5th Corps, were frequent visitors to the lines of the

17th Division, and the Commander-in-Chief had little to learn of the position in the Flesquières salient.

On February 24th the Divisional H.Q. moved from Ytres château to Bertincourt. That day the enemy's artillery was exceptionally active, and there was heavy fire of trench mortars from the German front system. These latter were silenced by our artillery, but all day and intermittently during the following night, our trenches were shelled by 7.7 guns and 10.5 howitzers, and the huge shells of the enemy's 15 centimetre howitzers were bursting continually along the north margin of Havrincourt Wood. It was just after the anniversary of Verdun, and many thought it might be the opening of a bombardment that would prelude the expected offensive, but next day was fairly quiet, with no sign of any exceptional movement on the enemy's side.

There was broken weather in the following week, and March " came in like a lion," with a cold wind, rising to a gale on the 1st, and snow on the 2nd. On the evening of the 1st there was a successful minor operation, when a derelict tank, one of the casualties of the Cambrai battle, was destroyed far out on No Man's Land north-west of Flesquières. It was near the German line, and it was believed that it had been used as an advanced base for his patrols on this side. A party of R.Es. went out late in the stormy evening of March 1st, covered by a strong patrol of twenty rifles. The engineers placed a good supply of high explosives at effective spots in and round the crippled tank, and withdrew after lighting the fuses without being discovered. An explosion followed that blew the tank into scattered scrap metal, and for awhile caused puzzled excitement on the German front with bursts of firing that suggested that he was repelling an imaginary attack.

On the 3rd, H.Q. was informed that the Division would be relieved within a few days by the 19th Division.

This order however was almost immediately cancelled, as the result of General Robertson urging that his Division should be allowed to remain in the entrenched position, which they now knew so well, to meet the expected attack, instead of putting in a new Division, to hold at such a critical moment a trench system that would still be strange to them.   A fortnight later there was again a talk of a relief, but this also came to nothing, for by that time G.H.Q. had information that indicated an almost immediate enemy offensive, and realised that it was better that it should be opposed by troops thoroughly familiar with this important sector.   The British High Command had remarkably accurate information as to the enemy's preparations, but during March, as the weeks went on and nothing exceptional happened, there was a tendency in less exalted circles to doubt if the long-talked of " great push " by the enemy was really coming.   The French persisted in their belief that the attack when it came would be launched, not against our front, but upon their front in Champagne.   Sir Philip Gibbs tells how he visited the greater part of our front in these weeks and found many even of the Generals commanding Divisions sceptical about an early enemy move on a grand scale. In the House of Commons Mr. Bonar Law gave it as his personal opinion that the Germans were indulging in a big bluff.   If men so highly placed were thus doubting, it is no wonder that many, who had no special information, began to think that after all the " great offensive " was a myth.

At the end of the first week of March the weather began to improve.   There was even a feeling of spring in the air at times, and on the 9th—somewhat prematurely and optimistically—" summer time " was introduced.   The slight rise of temperature had the drawback that heavy mists and restricted visibility became a more frequent feature of the early morning hours.   With a front line of posts, the defence of which depended largely on their crossing their machine gun fire over the near front, this might play into the hands of the enemy.

In the second week of March G.H.Q. circulated information, obtained by its Intelligence Department, indicating immediate German preparations for an attack. The enemy was installing gas cylinders along his front and indications were given of the chief points at which they were being placed in position. During the night of the 11th to 12th the artillery positions on the reverse slope of the ridge on both sides of the Canal, near its sharp bend south of Hermies, were bombarded by the enemy with H.E. and gas shells. The fact that mustard gas was not employed, though lately a favourite with the enemy, was taken to be a possible indication of an impending attack, for mustard gas poisoned the air and ground and hung dangerously in the hollows, making it unpleasant to advance across an area where it had been let loose. Then too the news was officially circulated that a deserter, who had come in on the 4th Corps front, reported that the attack was fixed for the early hours of Wednesday, March 13th.

Possibly he was sent across to our front to tell this story and this and the bombardment were part of a scheme for playing the game of " Wolf " and so putting us off the alert when the real push came. However, in case some big move was beginning, steps were taken to counter the German preparations. For some days fatigue parties had been busy bringing up " gas projectors " to selected positions in the Forward Zone. The " gas projector " was a new British device dating from 1917, and meant to replace by a handier method the heavy gas cylinder. It was a light tubular projectile, charged with compressed gas, and discharged from a tube buried in the ground. It broke open at the point where it fell and loosed a cloud of gas. At 4 a.m. on the 12th 1,402 of these " projectors " were hurled into the enemy's advanced trenches, along the Divisional front, and directed at the points where it was reported the Germans had installed their gas cylinders.   At the same time the artillery began and continued through the night a bombardment of these points, the heavies simultaneously shelling critical points in the German back areas and along the communication lines. This counter-bombardment of gas and shells was carried along over the whole front from Cambrai to St. Quentin.

The enemy's artillery replied, but their fire was not exceptionally heavy.   Our gunners continued the bombardment all through the next day, and at intervals during the night of the 13th to 14th.   Our fire ceased at dawn when it became clear that all was quiet in front and no attack was yet coming.

During the following days the enemy was very quiet, making only a feeble reply even to our occasional bursts of shell fire by night and day.   Between the 15th and 17th nearly 600 more gas drums were flung into his trenches, eight tons of stuff in all, without provoking any serious attempt at retaliation.   The quiet was, if anything, overdone, and warnings from G.H.Q. indicated that it must be considered to be the lull before the storm which was likely to break out on or about Thursday, the 21st.

In this third week of March the distribution of the infantry units of the Division was as follows: [1]

On March 9th the 50th Brigade had relieved the 52nd in the left sub-sector, and on the 18th the 52nd after having been nine days in reserve took over the right front from the 51st Brigade, which went into reserve.   On taking over, the 50th had put the Dorsets and the West Yorks into the front line with the East Yorks in support. The 52nd put the Lancashire Fusiliers and the Manchesters into the front line with the Duke of Wellington's in support.   The H.Q. of both Brigades were south of Hermies behind the ridge and between it and the Canal.

The 51st Brigade had the Sherwoods and its Brigade H.Q. at Bertincourt, the Lincolns at Hermies and the

[1] Cf. Map, p. 270.

Borders near the bend of the Canal about half-way between these two positions. Right and left of the 17th Division, the front of the salient was held by two Divisions with a fine war record—on the left the 51st Highland Division (Territorials) and on the right the 63rd Royal Naval Division.

In front of these three Divisions (51st, 17th and 63rd), holding the Flesquières salient, the enemy had concentrated eight Divisions in all. · On the whole front selected for the first attack, some fifty miles from north to south, there were 37 Divisions in the front line to open the assault and 27 more near enough to be sent into action in the first day—64 Divisions in all against 19 British Divisions in the line with 13 more in reserve as the first available reinforcement. The weather favoured the enemy's plans. Tuesday, 19th March, was a dull day with constant drizzling rain that thoroughly soaked the ground. On the Wednesday it cleared up. In the early hours of the day there was good visibility and there were reports of unusually active movement behind the German front, —mostly of large bodies of infantry. But the day was quiet. Towards evening with the warmer weather the ground was drying rapidly and rising mists covered its slopes and hollows, and darkened into a dense fog after sundown.

It was a cloudy night, with hardly any wind. What there was amounted only to a slight movement of the air from the north-east, which did not break up the haze, but blew from a favourable point for the enemy if he were to loose off gas against the salient. All was quiet till 4.45 a.m. when there came the sound of gunfire from the right in the direction of La Vacquerie, on the 6th Corps front. This seems to have been the result of some premature activity on the part of the German gunners in this direction. A quarter of an hour later, at 5 a.m. (the zero hour of the enemy's attack), a tremendous bombardment opened on all the fronts. It was still intensely dark, for the fog lay heavily on the ground and it was more than an hour before sunrise.   To those who looked out towards Cambrai from the Hermies-Havrincourt Ridge there came through the haze the glare of gunfire in a wide zone of batteries from the enemy's front trenches where his mortars were at work, far back to his heavy gun positions.   Officers and men who had a record of long service on the Western front, and with this many experiences of bombardments on a large scale, had now the impression that they had never heard a greater outburst of gunfire.   The massed artillery of the enemy was hard at work on a front of over fifty miles northward from the Oise valley.   But the bombardment was not confined to the coming battle front.   There were subsidiary bombardments eastward on the French front about Rheims, and northward on the British front covering Arras, and on the Lys and before Ypres, and heavy shells were flung into Dunkirk from a long-ranging giant gun behind the enemy's Belgian front—shells that at first were taken for naval projectiles, the forerunners of a raiding attack from the sea.   These bombardments right and left of the battle line were no doubt intended to make the Allied command doubtful for awhile as to where the main attack would be launched.[1]   There was a trench mortar barrage on our forward positions ; shells were showered upon the defence zones in its rear and on the roads by which the front would be reinforced.   This bombardment of the country behind our lines had a remarkable feature.   Not only were shells bursting over near centres like Ytres and Bertincourt, but long-ranging high velocity guns were sending their projectiles 20 or 25 miles beyond our front, their targets being important road and railway

---

[1] The heavy bombardment of the Rheims front had some practical effect. The French High Command was already persuaded that the enemy attack would be directed against the Champagne front, and that any movement against the British front, even on a fairly large scale, would be a subsidiary operation. The shelling about Rheims confirmed them in this view, and they were slow in sending any reinforcements to our hard pressed southern flank.

junctions.   Thus, for instance, before dawn shells were exploding in the streets of St. Pol and Doullens far west of Arras.

Our artillery had at once replied, firing through fog and darkness on the assigned but invisible targets of the enemy's trench system.   Later on we learned that this fire was effective and caused considerable loss to the masses of infantry concentrated for the coming assault. The evening before, far away to the south in front of St. Quentin, prisoners captured by patrols of the 18th Corps spoke freely of the next day's attack, and told how their trenches were filling fast with the troops brought up to form the first wave of stormers, and the villages behind the line were crowded with troops waiting to pass through to complete the expected success.

It had come at last.   The greatest battle of this war of tremendous battles was beginning.   Even without pre-liminary warnings from G.H.Q. there could be no doubt the raging storm of artillery fire was no mere feint but the prelude of the vast effort in which Germany was staking everything.   The official communiqués issued to the press in Berlin and all the great cities from the Rhine to the Vistula told that the " Kaiserschlacht "—the " Emperor's Battle "—had begun, the final effort of the German arms, which was to bring victory and peace to the Fatherland.

In our lines in the Flesquières salient everything was ready.   During the night, before the enemy's guns opened fire, the Forward and the Battle Zones had been manned.   There was no sense of surprise on our side. The expected had come at last and officers and men felt they were ready for it.   For many of the newcomers in the 17th Division it was their first battle, but they had been long enough at the front to catch the optimistic spirit that prevailed even among those who had lived through the disappointing experiences of the preceding year.   No doubt this cheerful optimism was partly the result of that

limited range of mental vision that characterises the average officer and soldier occupied mostly with thoughts of
how to get through the day's task, leaving all worry about
problems of higher strategy to "the brass hats," and
knowing little of the situation outside the sector where he
finds himself posted.   The General and staff officers
had been working out the plans for an ordered retirement
if fate should give a temporary success to the enemy, but
all this was "confidential" as yet, and those who manned
the defence zones in front of Cambrai were undoubtedly
in a very cheerful frame of mind.   One may take as
typical such an incident as the reply of a young officer in
a reserve billet at Bertincourt that morning as the first
roar of the bombardment was heard and shells began to
drop overhead.   "They are coming at last," said a
comrade.   "Good business.   They will get it in the
neck," was the cheerful reply.

On the Divisional front in the Forward Zone, and as
far back as the ridge, gas was streaming in through the fog
—phosgene, not mustard gas—masks had been put on
at the first sign of it, and it caused hardly any loss all
through the morning.   The fog hung heavily, made denser
by the smoke and dust of the bombardment.   Even when
the sun rose behind it the range of vision was nowhere
more than a hundred yards and in places was limited to
a few feet.   But for a long time there was no sign of an
infantry advance on this part of the front.

About 6 a.m. the bombardment of the Forward positions became less intense, but the heavy bombardment of
the artillery positions and of the villages on the ridge
continued.   By this time the only available reserves of
the Division were moving.   These were two battalions
of the 51st Brigade, which had already the 7th Lincolns
holding the Hermies defences.   There were also four
Maxims of the Machine gun detachment.   The 7th
Borders were delayed in their advance by coming under
shell fire and suffering some casualties.   Half the bat-

talion occupied the Havrincourt defences, the other half
battalion was posted to the left of the village at Fort
Robertson, a strongly entrenched spoil heap on the east
bank of the Canal.   The 10th Sherwood Foresters were
in close reserve on the Canal bank near the north-west
corner of Havrincourt Wood, while the Machine gunners
and the Brigade H.Q. were established close by.   Of the
three companies of the Pioneer Battalion one was with
the 50th Brigade on the left front, and the two others
were at Havrincourt and Hermies, the Battalion H.Q.
remaining on the north margin of Havrincourt Wood.

By 6 a.m. all telegraph and telephone commuuications
with the Forward Zone had broken down, as well as
several lines in the Battle Zone, and communications by
wire with the Divisions on left and right was partly
interrupted.   Visual signalling and the use of carrier
pigeons were impossible on account of the fog, and henceforth all communication was only by runners.   So far
there had been no infantry attack on the Divisional front
and the losses caused by the bombardment were not
serious.   At Hermies and Havrincourt the enemy's
gunners were making the villages their targets, and shells
were bursting freely in them, showing the Germans had
very carefully registered their gunfire in advance on
these points.   But this had been foreseen and the defenders were in the adjacent trenches, where they were fairly
safe.   The gas caused hardly any casualties.   There
had been frequent practice for all ranks in moving and
working for long stretches of time while wearing gas
masks, and the discipline on this point was so good as to
give almost complete security.   The troops had taken up
their battle positions in perfect order and without any
confusion, despite both the fog and the bombardment,
and as the dull daylight came there was everywhere a
confident feeling that the position was sound and the
outlook reassuring.

Shortly after 8 a.m. came the first signs of an attack.

Runners from the Lancashire Fusiliers in the front line on the right brought the report of an intensified trench mortar bombardment along the 52nd Brigade front, in Hughes, Stock and Owen trenches.   Our artillery put down a barrage in front of this line, and the Maxim gunners at Havrincourt reinforced this from time to time with a machine gun barrage towards the enemy's position about Graincourt.   For two hours the firing was heavy and considerable damage was done to the forward trenches, which in places were reduced to a tangle of shell holes.   At 10.15 the Germans attacked.   A rush came through the fog in several successive waves and though they were met by a heavy fire at close range, a part of Hughes Trench was seized and a lot of machine guns run up into its shell holes.   Next day we learned from a prisoner that at the same time another column of assault had been launched from Graincourt against Owen Trench on the extreme right of the Divisional front, with orders to push through to Havrincourt.   This attack however was caught in a storm of machine gun fire and never reached the trench front.   This was probably the result of our Maxim gun barrage.

The section of the trench thus lost was east of the Canal and on both sides of the boundary between the two front line brigades.   The West Yorks promptly counter-attacked from a sunken road near the Canal, bombed the enemy out of part of the trench, and established a stop. The Lancashire Fusiliers had organised a similar counter-attack on the section of the trench in their area, but orders came through countermanding it, with the reminder that the Forward Zone was to be regarded only as an outpost line, the line of resistance being the Battle Zone, and only delaying tactics were to be used in front of this.

Our line on the right now ran along Carey Trench and Ship Trench and Spin Alley (the support line of the Forward Zone), and then up Soap Trench to its junction with Owen Trench where a stop was established.   There were to be no further counter-attacks on this forward ground. The loss of part of Hughes Trench was treated as of no serious importance. It was afterwards learned that the enemy had incurred heavy loss in this advance, and they had many casualties during the day in the captured trench and never succeeded in getting any further forward.

Reports to Divisional H.Q. from the Royal Naval Division on the right were satisfactory. The R.N.D. held all its Forward Zone, except a small salient which the enemy had captured. But from the Highland Division on the left the news told of an enemy success of some importance. Between 10 and 11 a.m. the firing had been heavy on our left and rumours reached Hermies that the Germans had pushed through the ruins of Deni-court, about a mile to the northward and just outside the Divisional Boundary. At 11.40 Divisional H.Q. had a report from the 51st Division that the enemy had captured Doignies, a mile west of Denicourt, near the Cambrai-Bapaume road, and it was now the intention of the Highland Division to withdraw gradually to a line running south of Doignies through Monchies. This endangered the flank of our Battle Zone about Hermies. Half a battalion of the Sherwood Foresters and a company of the York and Lancasters were sent to the Hermies defences as a reinforcement. In the afternoon the remaining two companies of the Sherwoods were moved to the left. Until evening there was desultory fighting along the front and about 4 p.m. the Yorkshires improved their position in the west end of Hughes Trench by bomb-ing the enemy out of it up to the Brigade boundary.

At sunset on March 21st, the position of the 17th Division was practically intact, the only loss having been part of one trench in the Forward Zone. This was also the situation of the 63rd (R.N.) Division on its right. But these satisfactory conditions were exceptional. Everywhere else on the long battle front from the Sensée

river southwards the Germans had gained ground.   On
mile after mile the Forward Zone was gone and in places

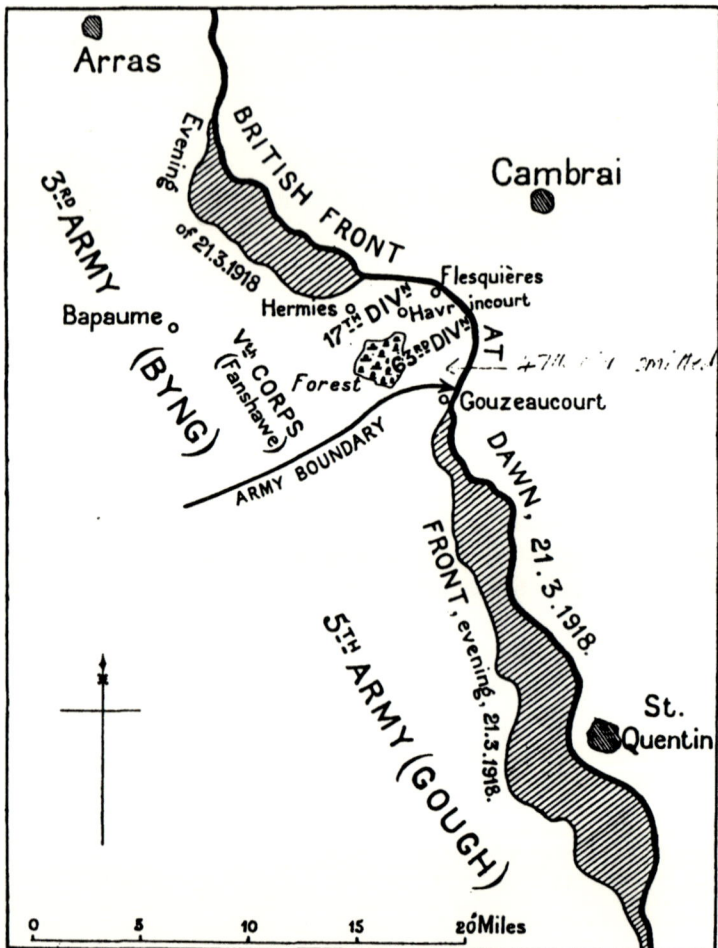

Sketch showing fronts held at dawn and evening, March 21, 1918
(Ground gained by enemy shaded).

the enemy's advance had broken into the defences of the
Battle Zone.

The fog, dense in the early hours, lighter in the afternoon, but always more or less limiting the range of vision, had favoured the enemy's new " penetration tactics."   It masked the first stage of the attack, making it all but impossible for the strong points of the Forward Zone to give each other the mutual support of cross fire for which they were designed, and at many places the columns that formed the vanguard of the assault found a way between them.   The storm troops that thus broke through the outpost line were abundantly provided with machine guns, and wherever they broke in they were rapidly supported by a constant stream of reinforcements that, working forward and to right and left under cover of the fog, frequently isolated the advanced posts which they had passed.   The advance thus became something that might be compared to a flood lapping in vain for a while against the rampart line of a breakwater along most of its front, but finding weak points and trickling through a fissure here and there and flooding the ground beyond, and extending the first narrow breach until presently a raging flood is widening and deepening beyond the crumbling barrier.   Early in the day the battle flood had thus rolled over the new and incomplete defences of our extreme right away towards the Oise valley, and poured into the Battle Zone.   There had been another break through before St. Quentin, and further north by Epéhy and Ronssoy, a little to the right of the Flesquières salient.   On the other flank of the salient, as we have seen, the attack had broken through the Forward Zone and forced a withdrawal on a front of some miles, menacing the left of the positions held by the 17th Division.

During the late hours of the evening Divisional H.Q. heard something of the general situation through the Corps H.Q., but the information was necessarily vague and incomplete.   It amounted to an intimation that along much of the line ground had been lost, though the Battle Zone mostly held fast, and nowhere had there been a break through its defences into the Rear Zone. But all that was known to the officers and men who held the salient was that some ground had been lost on their left, though their own front was intact, and few had any idea that the situation was at all serious. In great battles like this, most men outside the higher regions of command do not trouble themselves with any attempt at " appreciation of the general position." They leave that to their chiefs, and are too much occupied with what is happening in their immediate and narrow surroundings to trouble themselves with anything but the practical personal problems of the moment, and, for most of them, after a long day of strain and danger, the most important problems are those that concern food and rest. In the case of the 17th Division the impression that evening was that things were going well. During, the day all arrangements had worked smoothly enough. So far as the Division was concerned it seemed that the command was " carrying on " with the well-organised routine of holding against a somewhat half-hearted.'attack a position where every officer and man knew the ground from long familiarity, and was acting on a defence scheme that had been rehearsed for weeks. Carrying parties came along as usual after sunset bringing up fresh supplies of food and ammunition. It was only long after that it was known that supply arrangements had been modified during the afternoon, for early in the day the long ranging fire of the enemy had made the position of the transport base in Vélu Wood decidedly " unhealthy," and it had been moved back between four and five miles to a safer position at Bancourt, not far from Bapaume. The move was carried out in perfect order and on well devised lines. Main roads, which were swept at crossing after crossing by the enemy's shell fire, were avoided, and the columns made their way by country lanes and tracks across open ground, reaching their destination practically without any loss.

CHAPTER IX

THE RETIREMENT TO THE ANCRE LINE
(1918)

AFTER dark on the Thursday evening the enemy's fire had dwindled to intermittent shelling. There was no sign of any hostile movement in front and it seemed that it would be a quiet night. But for many it was a busy time, the first of a week of nights in which rest of any duration was hardly possible. It had been decided that in conformity with similar movements of the Divisions to right and left the Forward Zone was to be evacuated, and the Second System—*i.e.* the first line of the Battle Zone—was to become the Divisional front. Orders to this effect were issued at 11 p.m. The withdrawal was carried out in perfect order and without any attempt of the enemy to interrupt it. All stores and supplies in the Forward Zone were brought back, the dugouts in the trenches were thoroughly wrecked and at the last moment the building and retaining walls at Lock No. 7 and the bridge over the Canal cutting a little to the South of it were blown up.

The main position to be held now ran from the defences of Havrincourt to Fort Robertson on the Canal Bank and then to Hermies, with an outpost line beginning near Havrincourt and running by London Trench and Jermyn Street, across the Canal cutting to Bell Trench and then by Gong Trench and Liscloches Lane to the sunken road running back south-west to the Hermies defences.

The distribution of the troops, when all movements were completed, was from right to left: East of the Canal the 52nd Brigade had the 12th Manchesters in the

Havrincourt defences with one company in the outpost
line. The 9th Duke of Wellington's held Fort Robertson
with two companies in the outpost line, and the 10th
Lancashire Fusiliers in close support in and about City
Trench just behind Fort Robertson.

On the other side of the Canal the main defence line
running along Lurgan Switch was held by two battalions
of the 50th Brigade, the 10th West Yorkshires on the
right near the Canal, the 6th Dorsets on the left up to

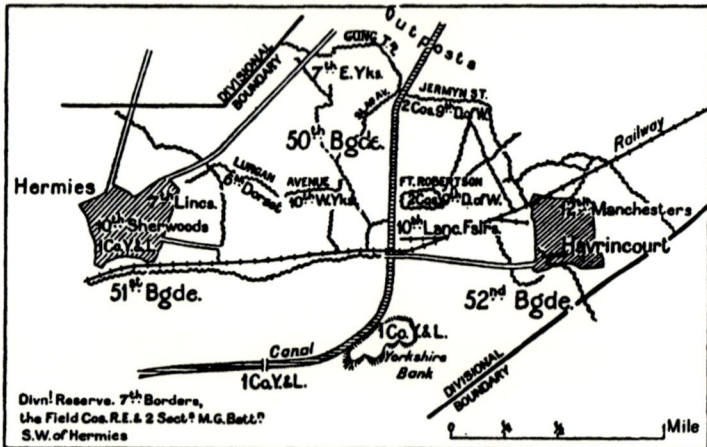

Position at Dawn, March 22, 1918.

the Hermies defences. The remaining battalion of the
Brigade, the 7th East Yorkshires, was in the outpost line.
The 51st Brigade held the Hermies defences as far as the
Doignies road with the 7th Lincolns and a Heavy M.G.
Company. On the extreme left were the 10th Sherwoods.
The remaining Battalion of the Brigade, the 7th Borders
was in Divisional Reserve near the bend of the Canal, with
a section of the Divisional M.G. Battalion, and a company
of the York and Lancasters (Pioneers). The other
companies of the York and Lancasters were in reserve
south of Hermies and at Yorkshire Spoil Heap, on the
west bank of the Canal near the bend.

There were thus in the lightly held outpost line a battalion and three companies; in the main position six and a half battalions (one of them less a company), and in Divisional Reserve a battalion of the 51st Brigade and two companies of the Pioneer Battalion.

It was not until after 5 a.m. that all these arrangements and movements were completed, and the last of the small covering force of picked officers and men was withdrawn from the old front line.   Dawn was coming, and again for awhile the haze hung heavily over all the ground.   It is not certain at what hour the enemy at last discovered that the Forward Zone had been evacuated in the night. In the early hours of the morning they threw some shells into it.   After sunrise as the mist lifted there were signs of considerable activity in the enemy's lines about Graincourt, but it was not till after 7 a.m. that parties in extended order were seen working forward from Hughes Trench, and cautiously and very slowly feeling their way into the abandoned trenches, the advance being covered by a shelling of the evacuated Forward Zone.   By this time there was firing all along both the German and the British front for many miles, and about 8 a.m. an intense bombardment was concentrated on the defences of Hermies.   This continued for some three hours.   Shells were also bursting freely behind the rigge, about the bend of the Canal and on the large spoil heap on its east bank.

It was about half-past nine that the enemy, advancing through the Forward Zone, made a first attempt on the outpost line of the Duke of Wellington's in Jermyn Street trench.   The attack was little more than a push of a strong patrol and was repulsed.   At 10.15 there was a more serious attack, but it also failed after a sharp fight. A few of the attacking party got into the trench but were driven out, leaving one prisoner in our hands, a private of the 234th Regiment.   He it was who gave the information already noted as to the attempted advance from Graincourt the day before and the heavy losses of his Division.

The enemy's attack west of the Canal now began to develop rapidly.[1]   There was some fighting in our outpost line at Gong Trench near the Canal bank as the result of contact with the German advance into the Forward Zone. But the enemy's chief effort was being made on the left of the salient.   Attacks in force, covered by a tremendous artillery fire, were being launched against the 51st Division, and the Highlanders were being steadily forced back to the 3rd system of the Battle Zone, further exposing the flank of the 17th Division about and to the rear of Hermies.   All day communication with the 51st Division was difficult, and the situation on this side was often very obscure.   All direct telephone lines had been cut. Some messages came through Corps H.Q., but what information the 17th Divisional H.Q. secured was mostly by sending officers to gain touch with the 51st and reconnoitre the enemy's advance on that side.

Shortly after 11 a.m. the first of many attacks on Hermies was launched from the direction of Doignies and

---

[1] A Victoria Cross was awarded to Sergeant Jackson of the East Yorks for his fine conduct in the fighting west of the Canal this day, and for other deeds of resourceful gallantry and devotion to duty during the retreat of the following days.   The official record runs thus :

" Sergeant Harold Jackson, 7th (S) Battalion, The East Yorkshire Regiment.   At Cambrai on the morning of March 22, 1918, this N.C.O. volunteered for a daylight patrol during a heavy enemy barrage preparatory to their first assault, and was successful in gaining touch with the enemy and brought back valuable intelligence as to their concentrations.   On the same morning, after the enemy had succeeded in entering parts of our front line, he held an important bombing-stop, and by his vigorous offensive forced them to withdraw.   He later stalked an enemy machine gun which was enfilading our line, and single-handed he bombed the crew and put the gun definitely out of action, killing or wounding the entire crew.   He fought with magnificent gallantry for the following seven days, during rearguard actions.   On March 31st, at Bouzincourt, he took command of his company after all his officers had become casualties, led them to the attack with splendid bravery and initiative, and withdrew when ordered to do so under heavy fire and took up a good new defensive position.   He afterwards repeatedly went out into the open and brought back badly wounded men under a murderous enemy fire.   His wonderful coolness and devotion to duty under the most trying circumstances has set the highest example to everyone."

Denicourt. The enemy came on very pluckily in wave after wave, throwing at least 4,000 of their men into the rush for the ruined village. They were held and repulsed with heavy loss, and as the fighting died down they left heaps of dead in front of our lines. Our machine gunfire was deadly, and the artillery gave admirable effective co-operation. But it was clear that with the retirement of the 51st Division on the left, this flank was becoming a danger point for the 17th. General Robertson therefore used his small Divisional Reserve to reinforce it, sending up to the 51st Brigade the 7th Borders and the two sections of the Divisional M.G. Battalion. Brigadier-General Bond placed two companies of the Borders and the machine guns at the disposal of the O.C. of the Lincolns in Hermies, and sent the other two Border companies to the 10th Sherwoods on the extreme left. All that remained of the reserve was now the three Field Companies R.E. One of these was kept at Hebburn spoil heap, and the two others were with the Pioneer Battalion, the three companies of which were sent back to Bertincourt. This was the first precautionary step taken in view of a retirement becoming inevitable. Locally the situation of the Division was sound enough, and there were reassuring reports from the 63rd R.N. Division on its right, but warning messages had come through from the Corps H.Q. indicating that the attack was gaining ground at many points of the general line, and if this went much further it might be difficult to extricate the Division from the Flesquières salient, now dangerously narrowed by the loss of ground to the north and west of Hermies. The Pioneers were set to work to strengthen the defences of Bertincourt and the Field Companies were busy for the rest of the day improving the somewhat rudimentary defences of the " Green line " on which the village was supposed to be a strong point. The " Green Line " had been marked out a week before as a rearward position, behind the main lines of the Battle

Zone. In the 5th Corps Area it began near Beugny on the Cambrai-Bapaume road, whence it ran south-west to Bertincourt, and then southwards by Ytres and Equancourt. So much labour had had to be devoted to the main defence lines that little had been done on the " Green Line." Nowhere were the defences completed, and in many places there was not a vestige of a trench, and only such natural cover as already existed was available in case it had to be held.[1]

Later in the day the 2nd Division, forming the reserve of the 5th Corps was coming into the line, and its 5th Brigade was placed at the disposal of General Robertson. He posted it in the third system of the Battle Zone in rear of the 51st Brigade and about half-way between Hermies and Vélu.

We now return to the story of the fight on the Hermies-Havrincourt ridge, where officers and men still had the confident feeling that they were holding their own, and knew nothing, or next to nothing, of the peril developing so rapidly in the general situation. After the failure of the first attack on Hermies, enemy pressure on front and flank of the outpost line west of the Canal made it advisable to withdraw the two companies of the East Yorks from the Liscloches and Gong trenches. With the rest of the Battalion they formed towards 12.30 a defensive flank, from Bell Trench to Slag Avenue, roughly parallel with the Canal cutting, and crossing its fire with that of Lurgan Switch. This flanking line was held through the afternoon.

Between noon and sunset persistent and determined attacks were made on the Hermies defences. In all, during the day there were six of these, and in the intervals the enemy kept up a heavy fire upon the village chiefly from the left front. Attack after attack was repulsed with heavy loss to the Germans. They tried to get some cover for their approach by massing in a sunken road

[1] See Map, p. 307.

running northwards from the west end of Hermies to Denicourt.   Under a well placed barrage put down upon it by our gunners it became a death trap for them.   At sundown the defence on the left of the Canal was intact.

Early in the afternoon there were signs that the enemy was preparing an attack east of the Canal.   His troops were massing in the evacuated trenches of the Forward Zone in front of our outpost line on this side, and at 2.45 p.m. a heavy bombardment of Havrincourt began.   By this time the weather was clear and hostile aircraft were scouting over the position and at times flying far into the back area.

About 6 p.m. the 50th Brigade H.Q. reported to the 52nd that the East Yorks had been withdrawn from the defensive flank of Bell Trench and Slag Avenue.   As it would soon be dark, and the enemy might cross the Canal cutting and work in on the rear of Jermyn Street on its east side, the outpost line of the 52nd Brigade was also safeguarded by organising a flank guard on its left to watch the cutting.   At 6.25 the enemy attacked all along the front on the east side of the Canal.   The two companies of the Duke of Wellington's still holding Jermyn Street repulsed the right of this attack, but on the left it was pushed up to the Havrincourt defences, but there it was successfully held, none of the enemy reaching our line.   A second attack upon Havrincourt was made at 7.30 in the dark, and another at 7.45.   All these attacks were easily beaten off by the Manchesters.   They were in touch with the 186th Brigade of the 63rd R.N. Division on their right, and after the final attack they received from them a report that they had held on all through the day, and so far as they were concerned the position was " very satisfactory."

After dark, carrying parties brought up rations and ammunition, the wounded were evacuated, and the men looked forward to a restful night with the feeling that they had put up a good fight and held the enemy all along their part of the battle line. But unhappily the general position that evening was far from satisfactory. North of the salient the enemy had gained ground during the day and was beginning a drive into the 5th Corps area from the line of the Cambrai-Bapaume road on its left. South of the salient the Battle Zone had been penetrated about Epéhy and Ronnsoy, and a flanking move was developing in a German push north-west that menaced our communications on this side. Further south, the whole line of the Fifth Army had been forced back and on this evening, March 22nd, General Gough had decided that the line of defence must be withdrawn to the Somme. With this general retirement right and left of them the two Divisions that stood fast in the Battle Zone of the salient would have to conform to the withdrawal.

In the long and detailed despatch, dated July 20th, 1918, in which the G.O.C. Sir Douglas Haig described the German offensive and the fighting retreat of the Third and Fifth Armies, he selected for special mention the determined fight made by the 17th Division in the Flesquières salient, in these first two days of the battle. In relating the events of March 21st, he notes that: " Astride the Canal the enemy was held up by the 17th Division under the command of Major-General P. R. Robertson, C.B., C.M.G., and made no progress"; and in relating the events of the following day he mentions the successful defence of Havrincourt, and he goes on to say: —" Further north, fighting was severe and continuous throughout the day. Shortly before noon the enemy attacked Hermies, and repeated his attacks at intervals during the remainder of the day. These attacks were completely repulsed by the 17th Division. Heavy losses were inflicted on the German infantry in the fighting in this area, the leading wave of a strong attack launched between Hermies and Beaumetz-lez-Cambrai being destroyed by our fire."

After having thus held the line so well, it was disappointing to have to give anything away. But late that evening the first steps were taken towards the retirement that was to bring the Division back in a few days across the war-wasted battlefields of the Somme to the west of the Ancre valley, the withdrawal—a fighting retreat—abandoning, in the face of overwhelming odds, ground the winning of which had cost six months of persistent battle in the Somme advance of 1916-1917.

In the evening of the 22nd, as a result of the general retirement of the whole line on the southward front, the Division received from the Vth Corps H.Q. orders to evacuate the Front system of the Battle Zone east of the Canal, swinging the line back from the bend of the Canal along the line of Metz Switch (a trench running southward through the eastern margins of the Havrincourt Woods, past the village of Metz-en-Couture, from which it took its name). The 63rd R.N.D. was at the same time to conform to the movement and hold the southern part of the Switch. The orders reached the 52nd Brigade about midnight. The retirement was carried out during the night and was completed by sunrise, when the left of the Brigade was established at Yorkshire Bank on the Canal, and its front ran back from this point to the Switch. The outpost line from Jermyn Trench to the Havrincourt defences was held till the move was all but complete. The enemy was very active during the night, pushing strong parties forward and making repeated attempts to break through the outpost line, with the evident intention of discovering if any withdrawal was in progress. These attacks were all repulsed, but it meant some sharp fighting, especially on the line held by the Manchesters in front of Havrincourt. Before the withdrawal from Fort Robertson was completed the railway bridge across the Canal cutting close behind it was successfully demolished at 4 a.m.

At this hour Divisional H.Q. received another order from Corps H.Q. directing a still greater withdrawal—

a move which was the result of the retreat, on the right, of the Fifth Army across the Somme. All the Battle Zone in the Vth Corps area was to be evacuated. A new defence front would be formed on the so-called " Green Line." It would be held on the left by the 2nd Division, in the centre by the 63rd R.N. Division, and on the right by the 47th London Division. The 17th Division was to retire through the Green Line and become the Corps Reserve. The first direction given was that the Division was to concentrate in the area west of Villers-au-Flos—(a village about three miles in rear of its present H.Q. at Bertincourt and a little more than a mile east of the Bapaume-Péronne road).

At sunrise on Saturday, the 23rd, the distribution of the Infantry Brigades was:

51st Brigade, still holding Hermies and the left of the line.

50th Brigade west of the Canal between it and Hermies.

52nd Brigade on south of Canal from the bend at Yorkshire Bank to the northern part of Metz Switch.

The 5th Brigade (temporarily attached) was guarding the flank between Hermies and Bertincourt. It had not been engaged, and was presently to rejoin the 2nd Division in the Green Line.

The only troops left in Divisional Reserve were the three Field Companies, R.E., and the York and Lancasters (Pioneers), who had been employed in strengthening the defences of Bertincourt and the line immediately north of the village. On the right the Division was in touch with the R.N.D. in Metz Switch, but on the left the enemy had pushed the 51st Division back to the Third System of the Battle Zone (the Beaumetz-Morchies line) and held the Second System on the flank of the Hermies defences. " The more haste the less speed," is sound wisdom of popular tradition, and the retirement was carried out with organised deliberation. At Divisional H.Q. preparations began as soon as the Corps order was received at 4 a.m. and after this there was no rest for the

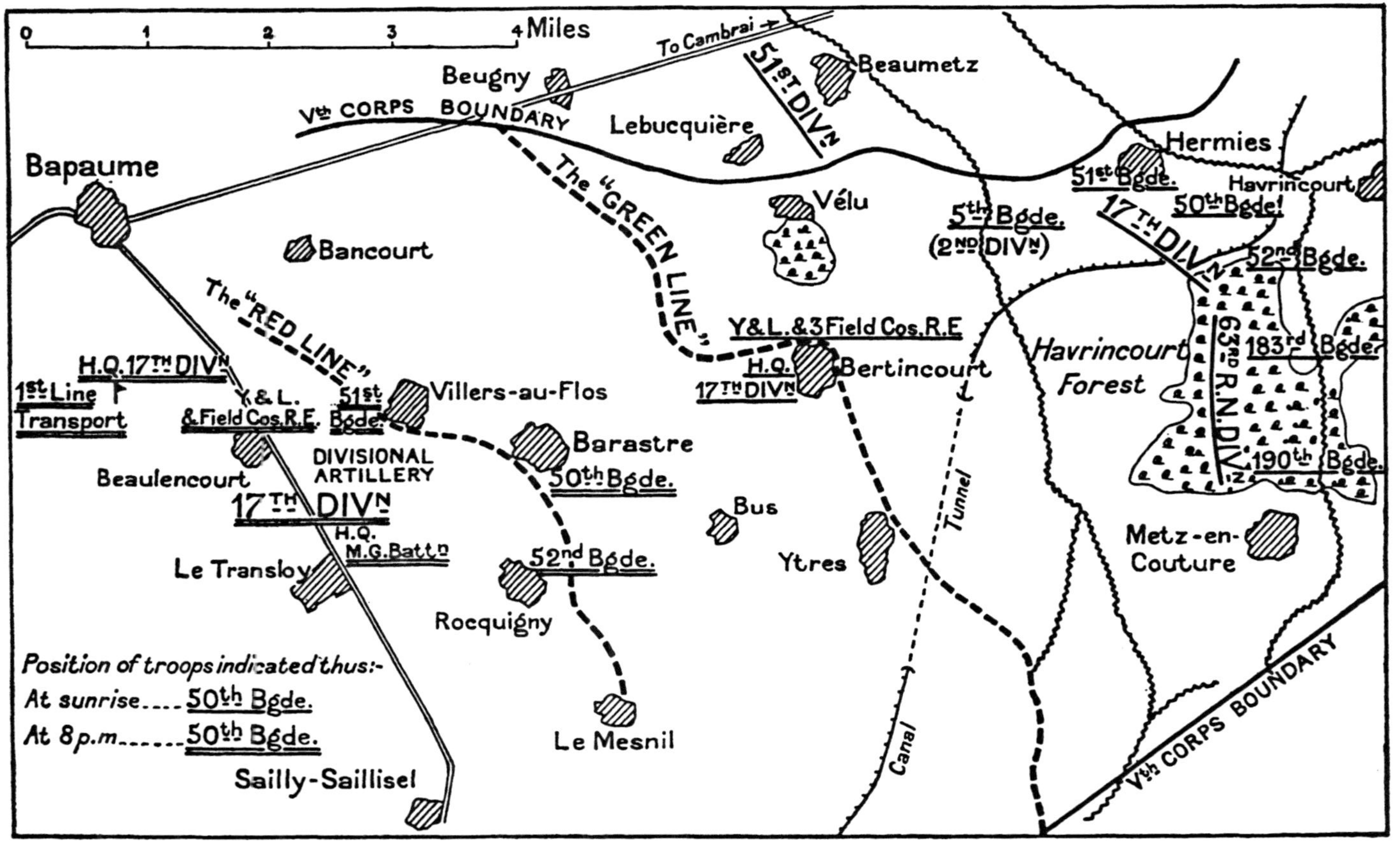
0 1 2 3 4 Miles
To Cambrai
Beugny
Vth CORPS BOUNDARY
Bapaume
Lebucquière
51st DIVN
Beaumetz
Hermies
51st Bgde.
Havrincourt
50th Bgde.
17TH DIVN
52nd Bgde.
Vélu
5th Bgde.
(2ND DIVN)
The "GREEN LINE"
Bancourt
The "RED LINE"
Y&L.&3 Field Cos.R.E
H.Q. 17TH DIVN
Bertincourt
Havrincourt Forest
63RD R.N.DIV.
183rd Bgde.
190th Bgde.
H.Q.17TH DIVN
1st Line Transport
Y&L. & Field Cos.R.E.
51st Bgde.
Villers-au-Flos
Barastre
50th Bgde.
DIVISIONAL ARTILLERY
Beaulencourt
17TH DIVN
H.Q. M.G.Battn
Bus
Ytres
Tunnel
Metz-en-Couture
Le Transloy
52nd Bgde.
Rocquigny
Position of troops indicated thus:-
At sunrise.....50th Bgde.
At 8p.m.......50th Bgde.
Le Mesnil
Canal
Sailly-Saillisel
Vth CORPS BOUNDARY

Retreat to the "Red Line," March 23, 1918.

G.O.C., his staff and the personnel of H.Q.   But the troops in the forward area were left undisturbed as long as possible.   It was not till 8 a.m. that they received orders to move two hours later.   To bring them back earlier would mean that they would pass through the Green Line before there was time to organise its defence.

At Bertincourt all the various centres of activity that had grown up during four months were being dismantled, from the offices of H.Q. down to the Divisional travelling theatre and cinema, and their manifold belongings where possible were packed and sent off for future use.   The scenery, dresses and properties of the theatre had mostly to be abandoned, but a lorry was found for the plant of the cinema.   As for the impedimenta of H.Q., there never was a war in which records and documents, reports and returns, maps and photographs accumulated at such a rate, and several lorry loads of office equipment and tin boxes of papers had to be got away to the new Divisional centre of directive activity.   A party of officers, clerks and orderlies went off with the first group of lorries to organise the new H.Q.   Shortly after 6 a.m. the G.O.C., who had been busy most of the night but looked as fit as if he had been having a good rest, turned into his office, where the last load was being got away, and remarked that it was time to be off, adding that those who could manage it might perhaps get a cup of tea but there would be no breakfasts till later.   The request to hurry the departure meant only that the general was anxious to start work at the new H.Q., but one at least of his hearers thought it meant that the enemy was pressing on very near at hand. There was already heavy firing away to the left front, and shells were dropping in Bertincourt.   One of them burst unpleasantly near General Robertson as he mounted his horse to ride away.

The first body of troops that followed him were the Field Companies R.E. and the Pioneers, the York and Lancasters.   The Battalion was relieved by the 2nd

Oxford and Bucks L.I. of the 2nd Division, and marched back the three miles to Beaulencourt on the Bapaume-Péronne road, near which the new H.Q had opened at 6.30 a.m. The H.Q. were installed in a deserted Casualty Clearing Station about a mile west of the village, in a hollow between two ridges near the plank road from Beaulencourt to Thilloy. A message had come through from Corps H.Q. directing that a defence line should be occupied east of the Bapaume-Péronne road, and the ground had been rapidly reconnoitred. It was part of what was known as " the Red Line " —a line partly made up of old German trenches dating from the last days of the Somme battles, and partly of a line of marks for new trenches better sited to meet an enemy advance from the eastward. The old trenches were in a ruinous condition, fallen in at many places and overgrown with weeds and brushwood. On the proposed new trenches no work had yet been done. The section of this line to be held by the Division ran from Villers-au-Flos eastward to Barastre and then south to Rocquigny, a front of between five and six thousand yards. After a hot meal and a short rest the Pioneers and the R.E. worked for about five hours on the trenches near Villers-au-Flos.

The retirement of the three Brigades from the Battle Zone was carried out successfully under at times very difficult conditions. The enemy was fairly quiet in front in the early hours of the morning, but on both flanks of what was now left of the Salient position the Germans were developing a plan for cutting off its defenders by breaking in on their line of retreat, and they counted on making a capture of one or more of our Divisions. Early in the day there began a determined drive against the 51st Division on the left, a push down the Cambrai-Bapaume road, the attacking force being largely made up of machine gunners and their ammunition carriers, and covered by intense bombardment. Here the plan was, as soon as the Third System of the Battle Zone was passed, to swing round to the left and break in to the rear of the whole battle position on that side, and on the flank of the Green Line. There was another push on the right from the southward through the ground about Fins, with Ytres and Bus for its final objectives.

Between these slowly closing jaws of the colossal pincers the retirement was carried through with deliberately-won success. Throughout the movement the 17th Division was always more or less in contact with and under the menace of the northern push of the enemy. That it carried through the movement, working by time-table with clockwork precision and with no serious loss, was due to the splendid spirit of all ranks. They felt they had held their own for two days and nights against heavy odds, and were now withdrawing, not because they had been defeated, but because things were going badly elsewhere. The men had perfect confidence in their leaders. As the G.O.C. of the Division put it, speaking of his men to a war correspondent a little later, " they were quite happy and were not worrying." It must be added that the success of the retirement was also largely due to the admirably efficient support given to the infantry by the artillery and the M.G. Battalion and also a section of the Motor M.G.s on the left flank. The gunners had a new experience, such as, till now, most of them had only heard or read of. They had been for months firing from fixed positions at long range, against carefully registered targets, usually invisible. To-day for the first time in France they were out in moving warfare, firing over open sights at short range against masses of the enemy, in contact all the time with the infantry, sometimes close beside them, moving with them, and as they ceased fire at one point bringing up limbers and teams to make a dash for another position at which to come into action again. There were times when the gunners held on almost too persistently in action and the move was a gallop under close fire.

The retirement from the Battle Zone began a little before 10 a.m. by each of the three Brigades sending back one of its battalions to the Third System to form a line through which the retirement of the rest would be made. They were to cover the withdrawal, hold on till 3 p.m., and then form rearguards to their Brigades till the Green Line was passed. The Duke of Wellington's (52nd Brigade) were on the right, the East Yorks (50th Brigade) in the centre, and the Sherwood Foresters (51st Brigade) on the left. With each Battalion there went back a battery of 18-pounders and a section of the Heavy M.G.s. At 10 the retirement from the main position in the Second System and the Metz Switch began, the first moves being from the Brigade on the right, which kept touch with the R.N.D. retiring on its flank. Rearguards were left in the Switch with orders to hold on if possible till 1 p.m.

From early morning the enemy had been making attacks on the front of the Division, but none of these were vigorously pressed, and all were easily repulsed. They appear to have been mostly the action of strong patrols feeling our line and watching for the first signs of a retreat. The real attacks were the flank drives towards the line of retirement. But once the withdrawal from the front line began the enemy attacks were persistently pressed and there was occasionally close fighting. The rearguards on the left about Hermies were forced back, and the 50th Brigade mostly effected its retreat by getting across the Canal to its south side. As they passed between the village and the canal crossing a party of the Dorsets had a curious experience. They saw a small body of what appeared to be British infantry approaching near the village. They were wearing British steel helmets, and their uniforms looked like khaki. One of the Dorset officers actually thought he could recognise in their leader one of the Battalion C.O.s of the 51st Brigade. But it was presently discovered that they were enemies, and after a sharp exchange of rifle fire they broke up and disappeared into the abandoned trenches near Hermies.

The most trying part of the retirement was after the Third System had been passed. The enemy's push along the Bapaume road had gained much ground. By 11 a.m. the Germans were into the village of La Bucquière. They cut off part of the 154th Brigade on the flank of the 51st Division, forcing some of the Highlanders to join up for awhile with our troops in the Third System. By noon the enemy was in Vélu, and soon after they occupied Vélu Wood. They had rushed up several of their field batteries to the flank of our line of retreat and a good many of their guns were in action south of the Cambrai-Bapaume road. The 52nd Brigade came back through Ruyaulcourt on the left, and did not shake off the enemy's attacks till it reached the Green Line, from which it continued the retirement through Bus. The other two Brigades came through Bertincourt with the enemy close on their flank. The gunners, moving back with them by successive bounds, protected their movement by action at short ranges, and repeated attempts of the enemy to issue from Vélu Wood were defeated by our artillery and motor machine guns.

The enemy's aircraft were very active all day, making daring flights at a comparatively low level. Few of our aircraft were available in this sector, and as the information they gathered went first through Corps H.Q. and only reached the Divisional H.Q. in this way, the reports mostly arrived too late to be of much use. General Robertson asked for a contact plane to be directly attached to his H.Q., but this was never available. Soon after Vélu Wood was occupied by the enemy one of the British airmen flew low over it, believing it to be still in our possession. He was caught in a blast of machine gun fire that damaged his aeroplane, but he managed to plane down south of the wood, narrowly avoiding a crash. He thus landed near a 17th Division field battery that had just galloped up and unlimbered. His hurried report to the Battery Commander was that the Germans were in force behind a rise of ground near Vélu and would soon be over. They were " thick as ants," he said, and he suggested that the battery had better get away to safer ground, as the whole crowd were coming on, " Are they ?' replied the gunner, " That's just what we're waiting here for."

By 5 p.m. the last of the Division was clear of the Green Line, and at 8 p.m. it was concentrated in its new positions on the so-called " Red Line."

That evening the distribution of the Division was:

50th Brigade, just west of Barastre.
51st Brigade, near Villers-au-Flos.
52nd Brigade, near Rocquigny.
Pioneer Battalion and Field Co.'s R.E. near Beaulencourt.
Divisional Artillery, west and south-west of Villers-au-Flos.
H.Q. of Machine Gun Battalion at the sugar factory on the Péronne-Bapaume road, half a mile north of Le Transloy.
The battalion was reorganising; its sections having been dispersed here and there in action during the day at many different points on the line of retreat and with all three Brigades.

The first line transport was immediately to the west of Divisional H.Q. The train and heavy transport had been sent back to Courcelette on the Bapaume-Albert road. This was in conformity with the Divisional scheme prepared in advance under which everything that was not immediately necessary for the fighting troops was to be kept well back behind the Division throughout, to eliminate as far as possible baggage delaying or hampering their movements.

At noon on the 23rd Divisional H.Q. had received a message from Corps H.Q. indicating that the higher command now regarded a long retirement as at least highly probable. It indicated the intended lines to be followed in this case—the 47th Division on the right through Sailly-Saillisel and Combles and then along the southern margin of the old Somme Battlefields by Montauban and Mametz on Bécordel; the 63rd R.N. Division by Le Transloy, Longueval and Contalmaison to Albert, and on the left the 2nd and 17th Divisions by Bapaume to Pozières by the Albert road, and then by Ovilliers to Aveluy in the hollow of the Ancre. It was a scheme of movements that it proved impossible to carry out. By the evening of the 23rd the situation was rapidly changing, and it was difficult to maintain the organised communication that would enable H.Q. commands to size up the actual situation at a given moment, much less to forecast movements for three or four days in advance.

That evening the information available at the 17th Division H.Q. as to the general situation on the Corps front was defective and in some respects misleading. At 8 p.m. it was understood that the 51st Division was covering Bapaume, with its right in touch with the 2nd Division in the Green Line. On the right of the 2nd the 63rd R.N. was prolonging the line to about Ytres, where the 47th Division continued the front with its right flank thrown back owing to a gap having occurred between it and the 9th Division, the extreme left unit of the Fifth Army.

It was a cold fine moonlit night. Out in front on the Green Line and away to the right front there was heavy firing. Here and there a red glare in the sky showed where abandoned hut camps set on fire during the afternoon retreat were still burning. On the right front a dangerous gap was opening. The 47th Division had fallen back, losing all touch with everything to right and left for a while, and the 9th Division was also withdrawing in the darkness. The Germans were pushing on into Lechelle, and towards Bus in the right rear of the Naval Division whose right was " in air " and saved only by throwing back a defensive flank facing nearly south.

About ten p.m. there was a tremendous crash followed by minor explosions. A huge ammunition dump at Ytres had blown up, and it set fire to a great dump of R.E. stores near it, and caused many casualties in a battalion of the R.N.D., which was holding the Green Line in front of it. The dump burned all through the night, lighting up the surrounding country. Before midnight the Germans were into Bus, and a single battalion of the R.N.D. was in position to bar their exits from it on the north side. But this meant that the enemy had gained a footing between the front of the 17th Division in the Red Line and the flank and rear of the 63rd R.N.D. in the Green Line. A message from Corps H.Q. informed the Naval Division that early next day they would be helped by a counter-attack of the 17th Division on Bus to clear the Germans out, but at 3 a.m. there came another order. The counter-attack was countermanded, and when morning came the R.N.D. and the 2nd Division were to evacuate the Green Line, and retire through the Red Line —the Rocquigny-Barastre-Villers position held by the 17th Division—to a position further to the rear not yet precisely defined.

This was one of the most critical moments of the whole long battle. During the 23rd far away to the south on the extreme British right the attack was gaining ground in the Oise valley. In the centre the Fifth Army had retired across the Somme and there was a fight for its crossings, some of which the enemy had already won. Further north, near where the 17th Division was engaged, there was a gap opening between the Fifth and Third Armies, and the enemy was pushing fresh Divisions forward to deepen and widen it. His superiority of numbers was now beginning to tell even more seriously than at the outset of the offensive. He was able to relieve the Divisions already engaged, while on our side most of the officers and men had endured the almost continuous strain of three days and nights of battle with scant and fragmentary opportunities of rest and all but unceasing toil and exposure. The strain was now dangerously near breaking point, and no relief was possible.

One may take this night of March 23rd as marking the close of the first phase of the great battle, and the beginning of an even more difficult period. All the prepared positions—Forward Zone, Battle Zone and Rear Zone had gone on a front of more than fifty miles. After three years of position warfare there were no longer any entrenched positions to hold under the protecting fire of huge masses of artillery. The whole front had become fluid. The troops were fighting under conditions of which most of them had no experience, and for which they had not yet been trained. For years they had acted under elaborate and detailed schemes and orders that defined even the movement of a small group of trench raiders, and set forth the targets of every gun brought into action to cover the operation. Their leaders had always had elaborate maps of every foot of ground, and had often rehearsed every movement even of a platoon. Now they were engaged in open warfare, not the open warfare of an advance, in which each objective could be marked out beforehand and every movement timed, but in a desperate struggle to hold a succession of fronts in a slow retreat under unceasing pressure from superior forces, and in which everything had to be improvised, often with defective knowledge even of what was happening near at hand. The elaborate system of communication, direction and control, which had developed since the autumn of 1914, had ceased to function under conditions that made it now impossible. The system of supply organised for fixed fronts had no application to a moving line held together more by the efforts of local leaders than by anything that the higher command could do. The marvel is not that there was a tremendous loss of men, material and ground, but that there was not an irreparable disaster.

The morning of Palm Sunday, March 24th was a

critical time in the opening of this second and more trying phase of the battle. The line was perilously near breaking point on the front where the Fifth Army and the Third were menaced with a loss of all connection between their flanks, and here much depended on the action of the 17th Division. It was supposed to be the reserve of the Fifth Corps, and without any really accurate information as to the situation, and with scanty and often belated messages from neighbouring formations and from the higher command, its chief had to take rapid decisions to meet each danger as it emerged from the surrounding obscurity.

During the night there was a good deal of firing away to the front, and a heavy outburst of M.G. fire towards 2 a.m. when an enemy attempt to advance north-west from Bus was repulsed by R.N.D. gunners near the Bus-Rocquigny road. At 3 a.m. Divisional H.Q. received a belated and not quite accurate report that the enemy had broken through the Green Line east of Ytres. The break was really well south of the place and had been effected by the German push on that side the evening before, and the R.N.D. had met the danger for the moment by throwing back its right to form a defensive flank.

South-west of Rocquigny, during the night, patrols of the 52nd Brigade had come in contact with German patrols. At 5 a.m. it was reported that there was a break in the line further south between Sailly-Saillisel and Mesnil. As a matter of fact the enemy had been moving in the night from the ground he had won south of Ytres in the Green Line, westward towards Sailly-Saillisel and the line of Péronne-Bapaume road, and there was a gap opening here between the Third and Fifth Army. At this time there was still telephonic communication with Corps H.Q. and orders came through for the 51st Brigade to move " to the high ground south of Sailly-Saillisel, and get touch with the 47th Division on its left and the 9th on its right."

Retreat across the Somme battlefields, March 24.

The Brigade moved off at 5.30 a.m. Day was coming, and it was a fine, rather warm morning with white mist on the ground. The sound of firing already came from the eastward, where the 63rd Division was still holding on in the Green Line. During the night they had repulsed several desultory attacks of the enemy, but the Germans were now becoming more active and had put down a heavy barrage on Ytres, and their long range guns were sending shells over the Red Line villages, some of which passed over the line of march of the 51st Brigade in their rear.

In a hollow behind Barastre the advanced guard of the Brigade formed by the Lincolns, came upon a peaceful scene. Some of the first line transport of the 63rd Division were in bivouac here and the men were busy cooking an appetising breakfast. " The air was thick with the smell of fried bacon," says one of the officers of the 51st Brigade, in telling of the episode as an instance of the matter-of-fact way in which our soldiers will set about the ordinary round of the day's work even under the strain and turmoil of events like those of the great retreat. The C.O. of the transport, on being informed of the mission of the Brigade and the gap in the line so close at hand, began to prepare for a retirement to safer ground, and as the Brigade was by this time none too well provided, handed over some rations to the Lincolns, including a share of the fried bacon. As the advanced guard moved on over the ridge beyond the hollow—the spur between Rocquigny and Le Transloy—it came upon a crowd of haggard exhausted men streaming back along a country road and moving westward. Some officers with them were doing what was possible to get them into some kind of order. They were about 1,500 in all, many of them wounded. It was a sign that for not a few the breaking strain was already past, and endurance had reached its limit.

At 6 a.m. the telephone brought through from Corps

H.Q. to the Division a message modifying the original order to the 51st Brigade and directing that its task would be now to fill a gap between Sailly-Saillisel and Rocquingy and gain touch with the left of the 9th Division. This cancelled the direction to occupy ground south of Sailly, and was the result of information that the enemy had reached Mesnil south of Rocquigny and there was now nothing between them and the 50th Brigade at the latter village. The order was sent on to the 51st Brigade, but before it received it, it had already discovered that the original order was impossible of execution. For Sailly-Saillisel was seen to be strongly held by the enemy, and north of it on the east side of the Le Transloy road the Germans were moving forward, though rather slowly and diffidently. It is fairly obvious that they had no idea of the existence of a gap in the British line immediately in their front, and they may have suspected they were being drawn into a trap. The gap was now being closed but only with a force far too weak to hold it against a serious advance of the enemy. The right of the Brigade was extended across the Le Transloy road and here came into touch with some units of the 9th Division, forming the left of the Fifth Army.

The enemy now ventured on some half-hearted attacks, which were repulsed by the rifle fire of the Brigade. But the situation was anything but hopeful. The thin line had as yet no artillery support, and a message was sent back asking for even a couple of 18-pounders to be sent along to knock out enemy machine guns. Presently low-flying enemy aeroplanes made their appearance. One of them came so low over the Lincolns that rifle fire was opened on it, but the German got away safely after retaliating by a burst of M.G. fire which wounded the O.C. of the Battalion, Lt. Colonel Metcalfe. The enemy must have learned by this time that there was no large force in his front. Patrols sent on by the 51st Brigade to its left front discovered that the enemy was in strength about Le Mesnil, endangering this flank. The line was therefore withdrawn to hold a front with its left south of Rocquigny and its right near the Sailly-Le Transloy road about halfway between these two villages.

With the 6 a.m. order cancelling the first directions given as to the move of the 51st Brigade, there had come an order for the 50th Brigade at Barastre to make a counter-attack on Bus with the help of a Brigade of Artillery, beginning at 6.20. At 6.45, when the preparations for the counter-attack were far advanced, another order came through countermanding it, and the Brigade was directed to form an outpost line running north and south in the old German trenches a little to the east of Barastre to cover the withdrawal of the 2nd and 63rd Divisions from the Green Line. The order added that the 63rd Division would take over the Red Line on the left of the 52nd Brigade and the 51st Brigade would prolong the line from Rocquigny to Sailly.

Communication with the Green Line was by this time interrupted, and the last clause of the order showed that D.H.Q. had not yet received the report that the enemy held Sailly in force. From this time forward communication lines were breaking, and orders and information passed slowly and irregularly from Corps to Divisional H.Q. and from the latter to the Brigades in the line. No orders had got through to the troops in the Green Line and its further defence was becoming impossible. The portion of it still held was turned on both flanks; a German kite balloon was flying close up in front of and almost over Ytres and directing the fire of batteries that were in action against the position with open sights. The 2nd Division fell back towards Bancourt, the 63rd R.N. Division, which had the enemy on its right rear at Léchelle and Bus, interposing between it and the 17th, retreated by making a flank movement to the left on Villers-au-Flos, moving under persistent enemy attacks and losing heavily. In many separate detachments the troops came through the 17th Division front about Villers and Barastre, and concentrated and reorganised between the latter village and Le Transloy, Divisional H.Q. being established at the sugar works north of the latter village.   It was near noon when the last of the Naval Division reached its destination.   The Division was temporarily out of action.   It was greatly reduced in numbers and a halt was essential to reorganise, hurriedly refit and give the men a brief rest.   Two battalions of the 47th Division with some small parties from other regiments had come into Rocquigny.   These were attached to the 52nd Brigade and held the line on its right, between its flank and that of the 51st Brigade.

Through the hours of the forenoon there was continuous fighting on the Red Line position, which was under heavy artillery fire, but it held good till the afternoon.   At 10 a.m. a determined attempt of the enemy to break in on the 52nd Brigade front about Rocquigny was defeated. At 11 intense machine gun fire from front and flank forced back the right of the 51st Brigade.   The enemy's westward push to the right of the Division was making steady progress and the 9th Division on this side was being gradually forced back.   There was continual danger of a new gap opening between it and the 17th.

A belated message which reached the Division from the Vth Corps H.Q. at 5.20 p.m. shows not only how rapid was the progress of the German flanking advance in the forenoon, but also how slow, uncertain and difficult was all communication.   It was timed from Vth Corps H.Q. at 1.10 p.m., but its information was the result of what the Corps Scouts had discovered as early as 10 a.m. It was to the effect that at this hour " the enemy was advancing on Combles apparently unopposed and had reached Le Priez Farm."   The farm was a little more than a mile south-east of the town.

On the northern flank of the Vth Corps the enemy was making a drive for Bapaume and gaining ground during the morning. The Germans were again in that place by the afternoon, and there was danger of another gap opening on this side. The position of the 17th Division was becoming a small advanced salient that would soon be turned on both flanks, and a further retirement could not be long delayed. The whole Vth Corps front was now held by a very " thin brown line " of tired men, standing up against the attack of the enemy forces newly flung into the attack. For the British the fighting was a succession of delaying actions fought to gain time for reinforcements to come in and for the French co-operation in the south to become effective. There was little prospect of the front being stabilised and the enemy's push brought to a standstill on this side until the line of the Ancre was reached and passed.

At noon the Divisional H.Q. were moved back to Courcelette, on the other side of the Bapaume-Albert road, and the second line transport was started off from that place to march by Albert to Hénencourt on the other side of the Ancre valley. The first line transport which had so far been kept near D.H.Q. was ordered to move to Méaulte by the main highway of the Bapaume-Albert road. It was escorted by a scratch force which had been improvised the day before as a guard of the D.H.Q. camp, at a moment when there was a false alarm that enemy cavalry had got through to the northward, and before any of the Brigades had fallen back as far as the Red Line. It mustered about 180 rifles. The men were organised in three small companies under an R.E. officer. They were N.C.O's and privates who could be spared from the A.S.C., with the transport, clerks and orderlies detached for the occasion from D.H.Q., some convalescents who had just rejoined from an evacuated rest hospital, and a few stragglers from various units. The transport and its improvised escort moved off under shell fire, avoiding the beaten tracks and working across the desolate waste of the old Somme battlefield to reach the Albert road near the Butte de Warlencourt.   One of the Padres of the Division, the Rev. W. Rushby, M.C., rode with the column, and in a narrative of the retreat he gives an interesting account of his experiences in the march with the transport column that Sunday afternoon and evening, a march of more than twelve hours in which a distance of only about as many miles was covered.   The story gives a glimpse of the conditions behind the fighting line in the final stage of the retreat.

It was rough going at first, over the old Somme battle-fields of 1916, past ruined villages and farmsteads and following for a while a planked track across a long stretch of shell-cratered ground, with, in all directions, tumbled-in and weed-grown German trenches, and lines of rusty wire, reminders of the months of battle in which these successive positions had been won,—now being lost again in a few days.   The huge tumulus of the Butte de Warlencourt by the Bapaume-Albert road, near the ruined village of Le Sars, was the guiding point of this first stage of the march.   There was a halt not far from it.   On the great mound three tall crosses stood out on the summit, sharply defined against 'the sunlit sky—memorials erected by Officers and soldiers of the Durham Light Infantry and two South African units to the memory of comrades who gave their lives in the long fight for the Butte in October and November 1916.   To the Padre the sight brought memories of the solemn anniversaries of the coming week. There could be no church parades that Palm Sunday, but during the halt he gathered the men of the escort around him, and spoke a few simple words on the lesson of self-sacrifice, and the need of trust in God even in the darkest times.   All that was now being abandoned, he predicted, would soon be won back.   He bade his hearers to keep a brave-hearted confidence in the future, and reminded them that the enemy's success was dearly bought, and the good fight the Division has made was an earnest of better fortune when the inevitable turn of the tide came at last.

The march was resumed, and the highway came in sight, packed as far as the eye could see with a crowded stream of traffic setting in the direction of Albert. It took some time to find a place for the column in the moving mass that was crawling at a snail's pace, with frequent checks, along the road. The pace was less than a mile an hour. Most of the stream of vehicles was made up of wheeled transport of every kind from several divisions. Here and there were Red Cross ambulances full of wounded, and peasant families with a few belongings piled on a cart or a barrow. From country roads on the right and left other minor streams of traffic came in to find a place in the main movement. On the left some tanks were retiring across the fields and at one point a battery was in action, firing eastward, and the rumour (a true one) told that the enemy was pushing forward from Combles along the ridge by Morval to Lesbœufs. Other rumours were circulating, for there were shell-shocked men among the parties of stragglers and walking wounded that had found a place in the long column, and some of them told strange stories of the enemy being close at hand on either flank. But there was a self-imposed order in the retirement, and no panic anywhere, no effort of anyone to push ahead at the cost of others, even when after dark the movement slowed down through the narrow streets of Albert, and German planes came droning overhead dropping bombs that shattered several vehicles and took their toll of life among men and horses.

There was a serious check in Albert when a bomb cratered a pavement and brought down a mass of *débris* from ruined house fronts and blocked the street. There was what seemed an endless halt while the traffic was diverted to a new line, and during this pause though the bomb attack continued drivers and wayfarers waited quietly in perfect order. At last the move began again, the town was cleared, and the 17th Division transport with its escort reached the new camp at Méaulte long after midnight. It was just a year and three quarters since Méaulte had been the jumping off place for the first day of the Battle of the Somme.

We now take up again the story of what was passing at the fighting front during the afternoon and evening of that day, before the Divisional H.Q. left its position near Beaulencourt to move back at noon to Courcelette. Orders were drawn up and sent out for a new disposition of the troops and a retreat by two stages to take up a new front between Bazentin-le-Grand and Martinpuich, about eight miles west of the Red Line.

These orders may be thus summarised: The York and Lancasters and the R.E. Companies were to move from their bivouac H.Q. near to the high ground immediately south-west of Gueudecourt.

The 51st Brigade was to fall back on a line between Rocquigny and Le Transloy, to cover the retirement of the other two Brigades from the Red Line. The 52nd Brigade was to take up a position about a mile south-east of Gueudecourt and a little to the north of the ruins of Lesbœufs. The 50th Brigade was first to take up a position covering Gueudecourt, and then move on the ground north-west of Ginchy. As soon as the 52nd was clear of Le Transloy, the 51st Brigade was to retire to Gueudecourt.

These movements would place the Division in a new position where it would be ready to deal with the German advance through Combles, as they pushed on towards Morval and Lesbœufs. But having thus got clear of the threat against its flank and rear the Division was to continue the retirement and concentrate on the line between Bazentin-le-Grand and Martinpuich.

The plan thus outlined was however not carried into effect. Indeed it seems that the only move actually executed was that of the Pioneers and R.E. to the spur near Gueudecourt. These units were in immediate touch with D.H.Q. As for the rest, the War Diary of the Division notes that " Owing to the difficulties in communication only verbal orders reached the 50th and 52nd Brigades who evidently misunderstood the orders." In a narrative of these operations subsequently drawn up by D.H.Q. this order of noon on the 24th is not mentioned, probably on account of its failure to reach effectively at least two of the three Brigades. But its general idea was the basis of another order issued in the afternoon.

One may perhaps suggest as a not unlikely explanation of the misunderstanding that the orders were taken to be not the direction for an immediate retirement, but an indication of the line to be taken when retirement at last became inevitable.[1]

One difficulty in the way of an immediate withdrawal from the Red Line was that the 63rd R.N. Division, which had no communication with Corps H.Q., was reorganising and resting near Le Transloy and not yet ready to move. It was not till near 3 p.m. that it, at last, marched westward in three parallel columns of route, its general direction being through Gueudecourt to High Wood. The German flank advance was reaching Lesbœufs and just north of the ruined village the R.N.D. machine gunners protected the flank of the retirement and held up the enemy.

Meanwhile from noon till after 3 p.m. the defence of the Red Line position was maintained, the 51st Brigade drawing back to the ground between Rocquigny and Le Transloy, and at 2 p.m. the 50th Brigade on the left drew in its advanced line and fell back to the west of Barastre.

Half an hour later Divisional H.Q. received a telephone message from Corps H.Q. to the effect that " the enemy had advanced westwards of Sailly, and had occupied

---

[1] This kind of misunderstanding arose in more than one instance in the case of other Divisions, and there was a misunderstanding of a somewhat similar kind with serious results on March 27th, when the 7th Corps took as an order to be at once executed one that set forth the action to be taken in event of a further retreat, and at once acted upon it, falling back prematurely to the lower Ancre south of Albert and uncovering the flank of the Fifth Army.

Combles and Morval and was moving to Lesbœufs. The 17th Division was to extricate itself as soon as possible, and move to the line Montauban—Bazentin-le-Grand and establish touch with the VIIth Corps at the former place." At the same time a report came through from the 51st Brigade that " the enemy was pushing northwards."

Divisional H.Q., now in touch by telephone with the G.O.C. of the Vth Corps, pointed out that with the enemy pushing up to Lesbœufs it might not be possible to reach the line indicated in the Corps order. The reply was that it was left to the Divisional Command to comply as far as might prove to be possible. At 3.40 D.H.Q. issued orders that were practically those of the noon scheme. They were sent by telephone to the H.Q. of the 51st Brigade, this H.Q. being now at Beaulencourt (it was the only one of the three Brigades with which the D.H.Q. was then in direct communication). Its Brigade Major reported that at that moment the left Brigade (the 50th) was moving past Beaulencourt, retiring from Barastre to Courcelette. He then took down the Divisional orders dictated over the telephone line to be communicated as soon as possible to the other Brigades. These directed that the 50th Brigade on reaching Gueudecourt was to move south to the position indicated in the earlier order, a line facing south-east across the Flers-Ginchy road and about half a mile north of the latter place. The 52nd Brigade was to take a position southeast of Gueudecourt, its retirement covered by the 51st Brigade holding the Rocquigny-Le Transloy line, the Brigade being in turn protected by the 52nd as it drew back to Gueudecourt. When the 51st reached this place the 52nd was to move into Flers, and the Pioneers, Field Companies R.E. and six M.G.s of the Divisional reserve were to take up a position between Flers and Gueudecourt. It was stated that two weak battalions of the 2nd Division were believed to be in Gueudecourt.

The whole Division having gained the above positions, covered by the Artillery Brigades which were to work in co-operation as far as possible, was to withdraw to the line Bazentin-le-Grand—Martinpuich.

After this transmission of orders through 51st Brigade H.Q., communication of any kind between D.H.Q. and the Brigades broke down completely, the last remaining link, the telephone line, being interrupted. The Divisional H.Q. narrative notes that " no further communications were received from the Brigades during the day and the situation of the Division was obscure until the following morning, except regarding the 51st Brigade, which by midnight was known to be at Martinpuich."

As to the movements of the three Brigades that afternoon and evening, there is even now only imperfect evidence available and it is sometimes contradictory. But in the light of definite statements as to the time and place of movements and halts given in available narratives, which when plotted on the map make an intelligible and consistent scheme of the retirement, one can reject some obvious errors in published and unpublished accounts, and trace the course of events from the afternoon to the midnight of this trying day.

The movements were mostly at a very slow pace; with at times long halts. The men were dead tired, many of them were short of rations. Water-bottles were mostly empty, and as the result of days of drought this chalk country of the old Somme battlefields showed mostly dry beds in its few and narrow watercourses. As for the wells and the former fountains of the ruined villages, hardly any were still available; the bombardments had choked them with *débris* and smashed up their headgear. So the retreat was the slow march of columns and smaller detachments of tired, hungry and thirsty men, plodding wearily westwards over rough tracks and broken cratered ground. At times the movement was amidst that of straggling parties from other Divisions, convoys of transport and other leaderless flotsam of the retreat. In some cases there was lack of clear orders, due to the general breakdown of communications, with temporary loss of direction. Little or nothing was known of the movements of other Divisions to north and south. There was the sound of heavy firing to the northward. From the eastward the enemy was following up the retirement, though as yet not closely, but there was occasional shelling from long-range high-velocity guns, and enemy aircraft came flying overhead, and dropped bombs or swooped down to deliver a burst of M.G. fire. Clouds of smoke came drifting along from the hutments and dumps that had been fired on the evacuated ground.

The enemy's pressure was chiefly from the flank movement on the south. The Germans had occupied Combles by 11 a.m. or shortly before that hour, and pushed on through Morval to Lesbœufs, which they held by 3 p.m. But they were moving only slowly and cautiously towards Montauban, where happily they had not discovered a gap in the line, but they were also at Ginchy in the afternoon and sending out patrols towards Longueval and Flers. During the retreat from the Red Line after the Bapaume-Péronne road was crossed the enemy's advance was held off by the Field Batteries working with each Brigade, which moved steadily from point to point, coming into action at each halt, though with a very limited supply of ammunition. The machine gunners co-operated. Several guns were knocked out by the enemy's shell fire, and others, pushed daringly out to the flank to cover the march, had to be disabled and abandoned. But the net results of these efforts and sacrifices was to impress the advance parties of the enemy with the idea that they had a formidable force in their front. Otherwise if they had shown more enterprise and hurried up reinforcements there might have been a disaster.

The 50th Brigade had been the first to begin the retirement. It drew out of the Red Line about 2.30 p.m.

and passed by Beaulencourt about 3.45 p.m., just as the last message from Divisional H.Q. was coming over the one surviving telephone line to the 51st Brigade and conveying the detailed orders for the retreat.   These did not reach the Brigadier commanding the 52nd.   He had given his Brigade the general direction to march towards Courcelette, where the Divisional H.Q. still were.   At this time the 51st Brigade was south of the line Rocquigny-Le Transloy holding up the enemy's advance from the southwards.   The 52nd was on its left, but its G.O.C. realised that he would soon have to retire, and had already transferred Brigade H.Q. to the road north of Transloy. He had intended to instal it in the sugar factory north of the village, but found this had been set on fire by the 63rd R.N.D. as the last of its columns marched off westward shortly after 3 p.m.   The fire was spreading to the adjacent hut camp.   The Naval Division marching on High Wood had nearly passed Lesbœufs at 3.45 and its machine gunners were holding back the enemy there.

A history of the 50th Brigade printed for private circulation in 1919 makes its retirement begin at 11 a.m. This is an impossibly early hour.   It was near Beaulencourt at 3.45 p.m.   It was moving very slowly and Gueudecourt was not reached till after 6.   It seems not unlikely that there was an intermediate halt in expectation of obtaining definite directions from D.H.Q. for the Brigade.   Meanwhile the Brigadier, General Yatman, had ridden on to Courcelette, where he met the G.O.C.

General Robertson had reached Courcelette about 3 p.m.   By some mischance, when D.H.Q. closed at Beaulencourt at noon, to reopen at Courcelette, he had become temporarily separated from his horses, and had made the journey across country on foot.   For some time he followed the telephone line connecting the two places. He tapped it near Ligny-Thilloy, east of the Bapaume road, and for a while remained there in touch by the wire with both Beaulencourt and Courcelette.   Soon after reaching D.H.Q. at the latter place he got in touch again with Beaulencourt, repeated the orders already given to the Brigade Major, 51st Brigade, who was speaking to him, and heard from him that the 50th Brigade was then passing the village. The G.O.C. told him to communicate the orders to the 50th. Shortly after communication ceased on the line, and the Staff Diary records that from 3.45 p.m. till midnight no communication from any of the Brigades reached D.H.Q.

When General Yatman arrived at Courcelette later on the G.O.C. told him of the orders already issued, under which his Brigade would be moving on Gueudecourt, and the Brigadier rode back to rejoin it there. He found most of the Brigade in position south-east of the place, but before he arrived his Brigade Major, Captain H. Ruthven, M.C., with the Brigade Staff and Signallers, had pushed on towards Courcelette, expecting to meet his chief on the way, but somehow missed him. To anticipate what followed—Captain Ruthven pushed on to Courcelette, with the Signallers, and was joined on the way by stragglers from various units, bringing his whole party up to 120 or 130 men. He reached Courcelette after D.H.Q. had left it for Méaulte about 7.30 p.m. and he bivouacked with his little detachment late in the evening near the Albert road, between Courcelette and Pozières.

The G.O.C. 52nd Brigade, after the retirement of the 50th on his left had begun, had got into touch with the 6th Brigade, the last unit of the 2nd Division, then retiring across the Red Line just north of his ground. From the Brigadier of the 6th he learned that orders had come through to the Division for " general retirement." Accordingly at 4.5 p.m. orders were issued to the 52nd Brigade:

" To conform to the general withdrawal then taking place on the line Gueudecourt-Courcelette, the initial stages of the retirement to be carried out in the general direction of Le Transloy,

on which the Brigade would pivot and from thence withdraw due
west. The Brigade would assemble at Flers and every effort was
to be made to keep in touch with units on either flank."

Having issued these orders the Brigadier got in touch
with the 51st Brigade, and from their Brigade-Major
learned verbally the details of the orders received from
D.H.Q. shortly before. He sent two of his staff with
the Brigade-Major to the 51st Brigade H.Q. then near
Beaulencourt, to obtain a written copy of the orders. On
reaching Gueudecourt the Brigade took up a position
covering the place on the south-east about 6.30 p.m.
The York and Lancasters and the R.E. Field Companies
had been in position on the spur south-west of the village
since an earlier hour in the afternoon. Flers was reported
to be occupied by the enemy—a premature and incorrect
report.

According to the orders from D.H.Q. the 52nd Brigade
was to have formed a flank guard about a mile south-east
of Gueudecourt with its right near Lesbœufs to cover the
retirement of the 51st. This ground was however now
held by the enemy, but the 51st had come through from
Le Transloy and was reaching Gueudecourt. All three
Brigades were thus in or near the village.

The orders from D.H.Q. gave as the final stage of the
retirement that day the occupation of a front from
Bazentin-le-Grand to Martinpuich, the 50th Brigade
forming a flank guard south-east of Flers towards
Ginchy as a prelude to this move. It was ascertained that
Flers was not yet held by the enemy, who was still south
of it. The Brigadier of the 52nd decided to go through
it to Martinpuich. It would seem that during the halt
at Gueudecourt the commanders of the three Brigades,
though close together, were not actually in communication
and their next action was taken independently. The
52nd moved on to Flers and by 7.30 p.m. was assembled
just north of the place, and threw out an outpost line
facing south-east. While taking up this line there was

a fight with a strong patrol of the enemy.   By 8.30 the head of the column of the 50th Brigade, coming from Gueudecourt, arrived and halted just north of the ground held by the 52nd.   The 51st Brigade had meanwhile left Gueudecourt and was marching by Eaucourt l'Abbaye on Martinpuich.

It was now night but there was bright moonlight. The enemy was becoming more active on both sides of Flers, and the outposts reported that there were mounted troops on the move with his patrols.   The C.O.'s of the 50th and 52nd Brigades met to discuss the situation, and it was decided that with the enemy in Lesbœufs and Morval, and showing increasing pressure about Flers, the best course to take would be a withdrawal through Eaucourt l'Abbaye to Martinpuich, where the 51st Brigade would probably be found.   " All Brigades of the Division would thus regain touch with each other and with Divisional H.Q."

By 9.30 p.m. the two Brigades and the detachment of R.E. and Pioneers were moving towards Eaucourt, the 50th Brigade leading, the 52nd supplying the rearguard. The enemy was content to occupy the ruins of Flers without following up the column.   The pace was not quite a mile an hour on the average.   At 11.30 there was a halt just north of Eaucourt.   At the cross-roads here it was found that H.Q. of the 99th Brigade was established. From these it was learned that according to information in Corps Orders to the 2nd Division (now in line to the north of Eaucourt l'Abbaye), the 17th Division was to occupy a position with its left just east of the village and its front running along the road from the cross-roads on that side to High Wood.   While the men rested for a while, orders were given for officers of the two Brigades present to reconnoitre this position and a Staff officer was sent to ride over to the Divisional H.Q. (still believed to be not far off at Courcelette), to report what had been done, and arrange for a supply of rations and ammunition.

The 51st Brigade had reached Martinpuich, and by midnight got through a message by way of Courcelette to D.H.Q. reporting its arrival there, but without being able to give any news of the rest of the Division.

At midnight the distribution of the 17th Division was:

D.H.Q. Méaulte (since 7.30 p.m.).
Detachment, B.M. and Staff officers, signals, etc., of 50th Brigade between Pozières and Courcelette.
51st Brigade at Martinpuich.
50th and 52nd Brigades, with the York and Lancasters and Field Companies R.E. halted on the road north-west and south-east of the cross-roads just north of Eaucourt l'Abbaye.
2nd Line transport and train at Hénencourt, west of the Ancre.

The 50th and 52nd Brigades had little rest that night. The position was soon identified and reconnoitred, and by 2 a.m. the two Brigades had occupied it—the 52nd on the right towards High Wood, and the 50th on the left up to the cross-roads west of Eaucourt. An hour later, while the Brigadier of the 52nd was inspecting his line, he met a Staff officer of the 63rd R.N. Division, who informed him that its 188th Brigade was just then marching up from Martinpuich to occupy this very front, the Division having been ordered to hold the line from High Wood to Eaucourt l'Abbaye. The information received from the 2nd Division was thus shown to be based on a misunderstanding. The Brigadier went to communicate with his colleague of the 50th Brigade and told him he intended to move the 52nd Brigade back to Martinpuich, but the Brigadier of the 50th, General Yatman, decided to remain in the line near the village, assemble his Brigade near Eaucourt l'Abbaye with the Poineer and R.E. detachments, and use this force to fill a gap which existed between the left of the R.N.D. and the right of the 2nd Division.

At the Divisional H.Q. at Méaulte on this night of March 24th to 25th it was known by midnight that the

51st Brigade, " the men very tired," was at Martinpuich and it was conjectured and believed that the other Brigades would be with it.   Under this impression General Robertson issued his orders for next day at 1 a.m.   The general situation on the Vth Corps front was:—What remained of the 47th Division was prolonging the line on the right of the 63rd R.N. Division from High Wood to near Bazentin-le-Grand.   On the afternoon of the day before a gap had opened in the line south of Bazentin. Reinforcements from the 1st Cavalry Division had been hurried up to fill it, and cavalry were now believed to be holding Bazentin and Montauban.   South of Montauban the VIIth Corps prolonged the line.   The enemy were believed to be in Longueval and Delville Wood, and later information showed they had penetrated into the east margin of High Wood also.

The orders for the 17th Division were that it would close the gap between Bazentin-le-Grand and Montauban, 50th Brigade on the right, 52nd in the centre, 51st on the left.   The Divisional Artillery would cover the front of the Brigade and the Pioneer Battalion and R.E. Field Companies would be at Fricourt in reserve.   All movements southwards from about Martinpuich would be carried out west of the road from Martinpuich by Bazentin to Montauban.   Movements to commence at 4 a.m. and be completed by 6 a.m.

Communications had not yet been reorganised and these orders did not get through to the Brigades till later than the times named for their execution.   At 2.50 a.m. a report came through to D.H.Q. from the Brigade Major of the 50th Brigade saying that he had gone on to Martinpuich, and was there with only the Signal Section and 120 stragglers of the Brigade, and was sending out parties to discover where the rest of it was.   It was 4.30 a.m. when the 52nd Brigade began its march back from Eaucourt to Martinpuich.   It arrived there at 6 a.m. An hour before this the 51st Brigade had marched off

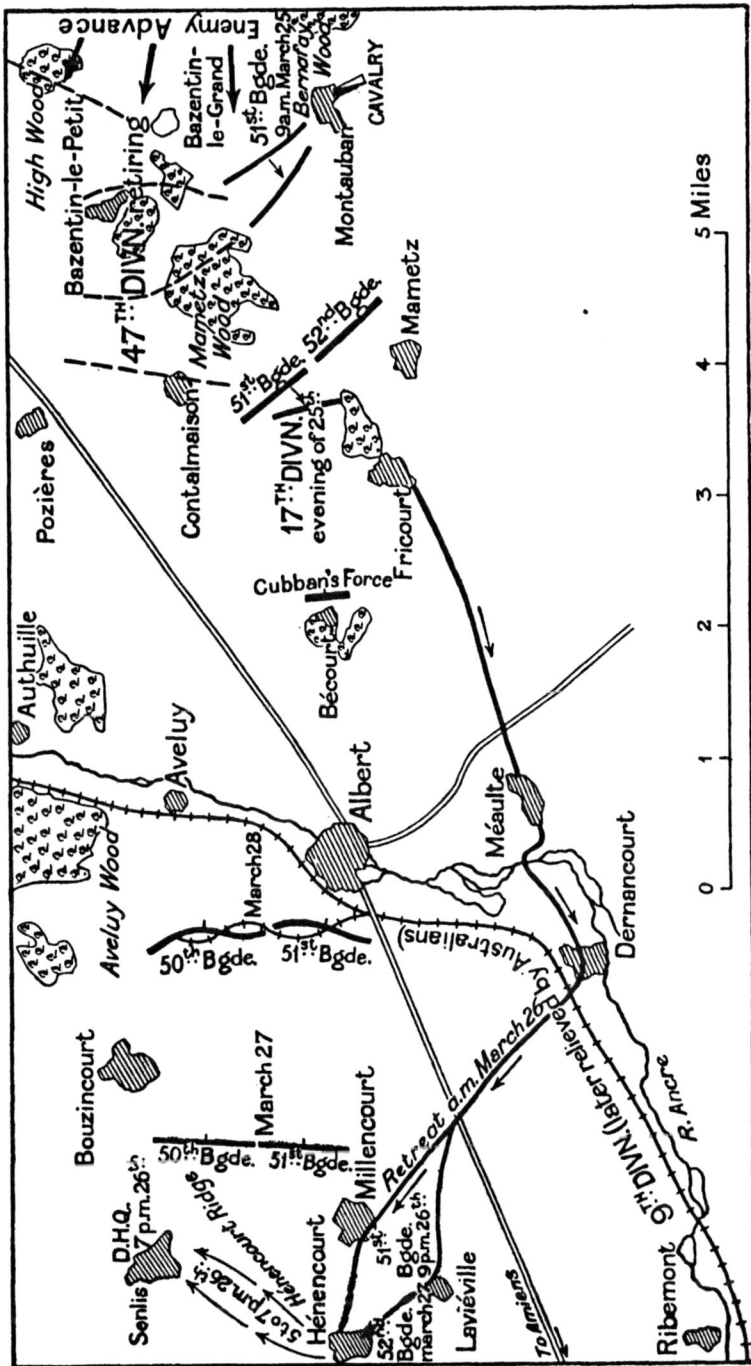

Retirement across the Ancre, March 25 and 26, and operations that followed, March 26 to April 3, 1918.

Map labels:
High Wood — Enemy Advance — Bazentin-le-Petit — Bazentin-le-Grand — 51st Bgde. 9a.m. March 25 — Bernafay Wood — CAVALRY — Montauban — 47TH DIVN. retiring — Mametz Wood — Mametz — 52nd Bgde. — Contalmaison — 51st Bgde — 17TH DIVN. evening of 25th — Pozières — Cubban's Force — Bécourt — Fricourt — Authuille — Aveluy — Aveluy Wood — Albert — Méaulte — Dernancourt — 50th Bgde. 51st Bgde. March 28 — Bouzincourt — March 27 — 50th Bgde. 51st Bgde. — Hénencourt Ridge — Millencourt — Retreat a.m. March 26 (later relieved by Australians) — 9TH DIVN (later relieved) — R. Ancre — Ribemont — D.H.Q. 7 p.m. 26th — Senlis — 50th Bgde. 51st Bgde. 9 p.m. 26th — 52nd Bgde. march 25 9 p.m. 26th — Hénencourt 5 to 7 p.m. 26th — Lavieville — To Amiens

0 1 2 3 4 5 Miles

southwards towards Courcelette.   Its bayonet strength was now only about 600.

The parties sent out by the Brigade Major of the 50th failed to get touch with the rest of the Brigade, so he decided to move back with his party southwards through Courcelette.   The 78th Field Company R.E. was also going south, following the 52nd Brigade.   Arriving at Courcelette, the Brigade halted for a while and the men, who had been very short of supplies, had breakfast, thanks to the discovery of a dump of rations near the road.   Here it was learned from the C.O. of a Field Ambulance at 7.40 a.m. that D.H.Q. were at Méaulte.

Thus in the early hours of Monday the 25th, the situation of the Division was:—At D.H.Q. there were only the staff and various details, with the improvised escort of the day before.   The 51st and 52nd Brigades and the small detachment of the 50th were moving down from the direction of Martinpuich through Courcelette, the 51st leading.   They were marching slowly, for not a few of both officers and men were nearly dead beat. Firing had already begun along the front of the 63rd and 2nd Divisions, holding the line from High Wood northwards.   General Yatman with his three battalions of the 50th and the attached artillery Brigade was holding a gap between these two divisions east of Le Sars, with the York and Lancasters on his left.   He had his H.Q. at Destremont Farm.

An officer was sent from D.H.Q. to Pozières on the Albert road to divert at this point the troops coming down from the northward, and send them on by the road running due south to Fricourt.   Other officers were engaged in collecting stragglers, and orders were sent to Hénencourt that all parties that had drifted there and any men that could be spared from the transport should be sent to Méaulte to reinforce the fighting line of the Division. It was an anxious time at Méaulte, for the gap to the eastwards, which the Division was to have occupied at dawn,

was watched rather than held by detachments of the
1st Cavalry Division, who were reported at Bazentin and
Montauban.

Of the main body of the 50th Brigade nothing was
heard at D.H.Q. till late in the following afternoon.
Here it may be noted that the Brigade was in action on
the right of the 2nd Division until, between 9 and 10 a.m.,
the line here was forced back towards the Ancre, and
General Yatman's detachment was involved in the retirement. The York and Lancasters had been fighting on
its right, holding old German trenches against an enemy
close in front in another old trench line. While they
held on here the battalion had for artillery support only
the fire of a solitary 18-pounder and a couple of trench
mortars. They had many casualties, including some of
their officers, and when the retirement on their left
developed they fell back to a line of heights on the east
bank of the Ancre, not far from Beaumont Hamel. In
the afternoon, finding themselves isolated and the enemy
appearing in force in front, they slipped down into the
gorge of the river, here now shrunk by the drought to a
narrow stream, and crossed it one by one over a fallen
tree trunk to the west bank. A supply of rations was
found in an abandoned camp close by and the men
—now about 300 of all ranks—had a much needed meal.

The 51st Brigade was the first unit of the Division to
reach Fricourt, and about 9 a.m. it was sent into the line.
It was impossible to get forward to the line Montauban—
Bazentin-le-Grand indicated in earlier Divisional orders,
for the right of the 47th Division had fallen back from
Bazentin and was now holding a line through Mametz
Wood. Montauban was however still held by the cavalry,
so the line taken up had its right on the high ground just
north of this place and its left near the south-east corner
of Mametz Wood. It was a front of about a mile, a long
line to be held by some 600 infantry covered by a few
batteries—the 78th and 79th F.A. Brigades. There

was indeed a good deal of bluff in the occupation of the position with so weak a force, but there were hopes that the line would be reinforced before long—hopes doomed to disappointment.   As the Brigade took up position it reported at 9.5 to D.H.Q. that a heavy attack was developing between High Wood and Delville Wood away to the north-east; the enemy had pushed on to the ground south-west of High Wood, and on the right front of the position an advance was developing from Trones Wood, east of Montauban.   Between 10 and 11 a.m. the left of the 47th Division was drawn back to Bazentin-le-Petit and there was a gap opening between it and the right of the 63rd Division north of High Wood.

The D.H.Q. staff was busy improvising reinforcements. A Field Company R.E. came in and the Brigade Major of the 50th Brigade arrived with his party.   Spare men from Hénencourt, officers and men from instruction schools and other centres now abandoned in the Divisional area, and stragglers from various units were got together, about a thousand men in all.   Then there was the improvised H.Q. escort of the day before.   At noon in Fricourt all these details were being organised in three battalions. They were placed under the general command of Major Cubbon, R.E. and it was directed that when ready they should fulfil the orders originally prepared for the 50th Brigade, and reinforce the line on the left of the 51st Brigade.   Familiarly known as " Cubbon's Force " the improvised detachment appears in orders and reports of the next two days as " the 50th Brigade."

Another useful improvisation was the formation of a mounted detachment of despatch riders, for communication purposes at D.H.Q.   The strength was only one officer and 16 other ranks.   The value of horsemen for this purpose had been lost sight of in the long months of trench warfare and within a year of its arrival in France the Division had been deprived of the Cavalry squadron originally attached to it.

A continuance of the retirement now seemed not unlikely. Shortly before noon D.H.Q. sent orders for the
transport and train to move west from Hénencourt to
Vademont. In case the Ancre had to be recrossed
Hénencourt was to be the new D.H.Q. position and the
centre of concentration for what was left of the Division.

The 52nd Brigade was now coming into Fricourt.
At noon its H.Q. were established at Fricourt Château,
but some time had yet to be spent reorganising before
the men could be sent into action. The 51st Brigade
was still the only unit of the Division in the line. It had
swung back its left as the 47th Division on that side was
forced back into Mametz Wood, exposing its flank.

About noon the 47th Division found they could no
longer hold on to the wood and fell back further to the
west of it towards Contalmaison. On the right of the
51st Brigade the Cavalry had to evacuate Montauban a
little later. The 51st Brigade began to fall back about
1 p.m. to a new position covering the north-east end of
Fricourt Wood. Five tanks of rather an old type had
been placed at the disposal of the Division at 12.30.
They were directed to go to the spur north of Fricourt and
be ready to protect any further retirement.

In the afternoon the situation was anxious. The
Divisional front was still lightly held. A gap opened
between the right of our thin line and the flank of the
47th Division. It was closed by the 51st Brigade
extending its left, just in time to stop the advance of a
party of the enemy from Mametz Wood. Major
Cubbon's force was sent forward to support the Brigade
on this side. There was another gap between its right
flank and the left of the 9th Division. This was filled
by Cavalry and a group of motor Machine Gunners.

After 5 p.m. the situation was improved by the 52nd
Brigade being brought up to prolong the line on the right,
between the flank of the 51st, and the Cavalry now
occupying a position about Mametz village.

The marvel is that the line held. Orders issued at
7.35 that evening gave the position of the Brigades thus:
—52nd on the right, from near Mametz village to the
north-east corner of Fricourt Wood, the 51st prolonging
the line thence north-west to the ground south of Contalmaison (where the Division had fought for days in July
1916). Major Cubbon was directed to send to these
two Brigades any men of his detachment belonging to
them, and with the rest to act as a reserve at Bécourt.
Before midnight touch was lost with the Cavalry at
Mametz, and it was afterwards learned that after dark
they had retired with the 9th Division on their right
under orders from the VIIth Corps.

At 1.15 a.m. on Tuesday the 26th, a Staff Officer
arrived at Divisional H.Q. with orders from the Vth
Corps that the retreat was to be continued at once. The
Corps was to recross the Ancre. One of its Divisions,
the 12th, was to hold Albert and positions on the bank
northwards to Hamel, and the 17th Divisional Artillery
was to support its right. The 9th Division (VIIth
Corps) was holding the line of the Albert—Bray road, in
touch with the outposts of the 12th covering Albert.
The 17th Division was to retire through the line of the
9th and cross the river below the town.

Divisional orders were at once issued. Major Cubbon's
force acted as a rearguard, and held successive covering
positions west of Fricourt till 4.45 a.m., when the last of
the long column of march passed through it. The retirement was unmolested, except at one point, early in the
movement, where the Lancashire Fusiliers, on the right
of the 52nd Brigade, and before it reached the first rearguard position, and had just left the line, were attacked
by a strong enemy patrol. There was a sharp fight
before the Germans were beaten off. This incident was
a result of the Cavalry on the right having withdrawn soon
after dark.

The march was by way of Méaulte, then across the

little river to Dernancourt on the west bank, and on to Hénencourt where the Division (less the greater part of the 50th Brigade still away to the northwards) was concentrated at 10 a.m.   An hour later all units were reported to be in billets.

Reorganisation began, and there were hopes of a brief respite after five days and nights of fighting and marching. But the troops were warned that the immediate outlook was still uncertain and all ranks were advised to take as much rest as possible.

There was confirmation of this warning in the fact that at Hénencourt, all the morning, heavy firing could be heard to the eastward, and at 2 p.m. hopes of a quiet time were dissipated by an emergency order being issued to the effect that the Division would move that day to Senlis, " at an hour to be notified later."   Meanwhile all units were to be ready to move off at half an hour's notice.

The afternoon was spent at Hénencourt, and during these few hours something was done in the way of reorganisation.   The whole fighting strength of the Division was now less than the full war strength of a Brigade.   The battalions in the 51st and 52nd Brigades were approximately each between 300 and 400 strong—say about 2000 rifles in all.   The 50th Brigade still consisted only of Major Cubbon's detachment—various details, a section of signallers, some of the Pioneers and the three Field Companies R.E.

At 4.30 p.m. came the order to move off; the head of the column was to pass the fork of the roads on the northern margin at Hénencourt at 5 p.m.   The 50th Brigade was to form the advance guard, and the 52nd, immediately followed by the 50th Brigade group, the main body.   The 51st Brigade followed the line of the Hénencourt Road, but as this ran partly on high ground under full observation from the enemy's positions about Albert, the main body marched to the west of it, by the margin of the Hénencourt woods and then across country to Senlis, keeping well below the crest of the Hénencourt-Senlis ridge. At 7 p.m. the Division was concentrated at Senlis and Divisional H.Q. established in the village.

This move north to Senlis placed the Division in a good position for reinforcing the front held by the Vth Corps, which now ran along the line of the railway on the west bank of the Ancre from Hamel to opposite Albert. But this move appears to have been actually ordered by the Corps H.Q. on the receipt of information which afterwards proved to be incorrect. A report had come in that the enemy was across the Ancre on the left of the line and close up to Hébuterne and Colincamps. There was even a story that he had got some armoured cars across the river. But though the line here was hard pressed, it was holding its own, and the origin of the armoured cars rumour appears to have been simply that some of our own new type of light " whippet tanks " (till now unknown to most of the troops) had been seen coming out of action, and mistaken for enemy armoured cars.

The information received on arrival at Senlis was that the danger was on the other flank towards Albert and south of it, where the front of the Vth Corps joined up with that of the 9th Division (VIIth Corps). Albert was reported to be " full of Germans " and they had got across the river both north and south of the town. They were on the low ground between the Ancre and the railway at various points from Albert to beyond Aveluy, and south of the town they had also crossed and were close to Dernancourt. There were even rumours that the enemy was across the railway line on the VIIth Corps left, and might be as far forward as the high ground between Dernancourt and the Albert-Amiens road.

Orders now received from Vth Corps H.Q. included a reference to this rumour. The 52nd Brigade was to move to a point about a mile east of Millencourt in the direction of Albert, and having cleared up the situation it was to be prepared either to reinforce the 55th Brigade —the extreme right Brigade of the 12th Division (Vth Corps) holding the line facing Albert—or to form a defensive flank on the high ground near the Albert-Millencourt road. The 51st Brigade was to follow the 52nd and be in support of it near Millencourt.

A mounted officer was at once sent off to the 35th Brigade H.Q. to obtain information, and by 9 p.m. the 52nd Brigade was assembled at the appointed place east of Millencourt and pushed out patrols towards the railway. The 51st was coming into Millencourt. At 11 p.m. the liaison officer returned with the report that there was no break in the line, but the 35th Brigade were being hard pressed, especially on their right at the road and railway junction west of Albert: the town was strongly held by the Germans. Arrangements were being made to reinforce the line, and the 51st and 52nd Brigades were requested to send up a battalion from each, but these movements had only begun when they were countermanded as the enemy's attack was slackening and the 35th Brigade reported its position to be now satisfactory. Reassuring news had also come in as to the situation on the right of the 9th Division. Here a patrol had gained touch with the 27th Brigade and brought back information that the rumour of an enemy break through on that side was unfounded. Dernancourt village and the railway were safely held by the Division, and there was no break between it and the left of the Vth Corps.

March 26th had been a day of "alarms and excursions," and the 51st and 52nd Brigades had marched more miles than in any twenty-four hours since the retreat began. The night passed quietly. At midnight Divisional H.Q. were moved back to Contay, on the Amiens Road, four miles west of Hénencourt. The distribution of the 17th Division at that hour was:—Divisional Artillery supporting the 12th Division; 50th Brigade (Cubbon's force) at Senlis; 51st at Millencourt; 52nd between that village and Albert. At 3 a.m. the 52nd was ordered to fall back to Hénencourt, and was in billets there by 6.40 a.m. on March 27th.

That morning commanding officers were warned to have their Battalions ready to move at half an hour's notice, but to see that officers and men had as much rest as possible. During the day the enemy made several attacks on the line on both sides of Albert and was able to bring a considerable artillery and machine gun fire to bear on the slopes of the high ground on the west bank. At 11 a.m. Divisional H.Q. notified the 52nd Brigade that it was placed temporarily at the disposal of the G.O.C. 9th Division. The Brigadier had already had a message to this effect from the 9th Division H.Q., which now sent orders that a Battalion and one Company of the Brigade was to take post in support south-east of Millencourt. A warning was added that they were not to get in the way of an Australian Brigade that was moving up to the Ancre front by the Amiens road.[1] The Lancashire Fusiliers and a company of the Duke of Wellington's were accordingly sent forward from Hénencourt, but they were not long in position, when at 1 p.m. the 52nd Brigade was informed that it had reverted to the 17th Division Command.

At 9 a.m. Corps H.Q. had telephoned to Sir Philip Robertson that, as soon as the situation permitted, the 17th Division was to take over the right Brigade front of the 12th Division (35th Brigade) on the front from the railway junction opposite Albert to the south side of Aveluy Wood. A little later he was directed to take general control of the defence on this line. At 9.30 an advanced report station was organised at Senlis, and a message came through from the G.O.C. 35th Brigade that his position was satisfactory and he could hold on till dusk. From 10.30 the Brigade came temporarily under the 17th Division command.

[1] This was the first contingent of the reinforcements now on the way to the right of the Third Army, which included an Australian and a New Zealand Division and the Guards Machine Gun Battalion.

But during the morning, despite reassuring reports from the 35th Brigade, it was realised that it was gradually losing ground under the heavy artillery fire of the enemy, whose infantry now occupied the railway line north of Albert. In consequence, at 1.30 p.m. the 51st and 52nd Brigades were directed to take up a position, on a front of about a mile and a half, from the high ground immediately west of Bouzincourt southwards to a point a little east of Millencourt, the 51st on the right, and the 50th on the left. When the order was issued the latter was represented only by Cubbon's Force at Senlis, but a welcome reinforcement was near at hand. Brigadier-General Yatman with what was left of his three infantry Battalions and various minor details of the 50th Brigade was rejoining from the northwards after having been in action for some days with the 2nd Division. This force reached Senlis about 2 p.m. and the Brigade was again reconstituted, and rapidly reorganised to go into the line. The orders were that the two Brigadiers were to send forward strong patrols to gain touch with the 35th Brigade and reinforce it if required. The 35th Brigade however was not being attacked and was holding a new line about a mile west of the railway on rising ground with a good field of fire, and in touch on its left with the 63rd R.N. Division. It was decided that it would be relieved by the 50th and 51st Brigades after dusk.

The 52nd Brigade had been kept in reserve at Hénencourt. At 3.30 p.m. it received a message from Divisional H.Q. that our aircraft reported that the enemy had forced the crossing of the lower Ancre about Ribemont (four miles west of Dernancourt), broken through the line of the 9th Division, and gained ground between Ribemont and Lavieville. The 52nd Brigade was therefore to take up a line south of Hénencourt and Millencourt, to form a defensive flank protecting the right of the position held by the rest of the Division. The three Battalions of the Brigade with " C " Machine Gun

Company moved out to the line indicated, and sent patrols southwards to gain touch with the 9th Division. An hour later these returned with the reassuring news that the line of the 9th Division was intact; the enemy had not passed the lower Ancre; and the aircraft reconnaissance report was one more of the mistaken rumours that characterised these anxious days. The Brigade accordingly returned to its billets at Hénencourt.

After sunset, the relief of the 35th Brigade began. It was completed by 4 a.m. on the 28th. The line taken over had its right on the Albert-Amiens road a little to the west of the point where the railway crosses it. It then ran northwards, partly east and partly west of the branch railway that starts from the main line at this point, and it continued to the high ground west of Bouzincourt, where it was in touch with the right of the 63rd Division. In front of the left an advanced post was established at an outlying knoll, which was the highest point in the vicinity. The 51st Brigade took over the right of the line, and the 50th the left. These two Brigades were supported respectively by the 78th and 79th Brigades R.F.A. The 34th Brigade, R.F.A. was in reserve, and the 52nd Infantry Brigade remained at Hénencourt. Before dawn the Field Companies R.E. and a detachment of the Pioneer Battalion were brought up from Senlis to begin entrenching the new line.

Its front was nearly two miles in length in a direct line, and nearly two and a half if one measured it along the curves of its trace. It was a long front to be held by two war-worn Brigades of tired men who had had scanty rest for a whole week, and whose effective strength in numbers was not much more than that of two complete battalions. But this weakly held front represented the end of the retirement, and the beginning of the establishment of the new general front along the west banks of the Ancre, from which, before the end of the coming summer, the advance to victory was to begin.

The first great German push had now reached its high-water mark, and its first driving power had become exhausted. Behind this part of the new German front, gained in a week of battle, there lay east of the Ancre the devastated and almost roadless region of the Somme battlefields of 1916-17. The enemy's supply arrangements were in a chaotic state and it would require some time for the organisation of a reliable system for moving up reinforcements, supplies, heavy batteries and the enormous reserves of munitions needed for a further push. On the day on which the 17th Division took over its new line, the enemy made an attack in force on the Arras front of the Third Army. General Otto von Bülow had concentrated twenty Divisions for this attack, which was launched on both sides of the Scarpe and southwards against our lines covering the Vimy Ridge. The object of the attack was the capture of this dominating ground and of the city of Arras. A success here would enlarge the huge wedge driven into the British front and open the way to a further advance over country that had not been reduced to the hopeless condition of the old Somme battle ground. But the fight before Arras resulted in a complete victory for the defence. The enemy broke into the lightly held " Forward Zone," but failed to make any impression on the " Battle Zone " and suffered enormous losses in repeated attempts to penetrate it. Von Bülow's defeat before Arras marked the final failure in the first phase of the German offensive.

On the day of the Arras battle the front held by the 17th Division was quiet, though north and south of it, at Hamel and Dernancourt, there was some fighting. During the night the work of entrenching and wiring the front was pushed on, and the 29th (Good Friday) was on the whole another quiet day until after dusk, when the enemy rushed and captured the advanced post in front of the extreme left of the line. During the day two sections of No 3 Battalion, Tank Corps, were attached to the Division (each of four tanks). One of these was posted at Bouzincourt to operate on the high ground, and the other at Hénencourt. In the night of the 29th to 30th the 52nd Brigade took over the right of the line and the 51st went into reserve at Hénencourt.

At dawn on the morning of March 31st (Easter Sunday) the 50th Brigade made an attempt to recapture the advanced post lost on the evening of the 29th. The zero hour was 5.30 a.m. and the attack was made by the 7th East Yorkshires, who were to have been supported by the Tank Section from Bouzincourt. But the four tanks were unlucky. One broke down at the start, two others were put out of action almost at once by their Hotchkiss guns jamming, and the fourth was knocked out by a direct hit of a shell. The Yorkshires came under a heavy machine gun fire from the enemy trenches and from the other side of the Ancre. They got into a trench on the right for awhile, but were unable to hold on and the attempt was abandoned. In the evening the enemy made two minor raids on the right of the Division. The first at 6 p.m. was made by a party of some thirty of the 3rd German Naval Division under cover of a trench mortar barrage. The raiders got into one of the advanced posts but were driven out, leaving several dead in the trench. The second attack, made half an hour later, under cover of a smoke barrage, never reached our line. On April 1st and 2nd all was quiet on the front, and on the night of the 2nd to 3rd, the Division was relieved by the 12th Division, leaving its artillery in the line, and also the Pioneer Battalion and Field Companies R.E. to continue the work of consolidation.

It was not quite a fortnight since the storm of the German offensive had burst upon the Division in the Flesquières salient. It was now drawing out of the line on the ground where our armies had concentrated, nearly two years before, for the Battle of the Somme. In those few days the gains of many months had been swept away, and the Division had lost two-thirds of its numbers. But it had not lost heart or confidence in ultimate success. The remnant that had survived the trial had in no way been broken by the toil, dangers and disappointments they had endured. Having faced all this there was nothing in the future that they were not ready to meet with cheerful courage. This remnant of the old Division would be the iron core of the reorganised Division that would help to hold the new front in the early summer, and share in the advance to decisive victory that would bring the long war to a triumphant close.

CHAPTER X

THE TURN OF THE TIDE
(April to August, 1918)

In the first week of April, 1918, the opening move in the great offensive of the German armies had been brought to a standstill. We can afford to face the fact that it was a defeat for the allied armies, the most serious reverse the British armies had ever suffered, and a success for the enemy. But it was a dearly bought success, and he had failed in his main object. The " Kaiserschlacht " had not brought the promised decisive victory. The attempt to divide the Allied forces had not succeeded. Their line was bent back for many a mile, but it was not broken. The new front was being consolidated. Reinforcements were pouring into France that would soon more than make good the enormous losses of the critical days after March 21st. But the initiative still remained with the enemy, and his effort was not exhausted. He struck again on the Flanders front with a drive for the Channel ports; he made another push for Amiens and strove to gain further ground towards Paris; and finally stormed the heights of the Aisne and once more reached the Marne. There were more than three months of these last efforts of the German armies. Each new offensive gained some ground before it was brought to a standstill. Meanwhile the enemy's forces were being worn down, and those of the Allies were growing in strength, until at last the moment came when the tide turned and the time was ripe for the Allied counter-offensive, which began in the first part of August and after a hundred days ended in decisive victory.

During the four months from the retirement across the Ancre in the first days of April to the British advance at the beginning of August, the 17th Division was upon a front where there was no fighting on a large scale. It was at first engaged in reorganising and refitting after the heavy losses of the retreat, training the reinforcements which were arriving to bring its numbers up again to war strength, and improving from day to day the new defence lines that were growing up west of the Ancre valley. The enemy was close in front and these four months were a time of reversion to the somewhat monotonous experiences of trench warfare.

Their record may be briefly told as a prelude to the stirring story of the victorious advance that followed. On April 4th, Divisional H.Q. were established at Flesselles, about eight miles north of Amiens, and the troops were billetted in villages east and west of the Amiens-Doullens road over a wide area, the 50th Brigade, farthest west at Halloy, being some nine miles distant from the 51st, east of the road at Pierregot. But in the next three days the Division moved into close billets in the villages east of the road, and the York and Lancasters and the 77th and 78th Field Companies R.E. rejoined.

They had been working under the commanding Engineer of the Vth Corps in the Forward Area on the consolidation—or rather the construction of the new front line. Their task was rendered more onerous on account of the shortness of every kind of engineer equipment and material, tens of thousands of tons of which had been destroyed or abandoned to the enemy in the last days of March.

Reorganisation and training began at once. Large drafts arrived from the home training camps and garrisons, with a number of young officers from the O.T.C. centres. Among the reinforcements there were also officers and other ranks who had already had some war experience, —some of them convalescents who had served in the Division, and some from several other formations. At this time men on leave at home, always a large number, had no certainty of returning to the units with which they had already served. They were attached in somewhat haphazard fashion to drafts which happened to be crossing the Channel when their leave expired. It was a gain for the Division that, until the advance in August began, it was employed in alternate tours of trench work on the Ancre front and rest and training in its back areas. This gave time for the remaking of the Division on the foundation supplied by the reduced numbers that had survived the fighting retreat in March. The first period of this training in the Flesselles area began in somewhat trying weather, with many dull, cold and rainy days.

On April 9th the Germans made their second great attack—this time across the Lys against the British northern front in France and Flanders. It was a drive for the Channel ports and at the outset the enemy gained ground rapidly. Hard fighting continued all through the month, and with less intensity during the first three weeks of May. During these anxious weeks of the battle on the Flanders border, the Ancre front was fairly quiet, though the enemy's artillery was frequently active. But a few hours after the offensive in the north began, reports of a probable German move on the Third Army front resulted in an order reaching the H.Q. of the 17th Division, directing that the Division was to be in the reserve of the Third Army and ready to move at four hours' notice. This suggested a coming break in its connection with the Vth Corps. But on the 11th orders from the Third Army H.Q. intimated that an attack on its front was expected at an early date, and the Division was therefore to move at once eastward to the left support area of the Vth Corps.

The weather had cleared up, and the march began under bright skies and on fairly dry roads. Divisional H.Q. moved that afternoon from Flesselles to Puchevillers. The 50th Brigade reached Raincheval and Ar-

quières; the 52nd and the York and Lancasters, Toutencourt; and the 51st, Talmas and Vicogne on the Amiens-
Doullens Road. The rest of the Division was well east
of this line. Next day the 51st Brigade moved forward
to Acheux and Lealvillers, and all the Brigade staffs and
Battalion commanders were ordered to reconnoitre the
left Corps front. The Division was now concentrated
close up to the new front and expecting soon to be again
in action, though its " rest " had been a brief one and it
was still below strength, with the final training of its
drafts incomplete. Warning orders were received that
it would relieve the 63rd R.N. Division in the line on the
night of April 14th to 15th on the left sector of the Vth
Corps front.

Accordingly on the evening of April 14th the relief
began and was completed in the early hours of the 16th.
The Divisional H.Q. were transferred from Puchevillers
to Lealvillers. The front taken over faced the enemy
positions on the west of the Ancre, where it makes its
long curve by Beaucourt and Hamel before running south
to Albert. The German line in this sector lay from near
Mesnil on the north side of Aveluy Wood to the high
ground about Beaumont-Hamel, a stronghold the enemy
had held through the earlier months of the Somme
Battles and regained in the last stage of his great offensive
in March. Our front here ran on the right near Mesnil
along the line of a light railway following a hollow in the
plateau, and on the left passed east of Auchonvillers on
ground slightly lower than that of the opposing German
line about Beaumont-Hamel. The 50th Brigade took
over the left of the line, and the 51st the right, the 52nd
moving up to a support position at Forceville.

The Division held the sector till the end of the first
week of May. The three weeks were comparatively
speaking a quiet time. The storm centre was away
northwards on the Belgian border, where there was
persistent fighting on a large scale. But the rumours

and warnings of a coming renewal of the enemy push across the Ancre and against Arras proved baseless. On neither side here was there any real infantry activity, though the gunners were busy enough at times. The Germans had got up some of their heavy artillery and indulged in intermittent bombardments, not only of the line, but also of roads and villages, far behind it from Englebermer and Auchonvillers back to Forceville and Toutencourt. Our batteries effectively retaliated on nearer targets both by day and night, often interfering seriously with enemy movements of reliefs and supplies between the Ancre crossings and the front.

Infantry patrols in No Man's Land were out night after night, but seldom encountered any of the enemy. A considerable amount of steady work was done in getting into effective condition the old British trenches of 1916, which formed the greater part of the forward line now held again. Further back the Pioneer battalion and working parties from the reserve Brigade were busy on second and third lines, in view of the possibility of this front becoming the scene of a serious enemy push. On several days low flying enemy aircraft were very active and enterprising, more than once raiding the artillery positions. A divisional order issued on April 29th called attention to the necessity of being ready to deal with such attacks. "The most effective defensive measures (it explained) consist principally in the infantry and artillery always having their machine guns ready for anti-aircraft action and making use of them. In the case of the artillery it is essential that machine guns be ready to open fire both in battery positions and on the march, and also in limber parks (the M.G.s will be mounted on the limbers). Further, all carrying parties and columns must take their rifles with them." In the second part of April the weather had been broken with mist and rain and limited visibility, and this facilitated these sudden low-flying swoops of the hostile aircraft.

On April 30th, orders were issued that from May 5th the plan for holding the line would be changed. All three Brigades would have each a Battalion in the front line, another in support, and the third in reserve, and on the night of the 4th to 5th this reorganisation of the defence was carried out. Rumours were again current of an impending attack and this was probably the reason for thus bringing all the Brigades into line organised in depth.

The change had hardly been completed when warning orders arrived that the relief by the 63rd Division would begin on May 7th. Divisional H.Q. were moved to a camp on the road between Lealvillers and Toutencourt, and in the night of May 8th to 9th the relief was completed. Just before the Division left the front a party of American officers and N.C.O.'s was attached to it to obtain practical experience of our methods. It was made up of Lt.-Colonel Rhea, Assistant Chief of the Staff, 77th American Division, who was temporarily attached to D.H.Q., and four Regimental officers and eight N.C.O.'s who were distributed among the three Brigades. This was the beginning of American co-operation with the British forces on the western front in preparation for the final offensive.[1]

The Division was out of the line for a little over a fortnight—till the last week of May. Divisional H.Q. were at Toutencourt, where the instructional school of the

[1] The American armies were already landing their advanced troops in the south-west of France, where they were forming large training camps and depôts and laying out ranges. The original idea was that they would not come into the line till the summer and then with only part of their eventual force. Their plan contemplated that the great Allied advance would not be possible till 1919, when an American army of four millions would be ready to strike the blow that would decide the war. The number of Colonel Rhea's Division suggested the large scale on which they were organising. From first to last the British Army had never more than about seventy Divisions raised in Great Britain and Ireland (besides seven from the Dominions), and several of these were in the East and on other fronts. The whole American force was to be concentrated in France, and it should be added that an American Division on a war footing was to have twice the strength of a British Division.

Vth Corps organised some months before gave useful facilities for special training. The troops were billetted in camps and villages in the tract of country between the Amiens-Doullens and the Doullens-Albert roads, now well known to many of the officers and men, as previous turns of " rest, refitting and training " had been spent there. The weather was all that could be desired,—the bright sunny days of the early summer of Picardy and Artois, with all the trees in leaf again, the ground dry, and the roads in good condition, and the warm air not yet too hot for strenuous work. That work was so arranged as to give welcome opportunities for rest and recreation. There were games, sports, meetings, horse shows. Reinforcements were coming more freely from home, and further drafts were incorporated in the various units. Lieut.-General Shute, K.C.B., C.M.G., who had succeeded General Fanshawe in command of the Vth Corps, held inspections of all three Brigades, and presented medal ribbons to N.C.O.'s and men who had been awarded decorations for the recent operations.

On May 25th, the relief of the 12th Division on the Ancre front began, and was completed in the early hours of the 27th, when the 17th Division H.Q. were transferred from Toutencourt to Raincheval. The sector taken over was the same that the Division held in its former tour of trench duty in April, facing the enemy stronghold at Beaumont-Hamel and his lines west of the bend of the Ancre. When the Division came back into the line here, there were some expectations that the Germans would soon attempt another drive on a large scale across the Ancre, and north and south of the Somme towards Amiens. Fighting had continued during May on the Flanders border, but by this last week of the month it was clear that the British, reinforced by the French, had brought the enemy drive to a standstill and were locally masters of the situation. It was known that the Germans had been accumulating very large forces in rear of the

huge salient now formed by their line in France, a salient
with its apex in the Oise valley only fifty miles from Paris.
It was certain that they were preparing for a third great
push.   It might be westward for Amiens, or southward
against some part of the main French front, or between
these directions it might be a bold drive towards Paris.

On May 27th, the very day on which the 17th Division
completed its taking over of the sector facing Beaumont-
Hamel, this third great enemy push began—and began
with swift and startling success.   It was launched against
the French front from Rheims to the old battleground
of 1914 on the heights of the Aisne.   At the outset the
enemy gained ground much more rapidly than in their
first great offensive against our front east of the old Somme
battlefields.   By the evening of the first day the Germans,
after clearing the ridge of the Chemin des Dames, were
across the Aisne and well southward towards the Marne.
Three days later they had reached its banks east of
Château Thierry.   They had captured thousands of
prisoners and large numbers of guns.   But French and
British divisions were holding them on their left and saved
Rheims.   As the enemy advance paused on the Marne,
the rumour spread again that there would be another
drive between Arras and Amiens.

But on the Ancre front the enemy attempted no serious
attack.   His activities were chiefly those of his artillery,
which on some days would rise for a while to such
intensity as to suggest the opening stage of a bombardment preparatory to an advance.   But during June the
enemy never ventured on any more important operation
than a raid on the 50th Brigade front in the early hours of
Tuesday the 4th.

At 2.30 a.m. that morning the enemy's gunners became
suddenly active, and at 2.40 a heavy barrage of artillery
and trench mortars was put down on the whole front line
of the Brigade, which held the trenches facing Beaumont-
Hamel.   As it lifted on to the support line, three strong

parties of raiders broke into the front trench. They retired after about ten minutes of sharp fighting, during which our losses were an officer killed and two missing, and of other ranks nine killed, 28 wounded and 13 missing. The retirement was made under heavy fire from our guns, but the raiders carried off their dead and wounded and patrols sent after them into No Man's Land could not secure any identifications.

General Gwynn Thomas and the 50th Brigade staff were already planning a raid on a much larger scale, and this was successfully carried out on the night of June 8th.

It was the most considerable operation of this kind yet planned by the Division, and all who took part in it were keen to " get a bit of their own back." On the night of June 6th the raiding force had a final rehearsal of the operation on the practice ground, and during the following night there was a move to the assembly positions. The force was made up of 18 officers and 500 men of the 7th East Yorks, commanded by Lt.-Colonel King, D.S.O., and the same number of officers and men of the 6th Dorsets commanded by Lt.-Colonel Weldon, D.S.O.

The front to be attacked by the raid was about 500 yards in length, forming a salient in the German line in front of Beaumont-Hamel, with its left or northern end by a huge mine crater dating from the operations of 1916, and on its right the deep narrow gully known as the " Y Ravine." The attack was to be pushed to a depth of 400 yards. All the officers and N.C.O.'s had been provided with large scale trench maps, and all ranks had attended lectures illustrated by lantern slides explaining every detail of the plan. Each one knew exactly his part in the raid. For the creeping barrage that was to cover the advance there had been detailed 107 guns of various calibres from heavy howitzers down to 18-pounders, besides 35 trench mortars and 96 Vickers machine guns.

At zero hour—10.5 p.m. on the 8th—covered by the creeping barrage—the Dorsets went forward on the right and the East Yorks on the left. The enemy's barrage came down about five minutes later on our front trench and support lines, but the advance was well forward before it began. The raid came as a surprise to the enemy. His front and support trenches between the crater and the ravine were cleared, and numbers of dug-outs blown in. Having pushed nearly up to the German reserve trenches the raiders retired just after 11 p.m. bringing back with them thirty prisoners, four machine guns and three trench mortars. The casualties in the attack were heavier than had been anticipated. This was partly the result of some of the men not only keeping close to our barrage, but, in their eagerness to follow up the enemy, going through it at more than one point.

The losses were ten officers wounded and two missing, and of other ranks 16 killed, 189 wounded and 34 missing, a total of 251. But the enemy's losses were believed to be much more serious. They had evidently been hard hit and it was not till 1 a.m. on the 9th that they reoccupied their front line, beginning their advance to it by bombing cautiously up the communication trenches, where they evidently expected to find some of the raiders still holding on. During the following morning the Third Army Commander, Sir Julian Byng, telegraphed his congratulations, saying:—" I consider this raid to have been very well prepared and carried out, and it reflects great credit on the two battalions."

In the following week warning came from Army H.Q. that the enemy was preparing an attack on our new front from Arras southwards to the bend of the Ancre, in which the Division would have to meet the advance of the German left. There were a few days of general expectation of serious fighting. On the evening of the 15th—the very day the warning message was received— the enemy put down a heavy barrage on the Divisional front, but no attack followed. Then for several days there was only intermittent activity of the German artillery and aircraft. The warning had been based on information that pointed to an attack being fixed for an early date, but the plan had been abandoned, perhaps because just at this time influenza was causing serious trouble in the German armies.

On the 17th the weather broke after a long spell of bright sunny days. There was heavy rain, and the nights were cold; and trench conditions decidedly unpleasant, but on the 22nd the relief of the Division by the 63rd Royal Naval Division began and was completed on the 25th, when Divisional H.Q. moved back from Toutencourt a couple of miles to Hérissart. The troops were in camps and billets in the now familiar training grounds east of the Amiens-Doullens road. It was notified that the Division, though still administered by the Vth Corps, was in G.H.Q. reserve, and must be ready to move at nine hours' notice, and also prepared to act as the right support of the Vth Corps front. G.H.Q. still thought it possible that the expected German attack might be made.

But though the possibility of another great enemy push was kept in view, and work was continued on the successive defence lines in rear of the British front, the Division was not called to meet any emergency during its fortnight of " rest and training." Instead of having to hurry up to stem some new German advance, it was called upon to lend some of its artillery and machine guns to other Divisions for a few days in connection with minor offensive operations, which proved to be the prelude of the coming general advance of the Allies. On June 28th, orders were received for the Divisional Artillery to be transferred temporarily to the 3rd Australian Corps, which was preparing for an attack on the German front about Hamel, south of the Somme. The gunners were to join the Australians in the night of July 1st to 2nd, and go into action with them twenty-four hours later. The first two batteries moved off on the evening of June 30th.

On the same day the four companies of the Divisional
M.G. Battalion, three batteries of Light Trench Mortars
and four heavy T.M.'s were lent to the 12th Division for
an operation the same night against the German position
in Aveluy Wood.

The attack on the wood was a surprise to the enemy
and at first was a complete success.   The 17th
Division units assisted in the barrage fire which covered
it.   The German front and support lines were captured,
and twenty-five prisoners were sent back, belonging to
the 243rd Infantry Division and the 3rd German Naval
Division.   Some of them gave very useful information.[1]
The daylight hours of July 1st passed quietly, but a few
minutes before 10 p.m. the enemy counter-attacked and
retook their support line, and later in the night the front
line, so that at dawn on the 2nd the position on the 12th
Division front was what it had been before the raid.
On the 2nd the 17th Division units returned to their
billets near Toutencourt.

On July 4th, the batteries of the Divisional Artillery
lent to the Australians for this occasion co-operated with
them in a more important and completely successful
operation on the Third Army Front, resulting in the
capture of the village of Hamel and the adjacent Vaire
woods with 1,000 prisoners.   This advanced our line
between Villers-Bretonneux and the Somme on a front
of nearly four miles to the depth of a mile and a half.

On the 9th the Division moved into the line, relieving
the 12th Division in the sector facing Aveluy Wood.

---

[1] The prisoners all declared that no preparations were in progress for any
attack on the Ancre front.   From information collected from them the enemy's
order of battle on the front from Albert northwards, including the Aveluy
Wood sector, was ascertained.   On the German left, south of the road from
Bouzincourt to Aveluy village, the line was held by the 243rd Infantry Division,
with the 122nd Fusiliers and the 479th Infantry in the trenches and the 478th
Infantry in reserve at Contalmaison.   North of the road the line was held by
the 3rd Naval Division, the units from left to right being the 2nd, 3rd, and
1st Marine Infantry Regiments.   It was against this Naval Division that the
17th Division came into line on its next tour of duty in the trenches.

The relief was completed on the 11th when Divisional H.Q. were transferred from Hérissart to Toutencourt.

The Divisional front lay along the high ground from near Bouzincourt to a point west and a little north of Mesnil. As this was the ground from which, a few weeks later, the Division went forward to begin the great advance that ended the war, a few words may be said as to the general character of the country immediately in its front, ground now held by the enemy, but most of which was in our possession two years before, on the eve of the Battle of the Somme.[1]

The Germans here held both banks of the Ancre. On the eastern bank of the little river the dominant feature was the high ground at the west end of the Thiepval-Pozières-Longueval ridge. The château and village of Thiepval were now mere ruins, and the park and wood a stretch of cratered ground with shattered trunks of branch-less trees. On the ridge the enemy had excellent positions for his heavy artillery. Below the Thiepval height the Ancre ran in a valley that here widened from its upper gorge as it flowed down to the more open ground about Albert. The flat valley bottom was a belt of marshy ground through which the river flowed, breaking into narrow branches and backwaters. In front of the sector held by the Vth Corps the enemy was established on the west bank, and the chief feature here in front of the 17th Division was Aveluy Wood, on a lower-lying under-feature of the high ground. It was a little more than a mile in length from north to south and nearly a mile across. The Germans held the railway on the west bank as their main line of defence covering the river crossings, with the wood as their citadel. North and south of it they had reconstructed the old British trenches dating from 1915 and 1916.

In this second week of July the enemy was engaged in an attempt to gain ground east and west of Rheims,

[1] Cf. Map, p. 370.

isolating the city or compelling its evacuation, and was preparing for a crossing of the Marne. General Foch and Sir Douglas Haig were discussing the plans of the Allied counter-offensive, but it was still recognised that the enemy might attempt a fourth offensive, and the front south of Arras and along the Ancre was considered a not unlikely objective for such an advance. West of the Ancre, in the three months since our new front here had been stabilised at the beginning of April, our defence had been organised in depth, so as to provide for all eventualities. Much the same system of successive zones as had been adopted on the British front before the great offensive of March was followed here. The scheme of defence was thus summarised in an instruction issued by Divisional H.Q. on July 11th:

" The system of holding the Divisional Sector for the tour is to divide the allotted area into three zones—the Advanced Forward Zone, the Main Forward Zone and the Purple System, and to hold each Zone by posts not less than 20 strong, each prepared for all-round defence. The Advanced Forward Zone is to be lightly held with the object of deceiving the enemy as to the strength and position of the defences, and of beating off raids, and, in the event of a serious attack of forming islands of defence to break up the attack. The Advanced Forward Zone and the Main Forward Zone each to be held by two Battalions of the two Brigades in the line, and the Purple System by one Battalion of each Brigade in the line. The Brigade in reserve is under orders, in the event of an attack, to occupy quickly the Purple System and to counter-attack from it under Divisional Orders.

" The work policy makes the Brigades in the line responsible for carrying out all work in the Advanced Forward Zone, and for finding parties for work between the Advanced Forward Zone (exclusive) and the Purple System (inclusive). The order of priority of work will be—(a) Wiring; (b) Construction of platoon and half-platoon strong points; (c) maintenance of necessary communication trenches between strong points."

So nothing was left to chance. But the tide of war was on the turn, and this was the last elaborate defence scheme to be issued.

In these July days on the Ancre front the enemy showed no sign of aggressive enterprise. His activity was limited almost entirely to intermittent artillery fire with an occasional bombardment of some point behind the British front—such as Senlis or Bouzincourt. On the 20th and 21st, by night and by day, patrols penetrated his front line near the Aveluy-Bouzincourt road, passing over an unoccupied trench following its line for some distance, and meeting with no opposition. One of the patrols brought back a straggler as prisoner. Another exchanged a few shots with a party of Germans that seemed by no means anxious to put up anything like a serious fight.

In this third week of July the enemy had failed in his attempt to establish himself south of the Marne, and Foch had struck his first heavy blow from the woods of Villers-Cotterets against the flank of the enemy salient south of the Aisne. The sensational gains of the third and last German offensive were crumbling. Sir Douglas Haig was preparing the double stroke east of Amiens and south-west of Arras. The Allied offensive was beginning.

On the Ancre front the Artillery of the 17th Division was busy, not in the desultory and somewhat aimless methods of the German gunners in the opposing high ground, but with persistent and systematic activity and a definite purpose. The infantry worked at the improvement of the trenches according to plan and kept up the routine of trench warfare. An interesting episode was the arrival of successive detachments of an American regiment, the 318th Infantry, and its commander, Colonel Ulysses K. Worrilow. The Americans spent a few days in the trenches in small parties attached to the units of the Division, and showed themselves keen learners and good comrades. But while the Infantry were having a comparatively quiet time, the artillery and machine gunners were carrying out a plan that soon made the enemy's positions on the west bank of the Ancre untenable. In each twenty-four hours the batteries of the Division fired 10,000 shells and the machine gunners 28,000 rounds. Part of this expenditure of ammunition was allotted to harassing fire distributed over the German trench system and Aveluy Wood, but constant targets for the shell fire were the causeways and bridges across the swamps and channels of the Ancre. These lines of communication with the west bank had been carefully marked down by our aircraft, and this persistent shelling of the river crossings made communication and supply exceedingly difficult for the enemy's troops on the west bank.

After dark on the evening of August 1st a party of the 10th West Yorkshires—four officers and seventy other ranks—made a successful raid, which had important results. The objective was a sunken road just inside the German left front—a portion of the road from Bouzin-court to Aveluy. Starting at 9.10 p.m. the raiders penetrated for 300 yards along the sunken road, blew in four dug-outs, killed a dozen of the enemy, and retired at 9.30, bringing back sixteen prisoners and a machine gun, the party having no casualties.[1]

Ten of the prisoners belonged to the 446th Infantry, the other six were men of the 358th Pioneer Company. On being examined the Pioneers told how, when captured, they had been detailed to lay charges for the destruction of the dug-outs in the sunken road in preparation for a general retirement across the Ancre.

On this information steps were taken to follow up the enemy and hustle his retirement from the wood. But it was presently ascertained that the Germans had been moving out of it all the evening of August 1st, and the West Yorkshire raid must have come in contact with one

---

[1] With reference to this operation Sir Julian Byng wrote : " The raid of the 10th West Yorkshire Regiment was exceedingly satisfactory. It was well planned and rehearsed and carried out in a determined manner. The identi-fications were most valuable, and the result seems to have dislocated the enemy's preparations for retirement. The Battalion is to be sincerely congratulated on its successful enterprise."

of the last of their covering detachments.   At 1.30 a.m. on the 2nd, a patrol of the 7th Lincolns—two officers and 40 men—pushed into the south-west front of the wood and met with no opposition.   Only dead Germans were found lying here and there in the abandoned trenches.   Other patrols were sent forward all along the front, and on the report from the 17th Divisional H.Q. the Divisions on the right and left also sent parties forward. Before dawn a trench line running north and south through the middle of the wood was occupied and was being consolidated, with outposts on the railway close up to the west bank of the river.

Two land mines exploded in the wood without resulting in any casualties.   Attempts had been made by the Germans to destroy their dug-outs, mostly without result. The fuses had failed to act, or perhaps the work had been done hurriedly and ineffectively.   There were no " booby traps."   When daylight came, messages left by the Germans before they abandoned the wood were found scribbled on scraps of paper, and fastened on tree stumps. Here are two samples written in English.   The first had a jocular allusion to our shells as " iron rations ":—

" MY DEAR TOMMY !
    Wenn are you coming, we are gone.   Many pleasure in our cottages.   Send not so many iron portions.   Eat them your selfst.
                        Make
                        peace
.....................next time !
    Have you not enough ? "

One word was illegible.   Another message, in somewhat better English, made an attempt at sarcasm:—

" DEAR OLD TOMMY—We congratulate you on your great success in taking Aveluy Wood and meeting many thousands of Hun prisoners.   We wish you will have a very good time here. Perhaps we take you a little bit of a better place some where else, and therefore good byee, au revoir.
                        Yours truly,
                        DEUTSCHE SEESOLDATEN."

These "German Sea-Soldiers" were a Marine Regiment of the 3rd Naval Division.

Daylight brought another discovery. As the sun came up it was found that the wood was not a place where anyone could have "a very good time." It was infested with swarms of horse flies. The men occupying it suffered terribly from their bites—hands, neck and face were often black with them. In the heat of the day they made life a misery.

The Germans had now abandoned all the ground west of the Ancre and were holding a new line on the east bank. On August 5th the relief of the 17th Division by the 38th (Welsh) Division began and was completed in the night of the 6th to 7th. Divisional Headquarters remained at Toutencourt and the three Brigades moved into the adjacent training areas to the west of the village.

Orders issued early on the 7th stated that the period of "rest and training" would probably extend to twenty-one days, after which the Division might be called upon "to take part in offensive operations, either attack or following up a beaten enemy." An outline of the programme for the coming three weeks set forth that training with troops was to be limited to four hours a day; the afternoons were to be devoted to rifle shooting and recreational training. A Divisional Rifle Competition would be arranged. In the evenings there would be lectures and tactical instruction; all training was to be directed to preparing for open warfare and offensive operations, and there would be tactical schemes without troops for Battalion, Company, Platoon and Section Commanders. This first day was given to reorganising and cleaning up, and time was found for the beginning of a Corps Boxing Competition. Everyone looked forward to a good long "rest and training" with the encouraging prospect of a successful advance in open warfare to follow.

Training began next morning. Some of the battalions

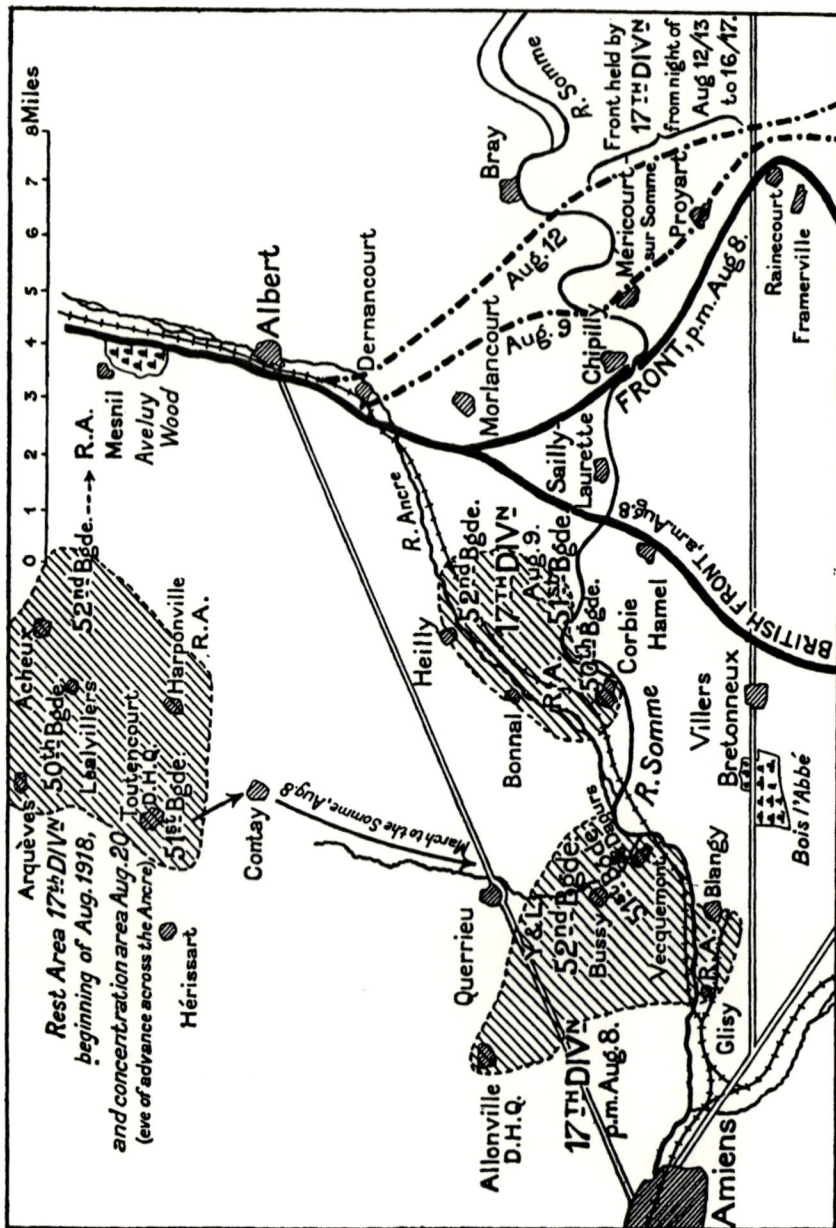

Allied Offensive, August 8 to 12, 1918, and operations of the 17th Division, August 8 to 20.

were route marching, others doing steady drill, when at
11 a.m. an emergency order arrived, and hurried messages
were sent out recalling all to billets and camps.

Since dawn there had been the sound of heavy firing,
not many miles away to the southward. But at this
stage of the war there was a general disposition to attend
to one's own business and not indulge in conjectures as
to what gunfire in another sector might mean—all the
more if one was out of the line. So it was a surprise to
learn that there was a battle in progress on both sides of
the Somme east of Amiens, and as soon as the men had
their dinners the Division was to " march to the sound of
the cannon." The move began at 2 p.m.—southwards
towards the crossing of the Somme at Vecquemont, east
of Amiens.

The 50th Brigade marched off at 2 p.m. followed by
the 51st at 3.30, the artillery at 5.30 and the 52nd at
7.30. It was a hot summer day, and a good number of
the men were hardly yet in training for this march over
the hilly country roads to the river crossing, but they
stepped out well, for they were in high spirits as the news
spread that they were on their way to a great battle that
had opened with undoubted success. As the afternoon
went on they met convoys of some thousands of German
prisoners, a sight that verified the current rumours of
victory on a splendid scale.

To sum up briefly the events of the day—at early
dawn, without any preliminary bombardment to put the
enemy on the alert—Rawlinson with the Fourth Army
had advanced on both sides of the Somme, the vanguard
of his attack being the onset of 400 tanks. British,
Canadian and Australian Divisions and an American
contingent followed them up. On the right Débeney's
French Army prolonged the attack to the southward.
The enemy was taken by surprise, and at first his line
seemed in a state of confused collapse, as the attack went
forward mile after mile, taking thousands of prisoners

and scores of guns.   For the first time in the war the
British cavalry got through and rode forward far beyond
the infantry.   As the day went on the Germans were
able to organise a serious resistance, but by evening the
British centre was ten miles east of its starting point and
a deep salient had been driven into the enemy's front.
Ludendorff in his Memoirs wrote of August 8th as " The
black day of the German Army in the history of the war."
It was the beginning of the end.

That evening the H.Q. of the 17th Division were at
Allonville, four miles north-east of Amiens.   The troops
were in bivouacs and billets on both sides of the Somme,
the 50th Brigade farthest south at Bois l'Abbé near
Villers-Bretonneux, the artillery on the south bank of the
river, the 51st Brigade in and near Vecquemont waiting
to cross over next morning, and the 52nd at Bussy a mile
and a half north of the crossing.

Next morning the Division was warned to be ready to
move at two hours' notice to reinforce any part of the
British line, which was still engaged, and gained further
ground during the day, though more slowly and in the
face of a steadier resistance than in the opening phase of
the battle.   It was not until late in the afternoon that
orders were received for a move, and in the evening the
Division was concentrated in rear of the left attack, at
Corbie and on the ground between the Ancre and the
Somme immediately east of the little town.   D.H.Q.
remained at Allonville.

For two more days the Division remained in reserve
while fighting continued, the battle extending farther
south as the French brought fresh forces into action, and
on this flank much new ground was gained.   By the
morning of the 12th the battle was dying down on the
Fourth Army front and the new line won in the preceding
days was being consolidated.   At 11.15 that morning
D.H.Q. received orders to relieve the 3rd Australian
Division on the front immediately south of the Somme

during the following night. The front thus taken over was about 5,000 yards in length—(just under three miles) —its general direction north and south, from the bend of the Somme opposite Bray, then east of Proyart village, to near Rainecourt, a little beyond the long straight highway that runs through Villers-Bretonneux to Vermand. Here on the south bank of the Somme, the plateau, which had been the scene of the battle, breaks into spurs overlooking the marshy hollow through which the river winds, and between them narrow valleys descend to the lower ground. The line held by the Division rose along the forward slope of one of these valleys, topping the plateau south of Proyart. It was not a good line to hold, though safe enough just now because, for the time being, any tendency to aggression had been knocked out of the enemy by his recent experience. But it was hardly organised for serious defence. In old German trench lines, nowhere deep or well revetted, a line of detached posts had been improvised. In front there was a wide No Man's Land beyond which the Germans were digging in. Their infantry showed no enterprise and only sent forward a few patrols at night, but day and night their artillery was busy. They had only heavy guns in action at long range and they sent over H.E. shells and great quantities of gas shells.

The 51st Brigade held the left of the line, the 50th the right, and the 52nd was in reserve well forward. A Machine Gun Company was attached to each Brigade. The York and Lancasters were at work improving the roads, the Field Companies R.E. were clearing out wells, organising water supply and repairing some damaged bridges.

The Division made a very brief stay in the line, and there were few incidents of note. On the first night just after taking over, patrols sent out by the 51st Brigade brought in a couple of prisoners. Next day the Brigade advanced their line on the left to the level crest of the spur in their front, but had to withdraw under heavy shell fire

and suffered some 700 casualties (including two Battalion
commanders) in the withdrawal, as they came back over
ground that had been deluged with gas shells.   After
this the high ground was watched by a few sentries in the
day and held by patrols at night.

On the night of August 16th to 17th the Division was
relieved by the Australians and next morning received
orders to rejoin the Vth Corps.   The return move was to
be made by night marches.   The weather was fine, and
the marches were made by moonlight beginning after
dusk on the 18th.   At 2 a.m. on the 21st the concentration of the Division in the reserve area of the Vth
Corps was complete, and part of the Divisional Artillery
was in action supporting the 21st Division, which with
the 38th was holding the line on the west bank of the
Ancre.   D.H.Q. was again at Toutencourt.   The distribution of the troops was: 50th Brigade at Lealvillers
and Arquèves; 51st at Toutencourt; 52nd at Acheux;
Divisional artillery at Harponville and near Mesnil.

Next day—August 21st—Sir Douglas Haig was to
strike his second great blow—this time against the
northern flank of the great enemy salient—Sir Julian
Byng going forward with the Third Army, the left
towards Bapaume, the right (Vth Corps) across the Ancre.

The 17th Division was to co-operate in this right
attack.   The hoped-for three weeks of training for open
warfare, that had been anticipated when it came out of the
line at the beginning of August, had vanished with the
emergency call to the battle-front south of the Somme,
and it was now to take its part in the open warfare that
went on continuously till the armistice of November 11th.

CHAPTER XI

THE VICTORIOUS ADVANCE

(1) FROM THE ANCRE TO THE CANAL DU NORD

(August 21st to September 3rd, 1918)

The victorious advance that was to end the war began
at dawn on Wednesday, August 21st, when Haig sent
Sir Julian Byng's Third Army forward on the front
south-west of Arras.   In the first hours of the battle a
dense mist hung over the ground.   It was like the misty
dawn of five months before when the first storm of the
German offensive burst upon the British front.   But
that day it was the cold mist of early spring: now it was
a hot haze that promised a sultry summer day.   On the
left and centre the enemy made a stubborn fight, but by
evening the British front had been carried forward from
two to three miles, and the Germans were making a stand
along the line of the Albert-Arras railway north of the
old battlefields of the Somme.   On the right the Vth
Corps had two Divisions in action and the 17th Division
still in reserve.   The 21st Division, on the Corps left,
attacking near the bend of the Ancre gained touch with
the advance of the centre, and secured a footing with two
companies on the further bank of the Ancre hollow, in the
trenches near St. Pierre Divion, just north of the great
shoulder of the Thiepval ridge.   The 38th Division on
the Corps right from Hamel to near Albert was held by
concentrated machine gun fire at all the crossings of the
swampy hollow.   The Ancre formed a serious obstacle,
a tangle of water lines, that made a broad ditch in front

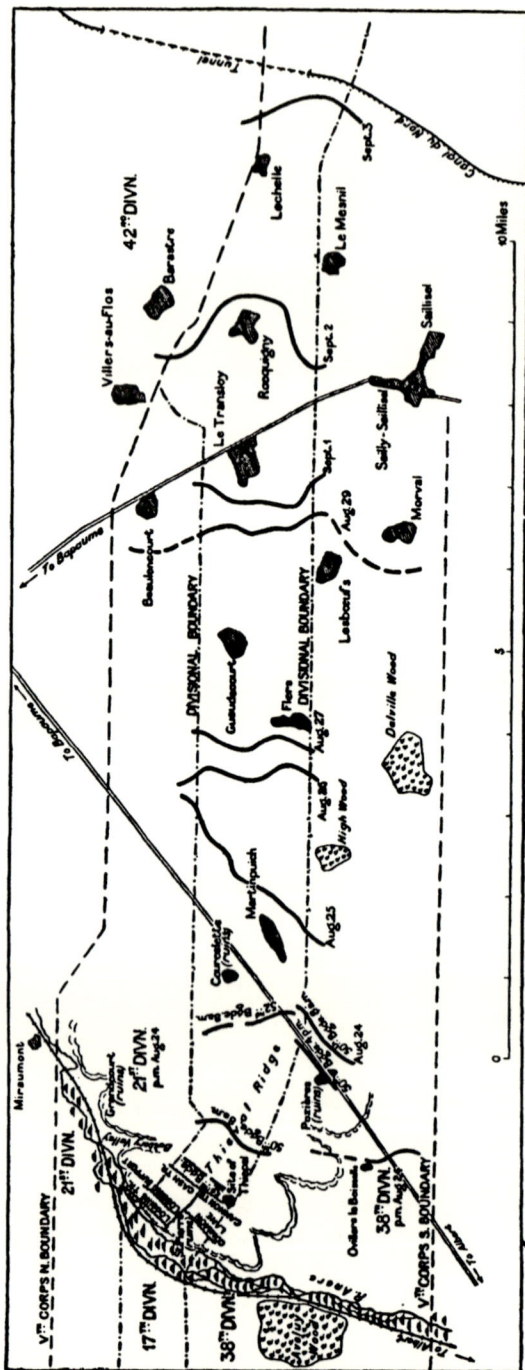

Capture of the Thiepval Ridge, and advance to the Canal du Nord.

of the rampart of the Thiepval ridge. The river was high, and had overflowed wide stretches of the long marshy islands between its branches, and the causeways and bridges over it had been damaged or destroyed by our gunfire, while the enemy still held the west bank.

The 17th Division placed its Field Ambulances at the disposal of the attacking troops and its Corps Artillery was supporting the attack of the 21st Division, mostly by firing flank and smoke barrages. At noon the three Infantry Brigades were moved forward into closer support—the 50th Brigade to the trench system between Englebelmer and Mailly-Maillet, the 51st to about Hédauville, and the 52nd between Beaussart and Forceville.

Next day, August 22nd, the battle continued on an extended front. On the left and centre further ground was gained across the railway towards Bapaume. On the extreme right, between the Ancre and the Somme, Rawlinson pushed forward towards Albert and Méaulte. On the Vth Corps front the enemy's artillery and M.G. fire was heavy, and the 21st Division made no further progress. Late in the afternoon the Divisional H.Q. received orders from Corps H.Q. that during the coming night one of its Brigades was to relieve the 110th Brigade (21st Division) at the river crossing, and prepare to co-operate in an attack on the Thiepval ridge in the night of the 23rd to 24th.

Orders were accordingly issued at 5.30 p.m. for the 50th Brigade to cross at the bend of the Ancre during the night, and General Robertson then took in hand the preparations for the attack on Thiepval in combination with the other two Divisions. At 8.30 p.m. preliminary orders were issued, with a map indicating the objectives and boundaries for the attack. A Company of the M.G. Battalion was attached to the 50th Brigade. The other three companies were to revert to the command of the Battalion O.C., who was to arrange to support the attack with M.G. fire. All movements of M.G. Companies were to be carried out under cover of darkness. The G.O.C. R.A. was to arrange for the barrage fire of the Divisional Artillery and such heavy guns as the Corps Artillery might place at his disposal. The G.O.C. 50th Brigade as a preliminary operation was to make good the trench line " Common Lane " and " Logging Support," reported to be already held by the 21st Division on the left bank of the river, and if possible, a line farther forward as the starting point of the attack. He was to have his infantry plan ready by 11 a.m. next morning, when the Officers Commanding the Artillery, the M.G. Battalion and the Signals were to meet him and work out all details. He was warned that at the outset only pack transport would be available, owing to the difficulty of the river crossings and the absence of roads east of the river. Arrangements would have to be made for water supply during and after the attack. Two Sections R.E. were placed at his disposal. The Officer Commanding the R.E. was to reconnoitre all crossings on the Divisional front early on August 23rd and commence work on making them practicable as soon after as possible. The coming operation was thus to be a " set piece " attack, but the time for adequate preparation was very short, in view of the difficulties of the crossings over the swampy Ancre valley.

During the night the 50th Brigade carried out the relief of the 110th. It was a trying operation. The enemy was continuously shelling all the crossings of the river and sweeping them with machine gun fire. His artillery made large use of gas shells, and particular attention was paid to the long crossing near St. Pierre Divion. The valley here was full of gas and the crossing was a narrow track over ruinous causeways and in places through the streams of the river and the flood that had risen over the marshes between them. By 5 a.m. the leading Battalion, the 6th Dorsets, had got across and taken over the trench line. The men dribbled over in small parties in single file and under continual fire. All were soaked to the waist and many to the armpits. As daylight was now coming the two other battalions, the 10th West Yorks and the 7th East Yorks, remained in the lines on the right bank, along the railway and by the river margin.

The position taken over on the east bank was a trench close to the river (named on the British maps, " Logging Trench ") about 900 yards in length with its right running into the broken walls and jumbled rubbish heaps that marked the site of St. Pierre Divion. In front, the hillside rose sharply for some 400 yards to another line already won from the enemy, "Logging Support" and its southward prolongation, "Common Lane." These trenches formed a front line for the Brigade nearly a mile in length. Above them the hillside sloped up for nearly half a mile to the second German line near the crest— "Cannon" and "Cash" trenches. The captured trenches now forming the British bridgehead by the riverside were not a very pleasant position for the single Battalion that held them; for the enemy looked down into them, and could enfilade their communication trenches. But the slopes above this line were under the fire of our supporting artillery and machine guns, which also covered the efforts made during the day to push on to Cash and Cannon Trench, so as to secure a better starting point for the attack on the ridge. This meant almost continuous skirmishing during the day, in which the Dorsets, though they could not reach the trenches on the crest, gradually worked their way until, by the afternoon, they established themselves 600 yards forward, improvising a new advanced line in shell holes and fragments of abandoned trenches, within easy reach of the enemy front. They were admirably seconded by covering fire of artillery and machine guns from the high ground west of the Ancre, and in this advance they captured eight machine guns and nine prisoners, one of them an officer.   It was a very fine piece of work.

Early in the morning the R.E. had reconnoitred the river line along the Divisional front.   There were three crossing points, the Mill Crossing (so named from a ruined water mill, on the west bank), the line by which the 50th Brigade had passed the night before; the Road Bridge Crossing, on the road to St Pierre Divion; and what was known as the Mule Crossing, a little south of it, a narrow path with a ruined footbridge.   At all these points the bridges were down and the old causeways, 200 to 300 yards long, were seriously damaged and at several points completely wrecked.   During the day the enemy kept all three crossings under such heavy gunfire that nothing could be done to improve them, but the York and Lancasters sent working parties to repair their bank.   At dusk the 78th Field Company R.E. started work on the Mill Crossing, and the 70th Company on the Mule Crossing.   At both points the working parties were under desultory shell fire, and at the former the work was rendered more difficult by the fact that troops were crossing during the evening and the following night. The West Yorkshires began crossing at 5.30 p.m. and by 11.30 were in position on the right of the Dorsets in the advanced line.   The East Yorks then followed and took up a support position in the trenches near the river.

By 1 a.m. on the 24th the Engineers had repaired the Mill Crossing sufficiently to provide a continuous road for infantry.   By 7.30 a.m. they had made it practicable for field guns.   At the Mule Crossing by 1 a.m. there was a practicable track across the river line and the swamps, made by using fascines and light trussed bridges at all the gaps.   During this work the Sappers discovered and successfully removed seven ground mines.

It was a moonlit night and zero hour had been fixed at 1 a.m.   According to the plan of the advance the 50th Brigade, after the first objective on the crest was won, would be in touch with and assisted by converging attacks of a Brigade of the 21st Division on the left and of the 38th Division on the right. Almost at the last moment it was learned that the line of advance assigned to the right of the 21st Division would leave for some time a very considerable space between it and the left flank of the 50th Brigade. A Company of the East Yorkshires was therefore brought up on the left of the Dorsets to prolong the front and guard the exposed flank.

At zero hour the barrage was put down and the advance began. The enemy made an obstinate resistance, and it was not until after daylight that the height was won. A first success came early on the right where, by a combination of pluck and good luck, a young officer of the West Yorkshires, 2nd Lieut. Braithwaite, M.C., either pushed on through the barrage or passed through a temporary gap in it, with a number of his men, went over the first trench line without much opposition, and though slightly wounded, made a useful diversion by attacking the enemy on the flank and rear. This helped the early success of the right attack, but on the left the Dorsets made slower progress, and presently came up against the tangle of trenches known as " Stuff Redoubt " in the earlier operations against Thiepval. It was only when the remainder of the East Yorkshires were brought up from the support line to extend the attack to the left and outflank this position that at last the Brigade, now with all its three battalions in action, pressed steadily along the heights and across the wilderness of shell holes, ruins and shattered tree stumps that once was the site of Thiepval village, château and park. At 8 a.m. it was reported that the " Red Line," the first objective on the crest of the ridge a little east of Thiepval, had been won, and consolidation had begun. Six officers and 208 men of the defending force had been made prisoners and were sent back across the Ancre.

But the intended combination with an advance of Brigades of the Divisions on right and left converging on the Thiepval height had not worked out " according to plan." The 110th Brigade, 21st Division, was reported to be held up in Battery Valley, a thousand yards to the left rear of the 50th Brigade. On the other flank there was no sign of the co-operation of the left Brigade of the 38th Division. It was rumoured that it was held near its starting line. The right Brigade of the Division was reported to be at Ovillers la Boisselle, near the Bapaume road and a good 3,000 yards away from Thiepval. The other Brigade of the 21st Division had reached the high ground south of the Ancre, near Miraumont.

Divisional H.Q. reported the situation to the Vth Corps, and orders came through at once for the 17th Division attack to be immediately pushed forward in the direction of Courcelette. The left of the 21st Division would move on the same point from the Miraumont height, and it was hoped this combined advance would cut off and capture the enemy force that was holding up the 110th Brigade in Battery Valley.

In pursuance of these Corps directions Divisional Orders were issued by 'phone for the 50th Brigade, closely supported by the 52nd, to push on to Courcelette. At the same time General Robertson ordered his Reserve Brigade (51st) to move forward to the trenches about Englebelmer and Mailly Maillet, so as to be in readiness to cross the Ancre if required, but he was anxious not to hasten this crossing, for supply would be by no means easy for the troops on the east bank. The crossings were still so difficult that it was not until the afterooon that the 52nd Brigade reached the Thiepval height.

Orders had been got through so quickly that at 8.30 a.m. the 50th Brigade was again advancing. Progress was still slow and it was not till four o'clock that it reported that it had reached the ruined village of Courcelette.

The 52nd Brigade did not join up in close support of the 50th till shortly before this hour. It had found the river crossing still only just practicable, and the subsequent advance was over trackless broken ground. Until the afternoon the attack had been supported only by long range artillery fire from the east bank, but the 18-pounder batteries of the R.F.A. had now been ordered to cross and give the advance closer support. They dribbled across during the afternoon, and it was an anxious matter to get them safely over the narrow creaking causeways and bridges. About half of them were over the river by nightfall. The rest crossed next day, but the heavy guns of the Divisional Artillery were sent round by a bridge at Albert.

Late in the afternoon a few of the 18-pounders were in action. It was the beginning of the exceptionally difficult and also exceptionally helpful work these batteries of the 78th and 79th Brigades R.F.A. did during the advance over the old Somme battlefields. Their ammunition supply was limited, the days of trench warfare when they could draw freely on huge dumps near at hand were over, and the arrangements for open warfare were only developing. Their support of the infantry advance was often so close as is seldom seen in modern war. Batteries or sections sometimes were actually in line with the Battalions with which they worked. They pushed so boldly forward that more than once, as day came, the gunners found themselves close up to the outposts, and took up improvised positions at short range. Officers and men passed the night in haphazard bivouacs, finding now and then shelter in old dugouts or ruined buildings. The horses were often watered at rain-filled shell holes.

To resume the story of the battle in the afternoon of the 24th: the occupation of the ruins of Courcelette had hardly been reported when there came a correcting message from the 50th Brigade. It was not at Courcelette, but at Pozières. At the outset in the attack on Thiepval the direction had been south-east towards Pozières. When the advance was resumed at 8.30 a.m. with new orders there had been, by some mischance, a failure to change direction with a half swing round to the left towards Courcelette. There was an impression that this was the ruined village out on front on the ridge crest, an impression so strong that the report was sent at 4 a.m. that Courcelette had been reached. It was explained as a mistake in map-reading on ground where all landmarks had been long since swept away. Perhaps a truer explanation would be that it was the outcome of the complete novelty of open warfare. Keeping direction from trench line to trench line up communication trenches in an assault rehearsal on model trench lines, explained in detail and marked out on large scale trench plans, was not an experience that helped towards guiding an advance over a desolate wilderness of ground like the battlefield of that day. The new advance had been hastily improvised, and it drifted along the ridge crest in the direction in which the Brigade had been fighting its way forward for hours.

There was both gain and loss in the mistake. As for the latter, touch had been missed with the 21st Division on the left, with the result that the Germans, who had been holding up the advance in Battery Valley, slipped away to the eastward by Courcelette.[1] But if the combination with the 21st Division had miscarried, the seizure of Pozières proved helpful to the 38th Division on the right and led to the retreat of another body of the enemy on that side being cut off.

At 4.30 p.m. when the 50th Brigade was busy consolidating the new line it had reached, facing generally south-east on a front of nearly a mile (the centre in Pozières, and the right and left slightly thrown back to the Bapaume road), it was fiercely counter-attacked by the

---

[1] The left of the 21st Division, the 64th Brigade, was heavily counter-attacked and failed to get forward from Miraumont towards Courcelette.

enemy, who all day had been gradually retiring before it. The attack was well supported by artillery and there was hard fighting before it was beaten off with considerable loss to the enemy's infantry. Its object was apparently to clear the Bapaume road for their comrades who were retiring before the advance of the 38th Division. A body of some 900 of these Germans soon after surrendered to the Welshmen, caught between their advance and our position at Pozières.

With the repulse of the counter-attack the long battle ended so far as the 50th Brigade was concerned. It had been in action for over seventeen hours, during which it had secured an advance of three miles and had taken 347 prisoners including 15 officers. The crossing of the swampy hollow of the Ancre, the storming of the heights beyond it, and the long advance on the ridge, made up a fine exploit. It was a day of victory, bringing success of an entirely new character. The Division had already had not a few successful days, but this differed from all that had gone before. It was no longer a case of winning a few trench lines and consolidating on the last of them with the enemy still close in front, unbroken and as strong as ever in his dogged resistance. Here at last was the long-hoped-for advance in open warfare, with success about which there could be no doubt or cavil. " That evening," writes an officer who took part in the advance, " I had a feeling of elation such as I had never known before in the war, except for a few hours on the first day of the Battle of the Somme. Those hours were of hopeful feeling that success was near at hand, but now there was a sense that we had reached it at last."

The feeling was well justified. The enemy was being steadily thrust back, and though there had been here and there sharp fighting he had made nowhere the steady persistent resistance of the old battle days of the Somme and the Arras front. He was bravely putting up a losing fight. He was going and must go further. For the long curving wave of the British advance was closing in from right and left of the great salient he had so rapidly won by his swift onset a few months before. He was fighting a huge rearguard battle, not to win victory but to gain time and avert menacing disaster. The tide of war had turned against him.

Successful as it was, the day had had its difficult experiences with its new problems for officers and men engaged in this, for them, novel kind of war. They had no previous experience of it, and their special training for it had been brief and much interrupted. On this half-desert upland it was not always an easy matter to say where the enemy was trying to hold on. With the moving battle-line it was not a simple matter to keep touch on left and right, and in these first days of the advance, the front on which at last the fighting ended was irregular and ill-defined. The line had to be improvised at haphazard. And night brought its new problems for solution. Supplies of all kinds had to be brought across the Ancre by the causeways, and carried to an ill-marked front over mere tracks that had once been roads, where it was easy to miss the way and blunder into a maze of ruined trenches and flooded shell holes. For the carrying parties to get their loads to the units for which they were destined was like a game of hide-and-seek in the dark. In inverse order there were the same problems for those who were moving the wounded and disabled men back to the collecting stations and the field hospitals beyond the Ancre. It is to the credit of all concerned that these difficulties were on the whole successfully met.

All day on the 24th the Pioneers and the R.E. companies had been busy improving the river crossings and repairing and marking the tracks up and along the heights. The 51st Brigade had begun crossing the Ancre late in the day. In the evening General Robertson, after receiving from Corps H.Q. orders for next day, issued by telephone his orders to the 17th Division. Already in the evening Corps H.Q. had directed the Division to take up a wider front, about 2,500 yards in all, extending it on the left so as to close the gap between its position about Pozières and the 21st Division. The pursuit of the enemy was to be vigorously continued eastwards, in the general direction of Gueudecourt, moving off at 4 a.m. D.H.Q. directed that the 51st and 52nd Brigades were to be in the front line with the 50th Brigade following in support, after being relieved at Pozières during the night by the left Brigade of the 38th Division. The 79th and 78th Brigades R.F.A. were to be affiliated respectively to the 51st and 52nd Infantry Brigades. Pioneers and Field Companies R.E. were to follow the advance improving communications.

When the advance began at zero hour the 51st Brigade had only just got into position. The ruined villages of Martinpuich and Courcelette, right and left of the Bapaume road, were occupied without meeting with any resistance. But eastward of these points the Germans began to offer serious opposition to the advance. Ground was gained on the left, and by 11 a.m. the two Brigades held a line just beyond the road that runs north-east from Martinpuich. A battery pushed forward through Courcelette in close support had a narrow escape, for a land mine exploded on the road just outside the village as the battery came through it, and there was a halt, with shells flying overhead while the track was made practicable. One of the gunner officers tells in his diary how just then " a strange figure appeared, clothed in a leather coat and sheepskin boots, an R.A.F. pilot; I gave him a drink from my flask and he told me he had been brought down by five Fokkers in No-Man's-Land, and had had to run for his life, being nearly shot or bayonetted by our fellows. He looked like a big toy woolly bear, in his flying coat and boots, padding down the King's Highway, and seemed, as was natural, more than a little dazed, but very cheery."

Serious fighting went on all the afternoon and progress was slow. The enemy's artillery fire was heavy, and along his line large numbers of machine guns, carefully concealed and difficult to locate, swept the ground, which was almost devoid of cover. Our artillery, with its very limited ammunition supply, could not attempt any counter battery work, and could not even dream of covering the advance with a barrage. The gunners pushing forward with sections, and sometimes even a single gun, were busy trying to spot and knock out German machine guns.

The only touch with the 38th Division was by occasional patrols. It did not get forward enough to combine with the right of our attack in a push against the position strongly held by the enemy on the rising ground about High Wood. The result was that the 52nd Brigade was held up a little east of Martinpuich, but the 51st on the left gradually got forward to near Eaucourt l'Abbaye. At 4.30 p.m. the enemy made two simultaneous counter-attacks, from High Wood and the valley south east of Eaucourt, but both were repulsed. Our line was somewhat disorganised by this time, and on the exposed ground the troops held on where they stood while daylight lasted, and were got into better positions on a continuous front in the twilight. In the evening, Divisional H.Q. were moved forward to Courcelette. During the day a squadron of the North Irish Horse (Cyclists) had been allotted to the Division.

Vth Corps orders for next day (the 26th) were that its three Divisions were to continue the advance, the 38th on the right against Longueval; the 17th in the centre on Flers, and the 21st on the left against Ligny-Thilloy and the line of the Flers and Ligny-Thilloy road.

A troop of the Irish cyclists was attached to each Brigade of the 17th Division for communication purposes, and the Divisional Artillery was reinforced by a Field-Battery, a 6-inch Howitzer Battery and a Battery of

60-pounders. These came into action near Courcelette and Martinpuich and did useful work, though still with a very limited ammunition supply. The advance begun at 5 a.m. again met with determined opposition. With the main attack of Byng's Third Army closing up to Bapaume, the enemy was making a stand to hold up the outflanking move of the Vth Corps south of the road. On the left of the 17th Division the 51st Brigade made early progress and won Eaucourt l'Abbaye, but the 52nd on the right was again held up during the morning, its right was in the air, and away to this flank, half-right, was the strong position of High Wood. The cross fire from this dominant stronghold so galled the Brigade that at last its right swung round, crossed the boundary of the zone of operations assigned to the Division, attacked the Wood and drove the enemy out. With its exposed flank thus cleared the Brigade was able to push on, and by sunset the Division held a front running north and south about half a mile west of Flers. During the day 118 prisoners were taken, mostly in the capture of High Wood.

Corps orders for August 27th assigned the following objectives to its three Divisions:—

Right, 38th Division.   Ginchy and Morval.
Centre, 17th Division.   The ridge 1,500 yards E. of Gueudecourt.
Left, 21st Division.   The high ground N.E. of Gueudecourt.

The battle was now a continuous advance, with fighting day after day, the zone of action assigned to the 17th Division having a front of just over 2,000 yards.

The front in which the Ancre had been crossed in the first day of battle was only 1,400 yards. General Robertson then put one Brigade in the front line, another in support, and the remaining Brigade was kept in reserve. He intended that this should be the normal order during the coming fighting advance, and that each Brigade should be in turn two days in the front line, two in support and two in reserve, so as to keep the Division as long as possible " fighting fit." It seemed the best solution of a difficult problem. For even the Reserve Brigade would often have what could be only comparatively speaking described as rest. The times were past when the Reserve lay well back in rear of the trench lines. It might now have to be moving forward each day in the wake of the continuous advance, bivouacking each evening in the open where it happened to be when the fighting ended.

In the afternoon of the first day when the 50th Brigade persisted in its original direction in the advance, the support Brigade had been pushed forward to the front to close the gap between the 17th and 21st Divisions. Since then, though the front had been shortened to about 2,000 yards, there had been each day two Brigades in the fighting line, the third in support and no reserve. The G.O.C. now decided to revert to his original plan. For the advance on the 27th the 50th Brigade was to pass through the front line and take over the whole Divisional front; the 51st was to follow in support at 1,500 yards distance, and the 52nd which had been longer in action was to withdraw to near Martinpuich for a brief rest.

The advance was to be in two bounds: (1) to the line Flers and northwards to the cross roads west of Gueude-court, (2) to Gueudecourt and the line of the Ginchy-Gueudecourt road. It was to begin at 1 a.m. This had the drawback that the time for circulating orders and getting through the difficult task of forming up the troops in the darkness was short, but there was the gain that the advance could be made by moonlight with some consequent immunity from the enemy's machine gun fire.

At zero hour (1 a.m.) all three Battalions of the 50th Brigade advanced in line, the 10th W. Yorkshires on the right, 6th Dorsets in the centre, and 7th E. Yorkshires on the left. Each was given its own objective. At first all went well. The West Yorkshires rapidly cleared the trench lines on the rising ground west of Flers, but then went forward more slowly, winning their way into the western side of the village and through the orchards south of it by dint of close fighting. By 4 a.m. two companies were east of the village, and two on the west side of it. The farthest advance was made by 2nd Lieut. Kirk, M.C., with a platoon and a half. He reached a sunken road 700 yards east of the place and held on there under heavy M.G. fire for two hours, when, with only six men left, he had to retire. In the centre the Dorsets cleared the northern end of Flers and joined up with the W. Yorkshires east of it. On the left by 3.30 the E. Yorkshires had reached their first objective on a rise of ground north of the village. In a hard hand-to-hand fight in a sunken road converted into a trench they took forty prisoners and 10 machine guns. The Dorsets, in the centre, had secured 3 trench mortars, 10 machine guns and 10 prisoners. In and about Flers the W. Yorkshires had taken 140 prisoners and 10 machine guns.

Daylight was now coming, and neither on right or left had the other Divisions got forward, so that the Brigade had both flanks exposed. The E. Yorkshires had hardly won the sunken road when they were counter-attacked from the north-east. They flung back a company to guard the flank and beat the attack off, but at 4.15 there was another counter-attack in front before which they had to fall back for some distance. There was then a lull till soon after 7 a.m., when the enemy opened a heavy artillery and machine gun fire on both flanks and from the high ground east of and commanding Flers. Before a new counter-attack the line was withdrawn west of the village. After this there was desultory fighting all day, and heavy shelling, but the new line was held. It represented only a gain of about 500 or 600 yards, a rather disappointing result for a day that had begun so well.

In the afternoon Corps H.Q. sent orders that the advance was to be suspended for the next twenty-four hours in order to reorganise the line generally, link up the three Divisions, and give the men some rest. Roads and other approaches were to be kept under fire, and if the enemy retired he was to be followed up. During the night our patrols kept touch with the enemy. His artillery was very active and daylight on the 28th showed no sign of a further German withdrawal. But later in the day our aircraft brought reports of fires lighted behind the German front, and this was taken to mean that supply dumps were being burned in preparation for a further retreat. Touch was regained with the Divisions on both flanks of the 17th and the day was a most useful time of rest and reorganisation. The 51st Brigade was ordered to relieve the 50th during the following night, the 52nd to come up in support and the 50th to go into Divisional Reserve at Martinpuich.

The Vth Corps orders for the 29th were that the 38th Division was to push forward on both sides of Delville Wood and gain the high ground east of Ginchy. The 17th and 21st were to stand fast, keeping their artillery and machine guns active, and moving forward on the first sign that the enemy's resistance was slackening.

It was a day of considerable and fairly easy gains of ground. Away to the left front of the Vth Corps the German resistance north of the Bapaume road was breaking before the advance of the centre and left of Byng's Third Army. That day the New Zealand Division took Bapaume and this outflanking success made it impossible for the enemy to hold on in front of Byng's right, the Vth Corps. Here the Germans were falling back from early in the day. Moving forward at 5.30 a.m. the 38th Division went past Delville Wood by its north and south without any contact with the enemy, and was into Lesbœufs by 11 a.m. Meanwhile the Germans were falling back in front of the 17th Division and the 51st Brigade pushed rapidly forward through Flers and Gueudecourt. The 38th then gained some ground beyond Lesbœufs and the 51st Brigade came up into line on their left facing Le Transloy. The 52nd Brigade moved up to Gueudecourt in support and the 50th was brought forward from Martinpuich to Flers. On the left the 21st Division prolonged the line of the 17th. Further progress was now checked. The Germans still held Morval, and from that direction, and from Beaulencourt kept up a heavy fire against both flanks of our advance, and his artillery was active in front beyond Le Transloy. But substantial gains had been secured. The Divisional front had been carried forward for nearly three miles. Orders for the next day were that the advance of the 17th Division was to be continued across the Bapaume-Péronne road in the direction of Rocquigny. The 21st Division would protect its left flank, and the 38th after clearing Morval move forward on its right.

But no progress was made on the 30th. The 38th Division failed to take Morval, the 21st was held up in front of Beaulencourt, and fire from both flanks and from Le Transloy made further advance impossible on the 17th Division front. During the night of August 30th to 31st, the 52nd Brigade came into the front line, the 50th falling back in reserve. Next day the deadlock continued. There was much artillery activity on both sides, and the enemy was heavily bombarding Gueudecourt.[1]

September 1st was another disappointing day. Le Transloy was the first objective, but it was strongly held by the enemy and our attack was checked early in the day and made no progress. But next day the onward sweep of our advance was resumed. At Le Transloy the enemy was still making a determined resistance, but

---

[1] On this day—August 31st—a troop of cavalry (one officer and 14 other ranks, 6th Dragoon Guards) was attached to the Division. It was always allotted to the leading Brigade, and did very useful service largely in liaison and orderly work.

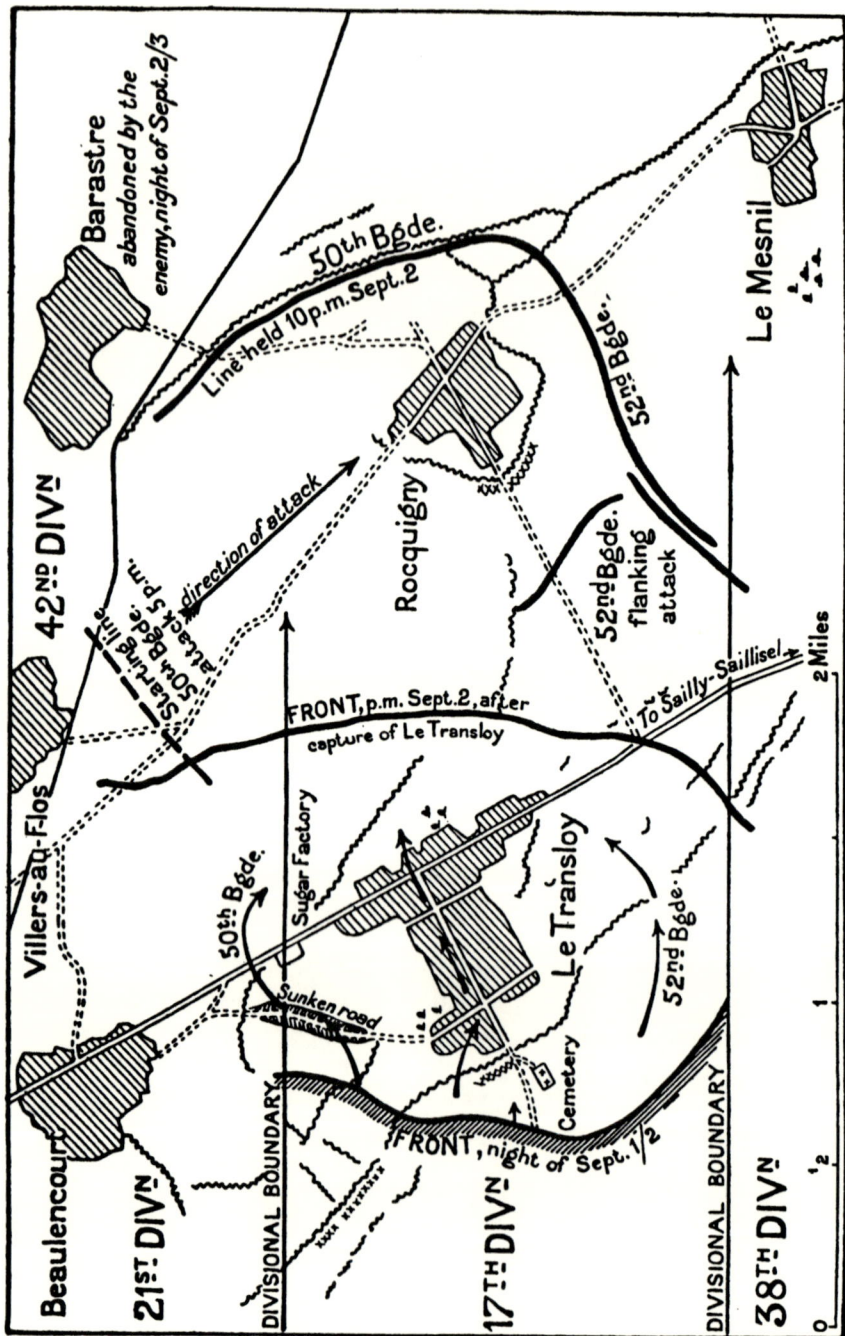

Barastre
*abandoned by the
enemy, night of Sept. 2/3*

50th Bgde.

Line held 10 p.m. Sept. 2

42ND DIVN

Villers-au-Flos

Beaulencourt

21ST DIVN

DIVISIONAL BOUNDARY

50th Bgde.

Sugar Factory

Sunken road

17TH DIVN

DIVISIONAL BOUNDARY

38TH DIVN

FRONT, night of Sept. 1/2

Cemetery

Le Transloy

52nd Bgde.

To Sailly-Saillisel

FRONT, p.m. Sept. 2, after
capture of Le Transloy

direction of attack

50th Bgde. 6 p.m.

Starting line

Rocquigny

52nd Bgde.
flanking
attack

52nd Bgde.

Le Mesnil

0   ½   1   2 Miles

Capture of Le Transloy and Rocquigny, September 2, 1918.

at 6 a.m. the 21st Division reported that it had taken Beaulencourt, and thus put an end to the interference from that flank which had been one of the difficulties in the previous attempts to clear Le Transloy and to get across the Bapaume-Péronne road. South of the village the right of the 52nd Brigade had by 9 a.m. reached the Péronne road and driven the enemy from a rising ground from which their fire had enfiladed our right attack upon Le Transloy. The 50th Brigade, which was in close support, sent forward two companies of the West Yorkshires to clear a sunken road north of the village, and drove out a party of the enemy, taking some machine guns, and then pushed on to the Péronne road. Le Transloy was kept under heavy shell fire by our gunners, and its defence gradually weakened. Shortly after 2 p.m. it was reported that parties of the defenders had been seen leaving it on its farther side. The East Yorks now pushed on round the north of it and the 52nd Brigade worked round its south end, while the Dorsets were sent directly forward to clear it. As the two flank advances joined hands east of the place, the Dorsets were into the villlage, where it was hoped a considerable part of its garrison would be surrounded and made prisoners. But only two stragglers were found. The Dorsets secured a trench mortar and some machine guns which had been abandoned as the last of the garrison bolted to escape the encircling movement round their position. By 3 p.m. the two Brigades held a line east of Le Transloy and the Bapaume-Péronne road, the 50th Brigade and the 52nd on the right. At 4 p.m. the Corps Commander sent through an order to the 17th Division to attack Rocquigny. The Divisional Commander issued detailed orders accordingly.

The situation was : on the left the Division was now in touch with the 42nd Division whose right held Villers-au-Flos. Rocquigny was reported to be protected on the west and south by a strongly wired trench line.

General Robertson therefore decided that it should be attacked from the north-west, so as to avoid these defences. The 50th Brigade was to push forward to the ground south of Villers-au-Flos, from which the actual attack on Rocquigny would be made at 8 p.m. It was to be covered by a creeping artillery barrage and the Divisional C.R.A. was to arrange with the 42nd Division to cover the left of the attack with its artillery. At 8 p.m. there would still be some daylight and the choice of this hour would give time for necessary preparations and the preliminary advance.

On the right the Division was not in touch with the 38th Division, which had been checked in its efforts to advance through Sailly-Saillisel against Le Mesnil. This latter village was strongly held by the enemy and there were indications that he might be massing there for a counter-attack. The 52nd Brigade was therefore ordered to occupy a new line further forward on which its left would observe the western side of Rocquigny and its right would form a defensive flank against any possible counter-attack from Le Mesnil. The 51st Brigade was brought up into close support at Le Transloy.

The attack was a brilliant success. The 50th Brigade advancing at 8 p.m. drove the enemy out of Rocquigny; and following up his retirement found the old trenches east of the village lightly held and cleared them after a brief hand-to-hand fight. By 10 p.m. the Brigade was consolidating east of Rocquigny. During the night its patrols discovered that Barastre was abandoned by the Germans. During the day's operations two field guns and about a hundred machine guns had been taken in the captured villages, and 160 prisoners.

September 2nd had been a bad day for the Germans. The British front from Arras southward to the extreme right, where it was across the Somme beyond Péronne, lay now nearly north and south, with most of the enemy's gains of March wiped out. On the left Horne was well forward east of Arras and had broken through the north sector of the Hindenburg Line. In the centre Rocquigny marked one of the extreme points of our advance. The enemy was falling back in our front to attempt a stand behind the line of the Canal du Nord.

Vth Corps orders for September 3rd were that, as the Division front was now narrowing, the 21st Division was to be withdrawn into Divisional Reserve. The 17th Division and the 38th were to organise advanced guards to press the pursuit of the enemy. General Robertson's orders to the 17th Division were that the 52nd Brigade was to stand fast in its over-night position and become Divisional Reserve. The 50th Brigade, with the 79th Brigade R.F.A., two troops of the Irish Horse cyclists, and two M.G. Companies, was to continue the advance. The 51st Brigade was to occupy the Rocquigny trench line as soon as the 50th moved on, and was to act in support. At noon D.H.Q. moved forward from near Martinpuich to Le Transloy.

At dawn the 42nd Division occupied Barastre on the left. Shortly after 8 a.m. the 38th Division, on the right, reported that it was through Sailly and into Le Mesnil. Touch being now established with the Divisions on both flanks the 50th Brigade went forward at 9 a.m. with the Irish Cyclists scouting in front. By 3.30 p.m. the leading regiment, the East Yorkshires, reached the high ground between Ytres and Etricourt and came in sight of the Canal du Nord in the Tortille valley beyond. Almost at once the enemy opened a heavy M.G. fire from its east bank. By 5.30 p.m. the Brigade had occupied the line of the railway on the west side of the Canal. Along most of its front was the open water line with all the bridges destroyed. On the extreme left it entered the long tunnel through which it passes under the high ground south-west of Havrincourt Forest. On the heights beyond the Canal the Germans held a strongly organised trench system.

Their machine guns and artillery of all calibres were busy through the rest of the day, and our gunners were doing their best to knock out the machine guns near the Canal. One of these hidden in a copse on the margin of Vallulart Wood (east of the tunnel) was specially annoying, until Major Marshall, D.S.O., M.C., galloped one of his guns to the top of a hill at close range in front, and firing over open sights silenced it in a few minutes. Our gunners on the sky line must have presented a good target to the enemy, but no one was hit.

The successful advance from the Ancre to the Canal du Nord line was an encouraging opening of the forward move to victory. Orders for September 4th were that the Canal line and the trenches on the heights beyond were to be attacked.

CHAPTER XII

THE VICTORIOUS ADVANCE

(2) FROM THE CANAL DU NORD TO THE SELLE

SINCE the coming of the tanks the enemy had set a higher defensive value on water lines of every kind, including canals and small rivers, for these were possible obstacles to the attack of the new fighting machines, especially if the waterline lay between steep banks or had marshy margins. The entrenched position on the heights east of the Canal du Nord was part of a defence line which had been selected largely on account of the obstacles of marsh, canal and river in its front. From the swampy flats round Douai it ran by the line of the Canal de la Sensée and the Canal du Nord to its junction with the Somme by the Tortille valley, and then along the upper Somme southwards from Péronne.

The 17th Division had now reached in its advance a point where it faced a sector of this line, which at first sight might seem a strong one. But it had a weak point on one flank and on the other was in imminent danger of being soon turned by the British advance further south, where Rawlinson with the Fourth Army had just got across the line of the Somme beyond Péronne.

The local weakness of the line on the Divisional front arose from the fact that on much of our Vth Corps front the Canal ceased to be an open waterline and ran underground for a few miles, in a tunnel that began a little to the south of the bend in the canal line west of the Havrincourt Forest. Here it burrowed under the broad rising ground of the long chalk range that is the final barrier between the flat lands of northern France and the upper valley of the Somme. After a six miles' underground course the canal comes out again into daylight in the valley by which the little river Tortille runs down to the Somme near Péronne.

The left of the 17th Divisional front faced the high, and in places wooded, ground above the exit from the tunnel. Along the rest of the front the water line lay in a deep hollow and above the slopes of the eastern bank was the German trench line. It was still far from complete. Round the large village of Equancourt there was a formidable trench system, but north of this, beyond the woods of Vallulart, the line dwindled gradually to a front line without any deep support system in its rear—this, too, where the gap on the water line made more developed defences all-important. Obviously the enemy had not had time to complete his entrenchments, and with the whole position turned by loss of the upper Somme line it was not likely he would now attempt a long stand at the Canal.

This was doubtless why the G.O.C.'s orders to the Division for September 4th had chiefly in view keeping close touch, feeling the enemy's defence and being ready to follow up his expected retreat. At the same time steps were taken to accelerate his departure, by a menace to his weak point. The 50th Brigade was to act as an advanced guard, and the orders were on the general lines of a continued forward movement. The day's operations were to begin at 6 a.m. Keeping the Canal line under fire the Brigade was told to make a push for Vallulart Wood, above the tunnel, and then work southward from the flank against the German trench system, avoiding however becoming involved in a serious attack if the enemy made a stand in force. If ground was gained rapidly the 51st Brigade would cross the Canal and co-operate and the 52nd move up from Rocquigny.

The 50th Brigade advanced at 6 a.m. covered by a heavy artillery fire against the enemy front. With patrols out it made its way through Vallulart Wood, and soon after 9 a.m. was established on a two-battalion front on its eastern margin. The advance was now continued for some distance south-eastward, but before long was brought to a standstill by a concentration of machine gun fire on front and flank. Attempts to get forward against the trench line south-east of the wood resulted only in serious loss. Orders were then given to dig in on the slopes beyond the wood and our artillery supporting the Brigade endeavoured to beat down the hostile M.G. fire. A gun was brought up through the Wood by the O.C. of B Battery, 78th Brigade R.F.A., run forward close up to the front, and, engaging the enemy at short range, silenced some of the machine guns. But all forward movement came to an end. The 51st Brigade was moved up in the afternoon to relieve the 50th after dark. The only gain of the day here was that the front was over the tunnel line a little beyond Vallulart Wood. There were reports (which proved incorrect), that on the left the 42nd Division was in touch. On the right, however, the 38th Division got two battalions after dark across the Tortille river and the Canal opposite Équancourt.

On the 5th the 38th Division was to attack the Équancourt defences from the Canal line, and, if the enemy still held on there, the 51st Brigade was to co-operate by attacking the trench line on the ridge north of the place from the north-west, covered by a creeping flank barrage that would sweep the trench line from north to south. The relief of the 50th Brigade was not completed till near daylight, so the attack by the 51st was not started till 9.30 a.m. It was made from an assembly position a little to the east of Vallulart Wood, on a single-battalion front, the 7th Lincolns leading. At 10 p.m. it was reported that the attack could be seen moving south, not far from the wood, and after this communications

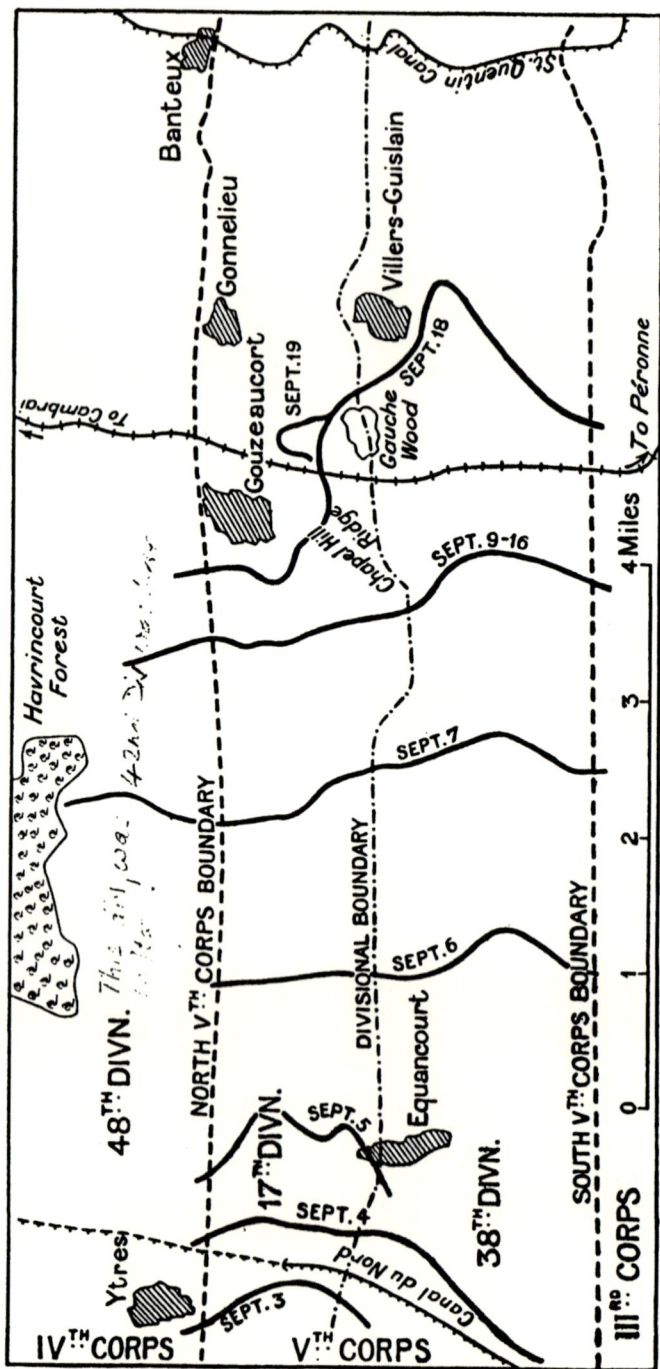

The advance from the Canal du Nord, September 1918.

with Divisional H.Q. were interrupted till a message, timed 2.45, came through, saying the attack was held up by heavy M.G. fire, well north of Équancourt on a line only about a thousand yards from its starting point. Orders were sent to hold on and renew the attack with the help of a barrage at 8 p.m.

Subsequent investigation showed that the Lincolns had been given an impossible task in consequence of the information available as to the position about the Wood being incorrect, either through an error in drafting it or in transmission. The line on which they took over was further north than the reports of the day before stated, and instead of the flank being protected by touch with the 42nd Division it was " in air " and under hostile fire from the north-east. On moving forward to the starting line it was found that enemy machine guns were close in front between the Lincolns and the starting point of our barrage. The O.C. of the Battalion however decided to fight his way forward, but gained very little ground before he was finally held up by M.G. fire in front and flank. In their limited advance however the Lincolns had captured fourteen machine guns and 15 prisoners.

The attack of the 38th Division on Équancourt had been repulsed, but when the 51st Brigade advanced again in the dusk of the evening with the 7th Borders in front, it was found the enemy had abandoned his position, using the coming night to mask his retirement.

During the afternoon, while the fight for the Canal line was still undecided, the Vth Corps H.Q. had sent through an important message to the Divisional H.Q. to the effect that " the policy of the immediate future would be not to conduct operations on a large scale, but to husband resources and improve communications with a view to the resumption of the offensive shortly; but that advanced guards were to continue to press the enemy and drive in his rearguards." Behind this confidential hint as to the immediate future probably lay the fact that at this time the British advance was nearing what was popularly known as the Hindenburg Line—a series of entrenched positions, the work of years, on which Ludendorff hoped to stand fast for the winter.   The British Government was counting on the war ending only in 1919, and there were influences at work that might have ended in staying our further progress in order to avoid a winter campaign, and give time for the American Armies to reach their full strength, and to accumulate for our own armies the munition supplies, and above all the projected masses of tanks and of motor transport, intended for the final effort of the war.   Haig was warned that heavy losses in an attack on the Hindenburg Line might produce a bad impression at home, and went to London to urge that now the enemy was going he must be kept on the move and his great barrier line smashed through.   He carried his point.

In any case, however, this great struggle for the German barrier line could not be opened without careful preparations.   So presently our advance slowed down.   For a few days after the crossing of the Canal du Nord it still went forward.   On the night of September 5th to 6th on the right the 21st Division relieved the 38th.   In the early hours of the 6th on our left the New Zealand Division relieved and passed through the 42nd and went forward through Neuville to Metz-en-Couture just south of the Havrincourt woods, following up the enemy retreat.   On the same day the 51st Brigade, without any opposition in its front, had pushed forward to the abandoned trenches on the high ground north of Fins, while its right, the 21st Division, reached Fins village after a slight skirmish with an enemy rearguard.[1]   Next morning, the 52nd Brigade passed through the

---

[1] On September 6th General G. Gwynn-Thomas, C.M.G., D.S.O., was recalled to India, and on the 8th Brigadier-General A. R. C. Sanders, C.M.G., D.S.O., took over the command of the 50th Brigade.

51st and, acting as advanced guard, went forward and occupied the old trenches north of Heudecourt, capturing an officer and 44 other prisoners. On the right the 21st Division took Heudecourt village and the New Zealanders came up into line on the left.

Patrols sent forward in the afternoon reported that the enemy was holding in force a position less than two miles in front, west and south-west of Gouzeaucourt.

This might be only one more instance of a strong, enemy rearguard waiting to fight a delaying action, but, as the events that followed showed, the Germans were prepared to make a serious and prolonged fight on what they had converted into an advanced line of the great Hindenburg system. The position in our front was entrenched along high ground, the German defence works being partly reconstructed trenches of our old " Battle Zone " through which they had forced their way in the March offensive. From the bend of the Hindenburg Line south-west of Cambrai they had improvised this new line, running generally south for many miles, using some of our old trenches and redoubts as the foundation for this new trench system. It took much strenuous effort before it was at last forced, and during this time there was a temporary reversion from open warfare to the old conditions of trench fighting.

The operations of the Division on September 8th were practically a reconnaissance of the German position, and a brief bombardment early in the day by the Divisional artillery was answered by very heavy artillery fire, and patrols sent forward to feel the front drew everywhere the fire of many machine guns. It was concluded that the Germans meant to make a serious stand, and arrangements were made for a combined attack by three Divisions, on the 9th—the New Zealanders on the left, the 17th in the centre and the 21st on the right.

The position occupied by the enemy lay along a ridge with several trench lines on its forward slope, and a second supporting reserve system on its reverse slopes. An out-lying hill just beyond its south end, known as Chapel Hill, from a wayside shrine, gave its English name to the ridge which was to be the objective of the 17th Division. From Chapel Hill another line of high ground, Revelon Ridge, ran south-westward. The Germans had a considerable force of artillery of various calibres behind the ridges, and these now indulged in intermittent shelling of our new front and its back areas. Night after night, enemy aircraft came flying over our ground and dropping bombs in a somewhat haphazard manner, but not without opposition. Searchlights, an air-craft gun and fighting planes of the R.A.F. were available to meet them, and on one night three of the attacking planes were brought down.

Our first attack on the German position revealed both its strength and the determination of the enemy to defend it so vigorously that it was clear we had no longer to deal with mere rearguard fighting. At 4 a.m. the 52nd Brigade advanced to the attack of the Ridge, with two battalions in its front line, the 10th Lancashire Fusiliers on the right and the 12th Manchesters on the left. The 9th Duke of Wellington's followed in support. The movement began in the dark, under a heavily clouded sky. After the event it was judged that it was too dark for the opening moves of such a long advance. Before describing what followed it should be noted that the entrenchments bore on our maps the names given to them when the line was marked out in the months before the great enemy offensive, when the whole system looked east, so that the attack of the Brigade was directed first against a line known as Heather " Support " and then against Heather Trench higher up the slope.

The New Zealanders were attacking the line away to the north, and on the right the 21st Division was sending one Battalion against the prolongation of the line (Lowland Support and Trench), and another against Chapel

Hill. At first all went well. In the dim early twilight, Heather Support and Lowland Support were won fairly easily, and Heather and Lowland Trenches after some stiff fighting. But as the daylight came the Germans attacked vigorously from the direction of Gouzeaucourt and after hard fighting recovered the second or " Trench " line. Our men then fell back to the Support line, and for some time devoted all their efforts to making good their hold of it, extending gradually north and south, and after much fighting gaining touch with the New Zealanders and the 21st Division. But this was not effected till the afternoon, when we held with a continuous line the whole of the front trench. By this time the 52nd Brigade had all three Battalions in the fight, the Manchesters in the centre of its front, with the Lancashire Fusiliers on the right and the Duke of Wellingtons on the left. We had taken 120 prisoners. At 6.30 p.m. the enemy, with a heavy artillery barrage, counter-attacked the right Battalion, and twenty minutes later the centre. Both attacks were repulsed.

Vth Corps H.Q. ordered the attack to be renewed on the 10th. The 50th Brigade had already been warned that it was to relieve the 52nd during the night, and if the enemy still held on to the ridge carry on at 4 a.m. the attack in combination with the 21st Division.

After sunset on the 9th the rain, which had been threatening all day, began and soon increased to a deluge, while the wind rose to hurricane force. In blinding rain, inky darkness and a driving gale the 50th Brigade moved out to the captured trench line. The ground had become a sea of mud. At 1.30 a.m. Brigadier-General Sanders telephoned to Divisional H.Q. that the attack could not possibly begin at 4 a.m., as his troops could not complete the relief in time. After exchanging messages with the Corps H.Q. and the 21st Division, General Robertson deferred the attack till 5.15. But even then it proved impossible to attack, for all the troops were not yet in line.

The artillery barrage was fired but there was no infantry advance. The barrage started the German gunners into action, and from that time all day they shelled our lines. It was not till 11.30 a.m. that at last the relief was completed, and in flooded trenches and a sea of mud the 50th Brigade had its three Battalions in line along Heather and African Supports and in touch with the Divisions to right and left. The Vth Corps H.Q. had already telephoned that our activities during the day were to be limited to consolidating the line already won, and harassing the enemy with patrolling, and artillery and machine gun fire. At 6 p.m. a counter-attack on the left front of the Brigade covered by a barrage was repulsed.

That afternoon Corps H.Q. had directed the 38th Division to relieve the 17th on the night of the 11th to 12th. Bad weather continued through the 11th. The enemy's artillery was very active all day, and his high velocity guns sent shells bursting here and there far back in the area behind our front. In the afternoon an attempt he made on our left against African Support was repulsed. During the day the Brigades behind the line were relieved by the 38th Division, and after dark the relief of the 50th Brigade began and was completed by midnight. When the Division passed into Corps Reserve, it had been almost continuously fighting for three weeks.

The casualties of the Division from the crossing of the Ancre on August 21st to the relief on September 11th were as follows:

	Killed.	Wounded.	Missing.	Totals.
Officers -	36	115	3	154
Other ranks -	443	2271	191	2905
	479	2386	194	3059

Besides these 9 officers and 422 other ranks were incapacitated by sickness, so that the total wastage during these first weeks of the advance was 3,490. The enemy prisoners taken during the same period were 1,303 (27 officers and 1,276 other ranks).

The Division spent the following days in reserve in the area of Rocquigny, Beaulencourt, Le Transloy and Lechelle. It had less than a week for " rest, reorganisation and training." As a matter of fact there was not much rest for anyone from the G.O.C. and the Divisional Staff downwards. It was a time of intense preparation for what in any earlier war would have been described as a tremendous battle, but in this war of giant armies was officially classed as a " preliminary operation," preparatory to the advance against the Hindenburg Line. On September 18th Rawlinson with the Fourth Army, assisted on the left by the right Divisions of Byng's Third Army, was to attack and clear the enemy's advanced positions in front of that main line of the German defence, by attacking on a front of about 17 miles from Holnon (west of St. Quentin), northwards to the ridges about Gouzeaucourt.

On the 14th, at a conference of Commanding and Staff Officers of the Division, General Robertson explained the part assigned to the Division in the coming battle. The Division was to clear the Chapel Hill Ridge, and the positions in its rear to the south-east of Gouzeaucourt. All three Divisions of the Vth Corps would be in line, and the 33rd Division was to be attached as a reserve. The 17th would take the centre of the attack, with the 21st on its right and the 38th on its left. The attack would start from the trench line captured on September 9th.

The advance was to be made in three bounds against successive objectives marked on the map as the Brown, Green and Red Lines. The first would carry the advance to the crest of the Ridge and the summit of Chapel Hill, the second would clear the trenches on the reverse slope and reach the hollow running south from Gouzeaucourt. The left attack (38th Division) would be carried no farther than the trench line close in to the west of Gouzeaucourt. But the other two Divisions would push on to the Red Line. This would bring the 21st on the right to the high ground south of and dominating the village of Villers-Guislan, while in the centre the 17th would press forward between this place and Gouzeaucourt, along a bold height crowned by Gauche Wood, the wood and the hill being both strongly entrenched. Its capture would leave Gouzeaucourt almost encircled by the general advance, and it was anticipated that the result would be its early abandonment by the enemy. It is no exaggeration to say that the 17th Division, in the centre, had the stiffest task of the day assigned to it. Divisional orders directed that it should attack on a single Brigade front, and by what was familiarly known as " leap frogging." The 52nd Brigade would take the Brown Line, or " 1st Objective; " the 50th would then pass through it to attack the Green Line, and when this was won the 51st would, in the same way, go forward to the attack on the Red Line.

This prelude to the coming great battle for the Hindenburg Line was itself to be a " set-piece battle " on a huge scale, elaborately prepared. Divisional orders were lengthy and full of detail, for with the enemy's successive positions defined by well-mapped trench lines there was a reversion to the earlier method of marking out in advance each stage in the conduct of the attack, and the special task of each unit employed in it. As there were, however, no deep belts of wire on this outlying enemy front, there was no need either for a prolonged wire-cutting bombardment, or the use of tanks as wire crushers. A couple of tanks were placed at the disposal of the Division, but they were not fighters but " carrying tanks," intended to bring up supplies of ammunition and abundance of engineer stores for consolidation as line after line was won. As there was no preliminary bombardment an effort was made to secure a surprise, by moving up the Division under cover of darkness to its assembly positions, and there were orders that, as far as might be, movement east of the Canal du Nord during the daylight hours should be avoided.

The orders included a detailed system of barrage support for the attack, with artillery trench mortar, machine gun and smoke barrages, the scheme being further explained and defined by time tables and diagrams. Aircraft were also to take their part in the advance, watching and reporting its progress, and giving warning of any impending counter-attack by dropping red smoke bombs on any point where the Germans were seen to be massing for this purpose. Everything was done to secure the ordered co-operation of all the units in action and of all the new weapons and appliances that had made their appearance since the days of what now seemed the old-fashioned battle methods of 1914.

Bad weather and shortness of time had hampered training, but something had been done, and the three Brigades were all the fitter for this very brief and imperfect period of rest—rest that meant chiefly change in the day's routine and undisturbed sleep when its work was over.

The forward move began on the night of Sept. 15th to 16th when the 52nd Brigade marched to Vallulart Wood, at the Canal crossing, and remained under cover there till after dark on the 16th. In the following night it took over from the troops of the 33rd and 38th Divisions, then holding that sector, the trench line in front of Chapel Hill Ridge (Heather Support, Lowland Support and the prolongation of the latter along the curving base of Chapel Hill). On the night of the 16th to 17th the 50th Brigade was brought up from Rocquigny to the old trenches north of Heulencourt, and on the night of the 17th to 18th the 51st Brigade was moved forward to near the same ground. There was heavy rain during the night, but by dawn the weather had improved though it was still dull and threatening.

At zero hour—5.20 a.m., on September 18th—the attack began—the 52nd Brigade advancing with all its three Battalions in line, in two closely following waves. The enemy's artillery had opened fire promptly as soon as our barrage began, but apparently the Germans were not prepared for the attack, and the first objective was captured very quickly, the trench system up to the crest of the Ridge being cleared with no very serious resistance anywhere. At 6.20 a.m.—just an hour after zero—the 50th Brigade, with all its three battalions in line, passed through the 52nd which was consolidating the position, and went on to attack the Green Line. On the right and centre this was all won by 7 a.m.: on the left the enemy made a longer stand. Here the sunken roads west of the railway had been converted into strong trench lines, and a German support Battalion had come up to assist the defence. It cost two hours of close fighting before the East Yorkshires were in complete possession. Meanwhile they and the left of the 52nd Brigade had begun to suffer from machine gun fire from Gouzeaucourt, which increased as the morning went on, and was brought to bear on the left of all our three attacks in succession.

The 51st Brigade now passed through to the attack of the final objective, the Red Line. It attacked in two waves, the three battalions having each two companies in front and two in support, ready to deal with any counter-attack. By 9.30 the right battalion reported that it had reached its objective and was in touch with the 21st Division on that flank. The left was delayed by having to assist the East Yorkshires in clearing the sunken roads. It thus lost the barrage and had to fight its way forward unaided. The centre Battalion came up against the strongest enemy position on the Divisional front. There was a cross fire from a communication trench to the right, and in front Gauche Wood was strongly entrenched. Just inside its western margin four derelict British tanks had been grouped together to form an armoured machine gun nest. (They were probably tanks captured the year before at Cambrai, which had broken down in attempts to use them as mobile weapons.) This improvised fort was finally knocked out by fire of some of our

6-inch mortars. But before it was thus reduced, it was turned by a flanking movement and some close fighting followed in the wood. The first of our men, who got as far as Lancashire Trench on its eastern side, were counter-attacked and driven out, but the trench was promptly recaptured by one of the supporting companies. A few minutes after 10 a.m., a report was sent to Vth Corps H.Q. that the Division had completed its task and held all the three objectives assigned to it. It had captured 1,069 unwounded prisoners, including 19 officers. Three field guns had been taken in Gauche Wood, and several machine guns at each stage of the advance.

The situation now was: the Divisional front formed a salient between Villers-Guislan and Gouzeaucourt, with its apex just outside the north-east corner of Gauche Wood. Its right front ran south to link up with the 21st Division in front of Villers-Guislan. Its left front ran along the north side of the wood and thence nearly due west to a point on the Green Line south of Gouzeaucourt, where it joined up with the 114th Brigade (38th Division). From this point the front of the latter ran back to the Brown Line, west of Gouzeaucourt, where the enemy was still in force and active with his machine guns. East of the village the enemy held a group of trenches with a work known to us as Quentin Redoubt as their strong point. The redoubt was about half a mile north of Gauche Wood on the slope of the ridge that runs north-east to Gonnelieu. Across the ridge ran a trench line to Villers-Guislan, connected with the line of Lancashire Trench, still held in its northern part by the Germans.

During the afternoon the enemy made three determined counter-attacks from these trenches, all of which were repulsed. Early in the afternoon Corps H.Q. ordered that after dark at 9 p.m., a Brigade of the 17th and another of the 38th Division should renew the attack against the enemy works north of Gauche Wood, and up to the southern outskirts of Gouzeaucourt. Divisional orders were issued at 4.15 p.m.

The 50th Brigade with " A " Company of the M.G. Battalion, was to attack on the right, starting from the northern margin of Gauche Wood. The 114th Brigade (38th Division) was to attack south of Gouzeaucourt. These attacks were to be covered by creeping and flank barrages of artillery, with a smoke barrage on the extreme right to mask the movement against view from Gonnelieu and Villars-Guislan. After a dull cloudy day the sky had cleared and the moon was near the full, so the attack was made in bright moonlight.

While moving up to the assembly position the 50th Brigade came under machine gun fire from Gouzeaucourt, and in the advance the left of the attack was harassed in the same way. The attack was made with the Dorsets and West Yorkshires in front and the East Yorkshires in support. Lancashire Trench was cleared of the enemy from south to north, and Quentin Redoubt captured by the Dorsets. They were presently isolated there for a while, in consequence of the company holding Lancashire Trench being driven out by a German counter-attack. The West Yorkshires were held by machine gun fire and the 114th Brigade failed to make any progress towards Gouzeaucourt.

Two companies of the Dorsets held on in the captured redoubt till morning, when steps were taken to open communication with them. Lancashire Trench was recovered on the right and on the left a post was established in the trench running down from the redoubt to the railway, and early in the day communication was established also along this line. Fifty prisoners and six machine guns had been captured in the night attack. Consolidation was now proceeding and the R.E. Field Companies and the Pioneer Battalion were ordered up to the front to assist. The enemy kept up a desultory bombardment during the forenoon. In the afternoon it became intense for awhile, about 2 p.m., and an attack was expected. But our aircraft spotted the enemy's concentration south-west of Gonnelieu; our artillery was turned upon it, and the Germans abandoned their projected counter-attack. At sunset it came however on a reduced scale. Lancashire Trench was attacked and for a while was in the hands of the enemy, but they were driven out by a vigorous counter-attack in the dusk of the evening.

On the night of the 19th to 20th a readjustment of the front was begun. The 21st Division extended its left and took over the front to the north-east of Gauche Wood, the 17th continued the line by Lancashire Trench and Redoubt and along the front south of Gouzeaucourt. Each day the enemy's artillery was active and machine gun fire came from time to time from the village. In the night of the 19th to 20th gas shells were used in the enemy bombardment, which extended to our artillery positions, and a good many officers and men were affected more or less. The stuff employed seemed to be a new variety of mustard gas " with a smell of smouldering petroleum."

On the morning of the 20th, Brigadier-General Sanders had gone up to inspect the front about Quentin Redoubt. After daylight he was returning to his Brigade H.Q., and as he crossed the railway was caught in machine gun fire from Gouzeaucourt and killed on the spot. Brigadier-General J. F. R. Hope, D.S.O., took over the command of the 50th Brigade two days later.

On the night of the 20th to 21st the 17th Division further extended its front, taking over the line from the 38th up to the Divisional North Boundary, west of Gouzeaucourt. Just after midnight a " Flammenwerfer" attack on Lancashire Trench was repulsed. Before dawn on the 22nd there was an unsuccessful counter-attack on our salient at Quentin Redoubt. On the following night we flung 200 gas cylinders into Gouzeau-court with a view to diminishing the machine gun annoyance from that side. The enemy's machine gunners were certainly less active next day. The 24th was also a fairly quiet day, and on the night of the 25th the 33rd Division relieved the 17th.

The Division moved back to the area west of the Canal du Nord for rest, refitting and training. The men were badly in need of rest. The weather had been trying, with frequent rain, during the recent operations and for many days and nights they had been lying out in shelter-less positions, on wet ground, exposed to frequent shell and M.G. fire. The losses of the Division had been:

	Killed.	Wounded.	Missing.	Totals.
Officers -	14	51	1	66
Other ranks -	243	1607	185	2035
	257	1658	186	2101

If we add wastage by sickness (10 officers, and 287 other ranks), the total loss was 2,398. Large drafts arrived during the rest period which lasted till the first days of October. They were good material, but with a deficiency of N.C.O.'s.

On September 28th the Germans evacuated Gouzeau-court and, followed up by the Vth Corps, began to retire towards the St. Quentin Canal. The greatest battle of the War—(and indeed of all wars)—had begun. On the Alsace-Lorraine front the German and French armies, in comparatively small force, still faced each other in positions they had held for years. But westwards and then northwards to the sea all the rest of the Allied Line was beginning to advance. The movement opened on the right where the new American armies were pressing forward on both sides of the Argonne and amongst its rocks and woods towards the Belgian border. Next the main mass of the French armies moved, on both sides of Rheims and up the valley of the Oise, their left curving round to link up with the main British advance against the Hindenburg Line. Then still further north British, French and Belgians pushed on from the old Yser line into the Belgian plain. It was a long curving line lapping round the great enemy salient on a front of nearly 250 miles. Four days after the first move of the Americans all that tremendous front was ablaze from the woods and hills north of Verdun to the level lands by the North Sea.

The 17th Division during the earlier stages of this immense battle was still in reserve and " resting," but warned to be ready to move to the front at brief notice. As was almost always the case the Divisional Artillery, instead of going back to rest billets, remained on the Corps front. It shared the advance to the St. Quentin Canal, but here there was no very serious fighting, for the enemy was falling back under the indirect effect of the heavy blow struck further north by Haig, towards Cambrai. On October 3rd, the 21st and 33rd Divisions on the Vth Corps front had reached the west side of the St. Quentin Canal. A battery commander of the 17th Division's artillery gives a striking impression, in his diary, of what he saw when he went forward to reconnoitre from the high ground above Honnecourt, commanding a wide outlook eastward:—

"Went on to the next crest, where we got an extraordinarily fine view of all the country the other side of the Canal, where lies the main Hindenburg Line. There was no mistaking it. The ground sloped up away from the Canal, and zig-zagging across it sepia-like coloured zebra stripes, were thick, dark wide lines, all wire, treble rows, and behind this deep lines of trenches, one mass of dug-outs as one knew, as hopeless looking a proposition as one was ever likely to see. Visibility was very good, but there was absolutely no movement to be seen. Everything was strangely quiet. A few 4.2's dropped into Honnecourt, just below us, but where we were on the crest, and in full view, we were moving about freely and no one shot at us—which was strange."

But the Hindenburg Line, formidable as it looked,

A.N.D.   o

cost no prolonged fighting on this part of the enemy front. This sector of it was already on the point of collapse under the heavy blows struck on both its flanks a few miles further north and south. On October 4th the Germans withdrew from their defences east of the Canal followed up by patrols of the 21st and 38th Divisions.

On the 5th both Divisions were across the Canal and had the strange experience of picking their way unopposed through the wire barrier and over the trenches of the abandoned Hindenburg Line. The 21st Division was on the left and the 38th on the right. The Divisional Artillery of the 17th was acting with the former. As the last trenches of the Hindenburg barriers were cleared, fighting began again with the retiring enemy rearguards. At 11.15 a.m. the Vth Corps H.Q. sent orders to the 17th and 33rd Divisions to move forward, the former in support of the 21st, the latter of the 38th.

The final stage of our victorious advance had now begun. The main line of the German defence had gone. All the war-wasted battlefields of the past years were behind the main British advance. The enemy still clung to a reserve line a few miles in rear of the last barrier. Beyond this he had begun here and there new lines of defence, but they were barely marked out. Henceforth he had to rely mainly upon the natural obstacles of the ground to assist him in fighting a series of delaying actions. It would be open warfare in country which the enemy had held as his own since the retreat after the first Allied defeats in August, 1914. Soon there would be for the victorious armies the unfamiliar sight of towns and villages showing no trace of shell fire; fields without craters; woods not reduced to mere branchless stumps of trees. At an early date in this new stage of the advance there came a change in the operation orders for the attacks on the enemy. Wherever possible the barrage fire of our gunners and the bombardment of hostile positions was arranged so as to spare the villages for the sake of the friendly French country folk still living in them to whom we came as deliverers.

The advance of this part of our front—that of the Third and Fourth Armies—had so far been almost due east. This had been the exact direction of that of the Vth Corps. There now began a gradual swing round to a new direction—the north-east. By a strange chance of war, the main British advance in the centre of the long Allied battle line was to be directed towards the lower Sambre and the district about Maubeuge and Mons, the very ground where the British Expeditionary Force had concentrated and fought its first battle in 1914.

The advance lay therefore through the country between the upper Scheldt with its Canal system and the river Sambre. It was country highly favourable to the delaying tactics of the enemy. On the small-scale maps of our atlases and tourist guide books it looks like a level, almost featureless country, an outlying region of the great plain that extends from Flanders eastward through all the north of Europe. But it has a marked character of its own, which in the existing military situation made it singularly favourable to the enemy. It is traversed by a number of small streams and small rivers, flowing to the Scheldt and Sambre, the general direction of nearly all of them being from south-east to north-west, that is more or less directly across a north-eastward advance. Some of them run between steep banks, below which they have cut a deep channel. Not only are the more important of these watercourses unfordable on long reaches of their course, but for lack of an easy approach they cannot be passed without difficulty, except where a road through their banks gives access to a bridge or ferry.

Their narrow valleys are divided by flat-topped ridges of the rising ground between the Sambre and the Scheldt. There are many clumps and patches of woodland and the most important of these, the Forest of Mormal, west of Maubeuge, extends for miles across what was to be the latest move of the British advance. It must be added that, as we have already noted, in this last phase of the war comparatively small rivers had acquired importance as a barrier against the new tactics of the tank. So though the enemy had no fortified lines on which to make a stand, this last stage of the war in open country cost much hard fighting and on one of the little river lines, the Selle, our advance was held up for several days.

On October 5th on receipt of the order to move forward the 17th Division began its concentration from its rest area and by evening halted a short distance west of the St. Quentin Canal. Next day there was no further movement. The news from the Divisional front was that the enemy was fighting a stubborn rearguard action on the last of their trench lines, a reserve position they had been preparing about four miles in rear of the Hindenburg Line. (It was known to the Allies as the Beaurevoir-Fonsomme Line, and for the Germans it was a sector of the " Hunding Position ".) The orders to the 17th Division were to support the advance of the 21st on the left of the Corps front, and be ready to pass through it when directed. The Division was now assembled in depth, the 51st Brigade leading. On the night of October 7th to 8th this Brigade crossed the Canal at Banteux and settled down in the old trenches of the captured Hindenburg Line on its east side.

At dawn there began heavy fighting out in front. The Vth Corps was attacking the German position, with the XIIIth Corps on its right and the IVth on its left. By 10 a.m. the news was that the advance on the three-Corps front was making good progress, and the 51st Brigade was ordered to move up into closer support of the 21st Division and accordingly went forward to the high ground between Montcouveux and Bonne Enfance Farms about three miles east of the Canal. In the afternoon the 50th Brigade crossed the Canal and occupied

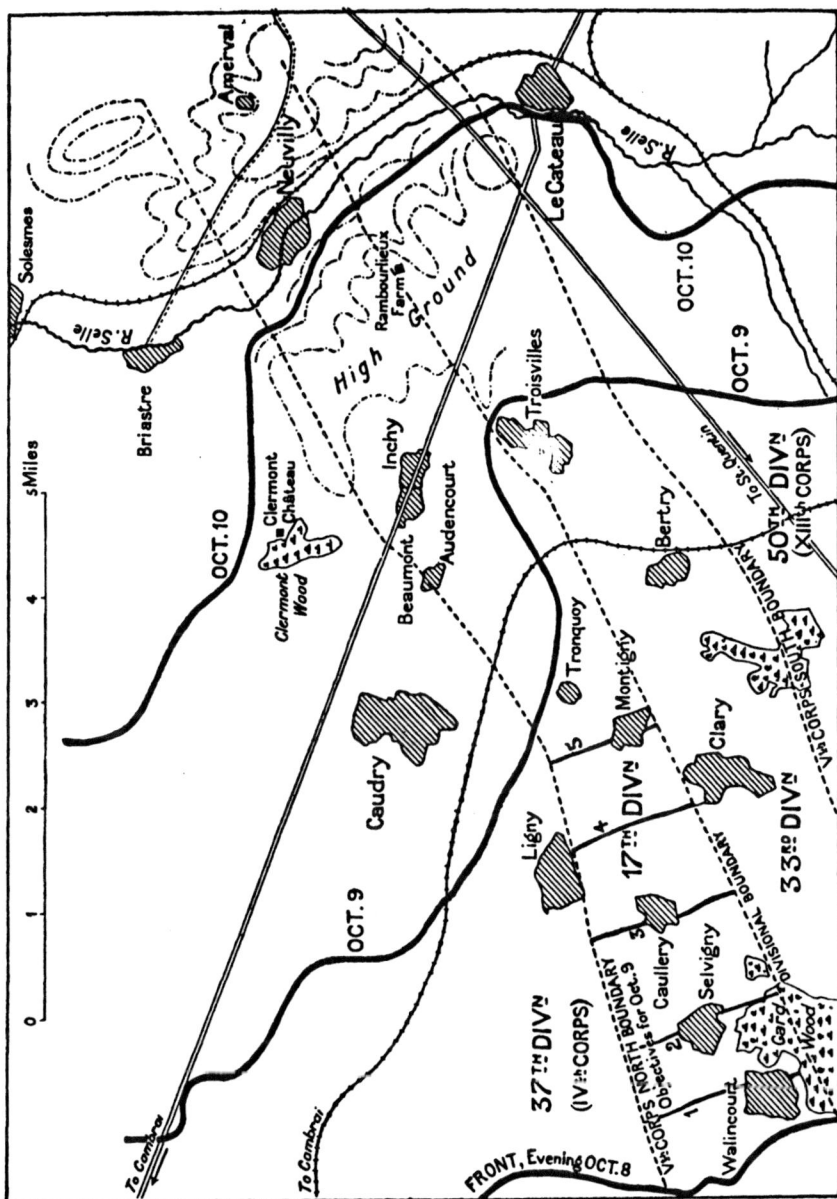

The Advance to the Selle : Operations of October 9th and 10th, 1918.

the Hindenburg Line on its east bank, while the 52nd closed up near its west bank not far from the crossings. At 8 p.m. orders were issued that the 17th Division was to pass through the 21st during the night, and continue the advance next morning.

It was to push forward by Selvigny and Caullery towards Montigny and Tronquoy. On its right the 38th Division would advance through Clary towards Bertry and the line of the Cambrai railway.

Orders from the G.O.C. 17th Division directed the 51st Brigade to act as advanced guard, moving forward so as to pass through the front of the 21st Division by 5.20 a.m., on October 9th. Attached to the Brigade would be the 78th Brigade R.F.A.; a section of the 77th Field Company R.E.; C. Company of the M.G. Battalion; four of the mobile 6-inch Newton Mortars; and a Cyclist Troop of the North Irish Horse. The advance was to be a succession of five " bounds," covering in all an anticipated gain of a little over four miles. The five objectives to be gained were:—

1. Walincourt and the high ground north of the village (if not already captured by the 21st Division).
2. Selvigny, the road running north from it, and Gard Wood to the south of it.
3. Caullery, L'Épine d'Andigny Farm, and the line of road running north and south from the village.
4. The Ligny-Clary road and the spur north of the latter village.
5. Montigny.

The 50th Brigade was to be at 5 a.m. on the line Angle Château to Hurtebise Farm (north of Villers-Outréaux), about 3,000 yards in rear of the starting point of the 51st Brigade's pursuit, and ready to move forward in support of it. At the same hour the 52nd Brigade would be on the line of Montcouveux Farm—Bonne Enfance Farm, occupied till now by the 50th. At 5.20 a.m. the 17th Division would take over its artillery that had been so far covering the advance of the 21st.

After dark on the evening of October 8th, the 21st Division had begun an attack towards Walincourt, but beyond a report that very little progress was being made no news of what was happening reached the 17th D.H.Q. and the 51st Brigade had no precise information as to the positions held by the troops it was to relieve and the Artillery and other units it was to take over. Much time was therefore occupied during the night in clearing up the situation, placing the troops in position for the advance, getting in touch with the gunners, the trench mortars and cyclists, and arranging for signal communications. But happily all was ready by 5 a.m. and twenty minutes later the 51st Brigade moved forward through the advanced posts of the 21st Division.

It was a bright autumn day, with a touch of cold in the early twilight advance and then pleasant warm sunshine soon after sunrise. The list of the five objectives to be won suggested a series of fights with enemy rearguards, but the Germans had begun to retire during the night— soon after midnight when the 21st Division had brought its evening attack to an end. They had got a good start on their way back to the line of the Selle where they were preparing for a determined stand.

So the 51st Brigade at first had the surprise of moving forward unopposed into peaceful country. There were no shells flying except on their extreme left, and these were British. The 37th Division on that flank had started off at 5.20 covered by a barrage, and some of its wide shots on the right caught the left of our Advanced Guard and caused a few casualties. When this firing was stopped, there was a strange silence everywhere for a while.

At first the Brigade advanced with prudent caution. It was hardly credible that there was not even an enemy patrol in front, but as soon as Walincourt was passed and the Gard Woods were found to be clear the advance was rapid.

The first man of the 17th Division to ride into Walincourt was a gunner officer pushing forward with a one-gun
detachment to find a line on which to bring up his
Battery.   He was one of those methodical people who
can manage to write up a detailed diary, day by day, even
amidst the strain of war, and his record of his experiences
that morning is well worth quoting, as a good sample of
the experiences of our advance into the country which had
so long been held by the enemy, behind the war zone of
trench fighting from 1914 to 1918.   This is how he
describes his ride into Walincourt and on to Selvigny:—

" At first I avoided the road from instinct. Roads were always
shelled. But there was a peaceful feeling in the air, which made
me think the Huns must be a long way away, so I took to the road
as it seemed quicker, and soon found myself in the village. Not
a sign of life was there, a deserted eerie place, and the sound of
horses' hoofs on the cobbles echoed all up the street. It was
strangely little knocked about, considering that we had shelled it
all night, only a window broken here and there and occasionally
the side of a house smashed in by a direct hit. I took a turning
to the left, marked ' Selvigny,' as this was the direction I wanted,
and just as I was getting clear of the village, got one of the shocks
of my life. I saw coming towards me a bent up figure in black.
I looked and thought again and realised it must be a civilian, the
first, during the whole war, seen by me while advancing. It was
an old, old man, and as we approached he looked up at me, smiled
and stopped. So did I, and said, ' Bon jour, Monsieur.' This
opened the floodgates and he was joined by an old woman who
appeared from nowhere. ' Ah, Monsieur, nous sommes délivrés.
Quel jour heureux ! ' was all he seemed able to say, but his eyes
said lots more. If ever I saw a man happy it was he. He had
been hiding in his cellar two days, he said, eating potatoes.
    " There was no time to wait, and I pushed on feeling mildly
excited. We soon reached Selvigny, and here the scene was extraordinary. Hundreds of old men and old women, young women
and children, were flocking into the street; tricolours, come from
heaven knows where, were hanging from the windows of nearly
every house; all were chattering, laughing, occasionally cheering,
and pressing round us asking so many questions so quickly that it
was impossible to understand. Bunches of flowers were produced

and given to everyone, our men grinning and making friends in a
way particularly their own. I felt excited and happy and wondered
where the devil the Hun had got to, and what I had better do
next. Then two men came up to me, very excited, and told me
the Curé ' veut beaucoup parler à un officier anglais.' So I was
led away up the street towards the church, where stood a grimy,
unshaved, cheery old man in a cassock, beaming through horn
spectacles. He came up to me, blessed the British Army, pressed
my hands, thanked me, and said a lot of nasty things about the
Bosch. But I hadn't time to wait long. I had to find out something so I went back, left the gun where it was, sent back a messenger for the rest of the Battery to come to that place, and pushed
on through the village, finding the cross-roads in the centre blown
up, only a huge crater remaining, the sides of all the adjoining
houses having fallen in. Fair warfare that, but it couldn't delay
us. With this fine weather one could take guns across country
anywhere."

North-east of the village he found the H.Q. of the
51st Brigade. Its infantry had gone forward over the
open country north of Walincourt and Selvigny as soon
as it was evident that these were clear of the enemy, and
it was now pushing on into Caullery, the 7th Borders on
the left, 7th Lincolns on the right and 10th Sherwoods
in support. The Brigadier had gone forward with them
and presently returned to his H.Q. and told how our men
were in Caullery, fraternising with the rejoicing villagers.
Some shells were falling about the place. Away to the
right front there was a rattle of machine gun fire from
Clary, where a German rearguard was temporarily
holding up the advance of our 33rd Division. It had
passed through the 38th at dawn and was advancing side
by side with the 17th.

It was now 9.30 a.m. Of the five objectives named
in Divisional orders three had been occupied without
opposition. But the enemy's rearguards were now
beginning to put up a fight. The Borders, supported
by the Sherwoods began to push on towards Montigny,
which the Germans were holding. The 7th Lincolns
swung half right to assist the 33rd Division in driving

the enemy out of Clary, and our batteries came into
action.   On the left the 37th Division had passed through
Ligny and was moving on Caudry.

Our advance now slowed down as the enemy's resistance stiffened, and in the latter part of the morning and
during the afternoon there was some heavy fighting.
On the left the 37th Division failed to reach Caudry and
at the end of the day were held up south and west of it.
On the right the enemy soon abandoned Clary and the
33rd Division reached Bertry in the afternoon.   By
1 p.m. the 51st Brigade had captured Montigny and was
advancing through the village and on both sides of it.
During the attack numbers of flags were hoisted on the
houses of Montigny.   At first these were taken to be
white flags, but the field glasses showed they were all
Red Cross flags.   The villagers had been told by the
Germans that if they hoisted them the British would not
fire on their houses.   The advance was pushed in the
afternoon through Tronquoy, and across the Cambrai
railway, in touch here with the 33rd Division, which
pushed on from Bertry into Troisvilles.   At 6 p.m. the
operations for the day came to an end.

Eleven prisoners had been taken by the 51st Brigade.
Two of these were brought into Brigade H.Q. just after
it was established, north-west of Selvigny, in the early
morning.   They had surrendered to a party of country
folk, and were evidently men who were anxious to get out
of the fighting.   Their captors brought them in, treating
them well, and there was only an exchange of not un-
friendly chaff between the Germans and the Frenchmen.
During the day the two other Brigades of the Division
had come forward step by step after the advance of the
51st.   In the afternoon, the 50th closed up in order to
pass through it at dawn on the 10th and act as advanced
guard.   The 52nd Brigade halted in and near Selvigny.
Both the 50th and 52nd Brigades, following up the
advanced guard, and making long halts on the way, had

abundant opportunities for fraternising with the people, and at every village and farm they had an enthusiastic welcome.

Orders from Corps H.Q. received in the evening assigned as the objective for the 17th Division on the 10th " Neuvilly and the high ground east of it," beyond the River Selle. Divisional orders were issued at 9 p.m. The 50th Brigade was to pass through the 51st and begin the advance at 5.20 a.m.

There was some rain in the night, and drizzling showers in the early morning, but later the sun shone out, and the clear air after the rain made it one of those bright autumn days when from every rising ground there are far-distant views—splendid weather for the gunners on both sides. In the twilight the 50th Brigade went forward, 10th West Yorkshires on the right, 6th Dorsets on the left, and 7th East Yorks in support. As they moved off a tremendous cannonade broke out away to the left rear. It was the barrage under which the 37th Division was attacking Caudry. But in front all was quiet.

Over the Cambrai railway went the advance, finding the track torn up on long stretches of the line. The scouts out in front reported Audencourt abandoned by the enemy. The Dorsets as they passed through the village amid the welcome of its people were reminded that they were on the very ground where their First Battalion had fought at the Battle of Le Cateau in August 1914. Then through a stretch of orchard land the Dorsets moved on into Inchy, where cheering crowds flocked out into the streets and tricolours appeared by magic at almost every window. The people said that the Germans had gone three hours before.

At the eastern exit of the place they had blown up the cross-roads as they went, making a huge crater 20 feet deep, and blowing some houses to bits. Between the wreckage and the crater edge there was just room to pass, and a crowd of villagers were at work filling in its edges to improve the narrow way on each side. Just beyond shrapnel were bursting, the first warning of coming opposition.

It was now 7 a.m. and the advance began up the slopes of the high ground that looks down upon the narrow valley of the Selle. On the right the 50th Brigade was in touch with the parallel advance of the 33rd Division, but the left of the Brigade and of the 52nd Brigade following in support was exposed, for the 37th Division had not yet cleared Caudry. At one time the 17th Division had its left thus " in air " for a length of some two miles.

Soon after leaving Inchy there came a blast of enfilade fire at short range (less than 3,000 yards) from the left. The enemy had brought into action a couple of field guns supported by a nest of machine guns east of Clermont Wood. A lively little skirmish followed. A gun of the Battery working with the advanced guard on this flank was knocked out by a German shell before it could fire, but the rest of the Battery galloped up and engaged the enemy over open sights, and after a few shots the German guns were withdrawn. Then, supported by our artillery fire, the North Irish Cyclists and a company of the East Yorkshires drove off the machine gunners. As the advance went up the high ground hostile shell fire increased. It came not only from the heights east of the Selle, but also from guns on its west side towards Briastre. A battalion of the 52nd Brigade and its M.G. Company were brought up to form a flank guard and the C.R.A. got some of his batteries into action to deal with the enemy's guns west of the river.

The supporting battalion of the 50th Brigade, the East Yorkshires, now passed through the Dorsets, and with the West Yorkshires on their right occupied the high ground by 9 a.m. Neuvilly was now in sight, though partly hidden by the farther crest of the height, from which the ground fell sharply to the deep trough of the valley. East of the river rose a bold line of heights, rising steeply over the houses beyond the Selle.   Artillery and machine guns opened from this strong position.   A glance was enough to show that there would be some hard fighting before the objective assigned to the Division could be won—" Neuvilly and the high ground east of the Selle," and the attack would have to be methodically prepared.   Awaiting further developments our men took cover and began digging themselves in, and the advanced guard batteries were brought up to carefully chosen positions on the western margin of the height.

The weather was clearing up and from the high ground there was now a remarkable sight away to the left and the left front.   On the railway near Solesmes several trains were moving.   Our gunner officers watched them with a regret that they were beyond the range of an 18-pounder. But the left battery found splendid targets within its reach.   Away to the northward on every road west of the river there could be seen columns of closed-up troops and long lines of all kinds of transport marching towards the crossings at Briastre and Solesmes.   Our gunners opened fire upon them, and soon they disappeared from all the nearer roads, moving out of reach by sheltered lanes or over the open country.

It was decided that in order to give the necessary time for preparation the attack on Neuvilly should not be made till 5 p.m.   During the afternoon the 37th Division having captured Caudry had advanced through Clermont Wood and gained touch with the left front of the 17th Division.   From this point the 37th Division front curved away to the westward.   On the other flank the 33rd Division had come up in line with the 17th.   During the afternoon the enemy kept up an intermittent shell fire, and our batteries were in action in reply.

CHAPTER XIII

THE VICTORIOUS ADVANCE

(3) FROM THE SELLE TO THE BELGIAN BORDER

BEFORE describing the prolonged fight for the crossing of the Selle at Neuvilly, it may be well to say a word about the general situation on this afternoon of October 10th. The German retirement was now reaching a critical stage. In Belgium, on the extreme left, our front was at last east of all the old battle ground of Ypres and the Yser line. The left of Haig's main advance was within a few miles of Lille; we had taken Lens, and were well beyond Cambrai. Now the push was for Valenciennes and Maubeuge in order to gain complete command of the link between the main German line of communication by the middle Meuse valley, and the main railway just within the French frontier on which most of the supplies of the enemy's armies on that side depended. This thrust would not only accelerate the enemy's evacuation of western Belgium, but also make his hold on French territory precarious and his retirement from it extremely difficult. On our right his armies in France were being pressed back by the French advance towards the Oise and across the Aisne and by the American attack on both sides of the Argonne.

The line of the Selle was almost the last strong position barring Haig's advance on Maubeuge, and his right was now facing the enemy here from Le Cateau to Neuvilly. Farther north our advance had still to reach the west bank of the little river that had now sprung into sudden importance. This river line was eventually forced by an attack on a long front from beyond Le Cateau to its junction with the Scheldt. But it was considered that it was sound policy to attack at once with the troops that had already got into touch with the enemy on its upper course, in the hope of forcing the line here and turning the position before the Germans had further strengthened their defences on the east bank.

In the orders issued for the attack of October 10th, the objective assigned was the road running south-east to north-west along the crest of the heights beyond the river (the country road from Forest to Briastre). The attack was to be covered by a creeping barrage of the field batteries, howitzers, and the heavy guns of the Divisional Artillery, and the Maxims of the M.G. Battalion. The barrage was to start upon a road running parallel to the river immediately west of the village, and move forward right and left of it sparing the houses for the sake of the inhabitants. (It was afterwards found that the Germans had already moved nearly all of them out of Neuvilly). The infantry was to attack on a two battalion front, each battalion having two companies in the first line and two in support. The remaining battalion of the Brigade would follow and " mop " up the village, when the attack had reached its farther side. The infantry were to be in position 300 yards west of the road which marked the starting line of the barrage, and they were to advance as soon as it began at 5 p.m. It was anticipated that the flanks of the attack would be protected by an advance of battalions from the 37th Division of the left and the 38th on the right.

While moving down the slopes to the assembly position the infantry of the attack came under heavy shell fire from the enemy's batteries east of the Selle. But moving in open order they had very few casualties. As they waited for a short time till the barrage came down on the enemy front there was a cheerful anticipation that, though there was a tough bit of work to be done, the Germans

Battle of Neuvilly, October 20th, 1918.

would soon be hustled across the river and over the hill-tops beyond.   After all the enemy was fighting a losing game.   In the last ten weeks there had been a series of fairly easily won successes and where the Germans had put up a stiff resistance and there was hard fighting it had always ended in their having to move on again.   This however was to be a more serious task than the Division had faced since the long drawn Battle of the Somme.   It would win through in the end, but it was a more difficult business than anyone realised that autumn evening.   A glance must have shown the enemy position was a very strong one, though many details of its strength were still to be discovered by the knowledge won in trying to master them.   Here let it be noted that to reach the objective—the crest of the opposing heights—there would be on most of the fronts of the attack an advance of about a mile and a quarter—first through the village on the west bank and over the ground north and south of it; then across the river in its ravine-like hollow; then over a road and railway easily converted into strong defence lines, the railway in a cutting for most of its length and then on a low embankment—the east side of Neuvilly would also have to be cleared—all this on the lower slopes east of the Selle, where every inch of ground was dominated by the heights; and these were a natural rampart, rising terrace above terrace with mostly steep banks forming the slopes between them.   On both sides of the Selle the houses of Neuvilly were detached buildings, even where they stood in rows on each side of the main streets, and there were between and around them walled and fenced gardens with patches of orchard ground,—the very place for hiding away machine guns.

The barrage, rapidly improvised in the afternoon, worked splendidly.   It came down, like a wall of fire, dust and smoke, along the road on the margin of the village, and swept steadily forward north and south of it. Wave after wave the two Yorkshire battalions went forward. On their right a battalion of the 33rd Division kept pace with them, but no flanking force appeared on the left. In the centre there was an immediate check. The enclosures on the west edge of Neuvilly had been made into an entanglement of barbed wire threaded through every fence and hedge and from tree to tree. The gardens and the houses behind them bristled with machine guns. The inner companies of the attack were held by the storm of bullets. But the outer companies worked round the place north and south, pushing for the river crossings above and below the village, and meeting with no resistance till they reached them, though they came under artillery and M.G. fire from the high ground beyond and rifle fire from trenches near the east bank.

South of the village the two companies of the West Yorkshires, as they pushed forward to the Selle, came under M.G. fire from the village and the east bank. They found the river flowing six or seven feet deep, and they edged away southwards looking for a possible crossing, till nearly half a mile from Neuvilly, they found it at the dam of a watermill. Here they forced a passage and joined up with the left company of the 33rd Division, which was attacking on that side. But repeated attempts to get forward up the slope beyond were checked by heavy machine gun fire from the railway in front and from the south side of the village.

On the other flank of the attack the two outer companies of the East Yorkshires reached the river and found a possible crossing-place about 600 yards north of the village. Here the Selle was 4½ to 5 feet deep, and 20 feet wide between steep banks. A couple of trees cut down by shell fire had fallen into the stream where their branches anchored them under the west bank. These were some help in crossing. So scrambling, wading and swimming across deeper patches, one company and a few men and officers of the other reached the east bank.

They took in succession a trench near the riverside, the crossing of the railway embankment and another trench 200 yards beyond it—a trench formed by deepening a a ditch running beside the Briastre road. Forty prisoners (an officer and 39 other ranks) were taken in this dashing attack, and the East Yorkshires claimed also the capture of seven machine guns.[1]

In the centre two companies of the Dorsets were brought up to assist the Yorkshires in the attack on the village. It made very little progress. Once our men got past the margin of the place they found themselves under close cross-fire from every house and wired enclosure, in a pelting storm of M.G. bullets. Thanks to our artillery having spared the village its strongly organised internal defence was intact. By 7 p.m. the attempt to clear the place was abandoned and Yorkshires and Dorsets, after having suffered considerable loss, were withdrawn to the road on its west front.

The attack of the 33rd Division on the right had also failed, and the West Yorkshires, unable to reach the railway and exposed to heavy fire in their position between it and the river, were brought back by the mill crossing to the west bank. On the other flank the East Yorkshire detachment that had crossed the railway was ordered to fall back over the river, leaving only posts to watch the crossing.

The first attack had thus failed, and the only result gained was a better knowledge of the enemy's position and defence organisation. It was decided that another attempt should be made two days later, on the morning of October 12th. The orders for the 11th were that, while preparations were being made for a renewed attack, the advanced guard Brigade would continue to reconnoitre the crossings of the river. After dark it would be relieved by the 52nd Brigade which was to attack on the 12th. During the day a line of resistance would be

[1] Captain O. Varley, M.C., who led this attack, received the D.S.O.

consolidated along the crest of the heights on the west bank, running north-westward from Rambourlieux Farm, and consisting of irregularly sited posts giving each other mutual support.

The day passed fairly quietly, but enemy snipers made any incautious movement on the forward slopes of the heights west of the village rather dangerous. After sunset, as darkness came on, attempts were made by the Dorsets and West Yorkshires to establish bridgeheads north and south of the village by pushing fighting patrols across, in order to facilitate next day's attack. A crossing was successfully made over tree trunks about 1,000 yards south of Neuvilly by a company of the West Yorkshires. They rushed three enemy posts and got forward to the road just west of the railway. The attempt to reach the line failed, as it was strongly protected by barbed wire covered at close range by machine guns and Minenwerfers, but the company dug in with platoon posts along the road, and a second company crossed and formed supporting posts between the road and river. Under cover of this screen the 23rd Field Company R.E. completed four light bridges before daylight.

The attempt on the north side of the village failed. It was made by a company of the Dorsets, under Captain Goodson, M.C., guided by two patrols of the East Yorkshires, who had crossed the day before and knew the ground. But the enemy was on the alert, holding in force a trench close to the east bank. An attempt to get a light bridge across failed, the party coming under heavy M.G. fire. Captain Goodson was shot dead while directing the attempt to bridge the river. Efforts were then made to secure a crossing farther north, but without success, and at 10.40 p.m. the Dorsets were ordered to leave posts watching the river, but make no further attempt to cross.

During the night there was a frequent splutter of firing where our posts on the east bank below the village were

in touch with the Germans holding the railway.   The
enemy's artillery threw some H.E. and gas shells into
the back area of our lines, some bursting as far west as
Inchy.   This however had happened on several recent
nights.   5 a.m. was the zero hour for the attack which was
to be made in combination with an advance across the
river of the 37th Division on the left, and the 33rd in the
right, each with a Brigade in the fighting line.

For the attack on Neuvilly the G.O.C. of the 52nd
Brigade had at his disposal, besides his own three Battalions, a Battalion of the 50th Brigade (the East Yorkshires), who were available as an immediate reserve.
Other troops of the 50th were to hold their ground along
and beyond the river till the advance had passed through
them.   On the basis of reports sent in by our patrols
on the evening of the 11th, it was believed that the enemy
had abandoned the part of the village west of the Selle.
This was a mistake.   Some of the Germans were still
holding on there near the river bank.   But it was now
known that the inhabitants had gone, so the barrage,
beginning at the river bank was to sweep the eastern side
of the place.

October 12th was a fine but dull day, with mist interfering with the view in the early morning.   The enemy
was on the alert, and when our barrage of artillery and
M.G. fire opened at 5 a.m. his counter-barrage replied
within five minutes.

It caught and inflicted serious loss on the rear company
of the 9th Duke of Wellington's, as they crossed the
river by the four light bridges south of the village.   The
Battalion pushed on to join up with the West Yorkshire
posts on the east bank and tried to rush the railway, but
they were held by a deadly cross-fire of machine guns from
the line and its barbed wire entanglements in front and
the orchards, enclosures and houses on the south side of
Neuvilly, from which they were enfiladed on their left.
Some distance away to their right, the 33rd Division

attack got across the railway, but as it pushed forward on
the slopes beyond, an enemy counter-attack came sweeping
down upon it over the ridge from Amerval, and it was
driven back to the riverside.

North of the village the situation was better. Here
the 12th Manchesters waded the Selle, cleared the trench
on the river bank, stormed the enemy's line along the
railway, and then fought forward till they reached their
first objective, on the Briastre road, north of Neuvilly.
It had been arranged that the Battalions attacking north
and south of the village were each to be followed by a
company of the 10th Lancashire Fusiliers, and as soon
as the river was crossed these were to wheel inward and
clear the east side of Neuvilly by attacking from both
ends of the village. The company that followed the
Manchesters fought its way well into the village, but there
was no sign of an attack from the other end of it. There
the company detailed for this operation was held up on the
west bank by the failure of the Duke of Wellington's to
get forward. In the face of a stubborn resistance
supported by M.G. fire from houses and enclosures and
a bridge over the railway, the Lancashires, thus left alone
in the village, fell back to the railway line near its northern
margin. Away to the left of the Brigade attack a single
Battalion of the 37th Division had crossed the river.

There was now a deadlock. It was past noon; the
right attack was still held up between the river and the
railway. The Manchesters were holding on upon the
Briastre road with the remains of a company of the
Lancashires on the railway to their right rear. They
were suffering heavily under the fire from the height.
The Battalion of the 37th Division that had crossed on
their left was extended on a long front, and unable to get
forward. Arrangements were in progress to reinforce
the left attack with the East Yorkshires and the two
remaining companies of the Lancashire Fusiliers, and
renew the attack in combination with a fresh advance of

the 37th Division.   But before the reinforcements had
got forward across the Selle, the enemy, at 2.45 p.m.,
put down a heavy creeping barrage on our left, followed
by a counter-attack in force.   It drove back everything
on this side.

The advanced Battalion of the 37th was pushed down
to the river edge.   The Manchesters were forced down
the slopes and across the railway and finally made a stand
along a bank near the riverside.   Here covered by our
gunfire they held on, while the enemy made good his old
position along the railway line.

After this there was only desultory exchange of fire till
dark.   The attack had ended in a disappointing failure.
The 51st Brigade was already moving up to take over
the line from the 52nd.   The situation at sunset was:
north and south of Neuvilly a Battalion was holding on
between river and railway.   The enemy held the railway line, and the village east of the Selle.   They had
apparently withdrawn from the west side of the place to
concentrate on the defence of the east bank.

For a week after this check no further attempt was
made to renew the attack, and the time was devoted to
deliberate preparation for another effort, as part of a
general forward movement of the 3rd Army along all the
river front.   Our artillery brought bursts of harassing
fire to bear upon the German position and the concentration areas behind the heights.   The enemy's gunners
retaliated by bombarding our front positions and back
areas with H.E. gas shells.   Inchy was a favourite target
for their guns night after night.

Covered by our artillery, our posts on the east bank of
the Selle north and south of Neuvilly were able to hold
on and consolidate these important positions.   Only once
did the enemy make a serious attack upon them.   It was
just before dawn on October 18th, when a detachment of
the 52nd Brigade holding the position south of the village
was attacked in force.   Our men were driven out of two

of the forward posts, but these were immediately regained by a counter-attack from the support line near the river bank.

Under the protection of these positions on the east bank, preparations were carried on for bridging the Selle at several points for the coming advance. Two tanks were to assist in the attack. These were brought up by night to carefully concealed positions behind the crest of the ridge on the west bank. At a point about 500 yards north of Neuvilly, where bushes and broken ground concealed the work in the deep hollow of the Selle from enemy view, the Engineers built up the piers for a tank bridge. On these, twenty-four hours before the attack, its frame work and track of girders bolted together was placed in position and carefully camouflaged.

A bridge was also prepared for the passage of field guns across the river, and a number of light portable foot bridges were to be carried forward at the last moment and placed in selected positions. The work on the defence line on the western ridge was completed—a precaution against the unlikely, but still possible, emergency of an enemy attack in force across the Selle.

All this heavy work was carried through by the Field Companies R.E., now assisted once more by the York and Lancasters. The Pioneer Battalion, after having been engaged since the crossing of the Canal du Nord in making good the line of communications, repairing railways and bridges, and filling up and making good crater damage on the roads—had been brought up to rejoin the Division on October 10th, and had its H.Q. at Audencourt.

Sunday, October 20th, was the day fixed for the attack. Officially that day's advance of the Third and Fourth Armies and the French left, on a front of several miles, is known as the " Battle of the Selle." For the 17th Division it is remembered as the " Battle of Neuvilly." The Division was to attack with the 38th Division on its right, and the 5th Division (IVth Corps) on its left. So far all the attacks on Neuvilly had been made by daylight. But zero hour for October 20th was fixed at 2 a.m. It was anticipated that a night attack would mean a surprise for the Germans, and this hope was justified by the event.

The general plan of the attack was: The advance was to be made by four " bounds." The First Objective would be the road running along the hillside, roughly parallel to the railway and just beyond it. All the eastern part of Neuvilly was within this, the " Blue Line." The Second Objective—the " Red Line "—was the road along the crest of the heights. The next bound to the Third Objective—the " Green Line "—would win the spurs and intervening hollows on the reverse slopes of the heights to a line beyond the little village of Amerval. The final push to the Fourth Objective—the " Brown Line "—would carry forward the left of the attack to a rising ground north of Amerval. The whole distance to be traversed by the advance from the Selle to the farthest point of the " Brown Line " was about two miles.

The attack was to be made by two Brigades. It would be covered by creeping barrages of 18-pounders, 4.5 and 6-inch howitzers, trench mortars and machine guns, with flank and standing barrages. The 50th Brigade would open the attack, pushing forward a battalion north and south of Neuvilly, each accompanied by two companies of its remaining Battalion. These last, on crossing the river, would wheel inward and make a converging attack to clear Neuvilly. Till they broke into the village its north and south margins would be kept under a heavy barrage. After winning the Blue Line the attack would move on to the Red Line. The 51st Brigade would follow its advance, and, when the Red Line was won, would pass through the 50th and attack in succession the Green and Brown Lines. The two tanks would cross the Selle in support of the left attack. Contact planes would fly over the advance. The attacks of the Divisions on the right and left would keep pace with the advance of the 17th Division and their objectives were, roughly speaking, prolongations of those assigned to the latter.

It was full moon on the 19th. But there was rain during the day and in the evening, and all night the sky was overclouded. This bad weather favoured the concealment of the attacking troops as they took up their jumping-off positions, but the rain made the ground heavy for movement on the slopes.

At 2 a.m. the opening of our barrage gave the signal for the advance. The enemy were evidently taken by surprise. By the time his counter-barrage replied the left and right attacks were pouring across the thirty foot-bridges above and below the village, and the German fire was wild and irregular. In half an hour the 1st Objective was won, but it was long after this before the east side of the village was completely cleared of the enemy.

On the right the 7th East Yorks advanced on a two-company front. The railway line was stormed after a sharp fight. The enemy had placed machine gun posts along it at intervals of 60 yards, with trench mortars between them. Beyond the railway the enemy held a second defence line along the road running parallel to it, covered by a single line of barbed wire on stakes. This obstacle was broken through by pulling up stakes here and there, and the Germans were driven from the road by a fierce bayonet attack. At 2.30 the East Yorkshires were reorganising and consolidating along the 1st Objective. On the left, north of Neuvilly, the 6th Dorsets attacked (also on a two-company front). They had a hard fight to overcome the determined resistance put up by the Germans entrenched along the road between the river bank and the railway, but after this the enemy did not make a serious stand, and the 1st Objective was won on this side about the same time that the right attack reached it south of the village.

Meanwhile the West Yorkshires, wheeling inward from south and north, were attacking the village. On its south side the Germans made a prolonged stand in the copses and enclosures of its margin, backed by machine gun fire from the houses. It was forty minutes before their resistance here was overcome. On the north side the attack got in more quickly, but after the village had been penetrated on both sides parties of the Germans held out in the houses at various points inside it, and it was not till 5 a.m. that it was completely cleared of the enemy. About 100 prisoners were taken. Other captures in Neuvilly included 34 machine guns, six trench mortars, three tool wagons and a wagon containing the travelling library of the 120th Reserve Infantry Regiment.

There was a ten minutes pause on the 1st Objective to reorganise for the continuance of the advance, which was now made by the East Yorks and the Dorsets on a front each of three companies covered once more by our barrage. The Germans did not make any determined resistance, except on the extreme left, where for a while the advance of the Dorsets was checked. The 51st Brigade was now crossing the river and the leading company of the Sherwood Foresters came up to reinforce the Dorsets on the left, and the enemy gave way. On the right the East Yorkshires were harassed by enfilade fire of machine guns from the flank, where the 38th Division attack had not yet got so far forward. But by 3.30 a.m. the crest of the ridge was won.

The 51st Brigade was now to pass through the 50th for the attack on the 3rd Objective (Amerval on the right and the line of the Amerval-Solesmes road on the left front). The 51st Brigade had assembled on the defence line of the western heights with its right on Rambourlieux Farm, and all three Battalions in line—the 7th Borders on the right, the 7th Lincolns in the centre, and the 10th Sherwood Foresters on the left. With each Battalion there were four guns of the M.G. Battalion. At 2 a.m. they moved down to the ground south-west of Neuvilly, and were ready to follow the right and left attacks as soon as the 50th Brigade had crossed the river. The Borders went across south of the village, and the other two Battalions north of it, and followed closely the advance of the attack on the 2nd Objective. By 3.40 they were in position near the crest of the ridge waiting for the barrage that was to cover their advance at 4 a.m. At that hour they went forward to the attack. They came at once under heavy artillery and machine gun fire. On the centre and left however ground was steadily gained, but on the right the Borders were long held up in front of Amerval, where the enemy made a well-organised and determined defence.

The two tanks had been directed to come to the assistance of the Borders. They had crossed the river during the second stage of the attack. It was rather a delicate operation. They had ploughed their way down the muddy slopes of the western ridge and across a sodden field north of Neuvilly, finding their way in a damp mist with the half-light of a moon muffled in cloud. Shells were whizzing overhead and exploding in the hollow of the river course and on the further bank, but it was a random fire and the enemy had not discovered the existence of the tank bridge. Those who watched the crossing looked on with mingled interest and anxiety as the lumbering machines in succession crawled carefully down the greasy ramp cut in the river bank, stopped for a moment and made a sharp right-angle turn on to the bridge, that seemed not to leave them an inch to spare on its narrow track. Then there was another sharp turn and a climb up a second muddy slope to the crest of the further bank. The tanks crossed the railway, went over the lower northern end of the high ground beyond, and began to move towards Amerval. But they never came into action. One of them was soon disabled by engine

trouble too serious to be set right by any hurried repairs.
The other got a little further forward before it was brought
to a dead stop by a German shell smashing its caterpillar
track.

In the attempt to push into the western margin of
Amerval, the Commanding Officer of the Borders and
his adjutant were killed by machine gun fire, and this led
to some delay in the reorganisation of the attack, but in
small parties officers and men worked their way forward
and succeeded in establishing posts close into the village
on its west, south and north sides. In the centre and on
the left the Lincolns and the Sherwoods had won their way
to the line of the Solesmes road, and by 6 a.m. the 3rd
Objective had been occupied on that side. In this stage
of the advance the Sherwoods suffered a good deal from
machine gun fire from the high ground west of Ovillers.
The enemy's main artillery positions were in rear of that
village, and the German gunners were keeping up a
scattered fire of shells of various calibres, now here now
there, over all the ground on which our advance was
being made, and as far back as the line of the Selle. Gas
shells in large numbers were pitched into the river
hollow and into Neuvilly, and for hours there was a lot
of mustard gas drifting in the valley.

At 6.45 a.m. the 5th Division, on our left, attacked the
4th Objective. It was a line running roughly parallel
to their front. Its right curved back to the centre of the
17th Division front, running north and south along a country road that linked up with the Solesmes-Amerval road
(the Green Line) west of the latter place. The Sherwoods
sent forward a company to assist the 5th Division, by
occupying this part of the Brown Line. But the advance
was brought to a standstill by machine gun fire and the
5th Division and the Sherwoods fell back to the Green
Line.

Just after 9 a.m. heavy fighting developed on this side,
the Germans counter-attacking against the Sherwoods

and the right of the 5th Division. The Sherwoods held
their ground successfully, though for awhile their left
flank was endangered by the 5th Division being driven
back from the Green Line. But a counter-attack of the
5th regained the lost ground. After this there was for
a while a lull in the fighting. Artillery and machine
guns were active on both sides. On the right of the
Divisional front the Borders were still trying to get
forward into Amerval, by pushing on gradually from
their positions on its west and south sides. Along the
rest of the front the positions won were being consolidated
in view of further enemy counter-attacks.

At 11 a.m. the general line was reported to be: On
the right the 38th Division was in the Red Line and in
touch with the Borders in front of Amerval. The
Lincolns and Sherwoods were along the Amerval-
Solesmes Road, and the former had outposts beyond it.
On the left, the right of the 5th Division was close up to
the Green Line and in touch with the Sherwoods. Several
of our Field Batteries R.F.A. had been got across the
Selle and brought up to the heights of its east bank to give
closer support to the infantry. It was decided to prepare
for an advance of our left at 4 p.m. in combination with
the 5th Division, to capture the Brown Line. The attack
was to be covered by a creeping barrage of all available
guns of both Divisions.

By 11.30 a.m. the Borders had at last fought their way
into Amerval, but they were then driven out of most of the
place by a counter-attack. They held on in the enclosures and buildings of its western outskirts, and gradually
gained some further ground.

The combined attack at 4 p.m. was a rapid and fairly
easy success. The Brown Line was won and consolidation began. Just as the attack went forward and its
covering barrage came down, the Germans launched a
counter-attack on the right through Amerval and on
both sides of it. They were caught in our barrage and

their attack was easily repulsed. At midnight the Borders with the help of a creeping barrage cleared the enemy out of Amerval by a well-organised attack, and got forward to the Green Line beyond it. By daylight the 51st Brigade was firmly consolidated on its final objectives.

The prisoners taken numbered 451 (17 officers and 434 other ranks). The machine guns taken were 120, besides a number of trench mortars, anti-tank rifles, waggons and other minor trophies. It was a very satisfactory day's work, an attack carried through according to plan, with complete success, against a very strong position.

During the 21st the enemy's artillery was active, shelling the forward slopes of the heights along the Selle and throwing H.E. and gas shells into Neuvilly and the river valley. But he made no counter-attacks. The R.E. Field Companies were employed with the York and Lancasters in improving the communications across the Selle, and substituting more solid bridges for the temporary structures used during the battle. Preparations were in progress for a new advance of the Third Army on the 23rd and the Divisional Artillery was being got forward to the east of the river.

On the 22nd the G.O.C. issued the following general order to the Division :—

" 17TH DIVISION,
22nd October, 1918.

" The Army Commander has requested the Divisional Commander to convey to all ranks of the 17th Division his thanks for and appreciation of the recent remarkable achievements of the Division.

" The Divisional Commander desires to add to that of the Army Commander his great appreciation of the splendid fighting spirit and loyal co-operation of all ranks, which have resulted in a situation of extraordinary difficulty—perhaps the most difficult which the Division has faced—being dealt with with complete success.

" The Divisional Commander wishes it impressed on all ranks that much still requires to be done to accomplish the defeat of the enemy, and that fighting will be much more open directly the final crust of the enemy's organised resistance is broken, and that open fighting of the nature anticipated will involve much more marching and will require great powers of endurance, strict discipline, determination and initiative. He is confident however that whatever tasks the Division is called upon to carry out it will do in the same splendid manner it has in the past."

The next stage in the advance of the Vth Corps was to be carried out by the 33rd Division on the right and the 21st on the left. On the night of October 22nd to 23rd these two Divisions relieved and passed through the fronts held by the 38th and 17th. The Divisional Artillery of the 17th was to continue its co-operation in the advance, and the R.E. and the Pioneers remained at their work on the Selle crossings. On being relieved the three Infantry Brigades concentrated about Inchy. D.H.Q. were at Montigny. The Division was to follow up the advance and be prepared to support the 21st Division, or pass through it to continue the advance when required.

During the operations from October 5th to the 23rd the casualties of the Division had been:—

	Killed.	Wounded.	Missing.	Totals.
Officers -	23	72	3	98
Other ranks -	358	1623	117	2098
	381	1695	120	2196

The advance of the Vth Corps in the next three days—October 23rd to 25th—covered in a direct line a distance of only about ten miles, from the heights on the east bank of the Selle to villages on the western margin of the Forest of Mormal. The character of the country was now entirely different from that in which the 17th Division had been operating since the advance from the Ancre began in August. Once Ovillers was reached it was no longer a land of open rolling uplands, where every rising ground gave in fine weather wide views over the country in front; it was a rich, highly cultivated country of small

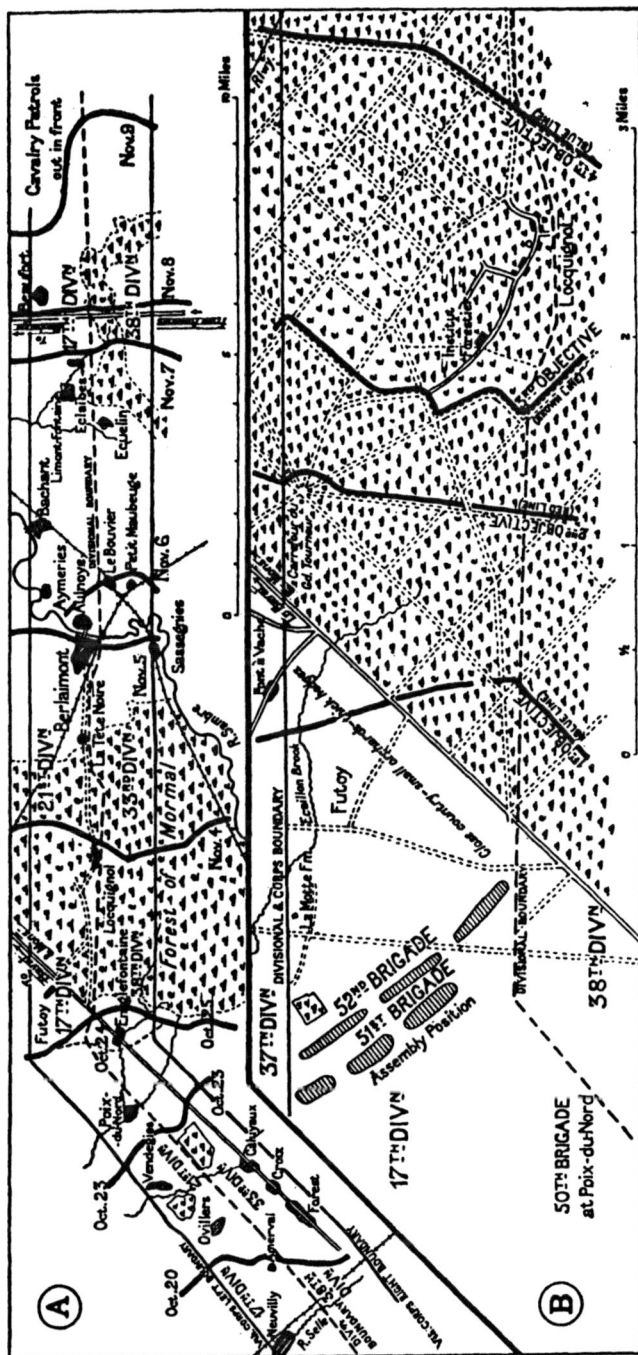

A. Final advance of the 17th Division from the Selle through the Forest of Mormal to the Belgian frontier.

B. The Division in the Battle of the Forest of Mormal, November 4th, 1918.

A.N.D.

fields and orchards, all with thick hedges and well timbered, so that in the distance it looked like a wide, far stretching forest. Late as the season was, the leaves were still on the trees. Everywhere there was abundant cover from view, making reconnaissance even from the air no easy matter. It was admirable country for an enemy engaged in a fighting retreat.

The advance, starting at 2 a.m. on October 23rd, made good progress that day. On the right the 33rd Division captured the villages of Forest and Croix and drove the enemy out of the wood of Vendignies. On the left the 21st Division took Ovillers and Vendignies village. The Infantry of the 17th Division had been hoping for at least a short rest at Inchy, but at 6 a.m. there came orders to move up in support of the 21st Division, and the 51st Brigade went forward to Ovillers, while the 50th occupied Neuvilly. All ranks were very tired that evening. But there was a day of rest on the 24th.

That day the Divisions in front went forward steadily, driving in the German rearguards, till by evening they held a line close up to the margin of the Mormal Forest, with the 33rd Division on the right on the western outskirts of Englefontaine. The village was captured in the following night. The 17th Division was now ordered to relieve the 21st in the night of October 26th to 27th. On the morning of the 27th D.H.Q. were established at Ovillers. The 52nd Brigade was in the line north of Englefontaine facing the forest, the 50th in support about and in the large village of Poix-du-Nord, and the 51st in reserve at Vendignies. " The troops were tired and in want of rest. The day passed quietly," says the diary of operations.

Preparations had now begun for the next and (as it proved to be), the final stage of the advance, in which the part assigned to the Vth Corps would be a push due east through the Forest of Mormal.

East and west of this great tract of woodlands the

British Expeditionary Force had retired at the outset of the retreat from Mons four years before this. The wheel had turned full circle and the victorious advance was soon to end where the retreat of 1914 had begun.

Mormal is a forest of oak and beeches, about nine miles in length from north to south and from three to four miles broad. The woodland roadways through it were mostly narrow tracks, unmetalled or at the best with a light layer of unrolled stones and gravel. These tracks generally crossed each other on lines from north-east to south-west and north-west from south-east, marking off the forest into large diamond-shaped blocks. But a railway line from Valenciennes to Avesnes passed through it in a direct line, at a smaller angle with the west and east direction than that of the forest paths. From Le Quesnoy the one good metalled road in the forest ran south-east to the village of Locquignol in the very heart of the woods and thence due east to its farther margin, near the point where the railway issued from it. This direct way through was an important feature in the scheme for the advance of the 17th Division.

Before the war the forest had been well cared for by the woodmen of Locquignol, a number of trees being felled each year, and replaced by planting others. But during the years in which it had been in possession of the invaders they had made, here and there, extensive clearings by felling trees to provide timber for their entrenchments, huts, bridges and other work. For some months this work had been done by gangs of Allied prisoners of war. In many of the clearings large quantities of timber were stacked ready for removal. It was curious that the felled trees were almost always piled in stacks running east and west. If they had lain north and south they might have been used as elements in the scheme for the defence of the forest. In the uncleared parts of the woods little or nothing had been done to check the undergrowth, and in some places it had grown up into dense

A.N.D.   P 2

thickets. But there were fewer of these obstacles than was expected.

The Division remained in the front line till the night of October 29th to 30th, when it was relieved by the 21st Division. During this short tour of duty the front was quiet, except for the activity of the German gunners, who however mostly paid attention to Englefontaine, held by the 38th Division, which they frequently bombarded. They also indulged in intermittent shelling of the back areas as far off as Poix-du-Nord.

It was now known that the 17th Division would form the left of the Vth Corps attack in the coming battle, advancing from this sector. The brief stay in the line gave the officers a useful knowledge of the ground immediately in their front. On being relieved the Division went for a very few days to the now familiar area on both sides of the Selle, the 51st Brigade to Inchy, 50th to Neuvilly and 52nd to Ovillers. The Divisional Artillery had already been taken out of the line for a short rest, the first they had had since the advance began in August.

All were soon back in the front, for the date of the attack had been fixed for November 4th. The move back to the line began on the 2nd and by 3 a.m. on the 3rd the 17th Division had completed the relief of the 21st. The 52nd Brigade was in the first line north of Englefontaine, the 51st in support in and about Poix-du-Nord, and the 50th at Vendignies. D.H.Q. were at Ovillers. The Division, when thus brought into the fighting line for its last battle, was far short of its regulation war establishment. Its three Infantry Brigades of three battalions each, plus the Divisional or Pioneer Battalion, would have meant, if their numbers were complete, an aggregate total of over 10,000 officers and men. A return dated noon on Saturday, November 2nd, shows that the infantry was nearly a third short of this strength—the available numbers being only just over 7,000. Other units also were under strength.[1] During the advance there had not only been the decrease by casualties in action, but for some weeks there had been a heavy toll of invaliding by sickness, during an influenza epidemic from which both the Allies and the Germans suffered seriously, and the reinforcing drafts for the Division had not made good this loss.

The battle of November 4th was to be an attack by the British First, Third and Fourth Armies on a front of some twenty-five miles from Oisy on the Sambre to Valenciennes on the Scheldt, pushing eastward towards Maubeuge and Mons. The Germans held a strong line of defence. Their left ran along the canalized river Sambre; their central stronghold was the Forest of Mormal; their right stretched through the flat country towards the Scheldt north of the forest—a district with tracts of marshy ground that were a network of streams, wide open drains and watercourses. Horne, with the First Army, was to deal with the enemy's right. Byng with the Third Army was to attack their centre and fight his way on a broad front through the Forest of Mormal; Rawlinson with the Fourth Army was to force the line of the Sambre to the south of it. On his right the First French Army was to cover his flank conforming to his advance.

[1] The figures were :

Units.	Officers.	O.R.	Totals.	Officers.	O.R.	Totals.
50TH BRIGADE :						
10th W. Yorks -	- 21	826	847			
7th E. Yorks -	- 25	843	868	74	2195	2269
6th Dorsets -	- 28	521	549			
51ST BRIGADE :						
7th Lincolns -	- 27	693	720			
7th Borders -	- 24	625	649	78	2014	2092
10th Sherwood Foresters	27	696	723			
52ND BRIGADE :						
10th Lanc. Fslrs. -	- 28	604	632			
9th W. Ridings -	- 25	740	765	74	1954	2058
12th Manchesters	- 21	610	631			
				226	6163	6389
7th York and Lancs				32	706	738
				258	6869	7127

In the attack of the Third Army, the special task assigned to the 17th Division was to clear a belt of the forest running west to east, about 2,000 yards wide, and to push forward for some four miles, to a line just east of Locquignol. When it reached this objective, the 21st Division would pass through it and carry on the advance to the further margin of the forest, and across the river Sambre about Berliamont.

During its advance the 17th Division would have the 38th on its right and the 37th on its left. All three Brigades would be engaged in succession, on what was familiarly known as the "leap-frogging" plan. Assembly trenches had been prepared along the front—for the first two Brigades to be engaged—the 52nd and the 51st. The 50th Brigade assembled about a mile further back, west of Poix-du-Nord. The work of the leading Brigade, the 52nd, would be to clear the enemy out of the village of Futoy and the close orchard around it and between it and the forest margin. Only its right would actually enter the woods east of the Englefontaine-Bavai road, which here marked clearly the forest boundary. The whole distance to the 1st Objective was about a mile and a quarter, and in the first stage of its advance the Brigade would have to change direction so as to face due east.

The 51st was to follow closely the advance of the 52nd, both having all their three Battalions in line. It was hoped that thus the two Brigades would be well forward before the German counter-barrage came down, and so escape any serious loss from it. Passing through the 52nd the 51st would fight its way forward through the woods for about a mile to the 2nd Objective, marked by a broad drive running south from the "Carrefour du Grand Tourneur," a junction of several forest drives and paths just within the northern Corps boundary.

The 50th Brigade would now be following up the advance, and it would pass through the 51st on the 2nd

Objective and go forward to attack the 3rd and 4th. The former of these, about half a mile farther east, was a zig-zag line running generally north to south but made up of sections of forest paths, crossing this general direction at a sharp angle. The 4th and final Objective was a mile and a half east of this line, which had been marked as a starting point for the attack on the intervening positions of the enemy in and around the village of Locquignol.

The capture of the 4th Objective, marked by one of the main north-and-south roads of the forest, and not far from its eastern margin, would complete the task of the 17th Division. Here the 21st Division would pass through, its mission being to clear the forest margins, push on to Berliamont and force the crossings of the river Sambre.

This was the only occasion during the great advance that our army had to engage in forest fighting on a grand scale, and in planning this novel operation some difficult problems had to be solved. The artillery plan was the subject of much discussion. It was anticipated that there might be danger to our infantry from premature shell bursts in the trees bordering the forest roads and paths, many of these being over 80 feet high. Eventually it was decided to use shrapnel barrages, and in order to reduce danger and get a greater volume of fire on the open spaces it was decided that the barrage should not creep through the denser parts of the woods. It would cover the advance along the forest drives and through the clearings, and the infantry were warned not to keep close up to it except in the open. After the 2nd Objective was won there was to be a pause in the advance, during which the Divisional Artillery west of the forest would move closer up to its margin to protect by a barrage the final stages of the attack.

Two sections R.F.A. were to go forward into the woods, after the 1st Objective was won, to give close support to the infantry. A few trench mortars were attached to the three Brigades. The M.G. Battalion was directed to support the attack of the 52nd Brigade with the barrage fire of two companies. Another company was attached to this Brigade, and two sections each to the 51st and 50th.

The infantry were to avoid being involved in close bush fighting in the denser parts of the forest. The advance was to keep to the drives and paths, the clearings and the more open parts of the woods. Dense patches held by the enemy were to be " pinched out " by out-flanking them and taking advantage of the many roads and paths that crossed the general direction of our advance diagonally and lent themselves to a converging move on a point in rear of the obstacle. In each stage of the attack posts for consolidation and communication purposes were to be established.

It was stated that three (and " possibly four ") tanks would be available to support the advance, but with the 17th Division tank support had been so far disappointing. On this occasion only one tank put in an appearance and it was knocked out by a direct hit of a shell while moving into position behind the assembly line.

The night before the battle was a very dark one, with a clouded sky and a heavy mist on the ground. The enemy seemed to have at least some suspicion that an attack was being prepared and the intermittent bursts of fire of his artillery were more frequent than on any of the preceding nights. Shells fell freely in Englefontaine— a favourite target. They burst, now here now there, on the ground behind our front, and there were some casual-ties among the troops moving up to their assembly positions. There were bursts of shell fire about the front line itself, but here the narrow and deep assembly trenches gave very satisfactory protection. By 4.30 a.m. the two leading Brigades were in position. At 5.30—zero hour —our barrage opened and the advance began.

There was still more than an hour before sunrise

and the troops went forward in darkness, deepened by the mist. The 52nd Brigade had its three Battalions in line, each on a two-company front—the 12th Manchesters on the right, the 9th Duke of Wellington's in the centre, and the 10th Lancashire Fusiliers on the left.

The many small garden and orchard enclosures with high and thick hedges, often wired, proved to be troublesome obstacles, and the enemy made a good fight. The misty darkness however handicapped their machine gunners. The Manchesters on the right had the shortest way to go, and a narrower belt of enclosures to clear in order to push into the corner of the forest between the 1st Objective and the Divisional boundary. The other two Battalions had to swing round to a new direction as they advanced. In the centre the Duke of Wellington's came under heavy machine gun fire as they crossed the Englefontaine-Louvignies road, and after fighting their way through the orchards had to clear the village of Futoy. The two leading companies worked forward north and south of the place, while the support companies went through it and " mopped it up." The Battalion had serious losses. It attacked with 15 company officers and 584 other ranks. Of these 13 officers and 226 other ranks became casualties. In the advance 180 prisoners were taken and sent back. After deducting escorts for these, stretcher bearers, runners, signallers and the like, the fighting strength of the Battalion was reduced to two officers and 200 other ranks. " That the final objective was reached successfully by those reduced numbers reflects highly on the determination of all ranks," says the diary of operations. On the left the Lancashire Fusiliers met with serious opposition in the large copse immediately in front of their starting point and then at La Motte farm. After getting beyond the farm they were delayed for a while by heavy M.G. fire on the left front, from the hamlet of La Vache just north of the Divisional boundary. Here their left was exposed, as the 37th

Division on that side had not as yet carried their attack so far. But even so, the Fusiliers were only a few minutes behind time in reaching the 1st Objective, on which the rest of the Brigade was established by 8.30 a.m.

Day had come during the three hours' advance, but it was a typical November day, dull and cloudy with much mist still hanging on the ground. The 51st Brigade had closely followed the advance, its three Battalions in line—7th Borders on the right, 7th Lincolns in the centre, and 10th Sherwood Foresters on the left. At 8.47 the Brigade began its advance against the 2nd Objective. On the left some orchard enclosures had to be cleared of the enemy before crossing the Englefontaine-Bavai road. After this the whole line was in the forest. The flank Battalions had three companies in line and the fourth in support. The Lincolns in the centre were on a two-company front. Progress in this part of the forest proved to be much less difficult than had been anticipated. Here there was little undergrowth; there were several large clearings and outside these in places the trees had been thinned. The barrage worked forward very well, and the enemy were steadily driven back. By 10.40 the long drive that marked the 2nd Objective was won, and with less loss in the attack than the number of casualties suffered by the Brigade from shell fire in following up the first stage of the advance.

There was now a pause of more than two hours to give time for the Divisional Artillery to move forward to its new positions for covering our further advance. At 9.30 the 50th Brigade had moved up to the line of the Englefontaine-Louvignies road. While the 51st Brigade was securing its objective, the 50th had begun its forward move through the forest. At first there were some casualties from hostile shell fire, and towards the end of its march also from the short shooting of some of our own batteries. By 11.30 it was close up in rear of the 51st.

As our patrols reported the woods immediately in front
to be now clear of the enemy, it passed through the 51st
and formed for attack just east of the road—the 10th
West Yorkshires on the right, the 6th Dorsets in the
centre and the 7th East Yorkshires on the left, each
Battalion on a two-company front.

At 1 p.m. the advance began again.   The artillery
barrage covering the attack of the 50th Brigade was
hardly a success.   It was reported to be good on the
right, but late in the centre, and on the left several
batteries were shooting short and there were some thirty
casualties from it among the East Yorkshires.   It was at
times difficult to say where the barrage was among the
tall trees.   The next Division on the right was not yet
up in line with the advance of the 17th and the East
Yorks had to use one of their companies to form a
defensive flank on that side, supported by the Lewis guns
of the North Irish Horse.   Hostile fire was not heavy at
first, and the advance to the Brown Line encountered
very slight opposition, but after that the enemy's resistance stiffened.   At 2.15 the right advance was held up
in front of a large group of buildings, north-west of
Locquignol, the Institut Forestier, and here the West
Yorks came under very heavy M.G. fire.   By 3 p.m.
this obstacle was outflanked and cleared of the enemy by
a direct attack.   Meanwhile on the left the East Yorkshires had been held by machine gun fire from the eastern
margins of clearings in the woods.   By 4.30 this opposition had been overcome, and twelve of the enemy's
machine guns captured.   There was a good supply of
cartridges with some of them, and these were successfully
turned on the enemy by the M.G. section of the East
Yorks.   At 4 p.m. the West Yorks on the right held a
line running north and south just beyond the Institut
Forestier and facing Locquignol.   The Dorsets were on
their flank north-west of the village.   It was strongly
held, and there was heavy machine gun fire from its

west and north margins, and from a clearing along a forest road north of it. A machine gun was firing from the village church tower.

There was no further progress that day, and daylight was soon over. Sunset was at 4.21 and darkness came on quickly under the cloudy sky and in the shadows of the woods. The G.O.C. of the 50th Brigade decided at 5 p.m. to reorganise his line and prepare for an attack on Locquignol later in the evening. Communication with the artillery was slow and difficult. They were asked to assist with a barrage, while another local barrage was to be organised with the machine guns and Stokes and Newton trench mortars attached to the Brigade. The hour fixed for the attack was 10 p.m. Preparations had been completed when, half-an-hour before the attack was to begin, a staff officer arrived with orders that as the 21st Division was to resume the attack next morning, passing through the 17th Division, and as they were to advance under a creeping barrage, the 50th Brigade was to take up and report a definite line by 10 p.m., so there was to be no further forward movement.

The cloudy day was followed by a pitch-dark night with torrents of rain. Active patrolling was kept up on the front. Just before midnight one of our patrols reported that Locquignol had been evacuated by the enemy. At 2 a.m. D.H.Q. was informed that the 21st Division would advance next morning without a barrage, and orders were sent to the 50th Brigade to move forward before dawn to the final objective. At 6 a.m. this line was occupied. At this hour the position was—50th Brigade on the Green Line; 51st on or just forward of the Brown Line; 52nd concentrated at Futoy. The troops who had passed the night in the forest under a downpour of rain had had a trying time after a long day's work. Between 6 and 7 a.m. on the 5th the 64th Brigade (21st Division) passed through the front to continue the advance.

During the day General Robertson moved his H.Q. from Poix to Locquignol. A week later he received by post from Paris a cardboard box, tied up with the striped " Allies' Ribbon." It was full of violets and enclosed was a card with the following message:—

> " Modeste hommage aux soldats brittaniques de la 17me Division et toute notre reconnaissance émue à leur grand chef.
>
>   " Famille Hurelle-Delfosse de Locquignol, Nord, reconquise le 4me Nov. 1918.
>
>   Paris, 33 Rue Bonaparte, VI."

On enquiry the General found that the Delfosse family had resided before the war at a large house near the west end of the village, and had left it in August, 1914, when the German invasion reached the district. They had seen the 17th Division mentioned in the papers as having retaken Locquignol. He sent them on his own behalf and that of all ranks of the Division a letter of thanks for this graceful tribute.

The day after the battle in the woods was a difficult time. The forest had proved to be a much less formidable obstacle than anyone had anticipated. The little patches of woods on the Somme battlefields had cost days of hard fighting. Places like High Wood and Delville Wood were remembered with horror. But our armies advancing on a broad front had swept steadily forward through the vast woodlands of Mormal with only here and there a temporary check, and the whole of it had been won in twenty-four hours, with little close or really severe fighting. The fact was that the forest had been very imperfectly prepared for defence. The Germans had gained a few days before the attack, on account of the elaborate preparations made for our advance, but once it began they had fought only a series of somewhat passive rearguard actions in the woods. There were no counter-attacks in the zone through which the 17th Division advanced on November 4th. There were very few anywhere else, and these were always purely local efforts on a small scale. By sunset the Germans had lost most of the forest, and after dark they began a general retreat.

The advance of the 21st Division, after it passed through the 17th at dawn on November 5th, encountered no very serious opposition. By 6 p.m. that day the front of the Vth Corps (33rd Division on the right, 21st on the left) ran from Sassegnies on the Sambre to Berlaimont, with patrols along the river line farther north. It was an advance of three miles since morning, and further ground would have been gained only that the river for the moment barred the way.

The Sambre is here a wide deep stream, with a strong current and carrying a considerable volume of water, rising with the deluge of rain that had been pouring down all day. The enemy had blown up all the bridges. His rearguards were holding the high ground around which the river curves east of Berlaimont, and he had guns of all calibres in position beyond its crest, which were pitching shells on to the roads and villages of the west side.

It was an indication of how thoroughly the enemy had been beaten that he made, after all, no serious attempt to defend this strong river line, a much more formidable obstacle than the Selle (a mere brook compared to the Sambre). The forcing of the Selle line had cost several days of fighting, culminating in a carefully prepared pitched battle on a front of many miles. There was only a brief delay on the Sambre, and it was the result not so much of any organised resistance by the enemy as of the difficulty of getting forward our artillery and the R.E. with their bridging equipment.

All movement of marching troops and transport was practically restricted for miles to the forest tracks, and these were fair weather roads with a surface that quickly went to pieces under heavy traffic in a steady downpour of rain. At several critical points they had been cratered with explosives during the enemy's retirement. At the eastern exit from Locquignol, on the best road in the 17th Division zone, the enemy had thus cratered the whole width of the roadway when they abandoned the village late in the evening of November 4th. On the 5th the road was blocked with halted or slowly moving columns, and there was an embarrassing congestion of troops in Locquignol. The 17th, 21st and 38th Divisions all had their H.Q.'s in the village. Part of the leading Brigade of the 17th and the reserve Brigade of the 21st were in and around the place, and transport of the latter Division was slowly struggling to the front. The 17th Divisional Artillery was to support the advance of the 21st, and enterprising gunner officers managed to get a couple of batteries through the woods north of Locquignol and out to the open ground near the little village of La Tête Noire.

After dark on the 5th a single pontoon bridge was thrown across the Sambre by the R.E. of the 21st Division while the Germans were shelling the town. During the following day a bridgehead was secured on the east bank by occupying Aulnoye and a front curving round east of the great railway junction south of it to the village of Petit Maubeuge. On a Corps order that the 17th Division should be ready to pass through the 21st (an order cancelled later in the day) the 51st Brigade was moved forward to La Tête Noire. This was the only move made by the Division. It rained steadily all day, and 50 per cent of the men were bivouacking in the open.

At dawn on the 7th it was found that the enemy had abandoned the high ground east of the Sambre and was again in full retreat. The 21st Division followed up the retirement, at first encountering very slight opposition from the enemy rearguards. As the morning went on his resistance stiffened and the Germans made a good stand beyond the hollow of the Grimoux Brook beyond which they had a good rearguard position on the hill to the east of it and in the orchard enclosures round the large village of Limont Fontaine. Their heavy guns had been drawn back beyond this ground during the night. At dawn they were shelling Berliamont, and a little later, just as the left of the 21st had occupied Bachant on the loop of the Sambre north-east of that place, and the people were crowding into the streets to welcome our men, big shells began to burst in the town, and there was a rush to cover on the part of its people. The German gunners evidently imagined that the Sambre had been bridged at Bachant and the town would be full of troops crossing there.

But so far the only available crossing on this part of the river line was the single pontoon bridge at Berliamont. A couple of the 17th Division batteries had pushed on to the Sambre and got across the bridge and under orders from the C.R.A. of the 21st they came into action just east of Bachant, firing " by the map " through mist and rain. As the day went on the congestion of traffic at the bridge and on the roads leading to it became appalling. The G.O.C of the 17th Division had received orders that it was to be ready to relieve the 21st during the night of November 7th to 8th and continue the pursuit of the enemy next day. He had made elaborate arrangements with D.H.Q. of the 21st for getting his Division well forward and across the Sambre during the 7th. But Corps Staff Officers on the road and in Berliamont made well-intentioned, but not always well-directed, attempts to improve the arrangements. The results were chaotic, all the more because the 38th Division began to push its troops and transport towards the Berliamont bridge, so that its approaches and the streets of the town were packed with the converging movement of three Divisions, the 21st, 17th and 38th. The 51st Brigade moving from La Tête Noire did not get across the river and into Aulnoye until 5 p.m. and even then, was without its first line transport, so that there were no rations to distribute; the 50th Brigade reached Aymeries (on the east bank between the bridge and Aulnoye) at 7 p.m.; hours later, during the night, the 52nd Brigade reached Berliamont.

The advance had made good progress during the day. Early in the afternoon the line of the Grimoux Brook had been won, and before sunset the 21st Division had captured the villages of Limont Fontaine and Eclaibes, and the 38th Division, on the right, had driven the enemy out of Écuelin and pushed well forward into the woods to the east of the village. The Vth Corps front now ran on a north and south line parallel to and about a thousand yards short of the Maubeuge-Avesnes road, which was held by the enemy's rearguards.

The Divisional orders for November 8th were issued at 4.50 p.m., when the latest information available was that the 21st Division was held up a little to the west of Limont Fontaine. The objectives assigned to the advance of the 17th, after passing through the 21st Division, named Limont Fontaine as the first of these, and then the line of the Maubeuge-Avesnes road as the second, and the village of Beaufort and the high ground just beyond it as the third. The 51st Brigade was to lead the advance and move off at 9 p.m. that evening. The 50th Brigade was to follow in support at an interval of 2,000 yards, and the 52nd was, for the present, to remain in Divisional Reserve at Berliamont.

The 51st Brigade marched out from Aymeries, where they had only arrived four hours earlier. There had been no issue of rations, and none reached them for another twenty-four hours. During this long interval they had only the " iron ration " and some scanty additions given to officers and men by the villagers on the line of march. Shells were flying overhead as they tramped forward through the darkness, but this hostile fire was high, being directed on Berliamont and the crossings of the Sambre. By 3.30 a.m., on the 8th, they were in position on the

line held by the 21st, just east of Limont Fontaine, and
the Brigade they were relieving was beginning its
withdrawal.

With all three Battalions in line, an attempt was now
made to push forward to the Maubeuge-Avesnes road.
After a gain of 500 or 600 yards the advance was brought
to a standstill by heavy artillery and machine gun fire from
the front and on both flanks. The fire from the right was
enfilading the Battalion on that side, the 7th Borders. It
came from the margin of the woods, which the 38th
Division had not yet cleared so far forward. The Borders
were forced to fall back. The other flank was also exposed,
for the 5th Division, on that side, had its right 2,000 yards
in rear of the front from which the 51st Brigade was
attacking. A defensive flank was formed on this side,
and the Brigade held on to the line it had reached, waiting
for daylight and the support of the Divisions to its left
and right. It was only soon after sunrise that the fighting
transport of the 51st and 50th Brigades reached them.
Time was needed also to organise an effective covering
barrage for the attack, and get as many of our guns as
were available of the batteries of the 17th and 21st R.F.A.
forward to closer range. The enemy was evidently
making a serious stand, and his rearguards had splendid
cover in the orchard country in front and the woods on
the right. It was decided to make the next attack at
2 p.m.

That attack however failed to reach the line of the road.
Our men made a good try to get forward under very heavy
artillery and M.G. fire, but they were evidently dead-
tired, and nearing the limit of endurance. The sun set at
4.15. The 38th on the right was now in touch and working gradually forward through the woods and the 5th
Division had come into line on the left, so another attack
was made in the twilight. This also was stopped short
of the objective, but on the left the 38th pushed through
the woods up to the line of the road. Darkness came on

rapidly, and the fighting came to an end. There was only desultory firing here and there along the front, and the German artillery fire gradually died down.

The G.O.C. of the Division had decided to relieve the 51st Brigade during the night, and renew the attack at dawn next day, and for this purpose sent forward the 52nd Brigade, which had had a day's rest at Berliamont. But during the late hours of the evening of the 8th the 51st Brigade had kept patrols out in front and at 9 p.m. these reported that the enemy had abandoned the line of the Maubeuge-Avesnes road. The Brigade then moved forward, with patrols working in its front and at 3.30 a.m. held a line 500 yards east of the road. Here the 52nd Brigade passed through and took over the new front.

The weather was clearing up. At sunrise (6.50 a.m.), there was a clear sky, the herald of a fine bright autumn day—a happy relief from the unceasing rain of the preceding days. There was a strange, almost unreal, feeling of peace and quiet, no shots ringing out in front, no shells screaming overhead. Evidently the stand made by the enemy on the Maubeuge road was the prelude to another long withdrawal. The orders to the 52nd Brigade were to push on to Beaufort and the high ground near the village. It was reached without any opposition whatever. An outpost line was placed in position covering the village and cavalry and cyclist patrols pushed out eastwards to regain touch with the German rearguards.

They rode forward by the cross lanes through close country to Damousies, two miles east of Beaufort. No sign of an enemy anywhere. The villagers told them that all night the Germans had been marching past, and the last of them had gone before sunrise. Damousies looks down on the long hollow of the Solre river, running northwards to the Sambre. Here was the very place where one might expect to find a hostile rearguard holding the eastern slopes beyond the narrow valley. But the

bridge over the river was intact and the villagers of
Obrechies, on the farther side, were flying little tricolours
from their houses and gave another enthusiastic welcome
to our men as they rode in.   For six miles more our
patrols went on now through pleasant woodland country,
with more welcomes at every village and farm.   At
last touch was regained with the enemy.   A German
rear-guard was found to be holding Hestrud, the
last French village, just outside the Belgian frontier
line.

That bright autumn day of November 9th, the Allied
front in Western Belgium ran from Ghent along the
Scheldt to Tournai.   British troops were on the margin
of the old battlefield of Mons.   They held Condé and
Bavai.   They were in Maubeuge and Avesnes.   The
French had passed the great junction of Hirson and
were well forward on Belgian ground in the Gap of
Chimay.   On the Meuse they held Mezières, and
Americans were in position on the heights of its southern
bank looking down on Sedan, from the very ground
where King William had watched the battle in 1870.
The war was within two days of its end.   The patrol
to Hestrud was the last military operation of the 17th
Division.

That day orders came that for the present there was to
be no further advance on the Divisional front.   Beaufort
was to be held with a forward line of standing patrols
along the Solre river, supplied by its small mounted force.
The bar to any further advance, for the time being, on
this sector of our front was not any possible resistance of
the enemy, but the question of communications and
supplies.   The railways as far back as Cambrai were not
yet fully repaired, and we had advanced far from the
nearest practicable railheads.   It was only with the utmost
difficulty that the necessary movement of supplies could
be maintained by road, and there were many miles of
these which had been reduced to the state of tracks on

which any rapid movement of wheeled traffic was impossible.

Sunday, November 10th, was in every sense of the word a day of rest for the Division. Persistent rumours of coming peace were circulating. On the Monday morning at 7 a.m., D.H.Q. received the order that all hostilities were to cease at 11 a.m. The Armistice between the Allies and Germany had been signed. The great news was circulated to all units of the Division. It was the best of good news, but it was received in a very matter-of-fact way. There was more excitement among the civil population in London than among these soldiers who had come through the long weariness of war, and now heard that there was to be rest at last and the return home before very long. A typical incident noted in the diary of a gunner officer tells how that morning, as he was riding to the billets of his battery at Limont Fontaine, he met a detachment of our infantry on the march:—

" I asked them where they were going, and someone said, ' Home ! ' They looked rather happy and I wondered if it could be true. Then an extraordinarily happy-looking Brigadier rode along and I asked him if it meant peace. He said, ' Yes. I've just been talking to Corps H.Q. It's official.' So I went to the Battery and told the Sergeant-Major to fall them in in the orchard. They all seemed to know what it was and fell in in a hollow square, grinning and expectant. Just as I was going to tell them, an orderly appeared with a message which said: ' Hostilities will cease at 11.00 hours,' so I read that. Nothing much happened, they cheered, not wildly; we all felt it to be so very unreal; and in a short time they were back at work, cleaning harness and guns and grooming the horses."

During the day the 21st Division relieved the 17th and the 50th and 52nd Brigades marched back across the Sambre to Berliamont, and the 50th Brigade through the Forest to Englefontaine, with the cheerful feeling that it was the first stage on the return home. That evening, the following message from the Third Army

Commander was circulated among all units of his Command:—

SPECIAL ORDER OF THE DAY,

By Sir J. H. G. Byng, K.C.B., K.C.M.G., M.V.,

Commanding Third Army.

To All Ranks of the Third Army:

The operations of the last three months have forced the enemy to sue for an armistice as a prelude to peace.

Your share in the consummation of this achievement is one that fills me with pride and admiration.

Since August 21st you have won eighteen decisive battles, you have driven the enemy back over sixty miles of country and you have captured 67,000 prisoners and 800 guns.

That is your record, gained by your ceaseless enterprise, your indomitable courage and your loyal support to your leaders. Eleven Divisions in the four Corps (Guards, 2nd, 3rd, and 62nd, 5th, 37th, 42nd and New Zealand, 17th, 21st, and 38th) have been continuously in action since the beginning of the advance, and have borne the brunt of the operations. Other Divisions have joined and left, each adding fresh lustre to its history.

To all ranks, to all Corps and formations, to all administrative and transport units, I tender my thanks. May your pride in your achievements be as great as mine is in the recollection of having commanded the Army in which you served.

(Signed) J. Byng, General.
Commanding Third Army.

During the fighting of these first days of November the losses of the Division had been:—

	Killed.	Wounded.	Missing.	Totals.
Officers -	12	47	—	59
Other ranks -	138	980	62	1180
Totals -	150	1027	62	1239

The total number of prisoners taken by the Division during the advance from the crossing of the Ancre to the

Armistice was 73 officers and 3,428 other ranks. The enemy guns captured were 563 machine guns, 35 trench mortars and 14 heavy trench mortars, two heavy 4.2 guns and twelve field pieces (two batteries).

The Division was now ordered to concentrate west of the Selle about Bertry and Inchy in country where it had spent many days in October, during the pause in the advance before the victory of Neuvilly. In three or four days the troops marched back over the battlefields of the last stage in the advance, which had meant a month of marching and fighting. On November 12th, D.H.Q. were transferred from Aulnoye to Inchy. The 52nd moved back to Vendignies, and the 51st to Locquignol. Next day the movement continued, the 50th Brigade reached Bertry, the 51st Troisvilles, and the 52nd Inchy. The Divisional Artillery marched back through the Forest of Mormal, part of it halting at Englefontaine, the rest going on to Vendignies. On the 14th the Pioneer Battalion, the York and Lancasters, marched from La Tête Noire to Bertry and the Divisional Artillery concentrated a couple of miles farther west at the town of Clary.

The Division spent the next three weeks in this area. There was abundant billetting accommodation, much of it in the large well-built barns of the district. The people were helpful and friendly, rejoicing in having the British amongst them after four years of German occupation. Steady drill began again, but there was plenty of time each day for football and other sports, and concert parties were organised for the evenings.

On December 4th, the Division was honoured by a visit from His Majesty the King, accompanied by the Prince of Wales and the Duke of York. The wintry weather was beginning and it was a cloudy day with frequent rain showers. It was announced that the visit would be an informal one, and there would be no inspection or march past, and the troops, formed up along the

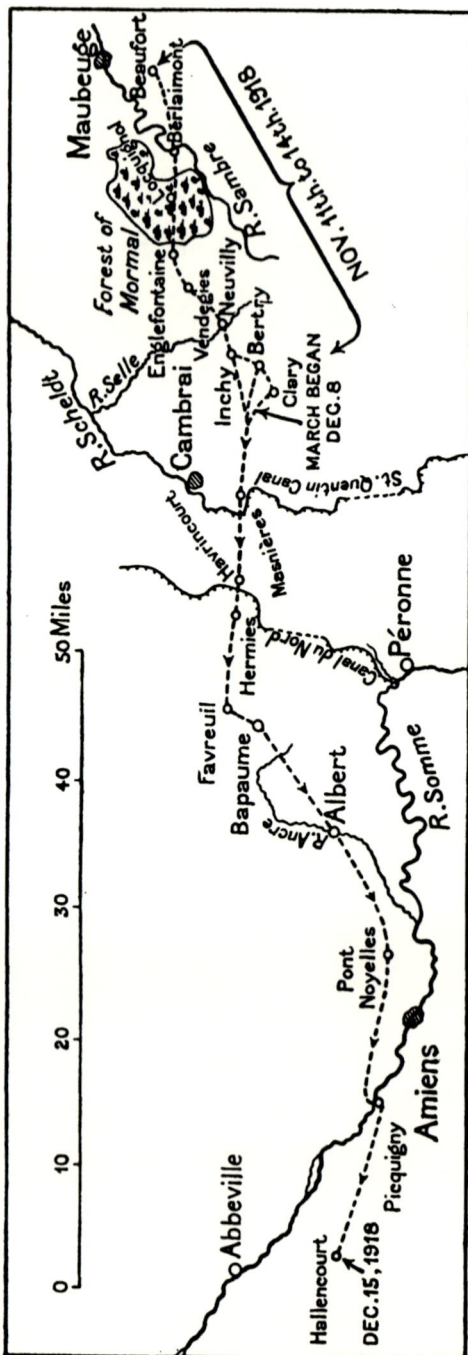

Last Marches of the 17th Division. "Homeward," November and December, 1918.

Inchy-le-Cateau and Inchy-Neuvilly roads expected that they would only have a glimpse of the King as he passed by in his motor car. He drove along the line receiving the salute of each unit as he passed, and then went on with General Robertson to visit the battlefield of Neuvilly. On his return journey he found unformed masses of officers and men along the roadside east of Inchy, and alighted from his car, and walked amongst them speaking to several of them as he went by and greeted by their enthusiastic cheers.

Rumours had been current that the Division would soon move to the neighbourhood of Abbeville, and after the royal visit these were confirmed by warning orders to prepare to proceed by march route to the Hallencourt area, starting on December 8th.

There had been expectations that the move would be by railway, and it was disappointing to hear that under existing conditions neither trains nor motor transport would be available, and the long march would mean a tramp of nearly a hundred miles, in weather that promised to be dull, cold and rainy—a promise that was fully realised.

But there was the consolation that it was the last march of the Division, a homeward march with faces to the Channel shores and the sea that was the way to England. It was a seven days' march, much of it over ground that was already familiar and associated with memories of harder things than a long route march in rain and mud. Sheltered billets in house or barn and shed were available at the end of each stage and advanced parties were pushed on in front to make all ready for a good meal and a night's rest under a roof for all ranks.

The march was first towards the Cambrai region. The Canal du Nord was crossed at Masnières, and then the route was by Havrincourt and Hermies, scenes of the splendid stand made by the Division against the tremendous German onset nine months before. Then the

northern fringe of the Somme battlefields was crossed
and the march was by the long road from Bapaume to
Albert and the Ancre valley; then by Pont Noyelles and
past Amiens to cross the Somme at Picquigny and reach
at last the Hallencourt area where the troops were
billetted in the villages of the district.   A few miles away
were Abbeville to the north and westward the Channel
shores.

Sanguine and optimistic spirits were dreaming of an
early voyage across that Channel, by complete units,
pleasant journeys through English country to the centres
where the battalions, batteries and other formations had
been raised; rejoicing welcomes from their own people
and old friends and neighbours—something of a trium-
phal progress; and then swift release from service.
But demobilisation was to be a long process, longer indeed
than the first formation of the Division in those far-off
autumn months of 1914.   It was part of an army of
millions, and these could not be dispersed by the stroke of
some magic wand.

There was leave in turn for some, with a warning that
they must report again in the Hallencourt area on its
expiration.   There was a call for coal miners, and before
Christmas a number of the northern men were released
under a special order.   Meanwhile the regular routine of
a " rest and training " area was resumed, but with more
time given for rest and recreation than to training, and
presently training classes for employment in civil life
became part of the day's routine.   Christmas was a real
festival, with the pleasant confidence that when it next
came it would be kept in England.

In January, 1919, the first drafts for demobilisation
started for the cross-Channel voyage.   During the month
there were a series of parades, at which the Commander
of the Division presented colours to the Infantry Battalions
and distributed medal ribbons, no medals being yet
available.   A little later drafts of officers and men who

had agreed to prolong their service were sent to reinforce
the Army of Occupation on the Rhine.   Gradually the
Division melted away, until at last there were left of the
Battalions only the small " cadres " of 4 officers and 46
other ranks, which were to take to England such stores,
equipment and other Battalion property as were to be
handed over on demobilisation.   Much of the miscellaneous equipment and transport of all kinds that had
accumulated since 1915 was disposed of in France.

In May the demobilisation of the Division was completed.   The last of the cadres crossed the Channel, in a
few hours officers and men had returned to civilian life.
For the infantry units of the Division the last parades were
later unofficial gatherings when the new regimental
colours they had brought back from France were hung up
in cathedrals and churches of their local centres as honoured memorials of the part they had played in an
achievement without parallel in their country's history.

That achievement was the realisation of Kitchener's
daring resolve to supplement the existing forces of the
country, not merely by organising new units of this or
that arm, but by improvising rapidly out of mere masses
of civilian recruits complete Divisions provided with all
the manifold organisations required by modern war.
The great experiment began in dark days when the
outlook was clouded with recent disappointments and
the peril of impending disaster.   There were serious
critics who doubted if it would end in anything but
failure.   After the needs of existing forces had been
provided for there was only a mere handful left of men
with any military experience to direct formation and
training of new Divisions, and it was a problem how to
arrange for their armament and equipment.   The only
things about which there was no doubt were the patriotic
goodwill of the new recruits and the splendid courage of
those who undertook to make them into soldiers.   The
result was a magnificent success.

Thirty such Divisions were formed, an aggregate force of nearly half a million. The record of the 17th Division might be taken as typical of them all. It had a few months of training in the south of England, and this training was completed in the stern school of war during the months it spent in the Ypres salient after its arrival in France. It stood the test well. Those improvised soldiers hardened into veterans. There was proof of the transformation when, after the first days on the Somme heavy losses under fire had reduced the battalions almost to skeleton cadres. All units were able to absorb large drafts of recruits who had only their training in England, and the fighting tradition already formed in the Division, and the comradeship and example of those who had already served through months of war enabled the new comers to bear themselves like men in the long-drawn series of battles which we remember as the " Battle of the Somme." Then came the long conflict beyond Arras, and the brief experience of utter misery in the winter swamps of Passchendaele. Finally there was the supreme test of the stubborn defence of the salient before Cambrai against the overwhelming onset of the German armies in March, 1918, and the dogged endurance of the fighting retreat that followed, and last of all came the victorious advance across the Ancre, over the wasted fields of the Somme through the Hindenburg Line, and over the Selle barrier and through the Mormal woodlands to the Belgian border. The Division had proved itself alike in patient endurance of hardship and failure and the glory of victory, and all who served in it had the right to look back on the years in France and Flanders with honourable pride in the memories of their part in this great achievement of the " new armies."

No memorial has been erected to its memory on any of the battlefields on which it fought. But its record is its best memorial.

THE END

INDEX

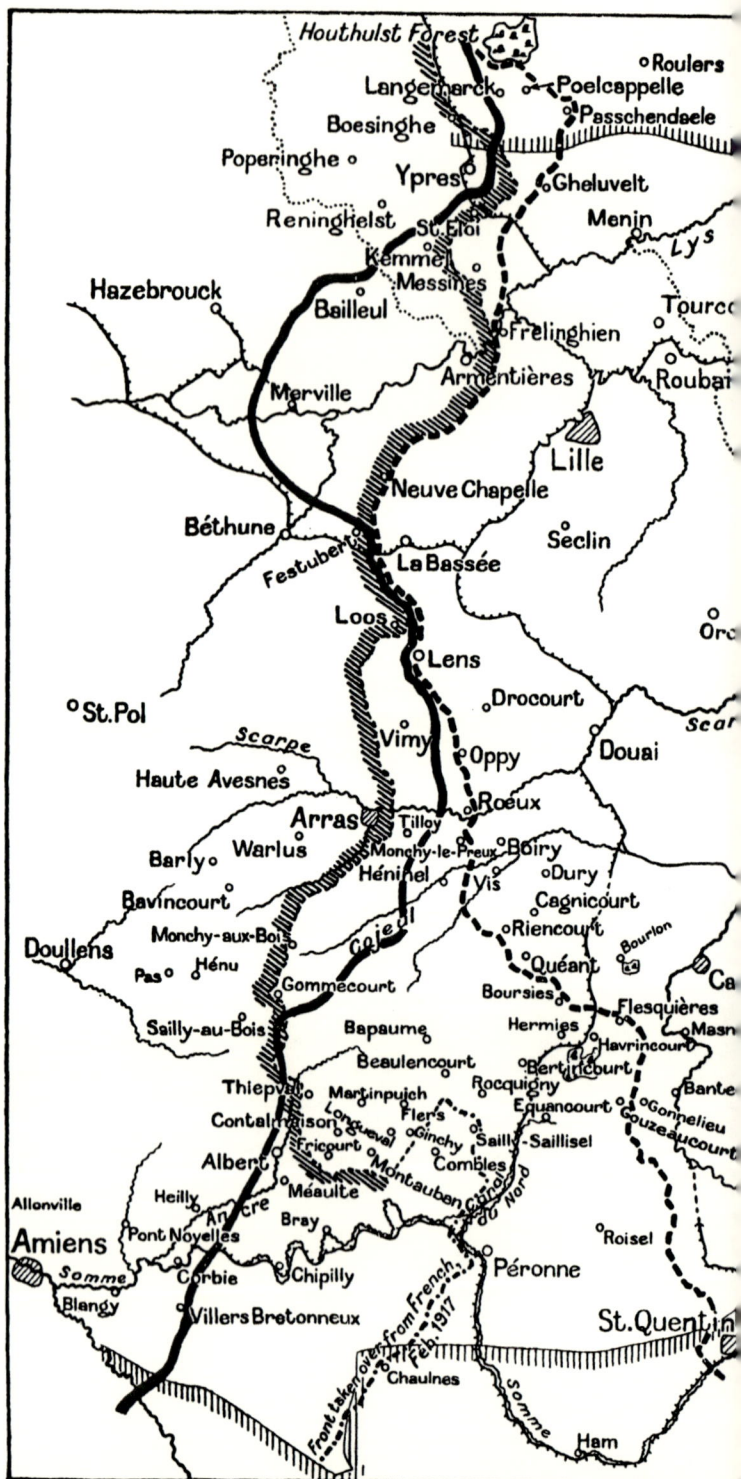

Courtrai

Grammont

Renaix

B E L G I U M

Tournai

Ath

Leuze

Scheldt

chies

Condé

Mons

Valenciennes

Scheldt

Selle

Maubeuge

Ecaillon Brook

Le Quesnoy

Forest of Locquignol

Sambre

oBeaufort

oEclaibes

Solesmes

Poix-du-Nord

Mormal

Berlaimont

ambrai

Vendegies

Caudry o

Neuvilly

Amerval

Avesnes

nières

Inchy

Landrecies

Montigny o

o Clary

Le Cateau

eux o

Walincourt

Beaurepaire

'b

Wassigny

Fresnoy

Scale of Miles

0   10   20

Approximate line from end of 1914 to July 1st 1916,
(before Somme Battles)..............................

Approximate line of March 1st 1918 (showing advances
of 1916 and 1917)....................................

Approximate line of July 1918 (showing losses by
German offensives of March and April 1918).....

Approximate line at Armistice, November 11th 1918 ••••••

Northern and Southern boundaries of British
Armies during final advance........................

Emery Walker Ltd., sc.

Printed in the United Kingdom
by Lightning Source UK Ltd.
124262UK00001B/301/A